The Sustainable Network

The Accidental Answer for a Troubled Planet

The Sustainable Network

The Accidental Answer for a Troubled Planet

Sarah Sorensen

BEIJING • CAMBRIDGE • FARNHAM • KÖLN • SEBASTOPOL • TOKYO

The Sustainable Network
by Sarah Sorensen

Published by O'Reilly Media, Inc. 1005 Gravenstein Highway North, Sebastopol, CA 95472.

O'Reilly books may be purchased for educational, business, or sales promotional use. Online editions are also available for most titles (*http://mysafaribooksonline.com*). For more information, contact our corporate/institutional sales department: (800) 998-9938 or *corporate@oreilly.com*.

Editors: Patrick Ames and Michael Loukides
Production Editor: Rachel Monaghan
Copyeditor: Amy Thomson
Proofreader: Rachel Monaghan
Indexer: Julie Hawks
Interior Designers: Ron Bilodeau and Molly Sharp
Illustrator: Robert Romano
Cover Designer: Monica Kamsvaag
Production Services: MacMillan Publishing Solutions

Print History: October 2009: First Edition.

ISBN: 978-0-596-15703-6
[LSI]   [2013-11-01]

The images in the chapter openers of this book are stills taken from the video blogs at Rocketboom.com, a New York City–based daily international news program that covers a wide range of information and commentary from top news stories to contemporary Internet culture. The author gratefully acknowledges Rocketboom.com for its assistance and generous permission to use these images to help wryly illustrate what some might consider a dry subject.

Thank you. Keep up your unique perspective on us!

Contents

Preface

*Real life is often more fantastic than fiction
if you just take the time to live it.*

—Thomas Harrison (the author's father)

I wrote *The Sustainable Network* late in the evenings. My husband and I would put our two girls to bed and then he would settle into whatever he was doing and I would sit down and try to write. I would start by thinking of the events and news of the day. It seemed the world was spoon-feeding me more and more examples of how the network has infiltrated our lives, our society, our culture. I can't tell you how many days I would read the morning headlines and find direct ties to what I was intending to write that evening. They were like signposts telling me that I was on the right track, that I wasn't just theorizing the sustainable network, but rather documenting its existence.

And as I went through the various stages of editing and production that O'Reilly and its staff handled so expertly, I struggled with wanting to update this book's pages daily with all that had happened in the world. "Yikes," I would say while reading some news story, "this is perfect for Chapter *x*." Right up to press time, I'm afraid I continued to badger the editors to include just one more little update. "Please. Pretty please. North Korea just launched a cyberattack against websites in Seoul…."

The network is a dynamic entity, as dynamic as the world itself, and ultimately I had to back off my desires for this book to represent that dynamic-ism in its most up-to-date incarnation. Ultimately I had to admit to myself that this book would be outdated the day it arrived. But that fact simply goes to prove that the sustainable network isn't just a vision, it's a reality. Every day there are examples of how all the various connections created, enabled, and supported by the network are sustaining new developments and opportunities.

So I hope that when reading this book, you too will start to recognize this network that is all around you, and maybe, by somewhere in the middle of the book, you will start to see its influence on the world and begin to understand your personal relationship with it. The network is in every political, economic, and social script that plays out on a local, regional, and international stage. It's in the way you live your life and do your job. And once it's called out and recognized for the role it plays—as a powerful tool that can be used to sustain change—there's a chance we can better address some of the tougher problems facing our planet today. At least that's my hope.

If this book can help open your eyes a little to the networking industry and this connective tissue called the network (sometimes boiled down to the Internet, but which is by no means indicative of all it entails), then I will have accomplished what I set out to do. Sure, the network is made of cables, routers, acronyms, and geeky things you may never care to know too much about, but it is important that you know enough to be able to understand its significance and then help shape the role it plays in our lives. That's why it's in the news every single day and terms like broadband, 3G, tweets, and smart grids are a part of our everyday vernacular.

In this book, I attempt to lay out the context and provide some background on the network that is rapidly changing the world. Only through greater understanding of this thing that connects us all in ways we never thought possible and helps us tackle problems we previously thought unsolvable does it have a chance to really make a difference.

Acknowledgments

The happiest moments my heart knows are those in which it is pouring forth its affections to a few esteemed characters.

—Thomas Jefferson

Many, many people have come before me, and many more will follow. But over the course of the past two years, some stopped to help me craft this book, and I am indebted to them all.

To start, I would like to thank Nir Zuk, a technology visionary who patiently explained the inner workings of the network to me, a nonengineer, and continued to listen and advise as I wrestled with the content of this book. I am also indebted to many others for their time and explanations over the years, particularly Kowsik Guruswamy, Ajit Sancheti, Jens Schmidt, Bryan Burns, Avishai Avivi, Rakesh Loonkar, Lee Klarich, Akhlaq Ahmed Ali, Kent Watson, Chris Cantrell, Eric Moret, Moshe Shaham, Glen Gibson, Arnit Green, and Mike Kouri, who helped me make sense of the "weeds." I would also like to thank Jonathan Zdziarski, Ted Ritter, and Chris Zimmerman, who took the time to read and provide insights into chapters of my book. I have also been fortunate to have great mentors in my career and would like to thank Robert Ma, Toby Zwikel, and Michael Hakkert for being such solid sounding boards on which I could always depend.

I am also thankful for the support of everyone in the Juniper Networks community. I appreciate the time offered by Leonid Burakovsky, Spencer Greene, Luc Ceuppens, Greg Friedmann, and Brad Minnis to read sections, and I am grateful to everyone who took an interest. Thank you Oliver Tavakoli, Mark Bauhaus, Andrew Coward, Dina Milazzo, Mike Banic, Manoj Leelanivas, Susan Ursch, Ronit Polak, Dorie Ravara, Susan Stover, Susan Lane, Gina Ahern, Michele Felder, Michelle Bhatia, Alan Sardella, Carolyn Rohrer, Penny Still, Trevor Dearing, Beth Gage, Michael Kluwin, Kristal Ferchau, David Asplund, Craig Strachman, Dean Hickman-Smith, Anya Harris, Nikhil Shah, and so many others. No matter how small or quick, your words of encouragement were like lifelines to me during this long journey.

Of course, the people at O'Reilly, who have held my hands through this process as a first-time author, have been invaluable. I am extremely appreciative of Mike Loukides's guidance and the support of Betsy Waliszewski and Sarah Kim, not to mention my copyeditor, Amy Thomson. I also want to extend a thank you to Nancy Koerbel for the careful reading and suggestions.

Then there is Patrick Ames, my editor. I am not sure I can ever thank him enough for all he has done for me and for this book. Without him, there would be no book. Thank you, Patrick, for believing in me and my ideas. Thank you for keeping me on track and being understanding of my quirks (no outlines). Thank you for your countless hours—I know you were up late at night right along with me—and the dedication you had to see this through. I am forever grateful.

Last, but certainly not least, I want to thank my family and friends. Their unwavering support and belief in me gave me the crazy notion that I could actually do this. While my dad passed away more than five years ago, he left me his trust in the possible, which kept me going when I had doubts. I want to thank my mom for her unconditional love, Uncle Ralph for his sanity checks, my in-laws for their enthusiasm, and all my family members and friends who in their own way helped me come to this point. To my husband and my girls, I do it all for you, with the acknowledgment that I will never be able to match all the gifts in life that you give me. I am very fortunate to have so many loving people in my life who inspire me to take leaps and be the better me. Thank you.

—Sarah Sorensen

Comments and Questions

Please address comments and questions concerning this book to the publisher:

O'Reilly Media, Inc.
1005 Gravenstein Highway North
Sebastopol, CA 95472
800-998-9938 (in the United States or Canada)
707-829-0515 (international or local)
707-829-0104 (fax)

We have a web page for this book, where we list errata, examples, and any additional information. You can access this page at:

http://oreilly.com/catalog/9780596157036/

To comment or ask technical questions about this book, send email to:

bookquestions@oreilly.com

For more information about our books, conferences, Resource Centers, and the O'Reilly Network, see our website at:

http://oreilly.com

To contact or learn more about the author, you can go to her author page on O'Reilly at:

http://www.oreillynet.com/pub/au/3718

or her website at:

http://www.sarahsorensen.com

or send an email to:

sarah@sarahsorensen.com

Safari® Books Online

 Safari Books Online is an on-demand digital library that lets you easily search over 7,500 technology and creative reference books and videos to find the answers you need quickly.

With a subscription, you can read any page and watch any video from our library online. Read books on your cell phone and mobile devices. Access new titles before they areavailable for print, and get exclusive access to manuscripts in development and post feedback for the authors. Copy and paste code samples, organize your favorites, download chapters, bookmark key sections, create notes, print out pages, and benefit from tons of other time-saving features.

O'Reilly Media has uploaded this book to the Safari Books Online service. To have full digital access to this book and others on similar topics from O'Reilly and other publishers, sign up for free at *http://my.safaribooksonline.com*.

I Am a Node

We cannot live for ourselves alone. Our lives are connected by a
thousand invisible threads, and along these sympathetic fibers,
our actions run as causes and return to us as results.

—Herman Melville

I am one of the more than 1.6 billion people in this world who is connected to the Internet, which is the world's largest public network. And like many of those billion or so, I spend a lot of time online, yet, for some reason, I had never really taken a step back to acknowledge the far-reaching implications of my ever-growing dependence on this connective technology. When I did, it hit me—*the network really is changing the world*. It's shepherding in the Digital Information Age that's shifting how we perceive, interact, and live in this world. And it's just the beginning. We are at a historic inflection point—one that our children's children will look back upon and study, like the Renaissance or Industrial Revolution.

You might be saying to yourself, "But the Internet has been mainstream for some time now; what's she talking about?" My point is that it's only within the last few years that it's become indispensable. It's only recently that we have come to accept it as an ever-present technology and use it to facilitate more and more of our daily lives. It was only a short time ago that it was *my* network, connecting *my* circle of friends and interests, and most other people simply used it the same way as me. Now, in a split second, it's different; now, it's a *global network* and I am one of billions of nodes (connection points) on it. We all are.

This is important. The *network* is any and all connections between computing devices. If you think of human anatomy, the network is like the intricate nervous system that takes messages from the brain to the rest of the body and takes feedback from the body back to the brain. It's responsible for processing critical information about the body and its surroundings to allow individuals to react to and regulate its behavior. The same is true of the network; it's a complex system optimized to transport and process all communications within its boundaries. The difference is really in the scale and scope on which the network can operate, which has no bounds.

Many people think of the network as the Internet. While the Internet is a network and certainly fits in the overall definition, the sustainable network discussed in this book is so much more. Just as there are the central nervous system and the peripheral nervous system in the body, you could say there is the public Internet and then all of the other networks in the world, which range from simple, connecting only one or two devices (say, your home network), to extremely complicated, connecting hundreds of thousands of devices and resources (say, a government, Fortune 500 company, or research network).

In a nutshell, the network is the foundation for the world's global communications infrastructure, which includes the Internet, as well as all the private domains of individuals, companies, governments, and institutions. The network supports all types of connections from all different types of computing devices (desktops, phones, and even building management controls). It facilitates conversations between people as well as inanimate objects (ever program your TV to record a show by using your phone?). It's a world filled with enough acronyms and unique terminology to make your head spin.

Wondering what I mean? Ever heard of LTE, IPTV, MPLS, or a PIM_SM bootstrap router? And this seeming complexity is one reason I would venture to guess that most of us would not be able to describe how the network works or what it really is.

The applications tend to get all the glory because they deliver the tangible "value" to you (ranging from email to a customer relationship management web tool to the massive role-playing game *World of Warcraft*), but it's the network that does the behind-the-scenes work. It's playing the connector role, fostering the relationships that are essential for these applications to maximize their value. And yet, this network, which is a part of every day of our lives, remains a mystery to most of us.

I thought of Thomas L. Friedman's book, *The World is Flat* (Farrar, Straus, and Giroux), and how he eloquently wrote about the new era of the individual, where everyone has the ability to participate, collaborate, and compete on a global scale. While there are a lot of forces at work impacting and shaping this "flattening," I couldn't help but think the deep dark secret in all this is the network. It's at the heart of it all. It's the enabling technology. It's fueling this era of rapid globalization and individual empowerment. It's changing the way we interact with our friends and family, conduct politics, and do business. It even impacts our planet.

You might ask, "So, why do I need to care about the network, when all I'm really interested in are the applications?"

Well, not only are we all nodes on the network, but the real worry is that if we don't care, we could miss a vital opportunity. The network represents a great platform for change because it establishes relationships between people, things, governments, and economies by creating, enabling, and supporting all the connections that have come to tie us together in one way or another. As such, it's one of our best tools for sustainable progress, change, and action.

It's a symbiotic relationship. The network offers us a sustainable platform for change, but we must in turn sustain it. The network's capacity to build, develop, and leverage these relationships enables it to take on a life of its own and perpetuate its growth—there are always new needs, interests, and connections to be made. Similarly, the more we are exposed to it (such as with the expanded availability of broadband), the more uses we find for it and the more we want and need it. But we must protect it and use it to its best advantage so that it can help as we tackle some of the hardest environmental, economic, social, and political challenges facing us.

Remember, we are all nodes on this network. It's the one thing that unites us all, no matter who you are or where you live. As such, it's a tool for enacting change. And it's one that already exists. We don't need to wait for its time to come—it's here. It has already set in motion changes that are infiltrating every aspect of our lives. Today, individuals, businesses, and countries can connect and influence people, ideas, and events in ways never before possible. By understanding the role the sustainable network plays in our lives, we can identify new extensions for this foundational technology and potentially derive more benefits and increase its influence.

But it's not all rosy. There are risks to the network that threaten its ongoing capability to provide a sustainable platform for change. And we need to understand those risks so we can mitigate and prevent them. To grow its reach and applicability, the network depends on investment. When money gets tight, it requires an ongoing commitment to invest in network buildouts that often have no immediate short-term payoff but are essential to long-term viability. And there's a dark side, too. In the wrong hands, these connections can be exploited and used to steal identities, blackmail, lure victims, infringe on an individual's rights, and, in the direst of circumstances, disable governments and endanger lives—the stuff of good crime shows and novels, only real.

Still, when I think about the network and all the implications of our ever-growing dependence on this connective technology, I am not afraid, but rather inspired, by the potential opportunities the network represents. I am electrified by the thought that *if people really knew what the network was and what it can do, we might be able to save time, energy, and effort on a scale that would actually make a dent in the world today.*

It's in this vein that I set out to shed light on the role the network plays as a sustainability agent to support energy conservation and economic, social, and political innovation. And to understand that, it's important to understand what the network is and what it isn't, its good qualities and the potential dangers associated with it. With a better understanding comes the opportunity to create better solutions, so this book sets out to demystify the network and provide examples of what it's already addressing and where it could be improved to enable greater change with greater impact.

The aim is to challenge every government, business, and individual to find their place in the global network. With this awareness, we can adapt to the speed at which things are changing, understand how everything is becoming interconnected, and recognize the new opportunities and challenges that come with living and working in this increasingly connected world. And then together we can develop more sustainable environmental, economic, social, and political models in this Digital Information Age.

The issues are complex, with many interdependencies. Real solutions will be developed from lots of small changes, new ideas, and many pieces working in concert—every node needs to play a role. There are also peripheral discussions and market and political influences that will shape the end state. But at its core, it's undeniable: the network plays the connector role, facilitating the relationships that will be instrumental to all our efforts to make this world a more sustainable one.

CHAPTER 2

What Is the Network: How Does It Work?

When we try to pick out anything by itself, we find it hitched to everything else in the Universe.

—John Muir

I t was just 10 years ago that the world started to see the network as a really new thing, even though it had been building momentum for years. Email began to replace faxes as a major mode of business and legal communication. Personal mobile phones started to really take off (until then, they typically were reserved for key executives as a perk and status symbol). Music was something you still went to the store to buy and listened to on a CD player. News was delivered to your doorstep. When you needed directions, you pulled out a map. When you wanted to see what was going on at your house or the street you lived on, you had to be there.

Today, it seems that everyone goes online to do everything.

Email addresses are as common as phone numbers. Cell phones are more important than landline telephones. You can hear a song in your favorite coffee shop, use your iPhone to identify it, buy it, and then listen to it on your way home. You can look up directions from so many different devices that sometimes you have to pause to decide which technology to use. You can see your street from your desktop at work and monitor your house from halfway across the world. You can turn on the lights, move the Nannycam, and schedule your TV to record a new program with the click of a button. You can buy anything in the world from your laptop, from cars to houses, trade anything away, or swap and sell what you don't want or need with someone online who does. You can play a game with someone in Russia and you can have a real-time video-conference with people in Finland, Texas, Singapore, and Zambia. And I haven't even scratched the surface.

Somewhere between the dot.com bust, when we all laughed at how an Internet company could be worth more on paper than General Motors, and now, a mere decade later, something has happened. We passed a tipping point in terms of uses and user adoption. Now, we use the network every day of our lives, whether we realize it or not.

Because of the network's pervasive and inevitable influence on our lives, it's important to understand how it works. With greater understanding, there can be greater possibilities, which can come in handy these days.

Linking Things Together

The network unlocks the value of all the computing devices and applications we use by linking them together. Take your cell phone, for example. If you can't reach anyone, it's nothing more than an expensive fashion accessory. It's the network that really gives it value. When you start to extend that value to your other connected devices, the vast expanse of the network starts to come into focus.

So, how does the network do this linking, and how does it work?

The answer is complicated, so let's use an analogy. Say you are writing a letter to your mother (I know, I know, but stay with me here). You start by getting out your stationery and putting pen to paper to compose your letter—that represents your application, say, your email program. It's what you (the user) actually interact with to do something—in this case, creating content. To take it a step further, the paper is your screen, or interface, and the pen is your mouse, keyboard, or keypad.

Once you have written the letter, you place it in an envelope and then address the envelope with a zip code to ensure that all those who handle the letter as it goes through the mail system know exactly where it needs to go. Then you physically place the letter into the mail system, either by handing it to a postal clerk or dropping it into a mailbox. At that point, the postal clerks (or machines) sort and mark the envelope with a routing code (often embedded in that bar code at the bottom of a sent letter) that tells all the mail handlers where it needs to go and the best route to get it there (Figure 2-1).

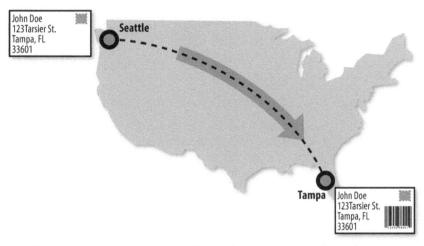

Figure 2-1. The network process is very similar to that of snailmail (the traditional postal system that can take days to route a package between sender and receiver).

Now let's assume you are connected to the Internet via your computer, phone, or other networked device and you are using the device's email application to create and send a message. When you click the Send button, the email application automatically packages your message (stuffing it into an envelope, so to speak) and passes it to the email server, which is like the post office clerk who marks the mail with the address and routing information that tells the system exactly where the mail is supposed to be delivered. The email server is a physical device that your email application is connected to via the network, and it is actually what you are connecting to when you access your email messages.

The email server plays a "translator" role, taking the content from your email application and transforming it into a format or language that is understood by the traffic-handling devices in the network (think of them like trucks or mail-sorting machines), ensuring that they have the right information to send the email message where it needs to go (Figure 2-2).

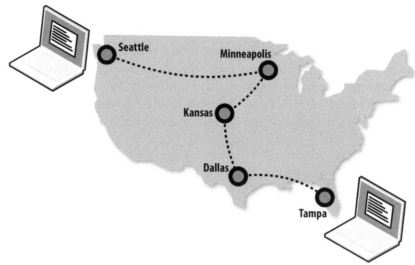

Figure 2-2. The reason they call it email is because the information is sent digitally across the network and uses electricity to do so (more about the network's electric needs later in this book).

Protocols

Just as there are specific ways to address your letter (use the recipient's name, street address, zip code, and country), there are specific ways to address the "packages" being sent across the network. These are called *protocols*, and they are agreed-upon standard formats that allow the various devices (mail handlers) to understand and interact with one another.

As I have already described, there is an ever-increasing number of computing device types connecting to the network, ranging from computers and phones to cameras, cars, TVs, and even refrigerators. These diverse devices can ultimately communicate with one another using the standardized set of protocols that govern the network, dictating how information should be received and transmitted across the network by all participating devices.

Just as there are conventions regarding what you should do and say when you first meet someone ("Hello, my name is Sam. Nice to meet you") and what to expect as a response ("Hi, my name is John, good to meet you, too"), there are conventions regarding what these network devices expect to see when they encounter a package and how they respond to that information once they encounter it.

This information is predictably contained in headers that are added to the content—in our case, the text of your email. These headers provide a variety of additional information that serves as pointers for the devices that handle and direct the traffic on the network to make sure your message is delivered to the correct place. In our case, the email server adds header information to the message before sending it to the network devices (Figure 2-3).

Figure 2-3. When you send information over the network, your computer or device adds a header to the package, and the network devices read and add header information as necessary.

Each person/role in the postal system requires different information. For example, the mail sorter is most interested in the zip code to make sure letters make it to the right part of the world, while the mail carrier is most interested in the specific street address. Similarly, different network devices handling network traffic require different header information, and each device bases its forwarding decisions on that information.

Just a Few More Terms: Hosts, Routers, Switches, LANs, and WANs

At the heart of the network lies a mesh of interconnected routers and switches, each capable of processing and forwarding millions of packets (think bite-size packages of bits and bytes) per second. These network devices operate the same way as all the handlers in the postal system. Your letter goes in steps to intermediate points, and workers at each intermediate point forward it on to the next point, which takes it closer and closer to its end destination. Network devices do the same thing. They are the traffic handlers in the middle of the country in Figures 2-1 and 2-2, and they are the means by which the network finds you among the billion-and-a-half network users across the world.

At the most fundamental level, *routers* and *switches* are responsible for making sure traffic packets get from point A to point B on the network, by reading the header information and passing the packets on. The differences between routers and switches are starting to blur, as functionality converges and network layers collapse, but in simple terms, they're distinguished by the types of information they evaluate when making their decisions on how to transport the traffic.

A switch on your local network typically keeps track of the host that's connecting to the Internet. The switch that is physically closest to you may be downtown at the DSL center or at the end of your roaming wireless connection. But when you connect to the network, a switch (somewhere) adds a record of your connection in a table that includes the hardware address that uniquely identifies your host and location (similar to your street address and zip code). That hardware address is called the *Media Access Control* (MAC) address (nothing to do with Macs or Macintosh computers). As a result, when the switch receives traffic for that particular host, it knows exactly where to send it to and can do so quickly.

Switches typically transport traffic between segments of a single *Local Area Network* (LAN), which is a network that is confined to a relatively small area, consisting of a single building or perhaps a campus with multiple buildings in close proximity. LANs are often private networks of companies or individuals.

Routers, on the other hand, connect at least two networks. These can be two different LANs, or a LAN and a *Wide Area Network* (WAN), which is a network that spans a relatively large geographical area and can be a mix of public and private networks. The largest WAN in the world is the Internet itself, which is sometimes referred to as "the cloud," and is often depicted in drawings as something like Figure 2-4. Why a cloud? Perhaps because there's so much going on in there that no one can keep track of it all (except for the world's routers).

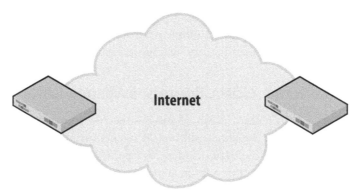

Figure 2-4. *The Internet is often referred to and depicted as a cloud. Here we have two switches on the edge of their connections to the Internet.*

Routers make decisions about how to handle the traffic they receive by looking (very quickly) at a couple of places for information. First, routers create and maintain internal tables that contain information on the availability of all the other routers they can forward packets to within their purview. Second, they look at the headers that describe where the traffic is coming from, where it is going, the type of application, and the priority of that piece of traffic. Based on their processing of this information, routers determine the best route to send the traffic to get it from point A to point B. You can imagine how quickly they must do this, and if everyone is online at once, the load becomes enormous. So, when the network seems slow, chances are, something between point A and point B is either not routing fast enough, is very busy, or could be down (by the way, when a router goes down, all the other routers in its purview instantly know, and they start to reroute traffic via another route).

When your letter gets to your mother's mailbox via the mail carrier, she will most likely open it, read it, and then respond in some way, potentially by sending you a letter or giving you a call to tell you she received your letter. A similar process takes place online. The receiving device—in this case, the email server of your recipient—opens the packet and sends it to the recipient's inbox for the next time she logs in.

A single email is not just a single packet; it is actually broken up into multiple packets for easier transmission, most often following the email Simple Mail Transfer Protocol (SMTP). These packets are then sent across the network and reassembled into the complete message at the other end—that is, unless you have been blocked by the recipient or the email server thinks your message should be classed as junk mail!

The recipient will then open and hopefully read the message. If she replies to you, the process will start all over again. The routers and switches that lie between you and your recipient manage the traffic and forwarding. Switches get you onto and off of the Internet and routers find the best route between switches. To borrow from the almost-so-old-it's-hip-again Information Highway metaphor, switches are exits and on-ramps, and routers are the highway interchanges.

All of this is seamless to you, the user, which in a lot of ways is very similar to the traditional postal system. Once you address your letter and drop it in the mailbox, you don't need to worry about exactly how it is going to get to your mother. You don't know whether it will travel by air or train or truck. You don't know how many stops it is going to make along the way. All you know is you have posted it and within a predictable amount of time, you can expect it to be delivered to your mother's mailbox. This is also how the network works. Once you send an email message, you don't think about how many devices are going to be touching it or the exact route it is going to take to get to the email server at the other end on its way to your recipient's email inbox. Just like in Figure 2-5, the cloud represents all these devices you don't particularly care about seeing (individually, that is).

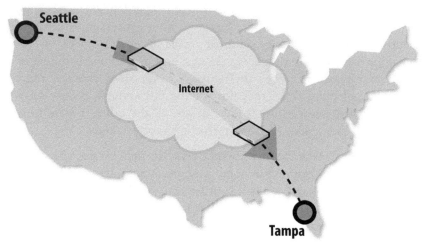

Figure 2-5. Switches and routers make sure traffic is routed around the world in seconds. Don't get hung up on the cloud's size here. In reality, it covers the earth.

It's a different story, however, when something goes wrong and the mail doesn't get to its destination. In the regular postal system, the letter you sent may be returned to you. In an email system, you will generally get a notice that your message is undeliverable. There are occasions when the mail simply gets lost. If this happens offline, there is not a lot you can do about it and not a lot of ways to track what happened. For the average individual like you and me, the same goes for the network. In both cases, there could be many explanations; most often, mail gets lost because of some sort of user error. Fortunately, it is fairly rare for mail to get lost.

There are many safeguards built into the network to help ensure that traffic gets from one place to another fairly reliably. However, there are some issues, both economical and technical, that may affect the availability and reliability of the network. We'll discuss some of these issues in later chapters. Most poignant are the investments that ensure that access can be extended to everyone, and security technologies and mechanisms that can lower risks in the digital world.

There is reason to be optimistic and believe that any network issue can and will be addressed. To date, there have not been any impenetrable barricades; there has only been acceleration on all of these fronts. The routers and switches and the backbone networks they support have all done their job and continue to compensate, so that, like the mailman, they can continue to deliver your messages, come rain or shine.

CHAPTER 3

Green by Accident

Where observation is concerned,
chance favors only the prepared mind.

—Louis Pasteur

Accidents don't always have to be bad. History has given us many marvelous discoveries and contributions to society that have resulted from accidents—from Coca-Cola, Viagra, and chocolate chip cookies to Teflon, X-rays, and penicillin (you can find even more accidental discoveries at *http://listverse.com/miscellaneous/top-10-accidental-discoveries*). Some of these contributions have had a greater impact on our culture than others; then again, it could also depend on your perspective whether the chocolate chip cookie is more important than Viagra (I'll stop right there). Anyway, the point is that in each of these cases, the accident solved a different problem than the one that it was actually intended to solve.

The genius of the inventors of these "accidents" is that they were able to recognize the unintended benefits that could be derived from their creations and transform them into something even better. They are perfect examples of the power of the often-overused phrase "thinking outside the box." It is an unteachable skill, to make simple observations and turn them into profound ones, to be able to see adjacent relevance for innovation and solve problems that deviate from the initial focus. Sir Isaac Newton may have come across the proof for gravity by accident, but once it hit him in the head (literally, if you believe the apple story), the world as we knew it changed forever.

The same could be said for the network. This book suggests some of the many ways it is forever changing the way we work, live, and play. It represents an increasingly invaluable tool that can help us address some of the world's toughest problems. But let's be truthful—the network wasn't intended to be green at all. Its original design goal was not to be a tool for sustainable action; it was never meant to be the catalyst for widespread change.

However, as with many great inventions, the network, which was designed to connect one computer to another, is now being creatively extended to address problems well beyond its original purpose. It may have occurred by happenstance, but its influence is nothing less than purposeful. It's the glue to all of our modern-day lives, creating, building, and supporting the critical relationships that underpin our personal, civic, and business activities.

So, is the network green?

Not really. It's a fallacy to say the network is a "green" technology; it is a technology that has environmental benefits and can be used to support more sustainable environmental practices, but it is not "green." As we'll see in other chapters, it uses electricity, wire, and lots of hardware (made of one material or another). So why the green terminology in this chapter? Why the hint of green-ness to an industry notorious for helping create the monstrous data centers that consume a few percentage points of our total energy consumption?

Because the network represents the possible. In fact, there are many examples and reports available that document the network as a tool for more sustainable habits, processes, and actions. For example, an analysis by McKinsey & Company estimates that information and communications technology (ICT), of which the network is a foundational element, has the potential to reduce global emissions by 15% by 2020.[1] So, while I readily admit I don't like the "green" term, I think it's appropriate to use it to start to frame the potential of the network.

The problem is that over the past several years, "green" has come to represent the environmental aspects of sustainability, focusing the discussions and often overshadowing broader sustainability topics. I think it has been overhyped and overmarketed to the point that it doesn't really mean anything. There is a lot of "greenwashing" going on; it seems every company these days slaps some sort of "green" label on its products. Ultimately, all these labels and advertising campaigns only serve to diminish the impact and confuse customers. I don't know how many times I've sat in a grocery store aisle trying to figure out which product is "greener," without really understanding what makes these products "green" in the first place. If I am having these problems with laundry detergent and hand soap, it's not hard to imagine the complexity and burden ICT workers face when buying their IT equipment and network infrastructures.

The reality is that very few products are green in the strictest sense; only those that have no impact on (or that positively impact) the environment over the span of their lifetimes—including creation, use, and disposal—should truly carry the "green" moniker. But since most products have some impact during a portion of their lifetimes, their manufacturers are leveraging "green" to indicate that they are more environmentally friendly and have less impact than previous or other competitive solutions in the market. As you can imagine, this is often a subtlety that is hard to prove, hence the confusion (and my extended grocery trips). It's like "fat free." To be fat free, a serving of food must have less than half a gram of fat. That's not exactly fat free, especially if the servings are extremely small, like five cheesepuffs (who eats just five cheesepuffs?!), but it qualifies for the label. So, with all the wiggle room and mixed messages around what is "green," we are left struggling to figure out what it all means.

As a result, I think it's important to expand the discussion to really reflect the goal of "green," which is to be more sustainable, not just environmentally, but in every aspect of our lives. I admit there is also much confusion around the term "sustainability." In absolute terms, it relates to the ability to maintain something indefinitely. Putting it in our current context, that "something" is the world we live in. How we maintain it needs to be addressed from a broader sustainability sense, in an environmental, economic, social, and political perspective. This book contends that the network can be used for sustainable purposes—it connects individuals, businesses, governments, and economies to sustain development, opportunities, and change.

The sustainable network is the *sustaining* network, playing a stabilizing role by creating and perpetuating the vital relationships needed to tackle the problems that most threaten our world:

- From an *environmental* perspective, the network can be used to take something physical and make it better or even replace it with something virtual. This is the accidental happenstance of the green network. In most cases, replacing something physical with something digital can be more sustainable. Examples include conducting a meeting among a dozen people online via a video web conference instead of flying those people to and fro to sit in the same room, or being able to stay home one day a week and telecommute instead of driving into the office. The network can be used to reduce waste and improve the efficiency of material consumption, the ready example being digital music rather than CDs. And there are more and more examples of ways that we can use the network to reduce our carbon footprint and environmental impact. In fact, there are many examples and reports available that tie worldwide CO_2 emissions abatement to the ICT sector. Remember, the previously mentioned McKinsey study estimates that ICT has the potential to reduce global emissions by 15% by 2020.

- From an *economic* perspective, the network can tear down boundaries and create opportunities for individuals and businesses to enter and participate in global markets. It can connect people to the resources and skills they need to be more productive in the workforce, fostering the competitiveness of individuals, companies, and countries alike. The network is being used to achieve productivity and operational efficiency gains in every type of traditional industry you can imagine, as well as creating completely new business ventures, products, and market segments from Google and Facebook to Hulu.com.

- From a *social* perspective, the network can be used to solve problems en masse, connecting the right people and resources to the "right" problems around the world. It can be used to locate and assemble resources and support for social causes. It can be used to improve many of the social services we rely on today—for instance, making healthcare and safety services more efficient and reliable. This is something those of us in the U.S. have heard a lot about lately, as "Health IT" plays a prominent role in the debate on how to reduce the costs and improve the quality of health care.

- From a *political* perspective, the network can amplify the voice of the individual (a prospect some ideologies may view as negative), giving people a platform from which to speak and air their opinions and grievances. It can create greater transparency and bring to light abusive or egregious behavior by governments or their policies toward citizens, as evidenced by the information unveiled and discussed at length in the millions of blogs that exist around the world. The sustainable network also helps bring like minds together, mobilizing them to better influence and shape public discourse and policy.

In many ways, today's network is the equivalent of the seafaring trade routes of past centuries, establishing new connections between continents and people, and whose ripple effects changed the world in ways never imagined by those who initially explored the seas. When you connect to today's network, you now connect to the world. And when you are connected, you establish relationships and access to a global wealth of information and resources that has the potential to change everything from the way you live and work to what you consume, to your social relationships, and even to your personal relevance to the world and its fate.

It is this ability to reach and connect people, devices, and places around the world, in what we must assume to be helpful and meaningful ways, that makes the global network the best tool for sustainable change of our time. It can tackle not only climate change and resource conservation, but the state of education and healthcare, economic stability, political involvement, and much more. It may not be "green," but it is a very "sustainable" tool for sustainable action (even if it was by accident).

CHAPTER 4

What Makes the Network Sustainable?

Describing the network as something that connects computing devices is akin to calling the Rosetta Stone a rock with words on it.

—Sarah Sorensen

Rahima Abdul Majeed lives in Kabul, Afghanistan. She needed a loan of $25 to expand her tailor shop. She didn't get the money from her local bank; instead, she received the money from someone halfway around the world who saw and funded her request on Kiva.org, a microlending site. Working with a local financial company that handled all the local logistics and serviced the loan, Rahima was able to use that money to buy an electronic sewing machine and increase the money she earns to help support her family. She also repaid the loan within its specified eight-month term, so that money can potentially be used to support the lifelong ambitions of another entrepreneur.[1]

Rahima is just one of the tens of thousands of entrepreneurs who have received a much-needed loan via Kiva.org to start or expand their businesses. Kiva's mission, to connect people through lending for the sake of alleviating poverty,[2] is an amazing example of the sustainable network's ability to reach out across all corners of the globe to establish connections and relationships that create change. It's something our tactile world simply could not have accomplished at this scale.

It is this pervasiveness that makes today's network one of the most powerful platforms we have. Its ability to spread out and infiltrate parts of the world that have typically been impervious to new technologies is simply uncanny. The network's ability to deliver equitable access to information and opportunity on a scale never before possible accounts for its rapid rise in adoption, especially over the past decade. Its ubiquity represents an unprecedented opportunity to reach, connect, involve, and impact everyone and everything.

If that last sentence seems a little outrageous to you, perhaps a little too politically correct or just pure starry-eyed optimism, you might consider that the network has already done it, and has done it *all* in a relatively short amount of time. While we have concerned ourselves over the past few years with the war in Iraq, or the rise and fall of our leaders, or the stock market crash and the subprime mortgage crisis, the network has been reaching out and achieving astronomical growth rates. New technology breakthroughs and network architectural evolutions have taken place, and the industry has found ways to extend broadband's reach and expand the offerings we all enjoy as users. So, the sustainable network isn't just about to happen. It just is.

After all, it was just 40 years ago, in 1969, when Leonard Kleinrock—the Christopher Columbus of the Internet and a computer science professor at the University of California in Los Angeles—and a group of graduate students connected to a computer at Stanford University and tried to send it some data. Theirs was the first real-world attempt to make the concept of Arpanet—the idea to connect computers over phone lines led by the U.S. Department of Defense's Advance Research Project Agency (ARPA)—a reality. They only got as far as "LOG" in their attempt to type LOGIN before it crashed, but there was no turning back.[3]

After a lot of work by luminaries such as Vinton Gray Cerf and Robert E. Kahn, and many innovations later, the first public demonstration of Arpanet was successfully conducted in 1972 among 40 machines. In 1970, Douglas Engelbart received a patent for a "computer mouse" (it would be years later when the inventor learned that it had been licensed to a little company called Apple for "something like $40,000").[4] Being of British heritage, I am pleased to say that Queen Elizabeth went online and successfully sent the first royal email message in 1976.

By 1981, Arpanet had 213 hosts, with a new host added every 20 days. The following year, the term "Internet" was first used to describe these interconnections among hosts; by 1990, the Internet was the de facto name for this network, particularly after Arpanet was decommissioned.

In 1990, Sir Timothy John Berners-Lee implemented the first HTTP (Hypertext Transfer Protocol) connection, which is the foundational protocol that defines how to retrieve interlinked resources, leading to the establishment of the World Wide Web (www). In 1991, the Internet became much more friendly for people like you and me, with the introduction of a "point-and-click" way of traversing the Internet (Gopher) and the first graphical browser (Mosaic) for the Web.

By 1995, the Internet was entirely in commercial hands, with 6.5 million hosts and 100,000 "www" sites. In 1996, Microsoft officially entered the Internet market with its introduction of its MSN browser, designed to take on the browser introduced earlier by Netscape Communications; at that time, there were 40 million people connected to the Internet. By 1998, that number was at 70 million.

Just 10 years later, in 2008, there were almost 1.5 billion Internet users in the world (*www.internetworldstat.com*; August 13, 2008). You do the numbers here—from 70 million to 1.5 billion in 10 years. That, I suggest, is a staggering adoption rate literally unknown to mankind. The significance of these 10 years is that it's indicative of the accelerating rate of adoption and change that we can expect to see continue as the world becomes even more connected.

While 1.5 billion might seem a potentially staggering number, all indicators are that the numbers will only continue to grow (see Figure 4-1). According to the *World Almanac and Book of Facts 2008*, between November and December 2007, 5.8 million new users joined the Internet; that translates to 193,333 per day, 8,055 per hour, 134 per minute, and roughly 2 people per second! Looking ahead, the total number of Internet users is expected to surpass the 2 billion mark by 2015 and the 3 billion mark by 2040, but it could be even sooner.[5] Perhaps more telling is that the growth of Internet usage in emerging, less developed countries is just as strong. In fact, there are estimates that the number of Internet users in the top 10 emerging markets surpassed the number of Internet users in the top 10 developed markets in 2008.[6]

Figure 4-1. Network adoption in the near future almost defines the concept of viral; the world map with the top 10 emerging markets shaded will shortly double our current network traffic.

We have already surpassed previous predictions that had the number of Internet users hitting 1.5 billion in 2011. In its report titled "Worldwide Online Population Forecast, 2006 to 2011," Jupiter Research anticipated "that a 38% increase in the number of people with online access will mean that, by 2011, 22% of the Earth's population will surf the Internet regularly" (*www.clickz.com/3626274*).

Broadband penetration, which is the physical high-speed network connection often required to support a satisfactory network experience, is also growing at a heady world-wide clip. Informa Telecoms & Media estimates that by 2011, there will be more than 1 billion broadband subscribers worldwide.[7] In 2012, 17 countries are predicted to have broadband penetration rates of 60%, up from 5 countries in 2007. Depending on market conditions, some countries could have a broadband penetration ceiling of 80% or greater.[8] Currently, the country with the highest penetration is South Korea, at 97%,[9] demonstrating the sheer range and potential of the network's reach into the homes and hands of people in *all* parts of the world. I don't have the numbers, but I suspect that's a higher penetration than in Silicon Valley itself.

What's caused this expansion? Some of these remarkable numbers are due in part to the fact that the network is not restricted to a singular device type; it's not constrained to just computers, as it was when Kleinrock ran his experiment. Rather, the past 10 years have been witness to a network that supports all types of devices that attach to a computer or have some type of computing power. While there are many varying estimates, the global number of Internet-connected devices is in the billions today; some estimate it's at 15 billion, with growth projections going into the trillions, potentially reaching 10 trillion over the next 15 years.[10]

Ten trillion devices does seem rather large, but consider that there are currently 4 billion mobile devices,[11] with forecasts up to 6 billion mobile subscribers by 2013,[12] and extend those numbers to the great range of devices we could be talking about—from phones and computers to TVs and refrigerators, traffic lights and cars, watches and, of course, the ever-present target, your wallet—it's easy to see how the numbers can get into the trillions.

There's another dimension to this perfect storm. These devices have become both increasingly powerful and very affordable, helping to ensure access to the network for an ever-swelling portion of the world's population. Perhaps you noticed it yourself during these past 10 years? Take the cell phone you had in the late 1990s. It's probably been replaced several times since, incrementally getting more computing power and functionality, until your present model. Now, you may have a smartphone that connects to the network and is more powerful than the full-blown computer or laptop you had just a decade ago.

In the days of the first computers, there were stories of entire rooms required to house the computer equipment to support a single application. Over time, we have seen processing power and memory capacity evolve, so that today, you can hold all you need in the palm of your hand. For example, when IBM invented the disk drive, the device used to store digital information, the prototype was approximately the size of a Mini Cooper and capable of storing the equivalent of two songs; today, an Apple iPod is about the size of a credit card and can hold up to 30,000 songs.[13]

The versatility of our new computing devices has also gone way up. For example, a decade ago, all you could do with your phone was make a call. Now, of course, you can take photos and videos, send and receive text messages, send and receive email messages, receive live news feeds, surf the Internet, and so much more. Smartphones are getting us ever closer to the reality of carrying our personal computers in our pockets. Palm's Pre, Apple's iPhone, and Google's G2, to name only a few, are no longer just the proven tools of the business road warrior. Now, Mom and Dad and their high-school offspring carry them, too. One million units of the iPhone 3G sold in the first three days it was available; by the end of 2008, Apple had sold more than 17 million,[14] with plans to make 40 million more phones from August 2008 to August 2009.[15]

Another factor in the soaring network adoption rates is the fact that as the technologies have matured, these devices have become less expensive to produce, and subsequently, are within the means of a larger consumer population. It wasn't too long ago that your computer had just a half a gigabyte of memory, and upgrades to get more cost hundreds of dollars; now, you can get 500 GB of memory standard. Web-enabled phones used to be hundreds of dollars, but now you can often get them for free from your mobile network provider or, at most, for a nominal price. On and on, devices that are network-enabled cost less, do more, and shrink in size at a rate that mimics the speed of their adoption.

This has all made it possible for the network to extend to segments of the population and emerging countries that might otherwise be left out because disposable income is extremely limited and a personal computer is beyond the average citizen's means, or where access is unsupported because there is no physical infrastructure (phone cables). The smaller, cheaper, more powerful devices enable the network to expand to segments of the world's population that might otherwise be left out.

Take a country such as India. There are 50 million middle-income families, but only 8 million homes with a PC. So, more than 30 million Indian consumers travel to cyber-cafés to access the network on a regular basis.[16] The mobile phone, however, offers a much more convenient and affordable alternative to the traditional computer. For about $10 a month, which seems to be the threshold price that Indian consumers can or are willing to pay per month for connectivity, they can have a mobile phone and all the possibilities that go along with having access to the network. This probably explains why India has been adding approximately 15 million new subscribers a month.[17] Soon they submit to temptation and pay a small fee to subscribe to SMS (Short Message Service) feeds, and it suddenly becomes the primary source of news for millions of subscribers in India.[18]

Or take China, which represents the world's largest mobile market. In November 2008, the Ministry of Industry and Information Technology placed the number of Chinese mobile subscribers at 633 million; that number represents less than half the population of China, but more mobile users than almost all of Europe's population,[19] and China is adding roughly 7.8 million mobile subscribers a month.[20] The typical investment of $10 a month represents 7% (or more) of the average Chinese user's monthly salary,[21] which consumers seem willing to pay as they adopt the technology as their primary communications tool for both voice and data.[22] Of particular note is that as the "base-of-the-pyramid" families generate more income, ICT[23] spending increases eightfold, while spending on food and housing rises only slightly.[24] I guess the network truly has become an essential.

The ICT industry refers to the full range of devices and applications that play a role in digital communication, ranging from monitors and cell phones to PCs and storage devices. This also includes all the different applications that enable the sharing or use of information, from email and online services to spreadsheets and video games, as well as the hardware and software needed to operate the networks that transmit the information, from the smallest home office to the largest global networks.

Another example can be found among consumers in the 17,000 islands that make up Indonesia.[25] Most use their phones to surf the Internet because other alternatives, such as high-speed cable, DSL, or regular phone lines are simply unavailable or too costly, even between the larger islands.

Then there's Brazil. Only 17.7% of the more than 192 million Brazilians have access to the Internet, but Brazil represents the fifth largest mobile market in the world, with approximately 100,000 million mobile subscribers in 2007.[26] It seems logical that for this market, Internet services will increasingly be delivered via the mobile phone networks. This theory is backed by the overall growth in mobile data traffic reported by the country's service providers and analyst predictions that Brazil's telecom market will increase at a compound annual growth rate (CAGR) of 18.26% from 2007–2012.[27] This is in relation to a 6% CAGR for the worldwide telecom/datacom equipment market during the same timeframe.[28]

There are many more examples of consumers using alternative devices, such as netbooks (which are cheaper than computers and are getting comparable in processing power), to be connected to the network all the time. As all computing devices become smaller, more powerful, and more affordable, the network access adoption rate will continue to grow and literally penetrate the circumference of the globe. It is becoming easier and easier to conceive of a world where it is possible to get a computing device into the hands of every single person and subsequently give them access to the network and the wealth of resources and opportunity that go with it. A decade ago, it was a pipe dream. Today, you can readily see how that could be implemented. A decade from now, we might say, "What took so long?"

I noted that the amazing thing about the network's reach and astounding adoption rate is that it has happened in a relatively short amount of time. To ground it a little, compare the network's adoption numbers with the adoption of television sets—another highly popular and successful technology, which was invented in the late 1920s. As of 2003, there were approximately 1.4 billion TVs in the world, with China (400 million), the U.S. (219 million) and Japan (86.5 million) leading the way.[29] It took the television industry 75 years to get 1.4 billion devices into the hands of consumers; in a little less than a quarter of that amount of time, consumers have purchased almost three times as many Internet-connected devices by all conservative accounts.

These numbers speak volumes on the ubiquity of the network and its ability to reach and connect large swaths of the population. As much as I would like to think this is a theory made up from my insightful analysis, it's not; it's simple arithmetic. In 1998, there were approximately 70 million network users. Today, there are more than 1.6 billion users and growing. It's been organic growth, simply feeding itself. Once introduced, the network has had the ability to take off quickly, making it a transformative platform easily embedded in everyone's daily work and personal life.

And in its wake, the network removes physical and geographical barriers and facilitates connections to people and resources that would otherwise be cumbersome or resource-intensive to maintain. In the past decade, it has truly leveled the playing field for the world's population. A farmer in India can be as wired as a VP in Silicon Valley. Again, this isn't theory; it's fact. The cost and availability of devices, plus the growth of the network and its services, has made the farmer and the VP equal in terms of access.

It's this all-pervading access and the different relationships that all these connections represent that make the network one of our greatest tools for sustainable change, development, and action.

CHAPTER 5

Broadband: What Is It?

...my birdfeeder Web cam

I feel the need, the need for speed.
—Maverick to Goose in the movie *Top Gun*

B roadband exists in our daily vernacular. It's in TV commercials from cable and phone providers that depict it as something like mercury, that, when applied to your shoes, allows you to outrace rockets and airplanes. It's on the radio as something you get for an amazing low price every month, with the first six months free. Even political leaders have used it as a rallying cry, promising to make it a part of their respective economic stimulus packages.

What is broadband, and why should you care?

In general terms, *broadband* is a high-speed network connection that allows you to do several things at the same time (each thing requiring a piece of that connection). For instance, with a broadband connection, you can download email messages with large pictures attached while watching an online video or listening to streaming music, while reading a blog and shopping on Amazon; you are not forced to do one thing or the other separately. And if the broadband is "broad" enough, the experience of doing it all will be pretty good (fast with no lag). It seems the more we get of it, the more we use it, and these new uses tend to demand more of the network, creating a self-perpetuating cycle that requires continual adoption and upgrading of our broadband connections.

So what's the big deal? Well, first and foremost, until just a few years ago it was not widely available. If you remember, in Chapter 4, when we discussed Kleinrock's initial Internet experiment, the connection went over the copper lines of a traditional, circuit-switched phone network, often referred to as the public switched telephone network (PSTN). This wired network, consisting of telephone poles and miles and miles of wire, supports reliable, high-quality, landline voice communications. However, with the introduction of Internet access and subsequent video downloads and other rich-media applications, the scope of what the sustainable network is now being asked to do is pushing the old telephone network to its limits.

Voice traffic, which is generated when you make a phone call, has specific requirements in terms of its information-carrying capacity and speed, otherwise known as *bandwidth*. When you add other types of traffic—say, video—onto these networks, it drastically changes the requirements. Consider that transmitting a minute of video requires up to 10 times the bandwidth of audio or more, depending on the quality.[1] That is a lot for the telephone network—optimized for audio—to handle.

This is why, if any of you still use a dial-up modem, you are frustrated by the slow speed of your connection (some readers may not know what a dial-up modem is; suffice it to say, it was popular at the same time in history when a 20 MB hard disk was all you needed for backup yet cost $200). In general, a connection of this type has the bandwidth of up to 56 kilobits per second (Kbps), which is a unit of measurement that quantifies the rate at which data can be transmitted from one device to another. Bandwidth is typically measured in these terms, which can also be called *throughput*. The data rates are measured in derivatives of bits and bytes. Bytes consist of 8 bits each. So, if a kilobit per second is equal to 1,000 bits per second, then a kilobyte per second (KBps) is equal to 1,000 bytes per second or 8,000 bits per second (it's actually 1,024 bytes per second and 8,192 bits, but I have rounded for simplicity's sake in this and subsequent calculations).[2]

A regular phone call requires approximately 8 Kbps to be of a good quality (8,000 bits/s). Compare that to compressed HDTV quality video, which can require 27 Mbps (27,000,000 bits/s). Just think of your telephone line as optimized for a VHS/Beta movie and broadband as well suited for a Blu-ray experience, and it's easy to understand why using the traditional telephone network via a dial-up modem is simply not acceptable for the varied requirements of today's much more demanding applications. The traditional telephone network simply doesn't have the bandwidth or capacity to support multiple applications at the same time—it's why you can't make a phone call when you are accessing the Internet using a dial-up modem.

Some Other Measurements You Might Want to Know (or Not)

- One megabit per second (Mbps) is equal to 1,000,000 bits per second
- One gigabit per second (Gbps) is equal to 1,000,000,000 bits per second
- One terabit per second (Tbps) is equal to 1,000,000,000,000 bits per second
- One megabyte per second (MBps) is equal to 1,000,000 bytes or 8 Mbps
- One gigabyte per second (GBps) is equal to 1,000,000,000 bytes per second or 8 Gbps
- One terabyte per second (TBps) is equal to 1,000,000,000,000 bytes per second or 8 Tbps
- One exabyte per second (EBps) is equal to one quintillion bytes per second

---

In 1994, a major research center with approximately 2,000 people working at a single location used one 56 Kbps modem for *all* of its network traffic, which was basically text-based email. Now, even if you're not streaming HDTV from Hulu.com yet, downloading a simple attachment to an email message on a 56 Kbps modem can seem a glacial experience (it's particularly disappointing when you find out it's porn-infused spam—absolutely hate that!).

What today's (and tomorrow's) users really need is a connection that allows them to have the flexibility to do several things at once, and quickly. We tend to demand the utmost in availability and performance because a few seconds' delay can affect how we experience the YouTube clip or online TV show we are watching. It can be the difference between closing a deal or losing the bid, having a good conversation or dropping the connection, and spending 1 minute or 10 to find something online.

We demand more. We want better, and we want faster, and this is what is driving the adoption of broadband. Broadband offers much more bandwidth than a dial-up modem, as well as the capacity to support multiple channels, which means users can do different things at once. Gartner Group predicts 77% of U.S. households will have a broadband Internet subscription by 2012, making the U.S. one of 17 countries worldwide that they predict will reach penetration rates of 60% or more in that same time period.[3]

Over the past 10 years, there has been a 600,000% increase (yes, that's 600,000%) in the total number of broadband subscribers.[4] In 2007, there were 340 million fixed broadband users worldwide, growing at 15% a year, with adoption hitting the 400-million milestone in November 2008.[5] That is phenomenal growth, primarily due to the evolution and advancement of the access technologies, which is the stuff you don't see, such as the hardware in the switching hubs and the cell towers on the tops of buildings, as well as the increasing availability of broadband across geographical regions.

While we may want it, we don't know exactly how much we need, nor what exactly bandwidth it is. And to tell the truth, there isn't really a single standard for the minimum bandwidth required to make broadband connections. That's because what is considered an acceptable minimum data transfer rate has changed with the times. Initially, most organizations placed the minimum rate for broadband at equal to, or faster than, 256 Kbps. In the U.S. in 2008, the Federal Communications Commission (FCC) defined broadband as anything above 768 Kbps. These adjustments have mirrored the offerings in the market. In 2000, broadband links in the U.S. averaged 500 Kbps. By 2007, the U.S. had seen a surge in broadband investment and an increase in average speed of approximately 3 Mbps.[6] In today's market terms, basic broadband is generally defined to be in the range of 786 Kbps and 1.5 Mbps.[7]

Let's drill down just a little to see how familiar you are with what you get through your home broadband service from providers such as BT, NTT, Comcast, or AT&T. As you may know, there are multiple broadband options to choose from, each with a speed and performance factor based on the type of connection you choose.

Some of the most common options available to you are Digital Subscriber Lines (DSL), cable modems, fiber cables, or mobile broadband. Each one leverages different physical lines to make its connections, resulting in different pros and cons.

High-speed Internet delivered via a DSL connection from a home or office to the telephone switching station is one of the most common. It leverages the copper wires of the telephone line to transmit data, but uses a completely different technology than audio data transmission, so it can achieve the required broadband speeds. It provides a dedicated connection, yet the speed can be affected by the distance of the subscriber (you) from the nearest switching station.

Something to note is that DSL connections are *asymmetric*, which means they don't have the inherent ability to send and receive packets simultaneously. This is a major technological hurdle, one that the first users of DSL connections experienced when they would have to stop sending traffic in order to receive something and vice versa. The technology has been improved with the use of amplifiers and virtual DSL access multiplexers (DSLAMs), which manage the connections and extend access to make the technological limitations less apparent to DSL users. These asymmetric connections also support different upload and download data transfer rates—the downloads are often faster than the uploads. There are a couple different flavors of this asymmetric connection, including ADSL, which is most commonly used in North America, HDSL (high data-rate DSL), and VDSL (very high data-rate DSL). There are approximately 74 million homes worldwide connected via VDSL2 networks, which can be up to 10 times faster than standard data rates.[8] Then there is SDSL (Symmetric DSL), which can send and receive packets at the same time and has equal download and upload speeds. It's most common in Europe.

A cable modem is designed to provide an Internet connection over the existing wires that deliver cable TV. It is typically faster than DSL, potentially up to twice the speed, due to the properties of the coaxial cable that it leverages. The downside of the connection provided by a cable modem is that it is a shared connection and can be affected by the number of subscribers connected at any given time. If you're on cable along with your whole neighborhood, chances are, it slows after the dinner hour.

The use of fiber cables to deliver services from a telephone switch directly to the home has been more available recently, providing much greater bandwidth and a connection that is less susceptible to potential interference than traditional metal cables. Unfortunately, the fiber cables are more fragile than wire and can be more expensive to install; as a result, they are not yet available everywhere, though they are slowly replacing traditional telephone lines. Currently, fiber cables seem to represent the best option to handle the future bandwidth requirements of home users, which is predicted to continue to significantly increase.

The Fiber to the Home Council projected the download bandwidth needed by the typical home, as shown in Figure 5-1, in the years 2010, 2020, and 2030, assuming what they consider will be a fairly typical scenario of three video and voice streams, one gaming stream, and one data/email stream per home, all, of course, simultaneously. The highest network requirement estimates for 2030 are close to 30 Gbps, due primarily to the coming 3D HDTV[9] that in two decades should be commonplace.

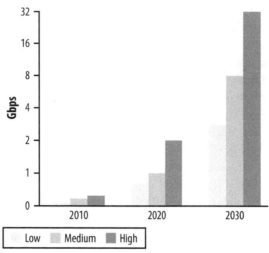

Figure 5-1. How hungry are we for bandwidth? In 20 years, your kids or grandkids might want or need 30 Gbps to send their avatars to virtual school each day.

There is likely to be a lot of investment in fiber over the next five years. Only 6% of all households worldwide have access to fiber cables, Fiber to the Home (FTTH) and Fiber to the Building (FTTB), which is an optical fiber that goes from a telephone switch directly to the home/building, representing approximately 98 million homes. Seventy percent of those homes are located in Asia-Pacific, with Europe and North America splitting the remaining 30%.[10]

Mobile broadband is also an increasingly viable way to connect to the Internet, particularly in communities and developing countries where cable or DSL is unavailable, or even within generational demographics (you can read that as our youth), where mobility is cherished more than almost anything. In September 2008, nearly 55 million people worldwide subscribed to mobile broadband services in 91 countries, and this number is expected to grow to more than 1 billion in the next four years.[11] And by 2010, well within the print life of this book, worldwide mobile broadband usage is projected to eclipse the aforementioned *fixed broadband* options.[12]

Mobile broadband uses the radio access network to transmit data and deliver services. Multiple frequencies make up the radio waves. Mobile providers buy the rights to transmit over a specific radio frequency, for example, 800 megahertz (MHz) or 1,900 MHz, within the spectrum associated with radio wave propagation. These rights are typically managed and sold by the government. You might have heard of "spectrum auctions"—this is what they're buying.

The types of applications, capacity, and speed supported by the mobile network are based on the "generation" (G) of the network. 1G is an analog network, while 2G is a digital personal communications service (PCS) network. Both are voice-centric, with the main difference in the voice quality, although 2.5G networks support some data services, such as mobile instant messages (IM) and push-to-talk (PTT) services. To date, most mobile broadband is offered via third-generation (3G) networks, which offer improved voice quality, spectrum utilization, and additional data capacity. 3G networks typically support data stream rates of 3 Mbps to 14 Mbps.

The next evolution is 4G mobile networks, and the simplicity of this naming scheme belies the future. 4G mobile networks promise to deliver speeds up to 100 Mbps, and are probably positioned to better support the applications and services of the near future than their hardwired brethren. One of the architectures and standards for these 4G networks is Long Term Evolution (LTE), which really is the "all IP" network, and it promises an enhanced Internet experience on mobile devices. More than 100 operators worldwide have already announced they expect to migrate their mobile networks to LTE starting in 2010 and beyond.

LTE is the next evolution of mobile broadband technology, utilizing orthogonal frequency-division multiplexing (OFDM)-based technology and a flat-IP core network to allow an enhanced Internet experience on mobile devices.

Another 4G wireless standard that is often talked about and is anticipated to take off in the next few years is WiMax (think Wi-Fi on steroids). WiMax is designed to have greater range (30 miles) and bandwidth (70 Mbps) as it travels over the radio access waves than the current wireless fidelity (Wi-Fi) standard. This means you won't have to go to the café for free Wi-Fi access, but can sit on your porch with a homemade cappuccino and still use the café's connection. (It also means the cafés will be populated with mostly single people.)

Currently, most of the services and applications in mobile broadband networks send the traffic *over the air*, which is open to anyone and everyone, making the performance, as you probably already know, somewhat erratic (we'll talk about the security breaches in another chapter). As a result, service can degrade based on the amount of congestion on the radio network (like everybody else in that traffic jam you're stuck in). Increasingly, however, the popularity of mobile devices is driving a trend to leverage the bandwidth provided by the backhaul and core of the network, which are under the control of the mobile service provider and therefore contain a lot of the same properties in terms of predictability, capacity, and bandwidth as the cable and telephone networks.

To clarify, mobile networks consist of cells, served by a fixed transmitter, called a *cell site* or *base station*, which receives the traffic sent from the mobile device over the radio access network. The more cell sites there are, the more capacity and the better the coverage. It is not uncommon for service providers to share cell sites. In fact, it makes sense because residents don't want to have multiple cell sites in the same location—they are neither energy efficient nor aesthetically pleasing—although some service providers try to disguise the cell site as objects (like trees) you might normally see.

Sustainable Network Law: The more broadband made available to network users, the faster sustainable network innovation occurs.

The *mobile backhaul network* is responsible for transferring the traffic between a cell site (base station) and the wireless service provider's core network, otherwise known as the *backbone*. If mobile devices can reduce the amount of over-the-air traffic and increasingly leverage the backhaul and core of the mobile network, service providers will be able to provide an overall better mobile broadband experience that will, guess what, fuel further adoption. This begs for a simple premise of networking. Let's call it the Sustainable Network Law: *The more broadband made available to network users, the faster sustainable network innovation occurs.*

The promise of all this increased bandwidth and broadband access fuels the appetites of the network's users, which in turn fuels the innovation of new applications that require more bandwidth, so that new services can be offered (at new rates or fees), which then fuels the rebuilding and upgrading of the infrastructure and all the access points of the worldwide global network.

There is a direct correlation between the rise of bandwidth and attainability of the sustainable network. And the more bandwidth we have, the more we will notice when it's running slow or not there. We're really still at the base of the mountain, where the adoption and innovation curve is up and to the right. A reliable, high-speed, high-quality connection is critical to any subsequent transformative solution made possible by the sustainable network.

CHAPTER 6

Can the Internet Hit a Wall?

*I predict the Internet will soon go spectacularly supernova
and in 1996 catastrophically collapse.*

—Bob Metcalfe, Ethernet inventor and 3Com
founder, in his *InfoWorld* column in 1995

The current prediction of bandwidth overload has a name—*exaflood*—and the potential inability of the network to handle such a load is the stuff of both cocktail-party conversations and serious boardroom discussions. While some may say it is doomsday, the-sky-is-falling talk, others warn that to not pay attention to the numbers would be foolish. As with most things, the appropriate level of concern is probably somewhere smack-dab between the extremes. And, of course, the entrepreneur sees it as a magnificent opportunity.

Let's start where everyone agrees: the global communications infrastructure, underpinned by the network, will continue to grow in importance and the volume of traffic will continue to grow at a significant rate. Whether the growth is linear or exponential will most likely be determined by the country and economic conditions, but it is reasonable, if not extremely conservative, to conclude that individuals, businesses, and governments alike will increasingly rely on networks worldwide.

There are predictions that have Internet traffic growing up to 11 times between 2008 and 2015. For example, take voice connections. The *Wall Street Journal* reported that as the 20 exabytes of data generated every year via telephone are transferred to video, those 20 exabytes could multiply "by a factor of 100 or more."[1] There are estimates that the annual run-rate of traffic in late 2012 will be 522 exabytes per year.[2] Exabytes may seem a bit extreme (an exabyte, if you're dying to know, is 1 quintillion bytes, or as Grant Gross in *PC World* estimated, "50,000 years of DVD quality video"), but when you consider that more and more content is being digitized and transferred online, it doesn't look like an unreasonable prediction. In fact, a zettabyte, which is 1,000 exabytes, could very well be the new term of the digiterati beyond 2012.[3]

Take the Laboratory of Neuro Imaging (LONI), which is a leader in the development of advanced computational algorithms and scientific structures for the comprehensive and quantitative mapping of brain structure and function. Located at the University of California, Los Angeles, LONI has the largest neuroimaging database in the world, with more than 25,000 unique scans, at nearly a petabyte in size (1,000 petabytes equals 1 exabyte). Hundreds of researchers work with datasets ranging from 20 megabytes to several hundred gigabytes.[4] And that is just one organization in one field of network use. The uses and bandwidth requirements are similarly grand and growing in almost every industry and aspect of our daily lives. A survey conducted by the Aberdeen Group found that companies, on average, expect to increase their bandwidth by 108% over a 12-month period.[5]

Some would argue that today's networks are simply not designed to support traffic increases of this magnitude. They hypothesize that the networks have not been built out to adequately handle the range of new, media-rich applications that are exploding in popularity today. Consider for a moment the scale and requirements of all the current *and* future users, devices, and applications—and they could be right.

In the recent past, network service providers created service-specific networks, meaning they created a network designed for a single application, such as voice or video, then offered you, the customer, a single service. All of these providers (such as your cable, local phone, or mobile provider) built their networks to deliver one specific service and prided themselves on their ability to do it well, making sure it was always available with no interruption.

Several years ago, that all started to change. As service providers added Internet access to their offerings, it opened up the network to all the different voice, video, and data applications consumers could access (this is often referred to as *triple-play*: voice, video, and data from one service provider). Boundaries between service providers began to blur. Email became accessible on a mobile phone, TV shows were viewable online, phone calls could be made via the Internet, a movie stored on a home device could be watched from a computer in an airport terminal. The lines between services, which had once been easy to discern, began to blur.

In response, there has been a great deal of convergence in the industry, both among the service providers themselves and within their siloed, service-specific networks. Many traditional phone, cable, and mobile phone providers acquired, partnered, or merged with one another in efforts to combine their service-specific networks and provide multiple quality services to customers. At the same time, these providers began to evolve their siloed networks into multiservice networks.

The problem is that because of the predictable performance of the service-specific networks, consumers have come to expect a certain quality. We rely on always hearing a dial tone whenever we pick up the phone; we expect emergency 911 service to always be available; we want a clear picture when watching TV; we require reliable access to email. While we are willing to make allowances for some of the obvious differences among the devices we use to access the content—for example, a picture on a 40-inch flatscreen HDTV is going to be different than the picture on a 12-inch laptop screen—we have little tolerance for any degradation of the overall experience. Let's face it: regardless of how we access a movie, we expect the picture to not be jumpy and the sound to not be choppy. And if it is, we jump ship from one provider to another.

As a result, the providers started announcing plans to build out their IP *next-generation networks* (NGNs) to evolve their current infrastructure to better handle the exploding growth of all the emerging IP applications and the network traffic being generated. This gets back to the question of whether the service provider networks are capable of keeping up with the exploding demands of all these new applications as they converge. And what about the ones we haven't even imagined yet? The Sustainable Network Law (Chapter 5) states that the more broadband made available, the faster network innovation occurs in a somewhat snowballing effect. So, provide a next-generation network, and in a few months you get next-generation applications.

It's highly probable that networks not originally designed to support multiple services will have problems dealing with the new demands of these applications, such as web conferencing and HD video, which require considerably more bandwidth than the pure data applications of even just 10 years ago. About 40 hours of HD video represent as much traffic as 1 million email messages.[6] A single iPhone can eat up as much bandwidth as 5,000 simultaneous voice calls, and HD video takes 35,000 times the bandwidth of an average web page.[7]

In fact, video is often cited as one of the applications driving network utilization and rising bandwidth demands. Take the popular video-sharing website YouTube. In 2007, users uploaded 65,000 new videos and viewed more than 100 million YouTube videos *daily*, representing more than a 1,000% increase from just one year earlier. Only a year later, in August 2008, YouTube was the world's number three site in terms of global minutes, and the number two global search engine, with close to 10 billion search queries a month.[8] In one month in the U.S. alone, users watched 12.6 billion videos, translating to 591 million hours online.[9] (The most popular video was downloaded 88 million times by people around the world by June 2008.)[10]

Given these types of numbers, it probably comes as no surprise that in 2008, Internet video made up approximately one-quarter of all consumer Internet traffic.[11] As video makes the move to HD (and perhaps even 3D at some point in the future), the requirements on the network go up significantly. There are estimates that sites such as YouTube could, by themselves, produce enough data to more than double all Internet traffic.[12]

The 2007 Bernstein report predicts that approximately 157 million Americans will watch video on the Internet at least once a month by 2010.[13] Others predict that in the foreseeable future, 100% of U.S. Internet users will view online videos regularly.[14] IP video is predicted to represent 80% of all video minutes in 15–20 years.[15] This represents a substantial amount of video content, particularly if you consider that the average time a U.S. home used a TV set during the 2007–2008 television season was up to 8 hours and 18 minutes per day, a record high since Nielsen started measuring television in the 1950s (and a statistic worth exploring another day!).[16] Then there are the mobile phone users, who spent three hours a month watching mobile video, a trend that many anticipate will grow significantly, especially in remote countries.[17]

As more people turn to the network, and more content is digitized, and the capabilities of the devices themselves continue to increase to support more of this content, it is perfectly feasible that the network infrastructure could start to strain under the demands. Keeping up with the bandwidth demands—in other words, being able to appropriately process all of the traffic at adequate speeds—definitely poses a challenge.

Keep in mind, however, it is a challenge that those who provision the network—telephone, cable, and mobile carriers—have been dealing with for some time now. Network traffic has been growing by about 50% year over year for the last decade,[18] and at this rate, the amount of traffic in 2020 will be 100 times what it is today.[19] Yet carriers have kept up over the past 10 explosive years.

The amount of Internet traffic in 2020 will be 100 times what it is today.

To see what carriers and providers in the U.S. have been dealing with since 2000, take a look at the predicted traffic demand shown in Figure 6-1. Can you imagine if your 401k graphed that well? The growth isn't that surprising when you consider people in the U.S. who used the Internet were online 27 hours a month (*www.tvturnoff.org*),[20] with predictions that 61% of the connected U.S. population will use the Internet daily.[21] Throw in all the things users do while online, from surfing the Web to watching video or playing online games (there are predictions that 33% of that U.S. Internet population will play games online),[22] and is it any wonder that this has been occupying the world's service providers for the last decade? It hasn't exactly snuck up on them. Their data centers and network operations hubs have been bursting year after year after year.

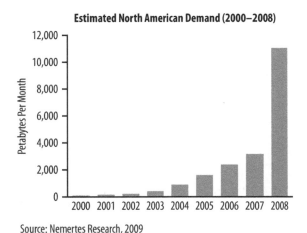

Source: Nemertes Research, 2009

Figure 6-1. North American Internet traffic from 2000 to 2008 increased slightly; the growth in 2008 makes one wonder if the presidential election had a little to do with it. (In case you forgot, 1 petabyte equals 1 quadrillion bytes.)

In fact, an overbuild of the network took place in the late 1990s and early 2000s that some providers never recovered from when the dot-com bubble burst. At that time, however, there was really only the promise of the adoption of users, devices, and a plethora of innovative IP applications and services. As this book postulates, the users, devices, applications, and services seem to have caught up. It isn't the "if we build it, they will come" field of dreams of the past. Today, there are already lines, thousands of rows deep, at the ticket booth trying to get into the game.

And while the network providers have been preparing for this moment, at least in their backbone and edge networks, the problem is that the rate of adoption and the ensuing network implications, particularly within the last mile (of the access network), may still have taken some by surprise. With IP traffic growth expected to continue, fueled by an explosion in video and other rich-media content as well as by mobile broadband growth, analysts are predicting bottlenecks and traffic jams on the network by 2012, especially in the U.S. Nemertes, an analyst research group, reported that demand on the network, which it estimated as growing roughly 140–150% year over year through 2013, could be gated by network capacity starting in the 2011–2012 timeframe. *Demand* represents what people would use *if* they could get it, while the *capacity* is the amount of traffic the network can actually handle (the supply). As with anything, when demand overtakes supply, problems arise. In this case, it can manifest itself in slow response times, disruptions to audio and video delivery, and even total unresponsiveness.[23]

We have already seen leading indicators. When pop legend Michael Jackson died in 2009, there was a huge surge in online traffic, with some sites seeing a fivefold increase in traffic that resulted in periods of slowness and even downtime.[24] Now, these were site-specific slowdowns, not network-wide, presumably due to the overload of those sites' web servers and their inability to adequately handle all the requests for information, but they illustrate how spikes and rapid traffic growth can impact the overall quality of network access.

It could be indicative of things to come, particularly for mobile carriers, which are potentially more susceptible to these bottlenecks because of the verifiable explosion of traffic resulting from the rapid adoption of smartphones. For example, it is not unusual for an iPhone user to consume up to 1 GB of data per month, which equates to the consumption of approximately 5,000 simultaneous traditional voice users. For network providers who have been accustomed to supporting those 5,000 users, to suddenly have to support a large number of iPhone users places incredible strains on the network (multiply 2 million new iPhones by 5,000, and those 2 million new smartphone users have just replaced 10 billion cell phone users, or about double the world's actual population). When that happens, real-time users can suffer from latency and lag time, slower downloads, and an overall less-than-stellar user experience.

Providers are working on reducing the amount of traffic flowing through the network. For instance, they are starting to offload smartphone traffic from the mobile network to a fixed one (phone/Internet service) as soon as the user enters her office or home. This automatic switch is only now possible due to the previously discussed convergence of the fixed and mobile networks that is taking place within and among network providers. The benefit is that users can receive a more resilient, consistent connection. We are also seeing developers work on the strain that devices themselves place on the network. For example, RIM has a network operations center that formats web content before it is forwarded to its BlackBerry PDA device. It seems to work, given that the typical BlackBerry user only consumes about 20 MB per month. It remains to be seen, however, whether this approach will maintain its benefits as more and more 3G BlackBerry devices reach the market.

There were some who predicted that if sales of 3G smartphones kept going strong, mobile carriers would run out of radio wave spectrum, which is required to add capacity to the mobile network, by the end of 2008. Now that timeline has come and gone, and there was no major meltdown.

However, there have been hints of the limits of today's mobile networks. On September 17, 2008, the Toronto *Globe and Mail* reported that AT&T, which sells Apple's iPhone in the U.S., is supporting RIM's BlackBerry Bold in 13 countries, but not the U.S. because, "both devices use the same next-generation (3G) network technology, but it now appears AT&T (T) wasn't prepared for the bandwidth-hogging Apple (AAPL) device and doesn't have the resources to launch the Bold until it cures its iPhone issues."[25] In September 2009, the *New York Times* reported that AT&T iPhone users in the U.S. were still experiencing "dropped calls, spotty service, delayed text and voice messages and glacial download speeds," due to the strain the phones were putting on the network.[26]

In early 2009, the *New York Times* wrote a story on the U.S presidential inauguration in the nation's capital that focused on the fact that, "the largest cell phone carriers, fearful that a communicative citizenry will overwhelm their networks, have taken the unusual step of asking people to limit their phone calls and to delay sending photos."[27] They anticipated that the technology-savvy onlookers were going to flood the airways sending and receiving high-resolution pictures and long video cuts, as well as blog posts, tweets on Twitter, and the occasional "it's freaking cold out here!" texts.

Joe Farren, spokesman for the Cellular Telecommunications and Internet Association, was reported by the *New York Times* as saying, "If some of these estimates come true, people should anticipate delays with regards to sending text messages or making phone calls or getting onto the Internet...." According to the article, the group "asked people to send texts rather than make phone calls (text uses less bandwidth than speech) and to send photos only after the event."[28]

The Internet's top 40 sites slowed by as much as 60% by the time the inauguration ceremony started at 11 a.m.,[29] as unprecedented numbers of people logged in to try to watch the historical event online. This points to the potential capacity limits of the current network infrastructure, which strained and sometimes even froze under the spike in general traffic. There were no reports, however, of major issues with mobile connectivity during the January 2009 U.S. presidential inauguration. This could be due in part to the capacity that cell phone carriers feverishly added in anticipation of the onslaught of usage. They provisioned additional access points on cell towers and the necessary landlines to carry the extra traffic from the tower to the provider's backhaul and core networks. This begs the question of how long we can stay ahead of demand with just-in-time buildouts. Events and issues such as these may serve as a wake-up call for the entire industry.

Predictions place the telecommunications service provider infrastructure market at over $100 billion by the end of 2008,[30] but analysts place the specific investment in IP infrastructure at less than 10% of all service providers' capital expenditures. Many are even more conservative, placing the percentage of investment in IP at 4–6%.[31] That is well below some of the estimates of the investment needed to support the proliferation of users of Internet-connected devices and IP services and applications. But then again, Moore's Law[32] may come into play here, which describes the ability to double performance approximately every 18–24 months; it could mean that investment can remain fairly stable, yet still increase capacity at a decent rate.

However, Nemertes has predicted that the amount of investment service providers will need to make to build the IP network capacity required just to meet the projected gap (mainly at the edge) between supply and overall IP demand will be between $42 billion and $55 billion in the U.S. and $137 billion globally.[33] Without appropriate investment, some predict user demand could outstrip broadband Internet bandwidth availability in the next two to four years.[34] Will this happen? Maybe, maybe not.

Traditionally, the bulk of investment in the telecommunications industry has come from the network service providers themselves. However, new models may emerge for sharing the burden of the investment or ensuring that the telecommunications industry is given the proper incentives to adequately build out the network. For example, the emphasis on broadband buildouts, which is on the agenda of many governments, could help.

In U.S., the 2009 stimulus package could support $10 billion of investment in one year in broadband networks.[35] In 2008, the Chinese ministry said Chinese carriers were expected to invest about $41 billion (USD) in 3G mobile broadband networks over the next two years, with at least $29 billion (USD) to be spent in 2009. Australia has announced the buildout of a national broadband network with plans to invest $43 billion over eight years to connect 90% of Australian homes, schools, and workplaces.

Only time will tell if these investments are enough to meet and stay ahead of demand. As discussed in different segments of this book, a lot goes into upgrading the network. Investment includes laying more wires and more fiber-optic cables—particularly, in the last mile, which some say is the biggest lag behind demand[36]—as well as investing in the routing, switching, and security infrastructure, among other technologies, to ensure optimal operation. New developments in architectures (data centers), protocols, and standards (such as Multiprotocol Label Switching—MPLS), and advances in addressing (IPv6) and security, will also be critical in the years ahead to ensure that the network can keep up.

However, it must be said that history is on the side of the network, which has been very adept at finding ways to support the ever-increasing number of users, devices, and applications that want to connect. We have just begun to tap into the promise of the network. What it can do is still to be imagined. It's why the network must continue to scale to demand and not hit the wall. The world's societies, economies, and governments have to be up to the challenge.

CHAPTER 7

The Mobile Me

It's opener there in the wide open air.
—Dr. Seuss,
Oh, the Places You'll Go!

U biquitous connectivity is the dream of the sustainable network. "Anywhere access" to the world's information resources enables you to touch everything, at any time, from anywhere. It opens up a world of possibilities we have only dreamed about and seen in sci-fi movies and books. Mobility allows the network to overcome the constraints of being tied to a specific location (as with a modem line), and actually lets you take your connections with you wherever you go.

It's also fueling the network's extension to parts of the globe previously locked out because of the lack of physical infrastructure (such as phone cabling) available to support access. In many parts of the world, the infrastructure is simply not there, but a cell tower can be erected and all of a sudden the population is connected—they now have unprecedented access to the world's resources. It's because of this ability to infiltrate all corners of the globe that mobility amplifies the network's flattening effects. It makes no difference whatsoever whether you're in Mumbai, India, or Mobile, Alabama. The same resources are available to you no matter who you are or where you're located. This helps explain the direct correlation between strong GDP growth and the growth of mobile subscribers in developing countries.

Microsoft's recent ad campaign around "Life Without Walls" captured some of the possibilities of this flat world well. Images of a roller coaster, a shooting star in the night sky, a boxer taking a punch, a fisherman holding up his catch—in other words, life's happenings—spill from one device screen to another device screen, from a laptop to a mobile smartphone to a TV. The spilling seems effortless, demonstrating the mobile network's ability to hand off connections between devices, which, when put together, give the total story meaning.

For the sustainable network, being able to take the network with you, wherever you are, whatever you are doing, makes it easier for more people to use the network in more ways. And the number of people who currently turn to their mobile devices to access network services and applications continues to grow. For example, there were 2.3 trillion mobile text messages sent as of mid-2008,[1] and you could say some people are obsessed—the record for the most text messages is 217,000 in one month.[2] If you're trying to do the math, that's one text message every 12 seconds!

Estimates place the number of *new mobile connections* around the globe at 1.3 million *every day*.[3] In fact, in December 2008, the mobile industry hit a big milestone, surpassing a worldwide total of 4 billion connections to mobile devices, representing 60% of the entire global population.[4] That number is expected to rise to more than 5.3 billion connections with annual revenues topping $1.03 trillion by 2013.[5]

What Is Mobility?

Generally speaking, *mobility* is made up of two components—the portability of the devices that are able to access the network and the roaming access of the network itself.

Portability refers to our ability to carry these computing devices and resources with us wherever we go. They may fit in our cars, backpacks, or pockets. The key is that they are not rooted to a single location. Some mistakenly assume, however, that because a device can come with us, it can automatically access the network from wherever we are. This is not necessarily true; the device may still need a physical connection to the network, which in turn would "root" it to whichever network we are accessing. A good example is when you connect your laptop to the network from your hotel room using the physical cable that is provided by the hotel. The device is portable, but the network access is still fixed. The Code-Division Multiple Access (CDMA) smartphone you bought in the U.S., when taken to Europe, is another example, because Europe doesn't support CDMA connections.

Roaming is the second piece of mobility. It is the ability to access the network from wherever you are; in other words, without wires or a physical connection. Devices must support wireless access and a wireless network to transmit information (voice, data, video, etc.). The best example is when you use your mobile phone; you are using a wireless device that can connect to the wireless network provisioned by your mobile phone carrier, allowing you to make and receive calls and other information as you move from one location to another. A key feature of roaming is the capability of the device and the network to support *hand-offs*, which allow you to drive long distances and remain on the same call or session—the connection can persist as you travel between locations and between different networks' cell tower coverage.

When you combine portability with roaming, you have true mobility for convenient, anywhere, any way access to the network. The combo is priceless.

If you have a smartphone or perhaps a mobile broadband card for your laptop, you know what's driving the proliferation of mobile connections to the network. It's the confluence of lower price plans on increasingly powerful portable devices and the increasing availability of mobile broadband access. It's telling that even in tough economic times, smartphones were the only mobile phone segment to show unit and revenue growth in the second half of 2008, and the only segment predicted to continue to maintain annual growth over the next five years.[6] Along the same lines, the adoption of netbooks, which are watered-down laptops that generally have mobile broadband capabilities, have taken many by surprise. Predictions have more than 300 million netbooks being sold between 2009 and 2014.[7]

These devices are all tapping into the mobile networks. There were estimates that there were already more than 200 commercial mobile broadband networks worldwide in 2007.[8] In a year there was a jump of 125% in individual broadband subscribers between 2007 and 2008, hitting 210.5 million by the end of 2008.[9] The rapid adoption of mobile broadband will most likely make it the dominant connectivity method for the world (read that last sentence again—it's really rather amazing). And predictions have mobile broadband subscribers overtaking fixed broadband users in 2011, the same year broadband is estimated to reach 1 billion total subscribers[10] (some predictions put the milestone of topping 1 billion mobile broadband subscribers just a little further out, in 2013).[11]

Remember that the number of Internet users in developing countries was expected to eclipse the total number of Internet users in developed countries in 2008. The vast number of those developing-world users are accessing the network via their mobile phones. In fact, they are more likely to have their first Internet experience on their phones than PCs. People who might not be able to afford a landline, a computer, a car, a washing machine, or a toilet with running water are able to get online and access the wealth of resources of the network via their phones or other mobile devices. And it's a virtuous cycle: as more mobile broadband connections become available, more users will use them and start creating more innovative applications, which will create more demand and necessitate more mobile access in these emerging markets.

Analysis by Informa Telecoms and Media reported that the Latin American and Caribbean region continues to demonstrate steady consumer growth with 16% year-on-year growth and subscription numbers predicted to hit in excess of 440 million, representing a 76% penetration.[12] As noted before, Brazil is amazingly ripe for mobile broadband adoption, so it's not a surprise that it added the most mobile Internet users in the region, at 19 million. In terms of annual growth, Peru has been on the fast track with subscription growth of 33%, equating to 4.6 million new Internet subscribers.[13] Asia is also strong on the adoption curve, as evidenced by China Mobile Ltd., which reported that 25% of its total revenues in 2007 came from mobile data rates.[14]

The telltale sign of the effect that mobility is having on the way value is extracted from the sustainable network is its encroachment on those with fixed access to the network. A J.D. Power poll released in June 2008 found a significant number of people have "cut the cord." Twenty-seven percent of the wireless customers surveyed replaced their traditional landline phones with a wireless service and, of those, 61% have completely disconnected their home landline service. The *Economist* had an article that predicted the last landline in America will be disconnected by 2025.[15] Have you disconnected? Have you thought about it? And perhaps more interestingly, why not?

There are estimates that mobile lines will outnumber fixed lines nine to one by 2015. With that trend, there are challenges that we should understand. One relates to emergency calls. For instance, with a landline, the origin of a 911 (emergency) phone call is easy to pinpoint because it is, by its nature, fixed. With a mobile connection, it's a little trickier. Mobile service providers were legislated to ensure that they deliver the same 911 service, but it has taken a little time for them to get there. The point is to be aware of how these networks are different and mindful of how that may impact you.

On the flipside, mobile connections can make it easier for people who are out and about to get help if they need it , or help others that might be in trouble (many police departments are starting to ask citizens to send "text tips" of crimes or situations in progress). Additionally, future applications may emerge that allow individuals to carry personal medical information on their phones that emergency service personnel can access in an emergency.

Mobile devices deliver on-the-go computing coupled with new and innovative applications that can further amplify their overall convenience. For example, Google recently introduced Google Latitude, which allows you to see your friends' or family members' locations on a Google map by tracking the locations of their cell phones (using either GPS or triangulation between cell towers). If you have Google Maps installed on your smartphone, you can see everybody's location around town at any point in time, no matter where you are. By the time you finish reading this book, the number of innovative applications that use this tracking ability for other purposes will no doubt be in the dozens or perhaps even hundreds. By 2015, you might be able to see satellite imagery of your friend's real-time location as she visits the Eiffel Tower, and by 2020, you'll be able to have full video and voice companionship with your friend as she sails across the Caribbean. Maybe even sooner.

Mobile access to the network provides more than simply the flexibility and convenience of being able to access the network and its resources from wherever you are; it represents huge productivity gains, increased collaboration and agility, and new opportunities generated for individuals and businesses on a scale that simply dwarfs what has taken place in the past 20 years. Suffice it to say that mobility unlocks the power of the network in ways previously impossible or not yet imagined. Monstrously so.

CHAPTER 8

Take It with You

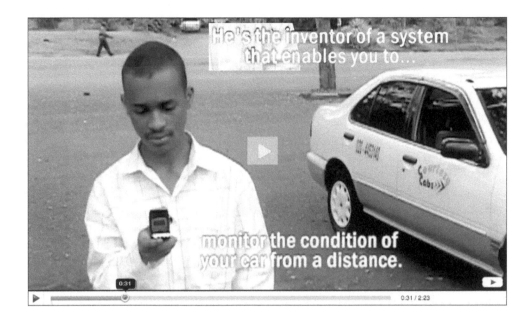

Twenty years from now you will be more disappointed by the things that you didn't do than by the ones you did do. So throw off the bowlines. Sail away from the safe harbor. Catch the trade winds in your sails. Explore. Dream. Discover.

—Mark Twain

Google has always had its eyes on the application layer of what the network delivers. It started with search and continues to revolutionize the services and applications we rely on as we go about our daily lives. The more we rely on those services and applications, the more we need the network to support them, fueling the exponential growth of its adoption, which in turn increases the use of the applications and services. It's a self-perpetuating cycle that represents the possible. And if you are thinking that these services and applications are starting to border on the sci-fi depicted in movies, cartoons, and graphic novels, you're right. Isn't it exciting?!

At a fundamental level, we have been spoiled by the rise of the mobile machines. We've experienced moments when we were able to access the resources we needed, using the devices we wanted, from wherever we were. It's a heady feeling the first time it works, and you don't want to go backward. We are empowered. We are all walking encyclopedias, able to answer almost any question with a just a few taps of a button.

And in the past few years, whether we are at work, home, the airport, or a coffee shop, we demand to be able to log in and get access to our email, online music, video library, the latest news or weather, or whatever else pushes our buttons. We demand it and get cranky when it doesn't happen. We want this communication to follow us wherever we go. The first cell phones did this with voice, but now we expect voice, data, and video access to be switched seamlessly and remotely between devices and locations. All in, what, the past 10 years? The corridors of Silicon Valley are littered with products and startups that didn't provide true mobility in their applications. They didn't get the simple premise. We want it all, all the time, wherever we go. Remember when two-day mail service was the gold standard?

Time will tell if offerings such as Apple's MobileMe, which automatically syncs contacts, calendars, and bookmarks on a Macintosh computer within a minute of the change being made on another (Apple) device, will provide the next-generation features that push technologies, such as Microsoft's Outlook server or the BlackBerry did for an earlier round of network usage (and that made us so addicted to mobility).

To see the capabilities network mobility offers, try looking at presence-based services (PBSs) that allow the connection to follow users, linking their different devices, such as a computer and mobile phone, so they can potentially be reached no matter where they are or which device they are using. Presence-based telecommunication services, including instant messaging (IM) and push-to-talk (PTT), are growing rapidly,[1] along with the burgeoning location-based services category.[2]

These services customize the content and potentially the advertising that is delivered to users, based on the user's physical location. Navigation services epitomize this category, such as your car's GPS navigator (or TomTom, which has more than 20 million subscribers in 28 countries in 22 languages), which provides personal, step-by-step directions to a specific destination and pointers to gas stations, restaurants, and other potential sites of interest.

> An interesting fact is that GPS was originally built by the U.S. Department of Defense for $12 billion and was only declassified in 1983, some say due to pressure from companies that saw the commercial applications for the technology. Others attribute the pressure to multiple plane crashes that were the result of the rudimentary instrumentation available to pilots who couldn't tell where they were.

Other location-based services focus on safety or security, such as tracking your children or calling for help if there is an emergency. One common example is the in-vehicle security, communications, and diagnostics system (such as On-Star) found in some vehicles. These services can locate stolen cars, open and start the car if the owner has lost his keys, call for assistance in the event of an accident, and more. (It hasn't happened yet, but we're waiting for some startup to allow cars to text you on your mobile: "I've just be stolen," or perhaps more importantly, "The meter just expired and the meter maid is 10 cars away.")

It's becoming more common for these applications to *leverage* your mobile phone rather than requiring a separate application-specific mobile device, which is a key difference. For example, if you had the right applications loaded on the right smartphone today, you could easily check the price of goods when shopping by scanning the bar codes to immediately see product comparisons, consumer ratings, and prices at competing stores. Visit Apple's iPhone App Store for a list of thousands of new applications that leverage the iPhone's features and connectivity—many of them are simply brilliant ideas of mobility and personal use. Other services, such as those offered by Loopt, Where.com, and Google's Latitude, can send information about the location of the people you care about to your phone, allowing you to track friends and family members as they travel around the globe (for those times when people don't want to be found, they can hide their locations or turn off the service). And the almost ancient Dodgeball.com (it's been around so long it was purchased by Google) lets you track your social scene, following friends and amours around at night and on the weekends.

However, there is another side to all of these personalized applications and services. To deliver optimal value, the applications need to collect personal information, such as your exact location at any given time. This has provoked some consumer advocacy groups to question where the line should be drawn to ensure personal privacy rights. If you drive by a fast food restaurant with your mobile phone on and get a text message offering a free hamburger, is that a service or an invasion of privacy? In 2008, the Center for Digital Democracy (CDD) and the U.S. Public Interest Research Group (PIRG), filed a complaint with the Federal Trade Commission charging that advertising companies should be required to provide more disclosure to mobile customers about the type and usage of data they collect.[3]

Typically, it is not the mobile service providers that are using this information, but rather the mobile marketing companies that are trying to target potentially receptive audiences (like our fast food example). There are opt-in guidelines that require marketers to get consent prior to carriers releasing any information. However, consumer groups are lobbying for more transparency in these opt-in guidelines to ensure that customers know exactly what they are authorizing and how information may be used. It may not seem like a big deal right now, just a message or two, but given current and anticipated adoption rates, it won't be long before your mobile phone knows you have a headache and recommends relief at a nearby pharmacy. Privacy will become a bigger deal as location-based applications and services become more prevalent and as the sustainable market connects everyone. If privacy and data integrity are not protected, the overall sustainability of the network is at risk. No one wants to be bombarded with marketing messages, and tolerance for intrusions into personal lives will wear thin extremely fast, threatening the very growth and possibilities for good that the network can represent.

We know there are best practices that reputable mobile marketers and providers follow—the real question is whether these practices will evolve at the same speed as the blistering network adoption rates to ensure the protection of the user. Can the industry get ahead of the issues or will it be forced into dealing with them through consumer groups? For example, many Internet marketing companies placed more stringent disclosure and data retention policies for behavioral and search data *only after* being pressured by the European Union and privacy groups.[4] We are starting to see pushback on marketing ploys that require personal information before you can make a purchase (ever been asked for your phone number or email address when trying to buy a product?). Only time will tell what is acceptable and when enough is enough. It's predictable, however, that the number of customizable applications available to enhance the overall utility and experience of the mobile network will continue to increase in number and imagination.

> By 2020, smartphones will be the primary Internet connection for most people around the globe.

And people everywhere are experiencing the possibilities, using the network to connect and develop relationships that are changing their lives. Users in both the developed and developing world are increasingly turning to their mobile devices to do everything from making phone calls to reading their email messages to searching the Web. The availability and adoption of increasingly powerful and affordable phones is putting network access within the hands, literally, of the world's population. A recent Nielsen report confirmed that users in developing countries are increasingly using their mobile devices as their predominant portal/browser for web access and entertainment—everything from reading news to playing video games.

And as smartphones become more readily available throughout the world, the variety of applications and mobile usage only promises to grow. Take the consumption of news—more than 10% of mobile users read the news on their mobile devices.[5] And approximately 20% of smartphone users perform mobile banking. Insight Research Corporation expects mobile financial services to more than triple between 2009 and 2014; these financial applications on cell phones will attract 2.2 billion users in that time, generating close to $124 billion for application developers and mobile operators.[6] Interestingly, among users with basic cell phones, fewer than 3% conduct financial transactions. This is a testament to the fact that the adoption of these more powerful mobile devices will lead to faster and greater adoption of more media-rich services and applications.

At the beginning of 2009, approximately a quarter of all cell phones in the U.S. market were smartphones,[7] with nearly half of all consumers planning to upgrade to a more advanced device within the next two years.[8] The switch to smartphones capable of accessing the Internet is causing a marked increase in the level of mobile search activity. Almost 40% of mobile users report that they access the Internet from their mobile devices. This represents a 6.5% increase since September 2007.[9] According to a report by Pew Internet & American Life Project, by 2020, smartphones will be the primary Internet connection for most people around the globe. But I think you would be safe to lay odds on cutting that time in half.

In large part, the mobility of the network enables greater personalization and subsequently makes the network more relevant for each individual user. It is a giant rolling snowball that is gaining momentum and size. Literally millions of people, and soon billions, are able to connect to the world for the first time, changing their economic, social, and political fortunes forever.

Is the sustainable network mobile? Yes. In fact, without mobility, half (if not more) of the world's population would not be participating. The numbers appear so skewed toward mobility that soon there will not be a distinction between mobile and non-mobile. It probably won't be long before generations will see connecting to the sustainable network with a wire as not only old school, but impractical. It won't matter whether you're mobile or not, just that you're connected. And we will have to determine what that means, in terms of privacy and future uses, for us as individual nodes on that network, as well as collective communities.

CHAPTER 9

The Network's Green Factor

It's not easy being green.
—Kermit the Frog

B eing green often comes with complications. No one is naïve enough to think that all this connectivity doesn't have an impact. It most certainly does; in fact, Gartner estimated the impact of the information and communications technology (ICT) sector at 2% of the world's CO_2 emissions,[1] while others place it at 3%. To put it in perspective, over the past couple of years, ICT, of which the network is a key component, has overtaken the emissions generated via the airline industry. That means there are more emissions from the ICT sector than all the airlines and jet fuel and vapor trails in the sky! That represents plenty of opportunity for improvement and a call to action for the industry to clean up inefficiencies and reduce consumption (a challenge that will be covered in subsequent chapters). But the underlying question still remains: is the network sustainable? Can the network help save the world and simultaneously save itself? As Kermit the Frog would vouch, it's never easy.

ICT needs to work to reduce its own emissions, but it also needs to help other industries streamline operations and reduce their overall emissions. The ICT sector is being heralded by governments and environmental advocates alike as an integral party to any climate-change solution. The World Wildlife Fund (WWF) has stated that a doubling or even tripling of the ICT sector's CO_2 emissions could be considered strategic *if* the overall benefits of ICT are fully realized within *other* sectors. A recent report, "Smart 2020," commissioned by the Global eSustainability Initiative (GeSI), with analysis by McKinsey & Company, estimates that ICT has the potential to reduce global emissions by 15% by 2020, saving the global industry more than $946 billion in annual energy costs and representing approximately 7.8 billion tons of CO_2, which is five times the sector's own footprint.[2] Insight Research Corporation places the value of "green offerings" within the telecommunications sector slightly higher, at approximately $1.2 trillion over the next five years, based on the estimated price of abated carbon emissions.[3]

McKinsey also released a detailed study, "Pathways to a Low Carbon Economy," which contains "more than 200 opportunities, spread across ten sectors and twenty-one geographical regions, that have the potential to cut global greenhouse gas emissions by 55 percent below 1990 levels by 2030, a reduction of 70 percent from the business as usual scenario."[4] The estimated cost for these measures represents less than one half of 1% of global gross domestic product. For example, in Australia, a Climate Risk Report identified the "use of telecommunications networks as one of the most significant opportunities to reduce the national carbon footprint."[5] The report estimated the opportunity at approximately 5% of Australia's total national emissions.

The basis for the network's environmental value lies in the very nature of the network—a global communications infrastructure capable of providing virtual access to people for all resources and all information. Its potential to reach and touch everyone on the planet is unlike any other existing tool humankind has. I know that sounds hokey, but it's absolutely true. Not only is it one of our best sustainable platforms to address environmental issues, but I also think it's the catalyst into the 21st century that we've been waiting for.

Those are big kudos, I know, but realize that the network can *unite* the world with its access to information to coordinate more sustainable consumption habits while *delivering* new applications that can help us reduce our unilateral carbon footprint. It's both the teacher and the school. Whether it is replacing something physical with something virtual or helping to drive efficiencies and conserve resources, network innovation can help us better manage our consumption. Even today, in what must be considered its infancy, the network is already helping businesses to reduce waste and streamline operations, while allowing cities and governments to control resource allocation (and more effectively manage those resources).

Other chapters in this book showcase how the network provides abatement opportunities (in tandem with the rest of the ICT sector) that cover transport reductions via remote office and web-conferencing capabilities, improved supply chain

The "Smart 2020" report estimated that ICT could cut annual CO_2 emissions in the U.S. between 13% and 22% through 2020, translating gross fuel and energy savings of between $140 billion and $240 billion, or a reduction of 11% to 21% in total oil consumption and a reduction of 20% to 36% in imported oil.

and distribution logistics, building management controls, smart grid technologies, and general dematerialization (where physical goods are replaced with their virtual equivalent).

This is where the carbon footprint becomes relevant, because it establishes a baseline for measuring progress. For example, consider individual household residential energy use and the use of nondiesel motor fuel for cars. Together, these items are responsible for about 1.2 billion tons of CO_2 each year in the U.S., making up approximately 40% of the U.S.'s 6 billion tons of carbon emitted each year.[6] While recognizing there are regional differences that can dramatically affect the percentages (see Chapter 10), it's fair to use these numbers to represent and measure the scope of the opportunities that are echoed, at some level, around the globe. If we can identify ways to reduce our emissions—for example, via better heating and power controls or reduced travel, most of which the network can facilitate—we have a networked way to better manage our consumption and measure it.

So, the network can help to dematerialize and make each and every citizen on the planet more efficient. It can also gather and distribute the data proving it. It can give us benchmarks and even program our devices to work within those parameters. It can give each of us individual sustainability plans based on our ages, locations, income levels, and digital acumen, then help us carry out those plans.

There are four factors that will either hamper or aid the network's ability to be a green factor:

1. The availability of high-speed broadband Internet access around the globe (Chapter 5)

2. The creation of effective telecommunications technologies that can credibly substitute large swaths of the need for travel, commuting, and face-to-face meetings (Chapters 14 and 15)

3. The continuing innovation of applications and services that can dematerialize how we conduct business and live our lives (Chapter 13)

4. The ongoing improvement of the network's own energy consumption to keep the impact of exponential network adoption at a minimum (Chapter 16)

Imagine the possibilities if we were to hit upon the right mix of all four.

CHAPTER 10

Carbon Footprints

You can't manage what you can't measure.
—Business and Management axiom

You can't improve what you don't know, and you have no way of figuring out if something is getting better or worse unless you can measure it. So, what's your carbon footprint? How about the footprint of the company you work for or the city you live in? How about the footprints of the companies you do business with? How about your car? Your bag of potato chips? Your favorite jeans? Don't know? Don't feel bad. The measurement standards are still in question and the debate for what constitutes a carbon footprint is currently playing itself out in the global theater.

Generally speaking, a *carbon footprint* is the amount of CO_2 emitted into the atmosphere via any given activity; it can be attributed to almost anything, from a single product or individual to the operations of a business, government, or an entire country. The issue revolves around the expansiveness of the carbon footprint—how wide do we throw the net when measuring all the ways in which we can possibly impact the environment?

Empirically speaking, we start at a disadvantage, because if I remember correctly from my third-grade science class, we humans emit CO_2 every time we breathe. Thankfully, we are forgiven for the factories that our bodies are, as calculations of our carbon footprint tend to focus on the carbon emitted as the result of all the energy (gas, heat, and electricity) we consume as we go about our daily lives.

Watch Your Weight

To figure out your individual or household carbon footprint, you would typically measure the emissions from your home and appliances (which can be extrapolated from your gas and electricity bills) and from your transport emissions (averaging your daily or weekly commute trips using both public and private transport and your air travel estimates) for the year. Let's follow carbon convention for a few more steps.

Within those steps, you'll find that the devil is in the details. I did a quick search on our beloved sustainable network (as opposed to personally driving to the nearest library and back several times), and I found a variety of calculators to determine my impact. I tried several of them. Each had different inputs and levels of detail and each seemed to return a completely different number. I consider myself a reasonably intelligent person, but I have to admit, I found many of the results downright confusing, if not obfuscated.

When confused, I race to the nearest expert I can find. So, being of British heritage, I found a recent study from the United Kingdom's Department for Environment, Food and Rural Affairs called "Defra 2007: Act On CO_2 Calculator Public Trial Version – Data, Methodology and Assumptions." This study estimated the average person's carbon footprint at 4.483 tons per year (approximately 9,885 pounds—sounds bad, eh?). 2.687 tons come from home and appliances and 1.796 tons come from transport.[1] Recognizing that a family of four doesn't emit exactly four times as much as a household of one, you can take some liberties and loosely extrapolate a household's footprint at

17.932 tons (39,540 pounds). While this is an interesting reference point, additional research explained that these numbers can't necessarily be applied on a global scale.

Measuring a Footprint

The U.N. Intergovernmental Panel on Climate Change estimates that human activity creates 32 billion tons of carbon dioxide a year, with 15 billion tons staying in the atmosphere and adding to climate change.[2] Different CO_2 sources have different calculations, some of the most common include:

- Emissions from gasoline. For every gallon of gas consumed, 20 pounds of carbon dioxide are emitted.[3] To convert miles per gallon (mpg) to liters per 100 km, divide 100 by (mpg/3.785*1.6093).

- Emissions from electrical energy consumption. This is usually presented on the basis of total mass (tons) and output rate, such as pounds per kilowatt hour (kWh) or megawatt hours (MWh); 1,000 kWh equals 1 MWh. For every kWh of power consumed, approximately 0.524 pounds of carbon dioxide (CO2) are emitted. Other terms used to measure the rate of energy use or production are watts and joules, which are equivalent terms representing the unit of energy expended per second; 1 kWh is equal to 3,600,000 joules (3.6 megajoules) or watts. These terms can be used to measure mechanical power, heating value, and electric energy.

- Emissions from heat dissipation (from heat or steam use). This may be calculated in British thermal units (BTUs), joules, therms, or pounds, all of which can be converted to kWh; 3.41 BTUs is the equivalent of 1 watt of power consumption.

Indeed, it turns out that one of the biggest determining factors of our carbon footprint is our pinprick location on the globe (where we live and do business, and whether that location relies more heavily on "clean" or "dirty" sources for its power generation, changes our output considerably).

On the spectrum of clean versus dirty pinpricks, coal is considered the dirtiest power source; natural gas produces half the CO_2 of coal, and solar and wind technologies are considered renewable energy sources that have low to no carbon emissions. Countries such as Amsterdam, which is leading the way in wind power generation, and France, which gets most of its energy from nuclear power plants, emit, on average, considerably less than countries that rely on more carbon-intensive power generation. Coal provides almost 50% of the power used in America and Germany; it represents 70% of India's power generation and 80% of China's.[4] In fact, China has overtaken the U.S. as the single largest carbon emitter in the world, building a new coal-fired plant once a week, while simultaneously setting a goal of attaining 20% of its energy from renewable sources, such as wind, by 2025.[5]

But it may not be as simple as determining whether or not your exact pinprick location is using coal or not, because the emissions from coal can also vary widely depending on how much nonflammable and sulfur material it contains. There are also coal factories with "scrubbers" that clean the air and gases they exhale. This is why the first input that most carbon footprint calculators require is the location of the individual or business, so that the makeup of the carbon emissions from the different power generation sources can be appropriately applied. Often, countries will factor the percentages of emissions generated via multiple sources and assign an average carbon emissions rate that people and businesses can use to calculate their emissions in that country.

So, since I'm at a pinprick location in California, the average household CO_2 emissions per year is between 37,921 and 41,853 pounds, which turns out to be in line with my family's outputs over in Great Britain. This is slightly better than other places around North America, such as New York, where the average is 48,357 pounds, or Houston, at 68,188 pounds.[6] Houston at almost twice that of California? Why such a big difference? Well, while the source of the power generation certainly influences the average carbon footprint of a particular location, it is not the only factor that plays a role.

Another influence is the natural climate, which may compel residents to want to use more or less heat or air conditioning at any given time of the year. Another is the proximity of resources, which may necessitate more or less travel. For example, if you can walk or use mass transit to get to your job or the corner store versus driving down the mountain or across half of suburbia, your carbon emissions will be lower. A related factor is the public transport infrastructure, which either enables or hinders the use of more environmentally friendly commute and travel options (regardless of whether you use them or not).

In addition, the level of disposable income found within the community can play a role, as upfront costs of more energy-efficient solutions may require deliberate investment (such as putting solar panels on your house). This leads to a less tangible but very important influence on the size of your average carbon footprint in a particular location—namely, the general mindset of the population and whether or not it perceives climate change to be a risk and a responsibility. Also, power consumption can be affected by the regulatory landscape and the goals of the governing bodies, which may be focused on education or imposing incentives or penalties around certain energy use behaviors. All of these factors can play a role in the carbon footprint of your individual or household pinprick because they can affect decisions about consumption choices.

While there is a basic level of agreement that calculating someone's household and travel consumption will provide a reasonable and easy-to-identify baseline, there are questions swirling around whether it is enough. There are discussions about whether it is as complete and fair a representation as possible. Are there other factors that should be included? What about all the stuff we buy during the year, and what it takes to make, transport, and dispose of those things? What about what you consume when you are in your place of work or while you are visiting another location? Some home workers have made the case that their household footprints are amplified because they are at home far more than a regular office-goer, consuming energy at home that the office-goer is using in his work setting. On the flipside, office-goers point out that their work environments are, in large part, out of their control, and their work emissions are accounted for within the business's own carbon footprint. You can see how it can become quite a dizzying discussion—and the complexity only grows when looking at the public and private sectors, where the scope and convolution can rapidly multiply.

Don't Forget to Take It to the Office

So what do organizations and businesses look at when calculating their carbon footprints? They take into account different *scopes* of emissions, which are categorized as follows:

Scope 1

These are "direct" emissions and include all greenhouse gas (GHG) emissions generated from sources actually owned or under the control of the organization, such as its own power plants, generators, or chemical processing facilities. These emissions are most commonly found in resource-intensive industries such as mining or energy. They may also come from the use of alternative power sources, such as backup generators.

Scope 2

These are considered "indirect," representing the emissions that are the result of gas and electricity that the organization purchased and then consumed. These emissions come from the power used to run everything under the organization's complete control, from the lights and temperature controls to the appliances and IT equipment.

Scope 3

These are also "indirect" emissions, and represent all other emissions created during the organization's lifecycle but not under the organization's direct control. Scope 3 emissions are probably the hardest to accurately track, as they can include everything from employee travel and commutes to supply chain emissions and the transport of finished goods.

The bulk of the emissions for most organizations is made up of Scopes 2 and 3; there may be some overlap in what is counted within an individual's own carbon footprint, as in the case of commute and travel. While this is something to keep in mind in its totality, it is generally considered of benefit for an organization to try to understand all potential impacts of its extended operations so that policies, procedures, and processes (such as supporting a network-enabled remote office or telecommuting) can potentially be put in place to mitigate those impacts.

Interestingly, many of the factors we discussed as influencing an individual or household's carbon footprint can also be applied in the business setting. The natural climate plays a role in the amount of energy the organization consumes to heat or cool its facilities, not to mention its data centers, which house IT equipment that can be adversely affected by temperature fluctuations. The proximity of offices to the workforce and the broader business community (made up of customers, partners, and vendors) and the accessibility of public transport can significantly influence the amount of CO_2 that is attributed to a business's carbon footprint due to employee commute and travel.

In many regards, the interest of the organization in understanding, managing, and ultimately reducing its carbon footprint and environmental impacts can be attributed in large part to business economics. Hopefully, a sense of responsibility may play into the decision-making process, but as with individuals and households, it is often constrained by an analysis of what the organization can and is willing to afford. While implementing energy-efficient practices and technologies can reduce the operational costs associated with running the business (in the form of lower heating and electrical bills), it often requires upfront investments. The motivations of the organization to consider the initial capital costs for longer-term gains are often tied to the macroeconomic climate and balance sheet of the business. There is also a vast landscape of environmental directives, legislation, and standards that the organization needs to contend with and adhere to in order to do business. The regulatory landscape, which includes activities on a local, national, and even international scale, may determine the types of considerations that the organization has to make regarding overall consumption and emission management at an individual and business level.

In addition to a business's operations, many are calling for a business's footprint to include the footprints of the services or products it delivers to market. Presumably this would consist of the consumption of those products and services while they are in use, estimated and detailed by some carbon footprint label attached to the product. There are also discussions of imposing carbon taxes and disposal fees on products that use excessive energy. So, a business that provides toasters might potentially have to charge for the product, its lifetime use of toasting energy (in the form of a tax), and a disposal fee for recycling the spent toasters and any toxic material recovery.

The Rules of Footprinting

The business standards that exist for GHG emissions cover environmental, social, and ethical components, but they tend to be very general and offer only basic guidelines. So the world's governments have stepped in through directives, regulations, or laws, making it a veritable maze to navigate. The rules can vary from country to country, with different governments placing different emphasis on different aspects of sustainability.

It is a benefit to business organizations to become more environmentally savvy and to pay attention to their carbon footprints to get ahead of any potential business impacts. There are ongoing discussions on the global stage, led by organizations such as the World Business Council for Sustainable Development (WBCSD) and the World Resources Institute (WRI). Emissions and footprints are also key topics of discussion during events such as the World Economic Forum, the U.N. Global Compact meetings, and the U.N. Climate Change conferences (which will strive to get commitments and clarity on where to take the Kyoto Protocol at the next major meeting in Copenhagen at the end of 2009).

The climate accords of the Kyoto Protocol call for the reduction of CO_2 by 50% before the year 2050. Industrialized countries set targets to reduce their collective GHG emissions by 5.2% compared with the emissions from 1990; national targets range from 8% reductions for the European Union and some others, to 7% for the U.S. (which did not sign the Protocol), 6% for Japan, 0% for Russia, and permitted increases of 8% for Australia and 10% for Iceland. Some countries have taken their reductions further:

- Japan has committed to reducing its CO_2 consumption to 6% below its 1990 level by 2010.
- The European Union has set a goal of reducing CO_2 by 20% by 2020.
- The United Kingdom has set a target of reducing CO_2 by 20% by 2010 and its net carbon amount by at least 60% from the 1990 baseline by 2050.
- The Netherlands has a goal of a 30% reduction by 2020.
- Germany set a 21% reduction goal by 2012.
- In the U.S., despite not signing the Kyoto Protocol, there have been efforts to reduce CO_2 levels, particularly at a local level. For example, over 500 mayors representing more than 50 million Americans have signed the Mayor's Climate Protection Agreement, pledging to reduce GHG emissions in their communities. And California is aiming to reduce its CO_2 by 80% by 2050. The 2009 Clean Air and Security Act proposes reducing U.S. emissions to 17% below 2005 levels by 2020 and 83% below by 2050 (the bill had passed the House and was working its way through the Senate at the time of this writing).

A Product's Carbon Footprint

It all begins with the carbon footprint *labeling* of products. However, there is no standard for what should be included in that label. Large retail establishments around the world have announced plans to place carbon labels on many of the goods on their shelves and in their racks (including the retail giant WalMart), but the timelines for delivery have stalled because of the complexity of scoping and then tabulating the carbon footprint.

For example, it is easy to identify how much electricity a product can reasonably be expected to consume and, consequently, the CO_2 it will emit when in use, based on the average energy draw and life expectancy. For example, a hairdryer emits about 57 pounds of carbon dioxide a year, a dishwasher emits 59 pounds, a central AC unit emits 4,067 pounds, and a TV emits 548 pounds.[7] You could multiply these amounts by the number of years they are expected to be in use, and you'll get the carbon footprint of the product. But is that single measurement representative of the true carbon footprint of those products?

What about its entire lifecycle from beginning to completion, from the research and development to the disposal of the product? This is often referred to as a product's *embedded carbon*, representing the carbon that was emitted to create it—it's the impact of its very existence, even if it is never used. In an ideal scenario, to truly understand the overall environmental implications of everything we purchase, use, and throw away, the carbon footprint label would include any and all CO_2 emitted or predicted to be emitted from the start to the end of the product lifecycle, activity, or operation.

But how far back do you go? How detailed do you get? Does it include the travel the sales rep did to talk up the product to the retail establishments that will eventually sell it? Does it include all of the retooling of the manufacturing plant that was done before production began? Does it include all the steps and energy expended in creating the components that go into the product? Does it include all the shipping and transportation required to get components from their manufacturing plants to the facility that's producing the product to the distribution house to the end destination? The list goes on and on, seemingly indefinitely.

And this is where the company—which makes thousands, maybe even millions, of these widgets—comes back into play in determining the carbon footprint. It is unclear as to where the lines will be drawn or even how organizations will get the visibility and accountability for certain aspects of their operations and product delivery that are not within their direct control. However, it is not unimaginable that some portion of an organization's carbon footprint will be included in the *lifecycle* carbon footprint label of a product in the near future, and vice versa; that the footprints of services and products will be accounted for, in some way, in the company's carbon footprint.

As a result, many businesses have invested in an infrastructure to calculate their carbon footprints and are looking at how to quantify the carbon footprints of their products in anticipation of pending requirements. For example, in March 2009, the U.S. Environmental Protection Agency (EPA) put forth a proposal,[8] under the Clean Air Act, that requires all major U.S. GHG emitters to report emissions in a national database. The proposal covers approximately 13,000 facilities, representing approximately 90% of the country's emissions, including fossil fuel and industrial chemicals suppliers, motor vehicle and engine manufacturers, and direct emitters of GHG that emit 25,000 or more tons of carbon a year. This process will require investment; the EPA estimates that first-year compliance will cost the private sector $160 million, with subsequent years costing $127 million. It's a sure sign of what's to come.

The Business of Reducing Carbon

To get ahead of the curve and reduce risks related to climate change, many businesses have started to report their own carbon footprints on a voluntary basis. The content may be contained in corporate sustainability reports, as part of the organization's financial annual reporting, or included in public repositories such as the Carbon Disclosure Project's (CDP) annual report, which houses the world's largest repository of corporate climate change information (*www.cdproject.net*).

In addition to reporting on their carbon footprints, many leading companies have also set reduction targets around the carbon emissions, implementing a variety of processes and programs designed to create consumption efficiencies. Some of these include using the network in efforts to reduce travel and commuting, as well as achieving general operational efficiencies. Some organizations, such as Google, Yahoo!, and Dell, have announced plans to be carbon-neutral.

Some companies have gone so far as to aim to be *carbon-positive*. Car service provider Ecoigo says it will offset double the emissions from all its vehicles, as well as the energy consumed by its office. Fiji Water has set a goal of offsetting its total carbon footprint by 120% (*www.environmentalleader.com/2009/01/21/eco-generosity-to-make-waves-in-2009/*).

So, how is it that companies, which are by nature fairly large in scope and in consumption, are able to make these claims or set these targets?

A business has to make a commitment to reduce its emissions from its operations and to offset what it can't reduce by investing in technologies or activities that are carbon-positive to make up the difference in its targets. Something that is carbon-positive actually reduces the amount of CO_2 in the environment—the most basic example is a tree, which can absorb an average of 50 pounds of CO_2 in a year.[9] In fact, a recently released 40-year study by the University of Leeds found that trees absorb nearly one-fifth of humanity's CO_2 emissions.[10] There are manmade examples out there as well, such as cement developed by British firm Novacem; the production of the cement creates 0.4 tons of CO_2, but during its lifetime it is capable of absorbing 0.6 tons of CO_2, making it a carbon-positive product.[11]

In the meantime, the best way to get ahead of the carbon curve is to begin to inventory and measure all impacts, to understand potential exposure to risks, and to identify opportunities for improvement and gain. To date, individuals and organizations are making estimates to the best of their abilities to try to capture a more complete carbon footprint, while keeping an eye on a realistic scope and ultimately results that are comparable and easily understood.

The key is coming up with a more holistic system that provides a clear picture of the environmental implications for each of our choices and actions. A system that avoids confusion and duplicate attributions is one that accurately and clearly defines what is counted, and who is responsible for what, whether that is an individual, a household, a public or private sector organization, a product, or a service. It is important to get it right, because only once we understand and quantify it can we seriously try to figure out what to do to alter our global course. Remember this chapter's epigraph: "You can't manage what you can't measure."

Oh, by the way, there is also the matter of whether carbon should be the only footprint factor. Water could arguably be a more precious and scarce resource than fossil fuels, or the issue of biodiversity, or even the climate change effects of other GHG emissions, such as methane, which is fairly prevalent and very long-lived. For example, should businesses have to report on how much water they use in their operations? Many wineries in California's dry climate do just that because the wineries are so water-intensive. On a personal level, you could look at your food intake. Theoretically, vegetarians should have much lower emissions than meat eaters because cows produce the GHG methane, plus it takes approximately 16 pounds of grain to produce 1 pound of meat. Should that be a part of an individual or household's footprint? (As an aside, $48 billion worth of food was thrown out last year, begging the questions: how can we create a more sustainable food distribution model, and how can the network help?)

According to the Footprint Network, the world's ecological footprint is currently 23% over capacity, and it takes about one year and two months to regenerate what we consume in a year. So, while progress is being made toward standardizing on a footprint measurement, the debate about what that measurement should include is far from over.

I've gone almost an entire chapter without mentioning the network. Hopefully, you already understand that everything we are about to do to measure, manage, and manipulate our consumption culture will be globally communicated and synchronized online. How else do you change a planet, except by using the only global tool we have?

CHAPTER 11

Net Efficiencies: Maximizing Resources While Minimizing Waste

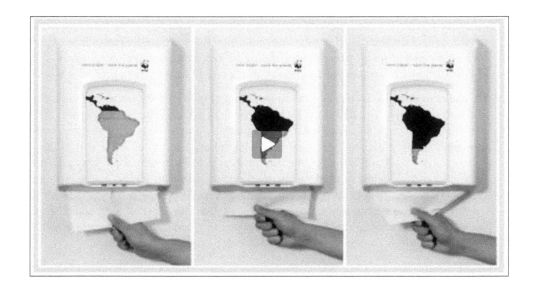

You have to think about "big things" while you're doing small things, so that all the small things go in the right direction.

—Alvin Toffler

The network makes all kinds of things possible to promote environmental sustainability—smart buildings, intelligent transport systems, just-in-time supply chain management, and the list goes on and on. ICT enables many efficiencies that are creating the forecasts for potential carbon emission reductions in the 15–40% range.

What's a Net Efficiency?

Can't envision what these efficiencies might look like? You swipe your key card to get access to your office, and it sends a signal to the automated building management system. You hear a click unlocking the door and then the lights and air conditioning units turn on. When you exit the building, the lights and air conditioning adjust; if it's the middle of the day, they simply dim, and if it's the end of the day, they turn off altogether.

Or you stop at the convenience store to buy a jug of milk and the transaction is scanned and automatically uploaded to an inventory system, which waits until a certain threshold number triggers an order for a replacement shipment of milk. The guesswork is removed for the store manager. No longer does anyone need to estimate when they will need to order more milk. In fact, the inventory system database might physically be in Atlanta, Georgia, while you are at the convenience store on Grand Street in Eugene, Oregon. The risk of too much milk has been reduced—all the waste associated with producing, transporting, and then getting rid of the milk that is not bought is minimized. Fresh milk brought to you by the network through a series of connections is the way of the world's supply chains, from tanker ships to vending machines.

There are thousands, if not tens of thousands, of examples of how the network is being applied to create efficiencies; some are as simple as adjusting a building's lighting and temperature controls, and others as complex as managing an entire energy grid. There are wireless water sprinklers that can communicate the ground's moisture level for watering only when a landscape actually needs it. There are whole-home systems that allow you to see what your house is doing while you are out. Every traffic light, car, and GPS mobile phone can be connected. City by city, state by state, and country by country, it can all be connected to share data, results, plans, and ideas that work. Smart houses, smart cars, smart stores, and restaurants, and hospitals, and schools are all within reach.

The network plays the connector role, linking resources and information to innovative applications and devices to better minimize, not to mention monitor, our every environmental impact. New net-aware applications are making for real-time understanding and analysis, as well as resource mobilization and planning. Due to the vast number and types of devices connecting to the network—phones, laptops, light switches, elevators, traffic lights, thermostats, even garage door openers—the network can measure consumption, report and analyze trends, and then program consumption reductions via all of these IP-enabled devices. In other words, the opportunity for one of those paradigm shifts is ripe—let's call them *net efficiencies*.

For instance, the concept behind Metropolis, a consortium of more than 100 of the largest cities around the world, is to use the network to track each city's resources and consumption and then model refinements in real time. Metropolis provides a forum for sharing and providing best practices as the cities devise plans to use technology as a means to become more efficient and to reduce waste and pollution. The applications cover the full spectrum of interest, as one could imagine covering over 100 different locales, from delivering information and services online to using technology to keep track of migratory animals in an effort to identify deviations that might indicate environmental disruptions or problems in the region. Some cities use the network to map more efficient garbage pickup or mail delivery routes, taking into consideration the impact that time of day and traffic patterns can have on drive time. Others use the network to get visibility into natural resource allocation, such as water or energy, or to collect and transmit information on commercial goods and food supplies. It might all sound standard issue, but none of it was plausible 20 years ago. It's all, literally, new ground.

Even if Metropolis's only efforts were to control internal city traffic patterns, you can just imagine what an effect that would have. The drain that vehicular traffic has on resources is enormous—Americans spend approximately 4.2 billion hours a year in traffic, which wastes the equivalent of 58 supertankers of gas.[1] In 2005, it was estimated that American commuters idling in traffic jams cost the U.S. economy $78 billion, up from $15 billion in 1982.[2] The European Commission estimates that up to 50% of its fuel consumption is due to congestion and nonoptimal driving behavior.[3]

What to do? The network can support dynamic route guidance systems (such as Google Maps on your mobile or the GPS in your car), which can be carried anywhere and linked into traffic information to provide up-to-the-minute instructions on the best way to avoid current traffic congestion or provide the best route to a new destination. Governments and industry are using applications such as those developed by Southwest Research Institute (*www.SwRI.com*) to improve the efficiencies of advanced traffic management systems (ATMS).

Cities that have sensors and computer-controlled traffic lights at intersections can leverage the network to monitor traffic patterns and quickly make changes to create more efficient traffic flows and reduce gas consumption. Stockholm's smart toll system was able to reduce gridlock by 20%,[4] reduce CO_2 emissions by 12%,[5] and increase public transport by 40,000 users per day. Australia is hoping to use smart traffic management tracking systems to slow the growth of its transport emissions, which have grown by more than 23% since 1990.[6] And the London Congestion Charging scheme, which keeps track of public transport options to facilitate planning and optimize capacity, is credited with a 20% reduction in emissions.

Other cities use network technology to monitor their water or electricity supplies, allowing them to identify potential issues and tweak resource planning accordingly. In 2009, as part of its greater Connected Urban Development program, Cisco Systems launched an Urban EcoMap designed to provide information on the GHGs generated through the transportation, wastes, and general energy use of a city's locale. In addition, "smart city" projects often include free wireless Internet access on public transport that provides updates on routes and other useful information, as well as remote, high-tech work centers that try to encourage people to stay local and reduce long commutes. Piloted in San Francisco (*http://blog.urbanecomap.org/*), the urban services platform creates awareness and a connection between the city and its people about their collective environmental impacts. Seeing is believing, especially when it's where you live, work, and raise a family, and applications like these are providing critical inputs to urban design and development.

Another, the EU's European Environment Agency, has a mapping, imaging, and data-visualization platform, which visitors to the "Eye on Earth" portal can use to access real-time information on the water quality of beaches throughout Europe (*http://www. eyeonearth.eu*). The system leverages environmental data provided by both the countries and beachgoers. The agency is hoping to extend the platform to cover soil, air, and ozone quality and general biodiversity monitoring information.[7]

In the U.S. and China, computer modeling is being used to monitor water basins for better planning and policies surrounding environmental impacts of industrialization and general land use on the water supply. The impacts of these programs can be great. IBM sells solutions that use sensors and analytical and modeling software to provide greater visibility and control over many of these systems. IBM used one of its factories to pilot technology to optimize water usage, reducing consumption by 27%, or 20 million gallons a year, while simultaneously increasing output at the plant by 30%.[8]

A great example of a technologically progressive city is Abu Dhabi. The capital and second-most populous city in the United Arab Emirates, it has the second-highest water use and carbon emissions per capita in the world. Abu Dhabi has set a goal to become a fully developed city by 2020, while simultaneously striving to establish a leadership position in the Middle East and the world at large in environmental responsibility and overall sustainability. As a result, it is relying heavily on technology and, more specifically, the network to foster more efficient, sustainable development.

Abu Dhabi's plans are ambitious. They include creating the world's first "carbon-neutral, zero-waste" city (Masdar City) and a unique sustainable philosophy (*Estidama*) that includes environmental, economic, social, and cultural concepts. It is drafting developmental regulations, building codes, and sustainability standards to align with its ultimate vision of creating a sustainable Arab world. Technology is central to many of the sustainability plans for the region. The Environmental Agency Abu Dhabi (EAD) launched a Green IT strategy project in January 2009 to harness the benefits of IT (IT Eco-Innovation) and address the ecofootprint of ICT (IT Eco-Efficiency) in an effort to create a comprehensive strategy that could be a net efficiency model for the world.

For example, you can imagine that the most limited resource in Abu Dhabi is water, and what there is of it is produced mainly from desalinization. Uncontrolled pumping of groundwater for irrigation is depleting existing aquifers, so EAD has developed a system for monitoring and managing all known wells, thus replacing the traditional system that required someone to visit the well, generally commuting by truck, every 90 days to manually collect and download data. This new wireless, real-time monitoring system is being rolled out to a growing number of important wells to ensure closer control and real-time management of the water supplies, while reducing the ecoimpact of doing it.

Abu Dhabi is also designing a waste system to remove many of the hazards traditionally associated with waste that is stored and then collected outside buildings. Basically, the city is piloting the use of large containers that are sunk into the ground, which passersby, street cleaners, and small-business owners can all use to throw away their trash. The containers have censors that will send an alert when the container hits a certain level. At that point, waste trucks can come and empty the containers, reducing unnecessary waste trips to maximize collection.[9]

Developing countries around the world would be well served to take a page from Abu Dhabi's book in using ICT and the network to reduce wastes around resource consumption. In fact, from an energy perspective, according to the McKinsey Global Institute (MGI), if developing countries increased their energy productivity, they could potentially slow the growth of their energy demand by more than half over the next 12 years. That could potentially drop the demand from where it would otherwise be by 25% in 2020. To put this number in perspective, MGI notes the reduction would be larger than the total energy consumption in China today.[10]

However, the window of opportunity for achieving these kinds of efficiencies is shrinking fast, mostly because these developing countries are building infrastructure now. In fact, over half of the capital building stock that will be in place in 2020 is in progress and will be built between now and then.[11] It's a significant opportunity that countries could miss out on if they don't make the proper investments today. MGI estimates it will take approximately $90 billion annually over the next 12 years to adopt automation technology and more environmentally friendly building practices that can reduce overall resource consumption over the life of the building. While the investment may seem significant to developing countries (where capital is hard to come by), the price tag could be looked at in another way. If countries don't invest in energy productivity, they will most likely need to spend double that on building out their energy supply infrastructures to keep up with growing demand. Unfortunately, the budgets of most of these developing countries are modest compared with that of Abu Dhabi. And, as is often the case, project decisions are based on fixed budgets and "right now" constraints—environmental or longer-range cost benefits are harder to quantify and may not even enter the decision-making process.

How do you tell these cash-strapped countries that for approximately $90 billion a year today, MGI estimates that the savings could total $600 billion a year by 2020?[12] What responsibility does the developed world have to support more sustainable building? If a building doesn't take advantage of natural air temperature fluctuations and flows or doesn't incorporate monitoring of resource utilization (such as water consumption, energy use, sewage and air pollution, and real-time management of those resources, via automated lighting, temperature, and power controls, among other things), the long-term energy efficiency will cost more as energy costs rise every year. That building will pollute and cost its hometown city dearly, and may have a potential ripple effect on the world at large.

Want proof of the return on investment in energy-efficient technologies? The data has been collected for years, and it's readily available for anyone to browse or download. For example, in the U.S., buildings account for 40% of the country's CO_2 emissions, a number ripe to reap benefits from efficiencies. Researchers define "energy productivity" as the total gross domestic product produced per unit of energy; the more efficient an area is, the greater the prosperity. We saw this in California after it passed appliance- and building-efficiency standards. These measures have paid dividends over the past three decades in the form of keeping the amount of energy consumed per capita flat. Throughout the U.S. during that same period, the energy consumed per capita has risen 50%. It is interesting to note that Californians use less energy but maintain a higher GDP than other Americans. In 2006, California created $2.17 of GDP for every 10,000 BTU of energy consumed, compared with $1.29 of GDP for every 10,000 BTU in the rest of the nation, and California citizens did it by using less than 7,000 kWh a year (3,668 pounds).[13] California's energy productivity is therefore 68% higher than the rest of the United States.

The European Union has quantified the data, too, and has found that building energy use also accounts for more than 40% of Europe's CO_2 emissions, more than half of which is used to heat, light, and run homes. It is estimated that close to a quarter (70 billion of the 400 billion kWh) of the energy consumed in homes could be saved through the use of building management systems, metering technologies, sensors, energy auditing, optimization software, and communication networks.[14]

Then there's the impact of efficiencies in the supply chain, which can also improve resource utilization and reduce the overall emissions of developing and developed countries alike. Between 40 and 60% of a business's total GHG emissions come from activities conducted outside of its direct control, in the supply chain.[15] These activities include the manufacturing, processing, packaging, and transportation of physical goods. For business, this is a huge opportunity for greater efficiency. For the community in which the business operates, it's an environmental responsibility.

Within the supply chain, transportation is one of the biggest generators of emissions. Beyond the obvious emissions generated via the planes, trains, and trucks—spurring companies such as WalMart, Ryder, and UPS to announce plans to test heavy-duty trucks that use hybrid technology and alternative fuels as part of their initiatives[16]— there is an opportunity to reduce emissions by generating efficiencies in the movements of those goods and fleets. This is where the network comes in, facilitating the real-time tracking capabilities of these fleets through product distribution management that can streamline orders and routes. According to Nokia Siemens, a 1% trucking efficiency or improvement could result in a savings of 3,400 tons of carbon dioxide.[17]

A great example of how organizations are leveraging the network to drive (pun intended) efficiencies through the supply chain and distribution comes out of the UK British Telecom worked with its customer BritVic, one of the country's leading soft drink companies, to streamline its beverage distribution. According to the BritVic website (*www. britvic.com*), "In 2006, Britvic sold 1.4 billion litres of soft drinks in hundreds of different flavours, shapes and sizes and delivers to over 4,000 customers and approximately 200,000 points of distribution." BritVic employees are based throughout the country, working out of its main offices, factories, or depots.

One of the ways that BritVic gets its soft drinks into the hands of its customers is through vending machines located throughout the country. A percentage of its employees are responsible for keeping these vending machines stocked. As you would expect with any delivery setup, an employee is assigned a particular area and is responsible for keeping the vending machines along his route well stocked.

The traditional delivery method consisted of the employee loading up his delivery van every day or every other day with all of the company's beverage products and then making the rounds to each of the vending machines and restocking as necessary. As you can imagine, a lot of waste is associated with this delivery method; sometimes there is no need to refill anything in a vending machine, and other times just one or two products need to be refilled. British Telecom worked with BritVic to develop a fuel force optimization model, which consisted of an intelligent monitoring system of the vending machines stock levels using wireless technology. Basically, the system keeps track of the beverages that have been sold, so employees know exactly what they need to restock. This system has enabled BritVic to achieve a 10% reduction in the number of visits employees need to make to each vending machine and has allowed the company to reduce its vehicle loads by 30%, because now it doesn't have to carry excess stock; this has resulted in a 15% decrease in gas consumption, which equals a 25% total reduction of costs. It's the story of one business, in one country, but a 25% reduction around the globe would be a really good thing.

So the question becomes, "Can every business reduce its carbon emissions simply by becoming more net aware?" The simple answer is yes—if the business is able to take that awareness and make better choices about the ways in which it operates, produces, and brings its products to market, with all the real-time information collected from a myriad of network nodes.

For example, by reducing carbon emissions, waste production, and natural resource demand in its 2009 fiscal year, Cisco's Global Supply Chain Management realized more than $3 million in annual cost savings just through manufacturing efficiency. That's not a small number. And one can expect it's even more in many businesses around the world. As such, senior management should understand climate change risks within their supply chains, how suppliers are managing those risks, and the opportunities for improvement.

Whichever way you look at this, the network is the tool driving the whole movement. With it, the business world can model, manage, and maintain close controls over its own supply chains. The network that runs modern-day business can also be the network that economizes its use of resources, energy, and inventories. It's the same connections, the same bandwidth. But with just a little entrepreneurial ingenuity and the foresight to see past immediate investments into the decades ahead, net-enabled efficiencies can significantly reduce total CO_2 emissions and one very large carbon footprint. A savvy business might be able a save a couple of million dollars to boot.

The data is out there, and it's becoming more convincing with every new piece of information. The very same network that fostered this world we've been discussing can also be the one that gives us these efficiencies in our personal, professional, and civic activities. It's not about what we have to do to the network, but rather how we use it. And if we use it to its fullest potential, the opportunity to maximize efficiencies and reduce waste and impacts is certainly sustainable.

CHAPTER 12

What's So Smart About an Energy Grid?

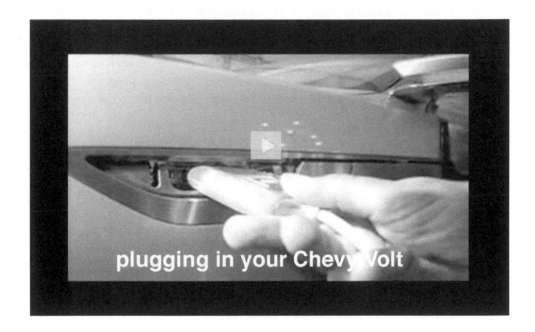

plugging in your Chevy Volt

I canna do it, Captain.
—Scotty, *Star Trek*

For most of the previous century, developed nations leveraged electrical grids to power their streets, cities, businesses, and homes. If you're reading this book, you've probably always had an electrical grid. A reliable energy grid is a badge of a prosperous community, enabling predictable learning and commerce. Just like the network, the energy grid (and the power it supplies) has become intertwined with everything we do, and our reliance on it only continues to grow as more and more of our daily activities require some type of power—from household cleaning to business communications.

I would venture to say that most of us in developed countries have come to take for granted the availability and abundance of relatively cheap energy to power our lives. However, we have seen demand for energy spike and stress available supplies. Living in California, I have experienced "rolling blackouts" in the summer months, when the power grid is simply under too much load and can't support the demand; by all estimates, problems like this are not going to go away and are more than likely going to get worse.

Projections place 2 billion more people on the planet by the year 2025, and a total of 9 billion people on the planet by 2050.[1] To accommodate all these people, who will all consume some amount of energy, the world must generate more. A lot more. Predictions see demand for energy growing 1.6% a year on a global basis—some have today's demand increasing by as much as 54% by 2025.[2] Regardless of which numbers you subscribe to, the increasing demands on the energy grid do not show signs of abating, and will most likely overtake supply in the not-so-distant future.

In the U.S. alone, electricity demand is expected to grow by 141,000 megawatts in the next decade, yet only 57,000 megawatts of new energy resources have been identified.[3] And when you look at the state of reliable sources of energy in developing countries, the picture is even grimmer; in many parts of the world, the energy grids are already close to maximum capacity. In these developing countries, it is not uncommon for facilities to be run off of backup diesel generators because the electricity grid keeps going down. It is also not uncommon for these facilities to close their doors until energy availability returns. This "energy poverty" results in chunks of the population who are unable to engage in overall development and who are completely shut out from the digital world. If you agree with the sustainability of the network notion and the idea that it only works if everyone around the world has access to it, you can see how the availability of viable energy sources is crucial.

Another stark reality is the nontrivial operating cost of producing energy. Now, let's be clear that the network and other ICT solutions are not the only things causing this ramp in energy demand, but they most certainly play a role. In some cases, the energy it takes to operate these devices is teetering on or has already overtaken the cost of the device itself. Specifically, from the network's perspective, businesses are finding that they are paying more for electricity than bandwidth; the cost of the energy and the cooling required for a core router over five years is approximately 8–12% of the capital cost of the router, and the percentages go up for smaller routers. And while it once took 30 to 50 years for electricity costs to equal the capital costs of a server, we are now seeing electricity costs of low-end servers exceeding the cost of those servers in less than 4 years.[4]

Green Power for Mobile

There are many initiatives underway by ICT companies and industry consortiums to create solutions that draw power directly from solar, wind, and sustainable biofuels in developing countries. One such example, the "Green Power for Mobile" program, has set a goal to power 118,000 new and existing off-grid mobile phone base stations in developing countries by 2012. This potentially represents a savings of up to 2.5 billion liters of diesel a year, which translates to a reduction of up to 6.8 million tons of carbon emissions.[5]

There are estimates that by 2010, almost 50% of the world's data centers, which house the servers, applications, and storage of a company (connected by the network), will not have enough energy to power and cool them.[6] There are stories of companies (such as Google and Amazon) building their data centers right next to power plants or near dams and water supplies so they can get the energy and cooling they need to keep their facilities going. Some companies have refurbished military aircraft carriers to house their data centers to take advantage of the natural cooling that comes from being hosted in the hull of a ship. Let me point out that this is happening in well-developed countries.

And with energy constraints and prices trending up, not down, the power requirements and costs of operating all these technologies will remain a long-term concern. In fact, it is because of these issues that the energy grid has come into focus of late. Many individuals, businesses, and governments alike are starting to look at how and when they use power from the grid, trying to understand the way power is managed and distributed.

The systems of today are highly centralized, with power supplied by a relatively small number of large power plants. They were designed to distribute power from a central location to the consumer (whatever or whomever that may be); it was not designed to be a bidirectional system to manage dynamic energy supply and demand. As a result, it is ill-equipped to manage shifts in supply and demand on a large geographical expanse. There is also very little built-in intelligence to balance the power loads and monitor how power flows across the grid.

As a result, there is much inefficiency associated with our current system. For starters, an amazing amount of power is "lost" during production and transport. It is not uncommon for a fairly significant portion of available electricity to be consumed simply during its transmission and distribution to end users (this is called *T&D loss*).

The amount typically ranges from 5% in OECD (developed) countries to 20% in developing countries.[7] In the U.S., for example, the power grid loses enough electricity annually to power India, Germany, and Canada combined for an entire year.[8] That, right there, represents significant opportunities for greater efficiency. In fact, there are estimates that if the U.S. was able to achieve even a 5% increase in efficiency in its energy transmission and distribution, it would be equal to eliminating the emissions of 53 million cars from the road.[9]

And this problem is only going to be compounded as the utilities add different power sources to the system. For example, in the U.S., there are many state mandates forcing utilities to incorporate clean energy into their processes. By 2030, they will need to add nearly 40 GW of energy from alternative energy sources,[10] which the current infrastructure is ill-equipped to handle. Interestingly, this is where developing countries may actually be ahead of developed nations. Because of the limited capabilities and availability of legacy energy grids in emerging countries, they are often on the forefront of efficient energy sourcing. However, from a cumulative perspective, many developing countries suffer from energy poverty, which can limit their overall growth and opportunities for improvement.

Each energy source has its own set of challenges, and as countries and utilities look at how to modernize their energy grids, it is obvious that they can benefit from the greater visibility and tighter controls offered by the ICT industry and its underlying network.

The generally agreed-upon starting point, however, is more fundamental. It focuses on building new power lines that can transmit clean, renewable energy from sources throughout any given region. Without these new lines, the ability to truly transform the nation's electricity systems to enhance their security, reliability, and storage capacities is hampered. This sentiment is echoed in a recent report from the North American Electric Reliability (NERC) (*http://earth2tech.com/2008/11/10/a-reliable-green-grid-could-need-2-trillion/*), which said that a lack of investment in the proper transmission infrastructure to accompany the increase of green power *will result* in an unreliable power grid.

So, what are we really talking about here? Think about a sea of solar panels in the dessert; how is the utility going to start getting that power from the desert over the mountain range to the homes and businesses that need it? Or what about a wind farm on the hilltops or even in the ocean? Unfortunately, the locations that host the most intense nature—heat, wind, waves, and geothermal—are locations that our population tends to avoid. We generally populate milder climates more densely.

Thus, not only does this power potentially need to be transmitted over long distances with variable terrain, it also needs to do it in an environmentally friendly way; otherwise, it will negate the efficiencies these "clean" sources are supposed to deliver.

> The other challenge in providing clean power is to do it in an aesthetically pleasing way; in other words, no one wants to look out on a beautiful expanse of land and see lots of ugly power lines. This is, by the way, akin to the issues that mobile carriers are facing because no one wants to have ugly cell towers dotted all around the landscape.

Another issue with the power lines is that they can be hard to scale, particularly when you are talking about trying to get power from individual homes and businesses back to the energy grid. For example, as more end users install solar panels on their roofs or parking lots to generate solar power, the utility needs to be able to efficiently take this power and add it to the grid for subsequent distribution. Germany was the first to establish a "feed-in" tariff, which basically allows an individual or business to generate and then sell energy to the utility, typically at a long-term, favorable rate.[11] Many countries have since adopted this distributed clean power–generation system, which, amidst rising concerns of the impacts of climate change, shows promise to only grow and expand (see Figure 12-1).

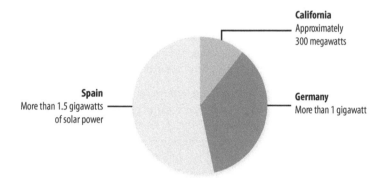

Figure 12-1. The installations of solar power in the top three regions in the world in 2008 amounted to almost 3 GW of new power; by 2030, the U.S. needs to generate 40 additional GW from alternative sources.

As mentioned previously, however, the current grids were designed for a one-to-many downstream type of transmission, not a many-to-one, or many-to-one-to-many, back-and-forth type of exchange, and they are straining under these new demands.

The time to deal with these issues is now. Alternative power generation is a burgeoning market that's not going to go away. Countries around the world are looking to reduce their dependence on fossil fuels and their carbon emissions. A lot of technologies are being developed to harvest energy. Wind and solar farms are probably the best known, but they are not the only games in town. Researchers are looking at geothermal energy, harnessing the power of the oceans, and using "kites" that fly in the atmosphere (around 10,000 feet up) to collect electrical charges. There are also "scavenger" technologies being developed that can capture and then recycle energy for reuse. Some energy companies are partnering with cow ranches to pilot methane capture programs using the cow manure to create an alternative energy source (which is as far as I am going to delve into that!).

Your Unsmart Home Grid

Estimates place the consumption of the networked home at approximately 4 kWh a day. This could be considered conservative, particularly if you look at the latest stats from Nielsen that put the average American in front of the TV for 142 hours per month (this is up 5 hours a month from just a year before,[12] and as I mentioned before, is a stat that deserves attention in another forum). It appears we are watching more "time-shifted" content, such as on-demand programming and content recorded via a TiVo, ReplayTV, and other Digital Video Recorder (DVR) devices, which offer the added convenience of being able to watch what we want when we want it. We are also watching more online video.

The problem is that there are a lot of inefficiencies currently in the network (modem, router, access point, TV, etc.). Take your DSL modem. It's probably on all the time. If it is connected to a desktop, it will ping the computer periodically and keep the Physical Interface Cards (PICs) and other aspects of the computer alive. This means that even if you're not using your desktop, it is consuming energy, often at 60–70% of its peak power consumption. If the idle consumption could be dropped by just 20–30%, that would represent a significant ongoing power savings for the home network, multiplied by the millions and potentially hundreds of millions of households that could be affected.

Imagine being able to use software on your computer or your cell phone to optimize the power management of the networked devices in your home, based on your usage patterns. For example, you probably have a smartphone, computer, and TV, all of which can be networked and are therefore drawing power from the network. You are probably not using all of your devices at the same time, so what if you could automatically power down devices that aren't in use? What if you could remotely control the air conditioning, lighting, window shades, and refrigerator temperature? The potential power savings would be great.

The U.S. has committed almost $17 billion toward investment in energy efficiency and renewable energy technologies,[13] which will bring it more in line with alternative energy programs in other countries. Currently, no really mature multisource generation markets exist. For example, if you look at solar power, you will find that it represents only a fraction of the overall energy capacity, even in Europe, which has been leading the solar market for the past decade. The takeaway is that now is the time to upgrade the energy system that was put in place over 50 years ago and build out the "smart grids" to support the inevitable growth of distributed multipower generation systems to scale with pending capacity and demand.

The goal of an Internet-based smart grid is to modernize energy generation and distribution to make it more efficient and more reliable. A true smart grid connects all different types of power sources to different power draws. It creates a real-time view of supply and demand, way beyond what we can imagine now. It ensures that the power sources, from traditional power plants and nuclear generation facilities to wind farms and solar panels, meet the power needs of a city, business, or home. These smart grids create greater transparency in the system for all, putting information into the hands of utilities and consumers alike. As a result, everyone can understand how power is being created and distributed, and can make informed decisions and recalibrate consumption to maximize its utility. The goal is to even out demand, cut expenses, and make the overall electric system more stable, through automation and the implementation of predictable controls that provide better management over power demand and supply.

Investing in the Grid

Google has estimated that the cost of building alternative power systems to stem global warming would be approximately $4.5 trillion over 22 years. However, it estimates that it would save $5.5 trillion over that same period, due to reductions in electricity costs and the building and ongoing operations of traditional power plants.[14] In the U.S., the Brattle Group predicts that to build an efficient power grid including transmission lines, it will need a $2 trillion investment, while others have set more conservative estimates at an investment of approximately $400 billion over 10 years to build a national smart grid.[15] To date, the U.S. has announced plans to provide $11 billion for improving the grid, funneled through the "Smart Grid Investment Program." This infusion of capital is designed to incentivize research and development, accelerate smart grid projects around the country, and increase federal matching grants for smart grid technology (up to 50% from the current 20%). The U.S. investment is expected to rise to over $20 billion by 2014.[16]

How does one build a smart grid, and where does the "smart" come from? A more intelligent energy grid starts with the installation of technologies that can collect and then feed more intelligence into the system (for example, check out *www.silverspringnetworks.com*). Smart meters are installed at the premises of buildings to keep track of the electrical, gas, and water consumption of that site. These smart meters are linked, via the network, from the building to the utility company, giving the individuals or businesses a real-time picture of the consumption in aggregate or of any specific location at any time of the day.

Gone will be the days of walking outside to the meter attached to the side of your house to try to make sense of the spinning dials that, even if you could interpret them, would only give you a lump sum of how much energy you consumed. Gone will be the days of trying to extrapolate your consumption and usage habits from your monthly bill, which is typically the only piece of information you get. And gone will be the days of the utility company sending out a technician to personally read the meters on a monthly basis, thus saving time and the travel impacts.

In its place will be a networked system that allows the utilities to receive and present real-time information—generally via an online portal, dashboard, or website—to customers about their consumption (Panasonic has already developed an intelligent meter that tells consumers how much energy is being consumed in a home with an easy-to-understand image of penguins on an iceberg that are either happy or unhappy, depending on consumption rates).

Providing all parties with visibility into real-time power consumption allows the utilities and end users to identify opportunities for efficiencies and reductions. Another change will most likely be in the pricing of electricity. To date, customers pay flat or average rates, but utility companies pay variable rates. They spend more for energy generated at peak times than during times of lower demand. So, making customers pay rates commensurate with the costs of their actual usage could increase awareness and help customers make decisions around consumption based on real-time costs and needs.

The goal is to stabilize the system and reduce energy grid consumption via a combination of education, incentives, and new "smart" service offerings. Users can go online and quickly create an energy consumption profile, receive an energy audit, learn tips for conservation, and find out about available rate incentives or rebates and environmentally friendly programs, all within a few clicks. There is also software available to encourage behavioral change, such as Google's PowerMeter (unveiled in 2009), which helps consumers take the information garnered from these smart meter–type devices and get a handle on their real-time electricity use.[17]

The not-so-distant future vision is that each outlet in your home will be connected to the network and subsequent energy grid, leading to even more detailed measurements about your energy consumption. These measurements could be at a macrolevel—say, room by room—or at the individual appliance/device level, so you can determine exactly what the impact will be if you change the temperature of your refrigerator up or down a degree or air-dry your dishes. "The Digital Home" has the potential to really increase energy efficiency. Just think about the possibilities when the network can link data effortlessly among all the devices in your home and integrate remote controls into their utility functions, allowing you to remotely control everything, including your TV, washing machine, air-conditioning, and heating units. The technology is already being used by businesses and it's coming for your home. It won't be long before you are able to see your consumption and then turn your devices on and off using your web browser or another application, even if you are halfway around the world. It's not the home of the far-off future; it's a reality that's just around the corner.

Studies have demonstrated that when people have information on their home energy consumption, behavior does, in fact, change, resulting in approximately 5–15% less use.[18] In the U.S., if you factor in that households consume an estimated 21% of the energy used, you can see how greater awareness could have a big impact on energy consumption reductions.

We have seen utility companies and municipalities try to leverage information, such as the state of California's "Flex Your Power" campaign, in efforts to make end users aware of and change their resource utilization. For a state such as California, which is striving to reach its goal of 80% CO_2 reductions by 2050 and has suffered from rolling blackouts that brought the state's energy issues to light (a little bit of irony never hurt anyone!), it is clear that the consumption of constrained energy resources needs to be managed better at all levels. But as previously noted, this is not a problem relegated to a single location or even region—it is one that almost every city, county, state, and nation is tackling.

This is one reason you've heard politicians clamoring about the jobs green technology can bring to the marketplace. According to estimates, the size of the market opportunity for a smarter power grid will create a $65 billion industry by 2013. The market for smart-metering hardware and software and networking technologies specifically—which are what make the smart grid smart—will grow from $2.7 billion this year to approximately $4.7 billion in 2013.[20] Morgan Stanley Research sizes the growth of the smart grid market at $40 billion by 2013 and $100 billion by 2030.[21]

And it's not a pie-in-the-sky dream or a politician's magical carpet ride—it's beginning to happen. Malta has committed 70 million Euros (roughly $103 million USD at the time of this writing) to build a national smart grid network, to be completed by 2012, that will serve 400,000 customers. It plans to install and connect a smart meter at 250,000 customer premises, be they individual homes, businesses, schools, or government agencies. It's going to be really interesting to see what the national utilities, Enemalta Corporation and the Water Services Corporation, will be able to see—and what they'll do with what they see. It could come down to delivering pricing based on the time of day, the day of the week, or the weather. There might be sales by the hour—set your electric clothes dryer to turn on at 2 a.m., and get a bonus kilowatt.

In the U.S., Washington state, in conjunction with the Department of Energy, demonstrated that 15% reductions are possible with a more intelligent energy grid, which, if extended nationally, could eliminate the need for up to 30 large coal-fired plants over the next 20 years.[22] We are starting to see projects around the country to this effect, like the SmartGridCity Project in Boulder, Colorado, which has installed a distribution and communications network for the city leveraging smart meters (close to 40,000) and a web portal to help customers understand and manage their energy use.

And Denver, Colorado is engaged in a project to extend computer control over the city's energy grid via a network of wireless devices (with up to 50–60 being deployed daily) that collect information from advanced household and business meters. That information is transmitted to the utility's facilities, giving them minute-by-minute information and future communications channels that allow them to interact with customers and make supply-and-demand decisions based on real-time information.

Business Responsibility

If greater awareness of energy use within the household leads to reduction, is the same true when applied to business? Suppose those responsible for the IT infrastructure could see how much energy they are consuming and, better yet, were made responsible for paying the costs of that consumption (through their budgets). It could go a long way toward developing more efficient practices within business itself.

Unfortunately, very few IT departments have that visibility or the sole responsibility for the charges of the electrical consumption of their IT infrastructures. Only 4% in North America and 5% in Europe responded that their IT departments were in charge of the electrical costs of their departments. On the flipside, 13% of North American respondents said they had no visibility, nor responsibility, along with 8% of European respondents. Most IT departments may have visibility, but tend to share responsibility for managing the electrical efficiency of the IT infrastructure with facilities and other departments. This is the case for 50% of respondents in North America and 56% in Europe. Twenty-two percent of North American respondents said they have visibility, but no responsibility, which is in line with their European counterparts at 20%.[19] As we have seen in home settings, when people have visibility and responsibility for their energy consumption, they tend to reduce their overall use. The same concept could represent a place to start for improving the energy efficiency of business and their internal networks.

Another starting point is to establish a baseline so that success with, or failure to improve, overall efficiency could be measured and validated. Often, this baseline will include a variety of factors, from energy consumption to carbon dioxide emissions to operational costs associated with running the infrastructure.

California's Pacific Gas and Electric (PG&E) program has worked aggressively to upgrade household and building meters, networking them directly to the power company's management systems to enable real-time monitoring of energy use. To date, PG&E has installed 440,000 smart electricity meters (and 1.4 million smart gas meters) toward its goal of more than 10 million installed by the end of 2011.[23] (I am pleased to report I just received mine this summer.)

An interesting side effect of these smarter energy grids is a change in the relationship between power companies and end users. In essence, the grid becomes a shared resource, with a wider constituency taking responsibility for it. Power companies are leveraging individuals and businesses as power generation sources and enlisting their help to better manage and even shed their load. This requires utilities to connect in different ways to a much wider set of consumers than in the past (which is where the network comes in, remember) and the relationship becomes a variety of downstream and upstream transactions.

A popular example of this upstream/downstream partnership is when energy suppliers partner with regional businesses. The utility company monitors real-time demand and when the load on the grid reaches a certain level, it asks its business partners to shed an agreed-upon amount, thereby reducing peak loads and ensuring that the energy grid can sustain the energy demands of the community. Because the cost of generating electricity during peak demand periods can be up to 10 times more expensive than during other periods (due to general supply-and-demand principles), it is particularly important to stabilize the load (100 hours of electricity at peak, which represents approximately 1% of the annual consumption, can account for as much as 20% of a utility's annual electricity expenditures). Such an event is triggered by a spike in electricity consumption, one that threatens the overall stability of the energy grid, which may be the result of a cold front or a heat wave.

The utility communicates via email, a networked visual signal, or automated phone tree to participating individuals and companies, who then reduce their load on the grid. To do this, most participating businesses have networked facility management systems that automate many of the processes, such as turning off lights, turning the temperature up or down a few degrees, closing or opening windows or shades, or evaluating equipment use and shutting down nonvital devices for the duration of the event. It is a fairly automated process that can have dramatic results, but it's proof of a larger, grandiose concept. What if sensors detected GHG emissions instead of heat waves? What if partnerships were formed with everyone, individual homes and factories alike? What if everyone had networked facility management systems?

There are already devices that allow a price information exchange to take place between a utility and a household or business; when energy prices fluctuate, based on supply and demand, the price of energy spikes, and the utility can wirelessly transmit that energy price to a smart thermostat in the home or business. The thermostat then automatically triggers a change in consumption. It's an approach that helps manage changes in energy consumption to prevent grid overloads. Think about it—you could have a "dollar-stat" instead of a thermostat, with a dial that tells you what you'd pay for energy on any given day.

There is a downside to the efficiencies that are created by all this connectedness, however. The energy grid represents a great big bull's-eye for hackers looking to cause a lot of damage, disruption, and manipulation of a new currency called energy. In January 2008, U.S. CIA senior analyst Tom Donahue confirmed that attacks on energy grids had resulted in disruption of service and power outages that affected multiple cities.[24] Attackers used the grid's Internet connections to enter the utilities and, in some cases, make extortion demands.[25] Intrusions into the electrical grid originating from China and Russia were cited by an unnamed senior intelligence official in the *Wall Street Journal*, as part of those countries' larger efforts to map the U.S.'s overall infrastructure.[26]

Bringing down the energy grid has a crippling effect on all activity. Governments and utilities worldwide need to make sure that the efficiency mechanisms they enable are not opening up the grid to undue risk. In the U.S., the Federal Energy Regulatory Commission (FERC) recently passed mandatory critical infrastructure protection (CIP) reliability standards to protect the nation's bulk power system against potential disruptions resulting from cybersecurity breaches.[27] The mandatory reliability standards require operators of the bulk power system to establish policies and procedures to safeguard both physical and network access to control systems. There's also a quiet effort to train personnel on security matters, to report security incidents, and to be prepared to recover from cybersecurity incidents.

The promise of an Internet-based smart energy grid is fast becoming a reality. It won't be long before we have more control over how we generate, consume, and conserve our energy, be it electricity, gas, or fossil fuels. Such implementation can deliver improved reliability and help us sustain our overall energy needs. Efficiency and security are not necessarily mutually exclusive factors, but the reality is that the cost associated with doing nothing is intolerable.

What You Can Do

If you have a smart meter, try to understand and manage your consumption habits through the utility company's portal (if it has one). If you don't have a smart meter, push your utility company or state government to adopt them.

Check out applications such as Tendril (*www.tendrilinc.com/*), Google's PowerMeter (*www.google.org/powermeter/*), or iControl (*www.icontrol.com/*) to understand and make better decisions about your energy consumption.

When replacing household appliances, choose more energy-efficient models; pretty soon, these devices will be network-enabled, so you can automate controls and remotely adjust consumption. Use compact fluorescent lightbulbs or LED bulb technology.

Turn off and unplug equipment that is not in use (don't just put your computer in standby mode). Remember that just because your LCD screen isn't on or your backup disk isn't turning doesn't mean they're not using electricity. Power them down when not in use.

Here are some other ways to get smarter about power consumption:

- How do you know you have too many things on? Take a walk around at midnight with all the lights turned off and count those little LED lights.

- Use a plug-in timer, like the ones commonly used for Christmas trees, that turns power off between 11 p.m. and whenever you wake up.

- Use power strips to make it easier to cut the power from groups of devices, such as your entertainment center.

CHAPTER 13

Dematerialization

*We ourselves feel that what we are doing is just
a drop in the ocean. But the ocean would be less
because of that missing drop.*

—Mother Teresa

The age-old mantra, "Do more with less" is particularly pertinent of late. In the current climate, less can refer to almost anything, from money to stability to environmental resources. In this book's case, it refers to all our physical stuff and the role the network can play to help reduce our consumption.

One of the most immediate, most identifiable benefits the network delivers is its capability to translate the physical into the digital (called *dematerialization*) to the point that we no longer want or need to use that physical thing. In fact, the digital product often opens a whole new world not tied to the physical restraints of tactile objects. And when the digital is able to substitute for the physical, it saves us from creating the entire lifecycle of the physical product, representing all that energy, pollution, and waste that is attributable to the making, use, and disposal of the "thing."

One of the easiest examples of the dematerialization benefits of the network can be found in the entertainment industry. Just think of downloading a movie to your computer instead of going to a store to buy a DVD. It makes sense; there are sustainability benefits to this network-enabled transaction. The most obvious is the reduction of the costs, energy consumption, and waste associated with producing and distributing the physical DVD, including the raw materials, packaging, energy used for assembly, and the emissions derived from transporting it from the manufacturer to the distribution center to the store to your home. There is the added benefit of not having to go to the store to buy the DVD.

As you know, there is also a similar revolution taking place in the music industry, due to the proliferation of MP3 players and Apple's extremely popular iPod family of products. As early as 2006, the Solutions Research Group reported that almost half of all Americans (45%) downloaded music one way or another. Apple has reported selling over 5 million songs a day—that's 58 songs every second! But while you can use these personal music players as a stereo (by adding speakers) or in your car (by using an adapter), they don't represent much of an environmental benefit yet. It should be noted that this is because they are constantly being updated, so they have a fairly short shelf life, which results in a lot of electronic consumption and waste.

However, they represent the potential of a more environmentally friendly way to listen to music. And as these individual devices converge—say, in a smartphone—and increasingly support video and other applications, the potential grows. And as digital music and video files replace the physical product, it means the raw materials and operational costs associated with producing, packaging, and distributing those products are eliminated. By some estimates, music and video downloads in 2007 saved 500,000 tons of CO_2 emissions.[1]

And while debates rage as to the future of the music and entertainment industries, similar discussions are taking place in almost every industry. Take the paperless office—will it ever really happen? It is certainly true that electronic reading and storage of files can reduce the amount of paper needed and wasted. To put the potential environmental significance into perspective, consider accessing a newspaper via a laptop versus getting the physical version. The digital newspaper has 1/600th the energy impact of actually printing and distributing the physical version.[2]

Spam Is Polluting the Planet

It should be noted that useless digital communications (spam) that flood our email inboxes, akin to the junkmail that floods our physical mailboxes, are not only nuisances, but waste energy. McAfee, which produces antispam technology, commissioned research on the carbon footprint of spam. The research calculated the global annual energy consumed in the transmission, processing, and filtering of spam at 33 billion kWh, or 33 TWh. This is the equivalent of the electricity consumed in 2.4 million homes and the GHG emissions of 3.1 million passenger cars (2 billion gallons of gasoline).[3]

While the entirely paperless office may still be a ways off, we have seen movements in that direction. GXS and Verizon Business offer a solution that converts manual, paper-based processes into electronic transactions among vendors, partners, and customers to automate supply chain processes. According to GXS, it processes more than 4 billion electronic transactions per year on behalf of its customers.[4] Assuming one transaction represents two sheets of paper, the potential paper savings generated by its customers equates to:

- 223 million pounds of CO_2, the equivalent of taking 22,820 cars off the road for a year or reducing gasoline consumption by 42 million gallons each year

- 132,000 tons of wood, saving the equivalent of 912,000 trees

- 1.5 trillion BTUs of total energy consumption, the equivalent of that consumed by 16,496 homes per year

- 745 million gallons of water, the equivalent of filling 1,129 swimming pools[5]

If you factor in the total worldwide number of annual business-to-business transactions (estimated at 40 billion) that could be translated from physical paper to digital, this type of automation represents a lot of opportunity for environmental benefits. Plus, these environmental benefits can reap financial rewards; Aberdeen Group[6] predicts that costs can be reduced by 60% for a company that previously manually processed 500,000 invoices per year. And the options for automation can be extended to many different processes.

Digital Books

Are you reading this book on a Kindle? On your laptop? On a Plastic Logic device? On a Sony Book Reader? Like the iPod, the book publishing industry has been on the verge of going digital, too. Most people in the book industry believe it's not a question of how, but rather when it will happen. Take this book. While it exists in paper, it is also available in an Adobe PDF format from O'Reilly Media (*www.oreilly.com*) and from the digital book service Safari (*www.safaribooksonline.com*). With almost 200,000 books published in the U.S. each year (about 100,000 in Great Britain), and each book having an initial printing of at least 2,000 copies, entire forests are being hacked down for such must-have-in-paper-format titles as *Thinner Thighs in Two Weeks*. The future will contain paper books, but they are likely to be the bestsellers from the digital editions, and then, what might be called "library editions" (for both the home library collector and the actual library market).

In the U.S., new foreign trade regulations mandated in July 2008 that everyone must file their export documents electronically using the Automated Export System (AES). Paper submissions will constitute a violation and penalties will be imposed. Now, I don't know how many export submissions the U.S. Foreign Trade Office processes every year, but a conservative estimate of 1 billion single-page submission forms would constitute a significant paper savings—approximately 10,416 trees or 14 acres of forest,[7] assuming 96,000 pieces of paper can be produced per 128 cubic feet of wood. In 2007, TurboTax e-filers in the United States saved more than 75 million pieces of paper, equaling approximately 900 trees and nearly 1,000 metric tons of carbon from reaching the atmosphere.[8] By filing their tax returns electronically, 30 million taxpayers saved 30 tons of carbon dioxide in 2007.[9]

By switching to electronic bills, British Telecom, one of the world's leading providers of communications solutions and services operating in 170 countries, saved 60 tons of paper each year. If you stacked all that paper, it would be three-quarters of a mile high. Chunghwa Telecom is also encouraging customers to opt for electronic billing to reduce its impact. In 2008, it billed more than 1.8 million customers electronically, cutting its resulting carbon emissions by 80 tons.[10] And those are just a couple of companies— granted, they are large companies, but a drop in the bucket just the same. They represent the magnitude of the opportunity to leverage the network to reduce physical consumption, because it is not just the end product we are talking about, but also the consumption up and down the supply chain required to manufacture and distribute various products.

Every form of human endeavor has its paper trail. The legal profession has a huge publishing industry behind it, accounting for all those books behind the lawyers in their offices. Medical, scientific, education, computer—you name your occupation, and there's a paper trail miles high. I was once told that the paper documentation for building a Boeing 747 fills up a Boeing 747. I can't verify that statement, but surprisingly, I don't flinch when considering its validity.

You can track your paper use online at sites such as PulpWatch.org, an independent website devoted to the environmental performance of pulp mills around the world. It strives to document the performance of the pulp and paper mills according to criteria of the Environmental Paper Network—a network of over 100 environmental organizations, large and small, dedicated to a sustainable paper industry and helping customers make informed consumption decisions. This brings us to another benefit of the network; it can be used to research companies and products to help inform our purchasing decisions and make a difference in our overall impact.

Some people have tried to make the case that simply purchasing something online is a more environmentally friendly approach to consumption. It's unclear if there is any real environmental benefit to an Internet purchase. The benefits potentially garnered by shipping the product directly from the distribution center to your house/office, which cuts out the transportation to and from the store, are probably negated by the individual packaging needed to ship the item to you. Typically, products are sent to a store in pallets, which is generally a more efficient use of materials from a packaging perspective. The production of the item remains unchanged, regardless of the channel you use to purchase it, so simply using the network to make your purchases doesn't have the same benefits as using the network to consume digital resources in place of physical ones.

The real benefit of the network is when it serves as the platform for something we call *dematerialization*, which enables the substitution of something virtual for something physical. Dematerialization is a concept that will continue to gain popularity with the expansion of broadband, the adoption of more powerful multifunction devices, and ongoing application innovation that ensures that the quality of the digital experience is on par or even better than that of the physical one. As these advances are made, the network will continue to help consumers everywhere develop more sustainable consumption habits.

What You Can Do

- Sign up for online banking without monthly statements—in fact, almost all of your bills can be managed and paid online.

- Have a straightforward path of archiving your digital files.

- Buy and listen to digital music; download and watch digital movies.

- Consider which publications (newspapers/magazines/books) you absolutely need to read in their paper form and which you can switch to online versions.

- Use online forms and applications whenever possible, taking advantage of both the convenience and environmental benefits.

- Visit catalogchoice.org to stop paper catalogs and junkmail services.

- Don't print email messages. When you do print something, make sure it's double-sided and consider printing multiple pages on one sheet of paper. Reserve color prints for those things that absolutely need them.

- Lobby your favorite companies to reduce their packaging and paper usage. Ask for a digital product guide, prospectus, annual report, online warranty, etc.

- Think about how frequently you upgrade electronic devices. Determine when you really need the latest and greatest, and make sure to recycle any electronics you discard (or better yet, look into donating it to someone to extend the device's life and extend the reach and resources of the network to someone in need).

- Use reusable shopping bags. Consider swapping or selling old items to extend their useful lives. Remember, one person's junk is another person's treasure. Antiques are the new green products!

- Recycle as much as you can—bottles, cans, paper, e-waste—and compost. Choose biodegradable options and purchase products made from more environmentally friendly materials, which can be found for almost everything from cleaning products to clothes (admittedly, it can be a veritable maze to navigate and very tricky to differentiate!).

- Research purchases online to make the best decisions. Educate yourself on what the network can do for you and how you can use it to improve your life and community.

- Make a commitment to learn how to make and use PDF documents using Adobe Acrobat. Attach to email, archive your paperwork, and keep a digital paper trail.

CHAPTER 14

Detravelization

He is happiest, be he king or peasant,
who finds peace in his home.
—Johann Wolfgang von Goethe

One of the more sustainable impacts the network can have is its capability to reduce the carbon emissions generated via human transportation and travel. The network's capability to connect people to the resources and information they need from wherever they are, using a variety of new applications and services, has exploded this past decade. Do you really need to travel for business? Is it absolutely essential to be in the same room for that meeting? How about going into the office every day? Remote office capabilities, web and video conferencing, and even "virtual worlds" allow individuals and businesses to substitute or reduce commutes and travel, and are predicted to yield between $15 billion and $30 billion in gross savings through 2020.[1]

Don't underestimate the amount of carbon emissions generated via the fossil fuels consumed to operate and maintain airplanes, cars, trains, buses, and other modes of powered transportation (approximately 2–3% of the world's annual carbon emissions). Detravelization can have a significant impact. For example, in the U.S., automobile emissions alone account for about 20% of the country's GHG emissions,[2] which is one reason green statistics in the media often use the phrase, "It's like taking *xx* number of cars off the road." Remember that transport emissions (both regular commute and long-range travel) are one of the major contributors to your individual carbon footprint (see Chapter 10, "Carbon Footprints"). And for businesses, transport emissions are often cited as the biggest contributor to that organization's Scope 3 emissions, which encompass all the activities that are outside of the direct control of the organization resulting in GHGs,[3] such as business trips and regular commuting by employees.

If we can use the network's online tools to replace the need to *always* commute or travel, the benefits could be amazing. There are a whole host of business reasons to use these virtual work environments—namely, improved productivity (up to 30% in recent studies),[4] better morale, enhanced ability to attract and retain talent, and improved disaster preparedness and recovery. However, the energy efficiency benefits are often cited as one of the biggest and most tangible reasons for virtual work environments.

As with anything, there are two sides of every "green" story. Critics cite the environmental impacts of the network itself (the power used to run and cool the network's devices and infrastructure) as negatively impacting or negating the benefits derived from detravelization efforts. So, let's look at that side—all devices on the network consume energy, from the devices you use to access the network (some of which need to be regularly charged) to each and every device that touches and forwards the traffic to its destination. Each step and stop along the way requires power.

There are a number of estimates on the CO_2 generated by a typical online search or by browsing the Web, and it's in the range of a fraction of 1 gram to 10 grams of CO_2. You could make your head spin trying to rationalize all the different studies into a single number set, but let's, as they say in the network world, drill down a bit:

- One study approximates that a single search on a large Internet search engine produces 7 g of CO_2; this same research places the CO_2 generated via browsing a typical website at around .02 g for every second viewed and up to .2 g per second for those sites with more media-rich content, such as video.[5]

- A different analysis places the CO_2 emissions of a search conducted on one of the largest Internet search engines within the bounds of a much greater range, somewhere between 1 g and 10 g.[6]

- Other research places the carbon emissions between 7 g and 10 g, assuming the user spends approximately 15 minutes on her computer searching and browsing.[7]

- The search engine companies themselves (Google, Yahoo!, etc.) have countered these claims, placing the CO_2 emitted during a single search at approximately .2 g.[8]

Due to the complexity and immense number of variables that can be factored into any calculation, it is fair to say that *all* of these numbers could potentially be correct, given a particular set of circumstances and underpinnings. The question really is whether these emissions are enough to negate the benefits of detravelization.

As far as I can tell, the answer that most have arrived at is, "No." For some context, boiling a kettle of water typically produces 15 g of CO_2.[9] Driving an average car one mile produces around one pound of CO_2.[10] The UK-based Low Carbon Lifestyle Guide found the emissions generated for an hour of flying was equivalent to the emissions generated by a TV that ran for 24 hours a day for 18 months.[11] Given this backdrop, it is easy to see how substituting a video conference for even just one trip a year via air could have significant benefits (if everyone did it), even when accounting for the energy consumption and emissions of the network.

You can imagine the benefits of forgoing the regular business convention of flying all the time to meetings and instead holding regular videoconferences. Don't get me wrong—there's nothing like a face-to-face meeting. There's something very powerful and beneficial in experiencing a gathering with all your senses to understand the context and other intangibles that can influence the ongoing business, but perhaps the routine, in-and-out travel could be replaced with a more efficient, more environmentally friendly method. When millions upon millions of people are traveling every single day all over the world, there is likely an enormous amount of detravelization possible.

Other Viewpoints on the Environmental Impacts of Remote and Virtual Work Environments

There are also impacts referred to as the *rebound effects* of telecommuting, or *telework*, as it is sometimes called in Europe. These effects are associated with the potential rise in energy consumption that comes from home office use, such as additional home heating or cooling, potential duplication of electronic equipment in the home and office environment, and the increase in nonwork-related technology usage, including trips of convenience (to the grocery store or coffee shop) and chores (doing laundry or making a pot of coffee). It has also been brought up that people who telecommute may end up living farther away from their offices, which creates greater carbon emissions when that individual does make the trip into the office.

While it is easy to throw everything into the same bucket, I think we are better off focusing on those things that the individual would not have done at all if she were not working from home. In other words, let's concentrate on only the additive activities that an individual would not normally do either in the office environment or at a different time of the day. These additive activities can reduce the overall benefits of telecommuting, but there are additional efficiencies to be garnered. For example, as organizations get better at supporting telecommuting environments, they can reduce duplicative energy consumption, creating shared workstations and reducing real estate overhead (electricity, heating, and other operational costs).

On a social front, those wary of virtual work environments often question the productivity gains; they wonder whether people will really be motivated to do their work when they are not in the office. It is true the temptations are there, and for some people, telecommuting simply doesn't work. However, studies show that if an individual's contributions and objectives are well understood, it is easy to determine whether someone is doing the job or slacking off. With the right incentives and work environment, individuals are often more productive when given the ability to perform their work in a more flexible structure. The benefit has been quantified by some studies at approximately a 30% gain in productivity. [15]

To the naysayers, I would argue that good business practices are required for any work environment, physical or digital, and an individual's ability to perform is most often derived from her motivations rather than her location. I would also point out that simply being in the office does not result in productivity.

That's business travel; then there's your daily commute. Do you think you could argue a case for the benefits of telecommuting? Let's make some general assumptions—an individual with a 10-mile commute in a car that gets approximately 20 miles to the gallon would save an equivalent of 20–22 pounds of CO_2, or approximately half a ton of carbon, on an annual basis if she telecommuted once a week.[12] Expand that to a company, a region, or even a country, and it becomes a compelling case for telecommuting policies. The Consumer Electronics Association found that telecommuting in the U.S. saves 9–14 billion kWh of electricity annually, reducing gasoline consumption by 840 million gallons. This represents close to 14 million tons of carbon emissions.[13] The European Telecommunications Network Operators Association (ETNO) estimates that 22.2 million tons of CO_2 emissions could be abated on an annual basis in the EU if 10% of the workforce were *flexiworkers*, under the assumption that they would avoid traveling 133 km by car and 60 km by train each week—this represents approximately 2.3% of all transport-related CO_2 emissions.[14]

As a work culture, we are just starting to recognize the benefits associated with telecommuting, mostly because the number of employees telecommuting and operating in remote and virtual work environments is still relatively small. For example, according to the U.S. Census Bureau's American Community Survey, 9 out of 10 workers, or 87.7%, drive to work, and 78% of U.S. commuters are solo drivers.[16] This helps account for the reason you are stationary, when you do commute, in the traffic lane of your choice. But as more individuals use online tools and more businesses embrace virtual work environments, we can start to realize significant reductions in the fuel emissions associated with daily commutes, as well as reap the economic benefits that result from better time management and resource utilization. (There's also the increase in productivity—just think of all you could do if you didn't have to sit in traffic!) There are already thousands of people and businesses that understand these benefits. Here are just a few:

- Accenture estimates that it has saved $8 million annually by substituting travel with telepresence systems, avoiding the production of approximately 2,000 tons of CO_2.[17]

- BT (British Telecom) has home-based employees that leverage video conferencing and remote access solutions, eliminating approximately 296,000 face-to-face meetings every year and 47,400 tons of CO_2 from travel-related emissions. This saves the company £128 million, or approximately $256 million USD.

- JetBlue Airways demonstrates how a travel company can effectively leverage a distributed employee base. The company uses web-based systems that allow its call center employees to work from home and control their work hours, resulting in a highly efficient staffing model that can meet call demands. The result is a highly motivated and productive employee base.

- Juniper Networks offers a remote office solution and reports that 90% of its employees telecommute at some point throughout the year, with 10% telecommuting on any given day. The company also has a policy that in regions where there are five or fewer employees, it provisions personal work offices instead of a corporate office, saving all the expenses and overhead emissions of a small office space (real estate, electricity, and pollution from commuting).

- Cisco Systems offers a virtual office solution that allows employees to work from home, either on a full- or part-time basis. Currently, more than 14,000 Cisco employees are using the solution, saving the average employee an estimated 2.81 hours of commuting time per week, and resulting in a reduction of 2.5 tons of CO_2 emissions per year, projected real estate savings of $82.5 million, and annual energy cost reductions of $0.6 million.

- Sun Microsystems has the granddaddy of successful telecommuter programs. Its Open Work program is a 14-year-old initiative in which more than half of Sun's employees, representing 20,000 individuals, work from home at least one or two days per week. In 2007 alone, Sun reduced its real estate holdings by more than 15% and saved approximately $68 million in associated costs, in part due to the 5,400 kWh annual reduction it realized for each employee who works from home a couple of times a week. Sun also saw a 30% reduction in initial and annual workplace costs for employees who work from home once or twice a week and up to 70% lower costs for those who are based out of their homes, as compared to full-time office employees. Sun estimates that employees save around $1,700 a year in fuel and car maintenance costs, and up to 2.5 weeks of work time per year due to the elimination of daily commutes. It estimates that the program reduces overall CO_2 emissions by 31,000 tons.[18] Perhaps Sun's spirit will inspire its new corporate owner, Oracle, to expand its programs.

What Are Some of These Detravelization Tools?

Let's start with *webinars*, which are seminars conducted on the Internet. Rather than driving to a specific location to hear someone speak on a topic of interest, the audience convenes online to listen to the speaker and watch some type of graphical presentation. SustainIT, researching the UK market, estimated that replacing physical conferencing with virtual conferencing could save over 2 million tons of CO_2 per year.[19]

In many cases, participants can ask questions (via telephone audio bridges or text-based chat) and provide input (via survey or polling mechanisms) during these seminars to make them more interactive. An additional benefit is that these presentations are typically archived online and available for on-demand viewing, extending the life and reach of the material. These online webinars also give the host something that every marketing practitioner is dying to get—the contact information (such as email addresses) of its watchers and participants for future outreach.

It's not just businesses using webinars to engage their constituents. City council meetings, Sunday sermons, adult education lectures, and even musical concerts are growing in popularity when offered as online webinars. U.S. President Barack Obama showed that the technology was mainstream when he held the executive branch's first-ever Internet conference in March 2009, bypassing the traditional media to speak directly through the Web to hundreds of thousands of citizens.

The technology can also be extended to on-the-fly and more intimate meetings. There are several online meeting services, such as Citrix's GoToMeeting, Mikogo, or Cisco's WebEx, that can bring geographically dispersed individuals together at a designated online location (a secure website) to meet and collaborate. On average, 7 million people a month use WebEx to host online meetings,[20] and that's just one service. Online meetings let participants share and work on documents together in real time; some services let users take control of one another's desktops (computing devices) in a secure manner, which can be invaluable for troubleshooting and cutting down on help-desk ticket resolution times and effort. As such, it is not surprising that these online services are becoming a regular part of business life.

Video conferencing solutions create visual interactions that closely simulate meetings in the real world and are available for PCs and Macs. For example, Apple's iSight embedded cameras and iChat applications enable conferencing with multiple participants and even offer a background creation feature to get rid of your kitchen cabinets in the background. Unfortunately, most video conferencing systems leave a lot to be desired due to what is called *network latency*. You know what I mean if you've ever been in a web meeting where there is a delay between sound and sight; or maybe, like my teenage niece, you feel compelled to text the person you are having a video conference with because you can't stand the delays in the conversations.

The technology to make these video interactions great is available; the problem is that it is not affordable enough, yet, to be widely deployed. The systems that provide an experience commensurate with the ones that you see on the *CSI: Crime Scene Investigation* TV shows are very expensive, often running into the hundreds of thousands of dollars for business environments. They also consume a lot of bandwidth, upward of 16 Mbps per endpoint, which requires additional investment in the underlying network; this is why only 1 in 10 high-definition video conferencing feeds today actually starts and ends in high definition.

These issues will be worked out, however. And when they are, it's safe to say that the technology has the potential to revolutionize the way we think about meeting and collaborating. In fact, the ramp-up is starting even as you read this book, as 63% of companies say they will be using videoconferencing and telepresence systems (essentially, a form of videoconferencing with high-quality images and audio) by the end of 2010.[21]

Large, technology-savvy companies with distributed workforces are also starting to invest in 3D virtual work and virtual world meeting environments. These new applications simulate the experiences of being physically present in a location, in hopes of increasing interactivity among the workforce to accelerate innovation and productivity (the reason we work together in the first place). Once people get used to the virtual work environment, it can truly enable detravelization, providing an affordable and more ecofriendly alternative to commuting or long-distance travel. Discussions and meetings held in Linden Lab's *Second Life* (a virtual world environment, discussed in Chapter 41, "Our Relationship with the Network") are free, while a persistent virtual workspace can be rented for less than $20 a month. There are also virtual environments that can be occupied on the fly, for a small fee, similar to on-demand web conferencing and teleconferencing technologies. Analysts predict that by 2012, more than 70% of organizations will use *intraverses* (private virtual worlds, as opposed to universes) to support internal collaboration and social interaction.[22]

> **The intraverses of tomorrow represent one of the greatest opportunities in our future to reduce travel, costs, and emissions.**

And then there are the Unified Communications (UC) solutions, which will further enhance detravelization efforts. In the strictest sense, UC solutions allow individuals to translate the information they send or receive into different formats and mediums. For example, if you leave a voicemail for someone, he could pick up that message on his phone or receive it as a text or email message. It's about integrating communication mediums so that individuals can communicate and access information in the way that is most convenient for them. These services, which contain both hardware and software components, can be deployed by an organization or hosted by a provider. Frost & Sullivan predicts that the total number of end users of hosted UC services will be around 2.6 million by 2014 (up from the 19,000 users at the end of 2008).[23] More aggressive numbers come from Wainhouse Research, which predicts revenues from UC solutions will reach $13.4 billion by 2013.[24] Ultimately, the speed of adoption for these different technologies will depend largely on the quality of the experience and affordability of the solutions. However, once in place, the possibilities for these virtual environments appear to be limitless. If people get used to going into the virtual world and conducting their lives as they would in the physical world, it has the potential to dramatically reduce physical consumption, waste, and transportation needs. It is these advanced technologies, in some form, that will ultimately enable the network to become the great detravelizer.

Now, I don't believe we will or even should replace *all* travel. I personally believe that regardless of how good the online and virtual worlds become, they cannot replace the sights, sounds, and physical connections you make when you are doing things in person. The sustainable network is about maximizing utility and minimizing waste. If you use the network and the aforementioned tools to eliminate as much of the unnecessary travel as possible—the daily commute, going to sit in an auditorium to hear someone speak, the trip to the two-hour internal meeting on the other side of the globe, a check-in meeting with a customer—then when you *do* travel, you can ensure that you get maximum value from the face-to-face interactions and experiences. You might actually enjoy the plane ride, too.

What You Can Do

- Find out what your company's policy is on telecommuting; what's the travel policy?

- Evaluate how much of your job you could do from home.

- Talk to your boss about setting up a regular telecommuting schedule—for example, one day a week.

- Look at your upcoming business travel plans; could you substitute an online meeting for any of them?

- Try the virtual conference option for the next show you are planning to attend.

- When you must travel, you can go home virtually and spend some time with your family. You really can be two places at once!

What's Being Done—A Glimpse at the Future

- Creating a custom, secure virtual world to work in, where you sit next to your colleagues, partners, or even customers in a virtual setting, obliterating the barrier of geographically distributed physical locations.

- Using an intraverse to support employee on-boarding and general training. Developing virtual classrooms or using online classes offered by universities to broaden resources available to an organization. It's enabling organizations to scale and provide individuals with the skills and information they need, all without having to invest significant capital in physical facilities.

- Virtual modeling environments for manufacturing are being used to identify opportunities for improvement and problem solving on issues that would typically require trips to the facility.

- Bringing architectural plans to life. Imagine being able to walk through a virtual building environment to see what the layout will look like versus trying to picture it in your head from a piece of paper. Virtual walkabouts of your next home are a lot better than static websites of facts and figures.

- Demonstrating products in virtual showrooms, allowing potential customers to examine products just as they would if they could actually touch and test products. For example, take a test drive in a new hybrid car or play with the new refrigerator you're thinking of purchasing.

- Hosting large tradeshows, conferences, and even concerts in these virtual worlds. These represent huge potential carbon abatement opportunities, including the travel and consumption usually associated with putting on and attending any one of those events. Virtual shows have the additional benefit of allowing you to attend a play, a concert, and a tradeshow convention all in different cities, all in the same day.

CHAPTER 15

What Is the Network: How Is Telecommuting Enabled?

Are we there yet?

—Your kids

The productivity and environmental benefits of being able to work and connect to the sustainable network will only continue as long as we feel that the connection is reliable and secure. Businesses, governments, and organizations in the public sector will only connect if their resources and intellectual property can be protected. Let's face it, even if virtual meetings reduce commuting and traveling, they are only viable alternatives if they can be counted on to deliver the same privacy that could be achieved in meetings behind closed doors. And this is where *virtual private network* (VPN) technology comes in. VPNs have been a boon for creating the sustainable network this past decade because they create a secure network environment where it's possible to conduct private conversations and business without participants having to be in the same room.

Originally, a whole decade ago, enterprises could only rely on service providers to deploy classic private network technologies, such as *point-to-point* or *circuit-switched* lines, and achieve the level of security they needed to reliably connect their employees. Point-to-point leased lines required service providers to lay physical links between locations, or points, which extended the deployment times into weeks and made changes to the network very costly and laborious. Because the enterprise paid for the entire line, not just the actual bandwidth consumed, the solution was expensive and made it hard to achieve redundancy. As a result, if a line went down, an enterprise had to wait for the service provider to physically come out and fix it before connectivity was restored. Plus, unauthorized users could tap into the user data streams without the knowledge of either the end user or the enterprise paying for the leased line.

Offerings such as asynchronous transfer mode (ATM) and frame relay networks (circuit-switched) made some improvement over point-to-point lines, yet still left the reliability and security of the private network in question. These lines reduced the cost by allowing enterprises to pay just for the bandwidth they used, not the whole line itself. However, service-level agreements to guarantee the availability of the bandwidth were usually cost prohibitive, which meant that enterprises often went without them and suffered reduced performance whenever the lines were under load. These offerings simplified deployment, partitioning the wire into logical circuits that could be added or removed with a phone call to the provider, as long as the wire to that destination already existed. But because the lines were partitioned, there was always the worry that the data could be delivered to an incorrect recipient, introducing another security concern.

Today, enterprises can deploy virtual private networks to solve these bottlenecks and security issues. VPNs leverage the cost-effective and ubiquitous connectivity of the Internet to transport secure private data. They use the public Internet infrastructure to quickly extend a private network across geographically distributed locations. While the Internet transfers traffic based on router hops, going from one router to the next between the source and the destination of the traffic, the VPN uses VPN gateways as its hops. This makes the multiple Internet routers seem to disappear and the VPN gateways appear to be virtually adjacent, which simplifies the network topology and makes it possible to create a private abstract one (Figure 15-1).

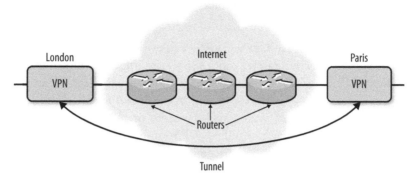

Figure 15-1. *A VPN tunnel is like having your own highway lane in the Chunnel all to yourself, leveraging all the work done to build and maintain the entire Chunnel under the English Channel. Thanks, England! Thanks, France!*

VPN gateways encapsulate the data into VPN tunnels to each other. These tunnels are set up for the exclusive transport of this data between pairs of gateways. Because an organization can forward traffic through these tunnels with internal IP addresses, VPNs also allow enterprises to connect remote offices and remote workers without having to reconfigure their IP addresses or pay for the dedicated IP addresses that are required for Internet transmission.

There are several different types of VPN technologies that enable organizations to take advantage of the ubiquity, cost efficiencies, and potential bandwidth of the public Internet (shown as the network cloud in Figure 15-1), yet retain the security and privacy characteristics of a private network. The most common technologies include IP Security Protocol (IPSec), Multi-Protocol Label Switching (MPLS), and Secure Socket Layer (SSL). Each has pros and cons and is best suited for different deployment scenarios. Let's quickly take a look at the options.

IPSec

IPSec is an Internet Engineering Task Force (IETF) standard that essentially defines an approach to providing a confidential and authenticated information exchange over an untrusted network. IPSec provides security services for encrypting and authenticating the data so even if the data is intercepted or delivered to the wrong destination, it is still safeguarded, since only the intended recipient can decrypt it. IPSec authentication prevents traffic manipulation as well as unintentional or malicious insertions into the data payload along the network path. This solves many of the security problems associated with the traditional leased and circuit-switched line technologies.

The physical network is constructed of network devices interconnected by routers, where the router determines how packets should be forwarded to the ultimate destination. A site-to-site IPSec VPN can be constructed of sites interconnected by VPN gateways, where the VPN gateway determines how VPN (encrypted and authenticated) packets should be forwarded.

It sounds complicated, but it isn't. IPSec VPNs achieve this tunneling using client software installed on the customer gateway in a site-to-site implementation (for example, a London office to a Paris office), or installed on the individual client PC in the case of a remote user installation (an employee working from his home office and logging on to the London office to get his corporate email messages or pull down the latest financial spreadsheet). Once the software is installed, VPN tunnels are set up for the exclusive transport of the private data between the pairs of gateways. It's almost like you have a tin can, and I have a tin can, and we string a wire between the two cans to tunnel through the void in between. Voilà. You and I can have a private conversation.

An organization can forward traffic through these tunnels with internal IP addresses because the private data of the overlay network never mingles with the public base network. In network-speak, that means enterprises using IPSec don't have to reconfigure their IP addresses or pay for the globally unique IP addresses required for Internet transmission. IPSec VPNs are often cited as the ideal solution for enterprises to connect remote offices and permanent home offices, because, as dedicated, always-on secure connections, they provide access to the company's networked resources and a user experience in line with what the employee would receive at corporate headquarters. And it isn't any coincidence that the usage of IPSec VPNs over the past decade has allowed telecommuting to enter into our daily business bag of tools and language.

MPLS

Another option in the VPN arsenal is an MPLS VPN. An increasing number of enterprises are outsourcing their WAN backbones to MPLS VPN service providers because the standard provides improved quality of service, reliability, and efficient network operations, while simultaneously optimizing network performance. In essence, the MPLS VPN working group task force (the IETF) takes a routing approach, while the IPSec working group takes a security approach to providing a secure and efficient VPN. Depending on who you are, what you need, and how much you use it, you'll prefer one over the other, especially when outsourcing some of your network options.

MPLS VPNs use *label switching* to affect how traffic is routed, forwarded, or switched to control where a packet is sent in the network. Instead of using the cryptographic techniques used in IPSec VPNs, MPLS uses a directed routing technique to ensure that packet transmission is private.

MPLS VPNs give network operators a great deal of flexibility to divert and route traffic around link failures, congestion, and bottlenecks, as well as to direct traffic to specified destinations in a more efficient manner (than the Internet). From a quality-of-service (QoS) standpoint, MPLS VPNs allow the network service providers to efficiently manage different kinds of data streams based on priority and service plan. For instance, those who subscribe to a premium service plan, or those who receive a lot of streaming media or high-bandwidth content, will see minimal latency and packet loss. For applications or services with demanding transmission requirements, such as video conferencing, which is sensitive to jitter and any latency in the transmission, MPLS VPNs are often cited as the best option. If you've ever been able to work on a MPLS VPN, it's hard going back to something else. The amazing thing is that it uses the same network infrastructure as your little DSL home networks; it's just very, very focused. However, MPLS VPNs can be complex to set up and manage, but there's hope that advances in the technology will allow you to telecommute in the very near future by simply maintaining your home MPLS VPN.

SSL

SSL VPNs are probably the most widely deployed VPN solutions for remote access and telecommuting. Instead of relying upon your networking knowledge to configure a client on your device, SSL VPNs use SSL/HTTPS as a secure transport mechanism, which just happens to be available on almost all standard web browsers. Using an SSL VPN, the connection between you and your destination resource happens via a web connection at the Application layer, as opposed to an IPSec VPN tunnel at the Network layer (see Chapter 31 and especially Figure 31-2 on the seven layers of the OSI model).

SSL VPNs are available wherever there is a standard web browser, and are independent of the underlying operating system of the device; this opens up the possibilities to a large variety of computing devices, such as smartphones. And it's very user-friendly. You do not need to configure or download anything onto the device prior to using it to access corporate resources. Most importantly, however, are the granular access controls that enterprises can use to ensure that users only see the resources and applications they are authorized to see. It's the biggest selling point of SSL technology, and this accounts for its popularity in small- to mid-size businesses. For example, your administrator can designate the URL, the files, and the server applications that you can access using the SSL VPN, thus mitigating the risks that an unprotected endpoint, untrusted network, or unauthorized user could introduce.

And because SSL VPNs operate at the Application layer, it is possible to offer extremely granular access controls to applications. This makes SSL VPNs an excellent option for providing extranet access to any audience from an untrusted network or unmanaged device, including remote and mobile employees, business partners, or customers.

It is not unusual for an enterprise to have all three types of VPNs (IP Sec, MPLS, and SSL) in its network environment to take advantage of the public network while maintaining the privacy and reliability of a private one for its various needs. VPNs are partially responsible for the explosive usage growth of the sustainable network over the past decade; whether the user is an employee, business partner, or customer, and whether he is working in a remote office, a coffee shop, or a hotel room, he can have easy access to the networked resources he needs when he needs them. And the adoption of VPNs to reduce daily commutes is just starting to have an effect on the sustainability of our planet. VPNs allow organizations to leverage the talents of a global workforce, to connect people and resources in a real-time way that can improve productivity, while reducing commuting and travel.

While telecommuting may be the most obvious of the VPN's virtues, the ability to have a private conversation and exchange information is critical to ensuring its ongoing use in meaningful ways. This level of control and security is required if the network is going to be a viable substitute for activities in the physical world, such as in-person or sensitive meetings. In this regard, the VPN is just like broadband and mobile devices—it has become a key ingredient of the sustainable network by broadening the range of its access.

Pushing the Boundaries

You must be the change you want to see in the world.
—Gandhi

As more and more activities are transferred to the digital world, it is inevitable that the overall energy consumption of the information and communications technologies (ICT), which includes the network, will grow and consume more. As the network attempts to keep up with the rapid pace of globalization, its technology and power consumption needs continue to grow at rates that are starting to outpace the space and energy available. By all estimates, the energy consumption associated with powering this digital world is nontrivial. Today, it is estimated that ICT consumes up to 10% of the world's energy and is responsible for 2–3% of the world's CO_2 emissions.

How do you balance 10% of the world's energy consumption with the network's opportunity to push the boundaries and redefine the world as we presently experience it? How do you balance 3% of the world's emissions with a promise to connect and reduce environmental impact on a scale that will improve our lives? Is the sustainable network unsustainable?

As our reliance on ICT increases, as evidenced by bandwidth consumption doubling every two years, the energy requirements to use that bandwidth also increase. To date, the bulk of the energy has been consumed by the connected devices, meaning the PCs, monitors, servers, and mobile phones (many with power adaptors that stay on whether or not they're charging, called *standby power* or *phantom load*). The network itself has only made up a relatively small percentage of the overall ICT consumption. However, as a colleague of mine likes to say, "A small percentage of a large number is still a large number," and the output, by some estimates, is already set to double by 2010.[1]

The main reason for the growth in the network's power consumption is, yep, you guessed it, the amount of stuff flowing through the network. When network providers need more capacity to support the demand (from all the data, voice, and video), they add more devices to accommodate the increase, and these additional devices add to the overall energy consumption. It's actually worse than that, because in reality, for every watt a device draws, it ends up consuming approximately 2.4 watts, due to the energy that is lost in its distribution and conversion and the energy required to cool it to a temperature that allows it to run optimally. Billions of packets a day tend to get routers warmed up, and they must be kept in air-conditioned rooms (it's one of the concepts behind data centers). Verizon estimates that cooling alone accounts for 38% of its energy expenditure.[2]

So, a goal of the sustainable network (versus an unsustainable one) is to stabilize and ultimately reverse the energy consumption trend lines. Doing that requires making sure that the exponential growth in traffic does not result in exponential growth in energy consumption. In other words, the network should be able to add capacity without adding a comparable load to the energy grid. It's a real trick, because you need to efficiently draw energy while minimizing heat generation, all without compromising the performance, reliability, availability, and security of the network. If any of these traits are degraded, the network's long-term viability as a sustainable platform is diminished because all the other benefits of the network, as discussed in earlier chapters, become restricted and therefore diminished.

A Country View—Japan

IT is having positive impacts in Japan, supporting its efforts to reduce energy consumption in other sectors significantly. For example, Japan has seen a 60% improvement in CO_2 rates over the last 15 years due to new electronic measurement technologies. It has also seen a 40% power savings in supermarkets and other stores through the unified management and coordinated operation of freezers and air conditioners, a 5% reduction in consumption in distribution and transportation through more efficient route allocations, and a 20% reduction in the operations of petrochemical manufacturers through the optimization of the oil refinery controls. However, the same IT that is bringing such sweeping improvements in Japan is also on track to become a bigger and bigger percentage of the country's overall energy consumption. [3]

In 2006, IT equipment, including network equipment, desktop devices, servers, and other electronic devices, reached 4% of Japan's total energy consumption. This represented approximately 50 billion watts and 26 million metric tons of CO_2 (equivalent to emissions generated by approximately 8 million automobiles). If left unchecked, Japan predicts that consumption from IT will be 5 times greater in 2025, and 11 times in 2050, representing 550 billion watts, or 300 million metric tons, of CO_2.

Japan has cited the primary cause of this drastic increase as the extended use of IT devices and networks. Japan's Ministry of Economy, Trade, and Industry predicts that by 2025, the amount of data traffic on the Internet in Japan will be 100–200 times what it was in 2008, which will require the deployment of additional devices to support the capacity demands. For example, there were approximately 600,000 servers in use in Japan in 2006, which the Ministry predicts will grow to three times as many in 25 years (close to 1.8 million servers). From a network perspective, to keep up with all the digitization and demand, the 20,000 routers deployed in 2006 are estimated to double in those 25 years to more than 40,000. As the performance of routers improves, Japan estimates that consumption will go up to 104 billion watts, which is 13 times what was consumed in 2006. [4]

Historically, the ICT industry has been able to make great strides in improving the overall energy efficiency of its equipment. While cutting carbon emissions was never an explicit goal until recently, it has always been a design imperative to create efficient technology (one of our accidental benefits), mainly out of necessity. To foster the adoption and use of increasingly powerful devices, such as laptops, mobile phones, and music players, vendors needed them to be capable of going wherever their owners went without running out of battery power (something can be small and still be inefficient). As a result, we have seen power advances in all ICT sectors. It's about how much work can be done with 1 watt of power. Perhaps the most noticeable advances have been in mobile devices such as cell phones; it used to take more than 10 watts to make a phone call 10 years ago, but today's cell phones can do it with around 1 watt. [5] Similar strides have been made in the network and need to continue into the future.

Let's Get Specific

Networking equipment has made efficiency improvements from 13 GBps/kWh in 1998 to today's equipment, which can deliver 163 GBps/kWh of efficiency (that's gigabytes per second per kilowatt hour), or about 150 gigabytes per second more for the same electrical consumption. Many of these advances have been born of necessity, such as attempts to overcome limits in data center environments, which require space, power, and cooling efficiencies, as well as the physical limits that have traditionally been placed by service providers for the past decade on the amount of energy any one device can draw. Service providers, such as telecom operators (British Telecom, for example), cable providers (Comcast, for example), and wireless providers (T-Mobile, for example), whose business is the network, have always demanded the most efficient solutions because the money spent on powering, cooling, and running network operations has a direct impact on the bottom line.

> The goal is to drive energy efficiency so that ICT can support the exploding growth, yet hold steady and actually start to minimize its own energy consumption.

These providers, on average, spend 18 cents of each revenue dollar on capital investments and 65 cents on operational expenses (costs directly related to running the network, such as power, cooling, management, and maintenance, as well as costs associated with running and promoting the business, such as billing, administration, sales, and marketing, among other things). This leaves approximately 17 cents for gross profit. If the network were optimized for power, cooling, and network operations efficiencies, there are estimates that service providers could save up to 8 cents of each revenue dollar. This represents the largest available source of savings in a service provider's operations, and could allow an operator to increase its capital investments or gross profits or any combination that adds up to 8 cents (which represents an increase of almost 50%).[6] This is one of the main reasons that virtually every network project or network product evaluation undertaken by service providers scrutinizes the efficiencies of the equipment proposed for deployment. And the overall network architecture design needs to be attuned to these equipment changes and streamlined to reduce excess deployment of equipment and overall operational inefficiencies.

So, to address their customer requirements (such as the scrutinizing service provider) and reduce the overall operational cost and environmental impacts of the network, network equipment vendors are eking out efficiencies within their solutions. Every component within a device needs to be examined for its energy consumption impact, from the power supply to the silicon to the processing engines. And all the interactions among those components in the system need to be scrutinized as well, to ensure that there is no duplicative or unnecessary processing that wastes cycles or energy. Let's drill down a little into these components.

Into the ASIC

Designing efficient network platforms is the first step in the new energy-aware networks. To become energy-efficient, a networking platform has to be meticulously designed to achieve advanced functionality within a limited energy budget. Starting at the component level, networking equipment vendors (Juniper Networks and Cisco Systems, for example) are evaluating each and every component that goes into their devices. They are looking at the impacts of swapping out power converters and fans, trying to understand the energy savings to be garnered from multicore processors, leveraging alternative chipset integration and fabrication, and evaluating the selection of memory to identify more energy-efficient approaches.

Everybody's Doing It

If, by chance, you haven't noticed, everybody has a cell phone. That means mobile network operators are finding their cell site transmission requirements continuing to rise into the foreseeable future. In 2007, the average site needed to support 6 Mbps, with high demand sites requiring 12 Mbps. By 2012, the transmission requirements of an average site will be 16 Mbps, and a high-demand site will need to support 36 Mbps.[7] These cell sites will require additional energy to support this increase in traffic. However, in many locations, energy availability is constrained or unreliable, forcing operators to look at more sustainable approaches, such as sharing cell sites with other providers to maximize the utility of the infrastructure or leveraging alternative power sources to keep their network operating. Many have started to power their base stations with solar power.

Similarly, consumer electronic vendors are experimenting with placing *photovoltaic* cell arrays directly on mobile phones or laptops to power the devices without relying on electricity from the grid. Basically, these cells convert solar energy into electricity, and there have been breakthroughs in the technology that allow these arrays to be printed onto surfaces as thin as a piece of paper. Calculators have been relying on solar power generation for years, so why not cell phones and mobile computers?

The breakdown of the energy consumed by a typical router is as follows: application-specific integrated circuits (ASICs) consume 48% of the power; memory, 19%; power conversion, 15%; other supporting chips, 10%; and the central processing unit (CPU), 4%.

Custom ASICs are highly specialized circuits, made up of hardware and silicon, that are optimized to perform specific tasks. ASICs provide many benefits over general, off-the-shelf processors, and are often the secret sauce that allows vendors to achieve the performance, capacity, and efficiency required of the network. As an added benefit, they can deliver better energy efficiency than generic processor or programmable circuits, since they optimize the "gate" count (the basic computing entity in a chip). You could compare designing ASICs to building sports cars—both are task oriented, focused, and fast. However, unlike track-bound sports cars, ultra-fast and purpose-built silicon yields better energy efficiency when compared to more generic, "family sedan" designs that mitigate go-to-market risks by being the masters of many tasks.

Given that ASICs represent the most power-consuming component of a device, vendors have invested a lot in research focused on driving ASIC improvements, such as designing the hardware to optimize its efficiency. In this regard, vendors strive to create the layout that enables the most efficient processing, use the best fabrication processes available (many ASICs started at 180 nanometers and have progressed to 65 nanometers (a nanometer is the unit commonly used to describe the manufacturing technology used in semiconductors), and ensure that the system is integrated as effectively as possible (for example, evaluating the use of silicon wafers, which are typically more efficient for energy transfer than discrete chips). Without throwing pages of details at you, networking vendors have so far been successful at ensuring that each new ASIC generation delivers additional efficiencies, while maximizing their traffic-processing capabilities. It's a real trick. But as the world becomes increasingly networked, the physical laws that underlie the technology's ability to keep up are being stretched. Because ASICs are a combination of hardware and silicon, they are generally beholden to limitations described by Moore's Law and Dennard's Scaling Law.

Moore's Law states that the amount of transistors on a die doubles approximately every two years, a phenomenon that has become a benchmark for the rate at which computing hardware capabilities will increase (this phenomenon has held for half a century and is expected to continue through the decade). However, with network service providers doubling and even tripling their capacity every 18 months, the network requirements are outpacing Moore's Law, and as the networks continue to expand, so will the absolute power consumption of the increasingly powerful devices required to sustain this growth.

The good news is that networking efficiency has been able to improve for the past 15 years. In fact, the reason this book exists is to herald this 15-year-old fact—that the network is advancing faster than our perceptions, and thus has created an opportunity never before revealed for humanity. For these past years, for every kilowatt of power used, the network equipment has been able to get more functionality or throughput. It's not only a marvelous technological advancement, but it has been a sustainable one.

At the highest level, energy-related improvements in network equipment design can be classified in two ways: organic and engineered. Organic efficiency improvements are commensurate with Dennard's Scaling Law, which states that every new generation of silicon packs more performance in a smaller energy budget. However, as experts increasingly agree, this law will cease to apply as silicon manufacturing processes evolve below 65 nanometers. At that point, networking devices need to turn to engineered energy efficiency improvements, such as new active energy management and device reduction schemes available at the system and architecture levels, respectively. So, let's change our drill bit and go sideways for a moment. By the way, we're deep in the heart of the Internet.

The System Level

The next generation of networking equipment is aiming at simpler designs, fewer components, better performance, and overall lower energy requirements. These can include gate count optimization, improved memory access algorithms, I/O buffer reduction, and other things that interest the networking engineer, but may make your eyes glaze over. However, an item of interest is the recent advances in dynamic power management. To date, because of the stringent requirements on the network, most equipment has been engineered for *optimal peak performance*, meaning it is most efficient when the device is at full capacity, processing a full traffic load. In other words, because the focus has been on the device's maximum capacity and throughput, networking vendors have built their systems to efficiently handle this peak load (without latency, loss of packets, etc.). However, the difference between the energy consumption of a device when it is under peak load and the energy consumption of that same device when it is hardly processing any traffic is only 10% in many cases.

The reality is that many devices are not used at peak capacity all the time. For example, the traffic at the home or service provider "edge" is much less predictable and lumpy (based on when people are at home) than the traffic in the core, where there is almost no real downtime (there is always someone using the network from somewhere all the time). Network edge devices typically have loads at less than 3% utilization, with bursts in high traffic. Enterprise core devices have a typical load in the region of 15% utilization, with fewer and less intense but more predictable bursts, and WAN core devices are often deployed with typical utilization up to 30%.[8] While the percentages may go up based on investment constraints or cyclical usage patterns, and while some parts of the network are run much "hotter" than others (such as a service provider's backbone network, where devices can regularly reach up to 60% utilization), the fact remains that only very rarely is a device pushed to its full capacity for extended periods of time, so there is a lot of energy potentially wasted during times of less traffic. As a result, dynamic power management that is *proportional to use* represents an opportunity to increase the overall efficiency of the network's energy consumption.

It has been suggested that different evaluation criteria need to be created, focusing on the actual use of the equipment. The thinking is that this could potentially reduce inefficiencies generated by overengineering a device to handle the worst-case scenario. There is some truth to this, but the real benefit most likely lies more in ensuring the appropriate sizing of the equipment that is deployed.

In reality, networking devices need to be capable of accommodating these peak loads, because, as this book continues to point out, traffic consumption is going to grow and we need to ensure the sustainability of the network via an ever-present, consistent, satisfactory user experience. So, the real problem is in ensuring that networking devices can efficiently consume energy in a way that is commensurate with the actual activity—in other words, adjusting energy use when the device is under low and peak traffic conditions. This requires new energy reduction schemes.

Let me introduce Barroso's Principle of Proportionality. It states that energy consumption should be proportional to the load. Since most devices in a network rarely run at peak power, yet still consume up to 90% of peak power in idle mode, the mode the equipment runs in most of the time also happens to be its least energy-efficient mode. Addressing this mismatch requires significant rethinking of components and systems. According to Barroso, energy-proportional designs would potentially double energy efficiency of equipment in real-life use, but it is an extremely difficult problem to solve because it requires focusing on a variety of factors to achieve efficiencies within the different modes:

Full load

Maximizing energy consumption at peak load requires looking at the silicon design, power design, and hardware design, including the choice of *all* the off-the-shelf components, *and* the software design, to make sure that tasks are performed only once and in the most efficient way. This is what networking vendors have been focused on to date, with fairly good success.

Idle load

This requires minimizing the energy consumption when traffic loads are low by placing the device or components of the device (such as interfaces that are not being used) into a certain "powered down" mode (similar to a hibernation mode, or sleep, used by PCs). It's an opportunity to more efficiently handle periods of predictably lower traffic by designing systems that allow parts to be run off of lower power draws or turned off altogether. Ideally, the system could be instrumented to allow the lower power modes to be automatically triggered when certain traffic thresholds are met or performed remotely based on real-time reporting of the actual activity of the device. The new hybrid cars do this, choosing when to run off batteries or start the gas engine.

Variable load

This requires scaling the energy consumption up or down automatically based on the load placed on a device. This is a relatively new area of focus, with some of the opportunities for advancement coming from lower clock speeds, idled CPU cores, and idled processing complexes on service physical interface cards (PICs).

One of the new mechanisms that could potentially reduce power consumption during periods of lower utilization may actually be enabled at the Physical level (refer to the seven layers of the OSI model in Chapter 31) by Ethernet (Ethernet is a set of wiring and signaling standards—it's generally the cable you plug into your laptop or desktop computer to connect to the network). This lower power consumption is part of the vision of energy-efficient Ethernet (EEE)—specifically, the IEEE 802.3az standard, which is currently being architected in the IEEE's working group and targeted for completion in September 2010.

IEEE 802.3az builds on the work from the Adaptive Link Rate (ALR), which was designed to save energy by quickly switching the speed of the network based on the amount of data being transmitted. Unfortunately, the transition times were in the tens of milliseconds, which could potentially disrupt voice, video, or multimedia transmissions.

The goal is to define a protocol that can coordinate transitions among different levels of power consumption in a transparent manner to the upper-layer protocols and applications (with no detectable delay or latency when transitioning from a lower level to a higher level), ensuring that the links are maintained (no dropped or corrupted packets). This would provide a foundational level of power consumption control at different loads, which could lead to additional opportunities to save power at the component level, device level, and network architecture level.

Now, instead of drilling down, let's move up to a level where we can see the whole picture or topology.

The Architectural Level

One of the biggest breakthroughs in network efficiencies is the overall simplification of the network's design. Any time layers in the network can be removed, significant space, power, and cooling efficiencies are created. If you can remove equipment that was typically required to perform a certain function—say, security or traffic aggregation—because that functionality can be absorbed into other equipment, the number of devices required to handle the traffic is reduced. As long as the device that is used to integrate the multiple functions is engineered to proficiently process the traffic and maximize the utility of that device, there are significant efficiency gains.

Networking vendors have introduced integrated platforms that allow devices to deliver multiple functions, removing the need to deploy multiple devices and saving on space, power, and cooling requirements. Most common is the combination of multifunction security solutions, which are increasingly being integrated with routing and switching technology.

There have also been some disruptive technologies—or game-changing innovations—that have created a completely new way of approaching the problem. *Virtualization* is one of these technologies. It allows a single physical device to be logically separated into multiple virtual instantiations of that device. So, instead of deploying multiple devices, you can deploy one device that is virtually partitioned and behaves the same way as multiple devices would.

From an efficiency perspective, virtualization has been paying huge benefits. A single server was traditionally deployed to support a single application and on average only 15% of that server's computing capacity was typically utilized. In a virtualized environment, a single server may support many different applications or consolidate multiple instantiations of a single application onto that server. As a result, virtualized servers often run with efficiencies upward of 80%. For example, when Citi's North American operations virtualized 10% of its environment, it realized a 73% reduction in energy consumption, which translated to a reduction of 56 metric tons of CO_2 per week (roughly 300 tons per year) and $1 million in annual savings.[9]

These types of savings demonstrate why virtualization technology has rapidly become part of a best practice deployment requirement. (It also explains the success of virtualization companies, such as VMware; *www.vmware.com*.) It is estimated that 50–60% of all servers are now virtualized, and the technology is being extended to storage and desktop devices to reduce inefficiencies and costs. For instance, virtual desktops use less power than a nightlight (approximately 4 watts) and 1/20th the consumption of a typical PC.[10] That's a huge savings when you might have hundreds or thousands of users and desktop devices. Forrester Research reported that these *thin client* alternatives to standard PC desktop assets can generate energy efficiency savings of up to 25%. This is probably why there are predictions that by 2011, more than half of users' workloads will be deployed in virtual machines.[11]

Administrators are also applying virtualization to the network itself, partitioning the network and leveraging it for maximum utility. Traditionally, service providers built out service-specific networks to ensure the performance and security of that service. But with everything converging onto a single IP network, providers have been able to combine services onto a single network infrastructure. Network virtualization brings a new dimension of flexibility and scalability to the network infrastructure. That's because network virtualization enables network convergence—it allows different departments, business units, and even different service providers to share infrastructure without having to change the organizational model of those providers. It allows the decoupling of the service from the infrastructure that delivers that service so that it can be controlled individually to achieve the same levels of performance and security traditionally attained via a service-specific network.

Network virtualization allows the sharing of infrastructure in a risk-free manner that has environmental benefits—namely, that the provider doesn't have to invest and build the infrastructure to support separate services. Rather, the infrastructure can be shared and can transcend physical boundaries with virtual, secure, individually managed networks. This reduces truckrolls (a technician physically driving to a location), duplicative buildouts, and general operational and energy use inefficiencies. It also enables new business models, such as *open garden* networks, networks as a service (NaaS), and network sharing. Network Strategy Partners estimated that virtualization in the network can save up to 40% in energy and potentially more than 50% in total cost of ownership of the network infrastructure.[12]

We are already seeing trends toward sharing network infrastructure. For example, Arcep, the French telecoms regulator, has called for the country's three mobile operators to reach an agreement to share infrastructure by the end of 2009. Arcep noted that providers in France are already sharing sites, buildings, towers, and masts that support their mobile networks, accounting for 20–40% of current sites, and called for further sharing due to the environmental benefits.

Lifecycle

The network's impact does not start or end with the in-use consumption of the networking devices. A true end-to-end solution comprises all the variables—not just the power consumed by routers and switches (which is a significant component), but also issues like truckrolls. As a result, the networking industry is looking at the entire *lifecycle* of its networking solutions to understand where efficiencies can be achieved.

This is where the carbon footprint discussion comes into play, as governments, industry, and customers struggle with how to quantify all of the environmental impacts of a product or service. Businesses are looking at streamlining their research and development efforts, supply chains, and distribution processes to reduce waste. They are also looking at what happens at the end of a product's useful life.

When Sustainable Life Media[13] conducted a survey on e-waste (old devices, routers, monitors, switches, computers, etc.), a full 100% of survey respondents said they were aware of their organizations' e-waste policies and practices; approximately two-thirds reported that their companies had a formal IT asset disposal plan, and about 15% admitted that their companies put e-waste into the dumpster.[14]

This may even be a low estimate of the amount of e-waste that finds its way into landfills. To minimize the impact, the UN has created a consortium (StEP) focused on solving the e-waste problem. In the U.S., the Green Electronics Council (GEC), in conjunction with the National Center for Electronics Recycling (NCER), has commissioned several research projects to identify opportunities to increase the cost effectiveness and resource efficiency of e-scrap recycling. The ideas range from improved product design to what they call "closing the loop," which is the tracing of recycling efforts, typically through a searchable database that can identify exactly where and when product materials are broken down and recycled, which, in theory, would get rid of the e-waste going to the dumpster.

To that effect, many companies have been adopting design for the environment (DfE) principles, which are guidelines and considerations to help organizations design products and manufacturing processes that ensure minimum impact on the environment. For the back-end of the product lifecycle, many companies have robust take-back and recycling programs to ensure that their own products are appropriately reclaimed, reused, and recycled.

In the ideal world, you would sell or give back your ICT devices to the manufacturer that made it, and it would end the lifecycle in a responsible fashion. For example, for the past two decades, Nike has had a "ReUse a Shoe" program, in which it takes back your worn-out Nikes. The company then grinds them up for other products such as other shoes, playground surfaces, buttons, and even track-and-field tracks to run on with your new Nikes (*www.nikereuseashoe.com*). Following in their shoes (sorry, couldn't resist), some of the things the ICT companies are doing to minimize their impact throughout the lifecycle include:

- Adhering to "green print" principles, which are designed to reduce the amount of physical documentation that gets shipped with each device. The documentation set for a high-end router can be up to 20,000 pages, depending on the complexity of its deployment, so most ICT companies provide a digital version instead, all downloadable and free.

- Consolidating products. This includes shipping multiple solutions in a single box or maximizing the use of pallets.

- Investigating changing the materials of their packaging to be more sustainable. A recent study by the Freedonia Group projects demand for rigid, reusable containers to grow 3.5% annually, reaching $6.6 billion by 2011 as businesses switch to reusable packaging.[15]

Perhaps the most innovative and important lifecycle aspect that ICT companies are looking at is expanding the usability of their products and solutions. With the average product lifespan between four and five years, there can be a lot of waste (the lifespan of consumer electronic equipment is even shorter, often 18 to 36 months). The industry as a whole has been focused on facilitating recycling and the reclamation of parts for reuse whenever possible. Juniper Networks has taken it a step further and dedicated engineering resources to developing solutions and techniques that can maximize the network device's lifecycle. Some chassis (a device's physical encasement) have been in use for 8–10 years, and customers have been able to upgrade them (by swapping out the routing fabric or interface cards) to double or even triple the capacity over that same time, extending the investment and diverting e-waste from landfills.

While there have been advancements within the network to improve overall efficiencies at every level and every stage in the network's lifecycle, becoming an even more sustainable platform for change will take a giant collaborative effort. It will rely on other industries as they advance their component efficiencies; it will involve disruptive technologies that were perhaps initially designed to solve other problems and can be applied to the network; and it will require out-of-the-box thinking and pooling intellectual property to continue to dramatically improve energy efficiency.

The return on energy investment is not always material. Being a pioneer is challenging and often expensive. The burden of developing resources and research will most likely fall on a few, and they will be expected to share, in some way, with all. But it is required to push the boundaries of the network in the coming decade. Interestingly, it also includes you, me, and all the end users of the network. It will take everyone leveraging technology to reduce waste—being aware of a product's impact and the manufacturer's level of responsibility, turning off equipment, implementing power-saving measures, and ensuring appropriate recycling and disposal.

The sustainable network can and will be relied upon to push the boundaries, so it can maximize dematerialization and detravelization, and reduce overall energy consumption and waste. It's a big responsibility, but the network's success will benefit us all.

What You Can Do

- Recycle your electronic equipment only at certified e-waste locations or events.

- Donate computing devices to schools, elder facilities, charities, etc., to extend their life.

- Turn off electronics that are not being used. Create a "charging station" where all your iPods, cell phones, cameras, and more are on a power strip, and when not in use, turn off the power strip.

- Instead of buying a new laptop, consider upgrading the memory and hard drive to extend its use.

- Buy energy-efficient products. Pay attention to claims of green.

- Write online reviews and include evaluations of energy efficiency. Demand better, more sustainable products and vote for them with your dollar.

CHAPTER 17

Data Center

X marks the spot.

W hy is everyone talking about data centers? Data centers comprise a mass of computing (servers/applications), networking, and storage equipment. A data center's purpose is to house and appropriately distribute all the digital information and resources of an organization. The data center is also a treasure chest (a big "X") of inefficiency. It represents a plethora of opportunities to reap the benefits of green IT projects, which makes it one of the first stops when anyone talks about greater network efficiencies.

In very recent years, data centers have grown in density and complexity like no other part of the network. This is due to efforts to consolidate data and centralize systems to achieve overall management and operational efficiencies at the same time that we are seeing more and more information and activities conducted online and translated to the virtual world. Add to that the escalating pace of innovation and the need to quickly adapt to changing business landscapes, and the result is a huge hodgepodge of different equipment hastily deployed to support different projects. All of these factors have combined to bring to the forefront issues around space, power, and cooling that we can anticipate will trickle throughout the network if they are not addressed.

In fact, power and cooling has become the number one problem for the data center, and accounts for up to 80% of a data center's costs.[1] It is estimated that the three-year operational expenditures of a data center, of which energy is one of the largest components, often exceed capital investment costs. And the number of devices in a typical data center has grown more than six-fold in the past 12 years,[2] with no signs of slowing. The storage needs of the average business are growing anywhere from 20–150% a year, with servers growing 11% and applications 10%.[3] As a result, data centers have seen a doubling of energy consumption and heat generation since 2000,[4] and this is on a trajectory to double again by 2010.[5] A typical 20,000 square foot data center uses 8 megawatts of power,[6] which is about the same amount of energy as 25,000 households.[7]

In 2007, the EPA issued a report to Congress on Server and Data Center Energy Efficiency, which noted that in the U.S. in 2006, data centers accounted for approximately 1.5% of the country's energy consumption, and predicted that the number would double over five years. No doubt it already has by the time you read this book. That same year, in the UK, data centers used approximately 2.2–3.3% of the country's total electricity;[8] in the Netherlands, they consumed around 2%;[9] and in Germany, they were found to use 1.6%[10] of the country's electricity. Data centers alone are expected to eclipse the airline industry as a top GHG polluter by 2020.[11]

Many of the facilities that house data centers are simply unable to keep up. Often, they cannot draw any more wattage from their utility providers. There are estimates that by 2010, almost 50% of the world's data centers will not have enough energy for power and cooling.[12] To combat this, many different organizations have created data center frameworks, such as those developed by the Green Grid or the European Commission's Code of Conduct for Data Centres, that outline energy-efficient best practices to help organizations better manage and ultimately reduce their data center power consumption. Typically, these best practices can cover everything from the physical layout of the facility to the devices that are housed in that facility. One example is rearchitecting the design of the data center to maximize air flows and power distribution or "intelligently refreshing" equipment that has reached its end of life with devices that are more energy efficient.

The typical data center is ripe for energy efficiency, or green IT, makeovers. *Makeover* is the key word here because a lot can be done to improve existing data centers without throwing up our hands and starting anew. The EPA estimates that, by implementing existing technologies and strategies, companies have "the potential to save up to $4 billion in annual electricity costs through more energy efficient equipment and operations, and the broad implementation of best management practices." A 2008 Data Centre Energy Resources Report found corroborating evidence that it is possible to revamp existing data centers to achieve energy efficiencies similar to those built into new, green data centers. When we are talking about spending upward of $1,000 per square foot for a new data center facility, the incremental costs of implementing some of these best practices and technologies can represent real savings.

Interestingly, many of the improvements have to do with the physical layout and management of the data center itself versus the IT equipment, starting with things as fundamental as how temperature is controlled throughout the facility and how power is distributed (the higher the voltage, the more efficient the power source). For example, a 208-circuit plug is more efficient than a 120-circuit plug and a 480-circuit plug is more efficient still, delivering maximum power savings.

Inside Versus Outside DC Energy Consumption

A Forrester Research survey found that, on average, the data centers of enterprises of all sizes tend to consume a similar percent of the enterprise's total electrical usage, at 24–25%. But it turns out that while it may be the single biggest consumer in an enterprise, 55% of an enterprise's total consumption still takes place outside the data center. The primary source outside of the data center is the enterprise's personal computing environment, which is why increasing the efficiency of computers and monitors has traditionally been an enterprise's highest priority and why interest in PC power management best practices, software, and more efficient thin-client architectures continues to rise.

Because energy consumed by devices in the data center creates heat, data centers must have heat removal, cooling, and buffering systems. When the temperature of the data center goes up, the integrity of the equipment can be compromised. While advances are being made to develop equipment that can perform at higher temperatures, the majority of devices in the data center still require a fairly consistent, relatively cool temperature.

The Uptime Institute reports that for every increase of 18°F above 70°F, long-term electronics reliability falls by 50%. This can account for the phenomenon of equipment located in the top third of a data center rack failing twice as often as equipment in the bottom two-thirds of the same rack (hot air rises).

Not only does hot air rise, but the entire data center room temperature can increase rapidly when not checked. For example, an Irish[14] data center–hosting company had all its chillers shut down in the middle of the day, and almost immediately the temperature began to rise by about 3.5°F (2°C) per minute. Within 15 minutes, areas of the data center were experiencing heat above 100°F (40°C). Servers began to shut down, and staff had to take drastic measures and power down the rest of the equipment to protect it from damage. As you can imagine, when something affects business continuity, it goes to the top of the purchasing list. That's why almost 50% of the power required by data centers is used for air conditioning, or what some define as "peripheral functions."[15] So, a large swath of power consumption of the data center is not used for actually accessing the resources and sending information to and fro, but for keeping the optimal temperature.

For new data centers, the general thinking is that it is best to start with an "on slab" design, meaning you place the equipment on racks that are directly on the floor versus a raised floor, which is how many legacy data centers have been architected. It may seem strange to be talking about "on slab" versus a raised floor, but it is a start in controlling the air flow in the data center. A lot of waste is created in the unconstrained mixing of cold supply air from the air conditioning units (HVAC units) with hot exhaust air from the equipment. If left unchecked, it increases the load on the cooling system and the energy needed to provide that cooling, thus reducing the overall efficiency. Cold-aisle containment can be easily and inexpensively retrofitted to most data centers, and can achieve noticeable benefits—upward of a 30% energy reduction.[16]

Organizations looking to perfect cold- and hot-aisle containment practices may install airside economizers, which use outside nighttime air to naturally cool the server rooms, or energy-efficient chillers that use a cold-water loop system to keep the temperatures down. Others are choosing locations in the mountains and in Greenland, which is touting itself as one of the "greenest" locations (pun probably intended) to house data centers, due to its ability to use ambient air to cool the facilities. When it works, it works, and data centers that leverage best practices are typically able to spend 15% for power and cooling versus the 30–50% of typical data centers.

Take Sun Microsystems, for example. Leveraging best practices, such as getting rid of the data center floor and deploying modular "pods" (racks with power, cooling, and connectivity), Sun Microsystems took its 496,000-square-foot data center down to just 126,000, reducing power consumption by 1 million kWh per month.[17] Then there's Telecoms giant BT, which has one of Europe's largest data centers and consumes close to 0.7% of Britain's total power output. By implementing energy efficiency measures, such as running its servers hotter and implementing fresh-air cooling, it reduced cooling costs by close to 85% and cut power use by more than 60% in recent years. And the investment payback took less than 18 months.

There are also out-of-the-box innovations that can support more sustainable data centers, such as newly invented scavenger technology. These tools can be hung in a data center (they look like a piece of paper) to capture the hot air released from the equipment and then convert it back to energy. The milowatts to microwatts of energy they recycle can be stored and used to power the lights or other electronic components of the data center. There are also data center–hosting companies that are retrofitting old ships and using them as data center sites to take advantage of the natural cooling effects of the water. Hey, every little bit can help, especially when land-bound data centers use 50% of their total energy just to keep things cool.

What About the Actual Equipment?

When it comes to the core devices within the data center (the servers/applications, networking, and storage equipment), overall energy efficiency comes from best practices—such as using variable speed drives, power-management tools, and virtualization technologies—that can reduce energy consumption and extend the facility's lifespan. Power management tools can include the following:

- Physical controls on the data center racks or aisles.

- Sensors that can automatically adjust power and cooling for specific equipment.

- Networked applications that collect information on power consumption and operating temperatures, similar to an electricity meter, to provide visibility into the energy used by different servers and storage equipment. Some of these applications can also allocate and bill the electricity costs to relevant departments, which ultimately helps people understand and be held accountable for their usage; an added benefit is that it helps create a consciousness that can often lead to conservation efforts.

Virtualization technology allows multiple software instances to run independently on a single physical device. Basically, it logically splits the device into multiple virtual devices, which operate as if they were separate physical devices. Since most servers are not used to their full capacities, organizations can maximize the utility of that physical device and minimize the space, power, and cooling requirements by consolidating multiple servers into one physical machine. Some researchers put the energy and cooling savings at up to 80%.

In 2008, according to VMware, a virtualization solution provider, 42% of customers worldwide require all new server deployments to be virtualized, up from 25% just a year before.[18] Microsoft estimates that its virtualization software has saved some business customers an average of $470,000 annually, reducing operations and capital expenses through reduced electrical power consumption and cooling in their data centers.[19] The biggest problem today with virtualization lies not in the potential, but the execution.

It isn't simple to meld virtualization implementations in servers, storage, and networking together into one cohesive, logical entity.

A shocking fact, in my mind, is that most of the devices running in the data center are used only about 15% of the time.[20] While virtualization technologies can improve this percentage over time, the immediate reality is that virtualization is happening more in silos, individually improving the utilization of servers, storage, or networking, but not all together in a singular way. In many ways, this is why *cloud computing* is so attractive.

The term "cloud" has been bandied about so much and used to mean so many different things that, for all practical terms, it has no real meaning at all. However, the basic concept is that people and organizations can leverage the Internet to access applications and services that are run in giant data centers hosted by cloud service providers (Figure 17-1). Thus, things you do are not siloed, or built just for one purpose, but are shared within the cloud. At the highest level, clouds let users share the costs associated with building out and running large data center–like environments. They also allow users to scale their applications and services and handle ebbs and flows in demand more efficiently without requiring them to overprovision or potentially waste resources to reduce energy consumption.

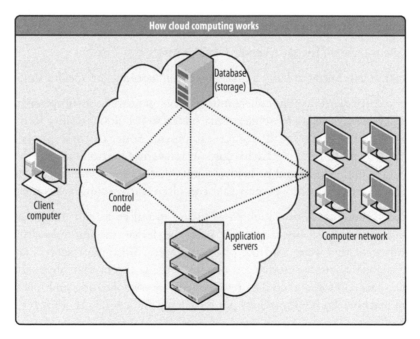

Figure 17-1. The promise of the cloud is that people can use the Internet to access applications and services that are run in a giant data center that is taken care of by someone else.

Another key concept that has the potential to create a lot of efficiencies in the data center environment is consolidation. Typically, in data center discussions, consolidation has referred to merging multiple physical data center sites into one or two. Now the same needs to be done within the data center environment itself. Virtualization will help consolidate servers, storage, and even networking devices, but the network can take it even further.

There are often multiple networking devices that make up different layers of the data center infrastructure. These layers start at the WAN edge (the edge where the traffic enters the data center); move into the core tier, the aggregation tier (which processes and secures the traffic); and finally end up at the access tier (which transports the traffic to the servers). One of the best ways to achieve efficiencies in the data center from a networking perspective is to collapse the layers, thereby removing physical devices and the associated space, power, and cooling needs. According to Juniper Networks, the benefits of a flatter network infrastructure can save up to 55% on space and 44% on energy and cooling costs.[21]

Similarly, when possible, data centers can also consolidate security functionality, either by deploying devices that deliver multiple functions in a single platform or by deploying devices that support higher capacity and density of a single function. It repeats the common mantra of data center efficiency—remove duplicate devices from the network and reap the associated space, energy, and cooling benefits.

Another way to drive efficiencies within the data center is to evaluate all of the applications, tier them based on their criticality to the business, then appropriately provision them in terms of the availability and quality of service truly needed. Data centers have typically been "one size fits all" and, as the heart of an organization's information technology infrastructure, that size tends to be big and is historically overengineered. There is a lot of redundancy built into data centers, with backup systems and duplicative processes that are designed to ensure the availability and integrity of the data. All of this redundancy requires additional equipment and processing, which in turn, consumes space, power, and cooling.

Tiering Backup Data

It's a fact that data centers require online storage disks to spin around the clock to ensure that all that data is readily available whenever it's needed. These hard-working disks need to be cooled to ensure optimal operation. And it all takes energy. The reality is that disks may be storing multiple copies of the same data or ancient files that are only very rarely needed. For files that are infrequently accessed, the data center can use offline storage, which is less energy intensive. By identifying the different requirements for different data, one can determine how best to store it, and whether it truly needs to be available at a moment's notice or is needed more as an archive of historical files.

This may not be possible, however, for certain types of businesses. For example, financial institutions often fall under legislative requirements that mandate the storage of live data, which is probably one of the principle reasons why many European and U.S. banks have been running out of power and space in their data centers.

The reality is that approximately 5%[22] to 10% of an organization's data is truly critical, meaning a delay of milliseconds makes a difference, so it's probably unnecessary to apply the same level of redundancy and performance parameters for all of an organization's data. The majority of data in data centers can handle a second or two of delay, and organizations that prioritize their applications and create different scenarios for different application tiers can more efficiently manage their resources and overall consumption than those that do not.

By understanding the differences in the criticality of applications, you can design your data center for optimal benefit. You can determine whether to invest in the infrastructure to support the applications themselves, leverage the infrastructure in the cloud and pay someone to host it and potentially guarantee the QoS, or take some sort of hybrid approach, all of which can help maximize investments and resources.

Increasing efficiencies in the data center can pay huge dividends. As data centers and cloud architectures continue to support and house the digitized content and services that the world relies on, it is important that they do so in a way that is sustainable, because in many ways they are the heart of the network.

Basic Consumption Reduction

Due to the explosive growth of the network and the sheer demand created by all the people and devices plugged in at your home, we are not that far away from home data centers. It probably won't be long before you are sporting a rack in your basement with its own cooling, like a wine cellar, or perhaps you will lease space at the neighborhood cloud. Before then, consider some of the efficiencies that the big boys implement:

General Tips for Facilities

- Automate building controls (from lights to building temperatures to timing of sprinkler systems) to make it easier to shed loads and make adjustments that can have significant energy savings.

- Work with your utility provider to determine the timeline for the installation of a smart meter at your home, or, if one's installed, start regularly checking on your daily (even hourly) consumption to understand and make more informed decisions about your energy use. Check out applications, such as iControl (*www.icontrol. com/*), that allow you to control all your networked devices from your iPhone to manage and reduce consumption.

- Install energy-efficient heating and cooling systems; apply double-sided window film or other window coverings to prevent large temperature fluctuations due to outside conditions.

- Phase out less efficient devices; choose energy-efficient solutions (printers, servers, desktops, monitors, and, of course, networking equipment).

- Encourage energy conservation; turn off lights when leaving a room and shut down computers and monitors when they're not in use rather than leaving them on standby. You can install power strips to make it easier to cut power to devices not in use and use sensors that recognize when you are not in the vicinity to automatically power down ambient devices (such as air, heat, and lights) or devices (such as monitors).

- Use compact fluorescent lightbulbs and leverage natural light as much as possible.

- Look at all aspects of the business, from the office space to the cafeteria to the plumbing, to identify more environmentally friendly practices, such as using bioware, "greening" the roof, or installing solar panels in the parking lot.

- Reclaim, recycle, and reuse:

  - Look to reuse components in production of products and services.

  - Recycle paper, plastic, and e-waste.

  - Reuse electronics and IT equipment; some companies have set up internal inventory portals that allow departments to shop for existing equipment that is no longer used (one caveat: sometimes the shipping of this equipment can negate the environmental benefits of its reuse). Consider donating or finding someone who can use your equipment to extend its useful life.

- Encourage printing documents only as necessary; set printer defaults to double-sided, use recycled paper and soy ink when possible, and encourage digital versions of collateral.

- Adopt environmental building standards, such as the Leadership in Energy and Environmental Design (LEED). While not something that can be done at the flip of a switch, these guidelines provide a wealth of opportunity to create efficiencies that can reduce both the ongoing operational costs and environmental impacts of your facilities. There are also green standards for residential buildings that cover almost everything from the insulation to the plumbing.

Tips for Data Centers

- Ensure that energy consumption can be measured at a granular level (at the device and rack level versus the overall building energy draw), to identify hot spots and potential inefficiencies.

- Maximize air flows and implement effective hot and cold aisle containment mechanisms.

- Install energy-efficient chillers; research whether ambient air can be used to reduce cooling needs or how hot the equipment can run before degradation.

- Automate building controls to make most efficient use of energy consumed.

- Choose energy-efficient devices—server, storage, and network equipment.

- Virtualize, virtualize, virtualize.

- Collapse the architecture of the data center to remove unnecessary equipment and layers.

CHAPTER 18

Energy Efficiency Measurement

The nicest thing about standards is that there are so many of them to choose from.

—Andres S. Tannenbaum

As noted earlier, you can't improve what you can't measure. When it comes to efficiency, you must first establish a baseline by which to measure your progress, or lack thereof. Unfortunately, to date, when it comes to the network, there is really no standard energy efficiency measurement available.

While there are a whole host of standards that cover how traffic should be handled on the network, developed by a whole host of standards bodies—from IEEE to ITU to GSM (that's how you know you are working in technology or the government: there are acronyms for the acronyms)—there is a void in standards associated with measuring the network's overall efficiency. And that lack of standards means there is confusion caused by different vendor claims based on different criteria. Those who are tasked with evaluating and then choosing networking equipment are left scratching their heads, trying to make sense of it all.

> Efficiency is the measure of power relative to the amount of work performed. When products use more power to perform the same amount of work, they are, by definition, less efficient.

Many existing environmental standards focus on pure energy consumption versus efficiency. This is logical, given that most of the regulations and governmental initiatives are focused on wholesale reductions of the emissions that result from consumption of energy derived via fossil fuel sources. For example, in the UK, many companies fall under the Carbon Reduction Commitment, which is set to start in 2010. These companies will be mandated to install a dedicated power meter for any device with electric consumption of 50 kWh or greater. While most networking equipment falls below this, in the 3–15 kWh range, customers will most likely look at the consumption of all their devices to try to ferret out the energy hogs and ensure that their overall energy consumption is as low as it can be.

While a flat energy consumption metric represents a good start to raise the visibility and understanding of a device's energy consumption, it doesn't address the overall *energy efficiency* of that device. What we need is a standard metric that customers can use to make meaningful decisions based on the true efficiency of the network solution or a device; it must take into consideration the function and overall capacity of the device. For example, if a single device is capable of doing the work of multiple devices, the additional functionality, capacity, and performance capabilities should be factored into the measurement so that this device gets "credit" for being such a workhorse.

There is plenty of precedent for these types of efficiency metrics. Consider your car. There is a pure consumption metric in the form of the number of gallons (or liters) of gas the vehicle uses, but most people will look at the number of miles (or kilometers) they can drive per gallon of fuel consumed (MPG) to understand the vehicle's efficiency. Many vehicle manufacturers break it down even further, providing MPG metrics for different driving conditions, such as in the city or on the highway. These kinds of metrics allow people to evaluate and make decisions on the type of car that makes the most sense for them given how they plan to drive it.

The same information should be available to customers trying to understand the energy consumption and efficiency of their network equipment. Ideally, the efficiency metric should take into account all the components of the device, the features and functionality that the device delivers, and the overall configuration for which it is optimized. The result should be a consistent, easily understood metric that customers can use to make apples-to-apples comparisons of equipment and choose the best option based on their requirements.

The problem is that there are a lot of parameters to consider. For example, a networking device that integrates routing and security functionality and is designed for deployment in a branch office or retail location would have different parameters than a device that focuses on a single functional feature set—say, routing—designed to deliver maximum density and capacity for the core of a service provider's network. You can't compare the two, because the purposes of the devices, the way they are architected, and the way you would use the devices are different.

What is needed is a metric that we can use to consistently compare the same device types or profiles. Ideally, the metrics for these different device types would be generated from a common framework, but somehow specialized to take into account the differences associated with each device type. Customers could then understand the metric at a high level and be able to make like-device comparisons. These metrics should evaluate *how efficiently* something is able to do the task it needs to perform and then put *an efficiency per packet value* on that task.

Unfortunately, the industry-wide vernacular, framework, and device profiles have not been agreed upon. As a result, the sustainable network lives in a gray area, not a green one, with vendors making claims that make it difficult for customers to compare competing products. Efforts are underway, however, to get rid of the confusion. There is activity across commercial companies, government agencies, and standards bodies to define a set of energy efficiency criteria and to develop a consistent way of measuring the energy efficiency of networking solutions and devices.

Other Sustainable Standards

While energy efficiency standards represent a critical commitment to the network's environmental impact, other sustainable factors must be considered, too, ranging from the use of hazardous materials to the ethical treatment of workers (the who-does-it-and-how-do-they-do-it standards). Nothing is exempt, and the ends do not justify the means. There are a host of regulations, directives, and guidelines for the networking industry, including:

- The Restriction of the use of certain Hazardous Substances, otherwise known as RoHS, regulates the use of chemicals and substances in the network and general electronics industries.
- The Waste Electrical and Electronic Equipment (WEEE) directive (EU Directive 2002/96/EC) is designed to reduce the waste associated with end-of-life equipment and encourages the design of electronic products with environmentally safe recycling and recovery in mind.
- The Electronics Industry Code of Conduct (EICC) outlines standards to ensure that working conditions in the electronics industry supply chain are safe, that workers are treated with respect and dignity, and that manufacturing processes are environmentally responsible.

One industry-wide measurement framework for network and telecom equipment originated from the Energy Consumption Rating (ECR) Initiative (*www.ecrinitiative.org*). This framework has been introduced to working groups within associations and standards bodies, such as the Alliance for Telecommunications Industry Solutions (ATIS) and the International Telecommunication Union (ITU) and the Broadband and IP/MPLS Forums. Through these industry consortiums and standards bodies, the goal is to refine the framework and establish a standard that can be used and, maybe even more importantly, verified by anyone.

The ECR initiative is by no means the only potential framework candidate. Verizon has proposed its own energy rating metrics, announcing that it will require vendors to reduce their power consumption by 15% in 2009. Verizon published an energy efficiency requirements specification document that it requires vendors to adhere to when selling to Verizon. It also requires vendors to have the energy efficiency measured by a certified lab.

We can only enjoy the benefits associated with energy efficiency metrics through their consistent application. This is hard to achieve when multiple flavors are in use or customized one-off measurements are required. Ultimately, the confusion will be removed when there is an agreed-upon vernacular and a standard as well as a way to enforce that standard to ensure its authenticity. This is where government entities can play a critical role.

International efforts (such as the Kyoto Protocol) and international bodies (such as the World Economic Forum and the United Nations Global Compact) have tried to step in to create some standards. Some progress had been made with international associations, such as the World Information Technology and Services Alliance (WITSA), which hosts the World Congress on IT. Another is GeSI,[1] an international strategic partnership of ICT companies and industry associations committed to creating and promoting technologies and practices that foster economic, environmental, and social sustainability while driving economic growth and productivity. GeSI, formed in 2001, partners with the United Nations Environment Programme (UNEP), which hosts GeSI's Secretariat and the International Telecommunications Union (ITU).

The problem is that while these types of efforts and organizations have increased awareness, identified opportunities, and put some basic goals in place, adoption hasn't been universal. The U.S.'s absence of adoption of the Kyoto Protocol is a good example, and enforcement, to date, has been on a voluntary basis. The European ecodesign for energy using products (EUP) directive will be taking effect soon and may go further than other efforts have in terms of mandating improvements, particularly for the worst offending solutions. Typically, however, the best success in driving consensus on efficiency goals has been seen on a country-by-country basis.

Take Japan, where there are well-known space and power constraints. As Japan works toward achieving its Kyoto Protocol goals to reduce CO_2 emissions by 50% by 2050, the NTT Group, the major network service provider for the country, aims to reduce electric power consumption by 2010 to the level it was at in 1990. If the NTT Group continues on its current consumption trajectory, it would consume 10 billion kWh by 2010. Instead, it is aiming to continue to grow its business while cutting its consumption to 3.4 billion kWh, which is its 1990 level—that's approximately a 60% reduction!

The Ministry of Economy, Trade and Industry (METI) is helping guide these kinds of reductions with its Green IT Project, which includes the goal of reducing router power consumption by 30%. Within this project is a Top Runner program. For every product category (networking and general IT), it picks the most efficient product and makes it the baseline by which all future product buying decisions should be made. In each selection round, it looks to increase the efficiency and move the baseline; it strongly discourages businesses and organizations from choosing any product that comes in 40% or more below that baseline. In fact, customers that choose less-efficient solutions may potentially incur costly tariffs imposed by the government.

Many countries have adopted the standards of other industries that could potentially be expanded to incorporate energy efficiency measurements of networking equipment. Indonesia recently adopted the UN technical regulation on auto energy efficiency, and Ghana has pioneered standards for household appliances in Africa. In the U.S., there are programs, such as the Leadership in Energy and Environmental Design (LEED), that provides a framework for evaluating the overall environmental impacts of buildings, of which the network could potentially be a component.

A more likely candidate for extension to the networking industry might be the U.S. Department of Energy and the Environmental Protection Agency's (EPA) joint EnergyStar program, which is a voluntary labeling program designed to identify energy-efficient products. Consumers have learned to look for the EnergyStar logo when buying refrigerators and dishwashers, but they may be surprised to learn that EnergyStar compliance is at the discretion of the vendor, with no formal certification by a third party (this is similar to gas mileage labels, for which there is no real certification, either). The EPA is now working toward the definition of a certification method for EnergyStar that would include test methodology. This will be a critical component for the extension of a similar program to more business-grade equipment. To date, this program has expanded to include office equipment, such as computers, printers, fax machines, and even servers, as well as consumer network termination devices, such as DSL and cable modems. It's not a stretch to imagine that in the near future it might include networking and telecommunications infrastructure equipment.

Another mechanism that represents possibilities for the industry is the Electronic Products Environmental Assessment Tool (EPEAT), which was developed by a grant from the EPA and is managed by the Green Electronics Council (GEC). It defines a set of performance criteria developed by the IEEE to help purchasers compare and select computer products based on their environmental attributes. It defines a lifecycle standard for the environmental impacts of electronic goods, with 51 criteria. Products can be included on the EPEAT registry once they are certified. If vendors meet at least half of the criteria, they are rated at a bronze level; additional criteria is required to achieve silver and gold levels. This standard has been adopted in principle around the world by many governments and organizations. For example, U.S. government agencies are required to acquire EPEAT-registered electronic products for at least 95% of electronic product acquisitions unless there is no EPEAT standard for the product. The value and credibility that tools like this can offer to the standardization of other types of equipment could be expanded to include the network.

It is absolutely critical to maintain the sustainability of the network with energy efficiency standards that are defined and applied to the network industry, and to establish a common vernacular and framework for measuring such energy efficiency in networking equipment.

The network is a disruptive technology. This book documents how it's changing the world, essentially turning business, politics, and social norms on their heads by creating connections that can serve as a platform for sustainable development and action. So, if the people who build and maintain the network are not able to measure, monitor, and minimize its impact—and yes, even disrupt it occasionally—the network will lose its special significance and value. It could become like a fossil fuel—useful but dated.

CHAPTER 19

Doing Good by Doing Right

> *You are not here merely to make a living. You are here in order to enable the world to live more amply, with greater vision, with a finer spirit of hope and achievement. You are here to enrich the world, and you impoverish yourself if you forget the errand.*
>
> —Woodrow Wilson

What is the role of business, and what is its responsibility to the larger good? For decades, some have argued that fostering economic opportunities and general prosperity is the only social role that businesses need to play—the jobs and money they bring into the communities, as well as the benefits derived from their products and services, are their contributions to the world. Others argue that monetary success needs to be balanced with a general respect for the overall impacts on the environment and the communities that their operations create; if businesses strip communities or landscapes of their inherent worth, they have a responsibility to replenish that value (and, ideally, would do all they could to prevent its depletion in the first place). There is still another argument that places the role of business in the middle of the social food chain, arguing that it is the duty of a business to proactively drive social and environmental improvements, sharing its knowledge and prosperity to prevent disproportionate wealth striations in society, and thereby creating a more productive workforce and environment in which to conduct business.

Regardless of which argument you subscribe to more, there is no questioning that the role of business in society is a complex one. Business does not exist physically in a plane where there are not people. While it may be a separate entity, it exists in the same world with the same resources as society as a whole. Considering the issues we are facing on a global scale, it is reasonable to assume that businesses need to play some societal role, if for no other reason than because it makes good business sense. And regardless of the business, ICT will be critical to the development of those more sustainable business practices.

Responsibility Viewpoints

"There is one and only one social responsibility of business—to use its resources and engage in activities designed to increase its profits so long as it stays within the rules of the game, which is to say, engages in open and free competition without deception or fraud."

—Milton Friedman

"The enlightened corporation should try to create value for all of its constituencies. From an investor's perspective, the purpose of the business is to maximize profits. But that's not the purpose for other stakeholders— for customers, employees, suppliers, and the community. Each of those groups will define the purpose of the business in terms of its own needs and desires, and each perspective is valid and legitimate."

—John Mackey

Companies perceived to be more sustainable than others can easily build on that good-will, impacting customer preference, loyalty, and even the company's ability to attract and retain talent. In fact, 85% of millennials (individuals in the 18- to 28-year-old range) want to work for companies that are good corporate citizens, and MBA graduates indicate that when all things are equal, they would take less pay to work for a company that was more responsible.[1] When interviewing, do you ask the company what it does for the communities and environment in which it is operating?

According to Nielsen,[2] "over 80% of the world's Internet users think it is important that companies implement programs to improve the environment and/or society," and an *Economist* article estimated that the "value of intangibles can be 20% up to 70%" of the stock price of a company. Do you make buying decisions based on what you have heard about a company's labor practices?

It should be no surprise that even the investment community is starting to scrutinize the operations of businesses and perform risk assessments to try to determine a company's exposure to unsustainable business practices, many of which can be mitigated through an ICT environment that brings visibility and accountability to the overall operations and impacts of the business. For example, in December 2008, the Carbon Disclosure Project (CDP), which has the largest global repository of carbon emissions from publicly traded companies, performed a survey[3] of individuals and financial institutions to determine how they use climate change data when evaluating organizations. The CDP found that:

> 77% of the respondents said they factored climate change information into their investment decisions and asset allocations, with more than 80% of those indicating it is an important factor relative to other issues for their portfolio. Almost half of the respondents (48%) are willing to ask companies to do more than just disclose information on climate change, and some have even asked companies for emissions reductions as part of their standard engagement efforts when investors feel there is threat to value.

Indexes like the U.S. Dow Jones Sustainability Index and the UK FTSE4Good Index series have been established to facilitate investment in companies that meet globally recognized corporate responsibility standards. And almost every big investment house manages "green funds" to provide investors with an option to invest in companies that do well by doing good. Do you investigate a company's stance on sustainability issues when thinking about investing in it?

There is also a whole host of lists that rank organizations on their programs and efforts. The annual *Corporate Responsibility Officer Magazine* publishes a "100 Best Corporate Citizens List," which bases rankings on only publicly available information. Of note, over the 10 years of publishing the list, more than 400 companies have made it, with only 3 (Intel, Cisco, and Starbucks) making all 10 lists. Another notable annual list is the 100 Most Sustainable Corporations (G100), produced by Corporate Knights, Inc., and Innovest Strategic Value Advisors, which evaluates organizations according to "how effectively they managed environmental, social, and governance risks and opportunities relative to their industry peers."[4]

The fact that people are paying attention could explain why many companies are implementing sustainability strategies that include using ICT to enable greater automation and operational efficiencies; reducing emissions, waste, and environmental impacts; and working to raise the visibility of their corporate responsibility activities. Companies like networking giant Cisco Systems have been very vocal in their global social commitments. Cisco CEO John Chambers has made strong statements to that effect, saying, "We know it's an aspirational goal that most people would think is impossible to achieve: to be the best company in the world and the best company for the world...But that's what our dream and vision are about."[6]

How do you know when your business is sustainable?

While there are some, such as Cisco, that have strong direction from the top, there are many more that are struggling with what it means to be a responsible or sustainable organization. Is it about compliance, or is it about innovation? Is it about doing just what you need to do to stay under the radar and keep everyone happy, or is it about going above and beyond to make a distinct mark on the landscape? To steal from sports, is it about making sure you are in the game and scoring your points, or is it about taking chances—going for the two-point conversion or just wasting time off the clock with as little risk exposure as possible?

How do you know when your business is sustainable? And can you ever really reach that point? The biggest problem is that there is still no consistent definition of what corporate responsibility or sustainability looks like, yet there is an endless supply of organizations and government entities weighing in on the confusion. There are associations and industry consortiums stepping in, trying to guide the policies and practices. They can be specific to a particular industry, such as the Green Grid, which focuses on environmental impacts of the IT sector, or the International Association for Soaps, Detergents and Maintenance Products (A.I.S.E.), which advances an agenda for improving the quality of life through hygiene and sustainable cleaning, or the U.S. Green Building Council (USGBC), which focuses on environmentally friendly construction. They can be more general, such as the World Resources Institute (WRI), Business for Social Responsibility (BSR), Study Centre for Corporate Social Responsibility (ORSE), and the European Committee for Standardization (CEN).

There are also a variety of metrics and standards that attempt to codify the *triple bottom line* (TBL). TBL refers to an expanded set of criteria that can be used to measure the success of an organization, including "People, Planet, Profit," or social, environmental, and economic metrics. There are multiple instantiations of the TBL, such as the Ecological Footprint, ecolabels, the United Nations International Council for Local Environmental Initiatives' ecoBudget metric, and the International Organization for Standardization (ISO) standards used in full cost accounting (FCA) and true cost accounting (TCA), which are often leveraged by public sector organizations to account for the costs and impacts of investments and projects. In 2010, ISO will have standards specific to corporate social responsibility.

If you just momentarily blacked out from all the wonkishness, you are forgiven. It's confusing trying to do good. Let's recap: our society wants to lessen the mantra of "profit at any costs," so we're encouraging good corporate citizens to invest in sustainable practices, but there's no common way of measuring the efforts, and if and when change occurs—there's no common way to advertise your investment and efforts unless you have the deep pockets of a Cisco.

So, many businesses attempt to capture and communicate their efforts in sustainability or citizenship in corporate social responsibility (CSR) reports. Some CSR reports are issued as standalone reports, while other businesses are incorporating them in their annual financial business reports.

In general, while they all tend to touch on the TBL, the depth and focus for each varies dramatically and the nomenclature is all over the board. Many follow guidelines laid out by the Global Reporting Initiative (GRI), but there are no absolutes. It is not unusual for different companies in the same industry to have completely different reports, even though they're basing their

CSR reports are becoming less of a necessity and more of a responsibility shared by all.

reporting on GRI's common framework. They may choose completely different things to report on or include different metrics in their readouts, all of which make this space incredibly difficult to navigate. Apples-to-apples comparisons are basically impossible.

The companies that traditionally have had the most robust CSR reports are those that are in resource-intensive industries, such as mining and automotive, or those with significant exposure to supply-chain integrity issues, such as garment and general retail industries. This makes sense, because the sustainable issues in these industries represent significant business risks (and can have real economic impacts on the value of the company). As a result, these companies need to reassure shareholders that they are doing all they can to understand and mitigate these risks. But with the elevated focus on general environmental and social issues, it is becoming less of a necessity for only a few industries and more of a responsibility shared by all. In fact, investors have started to call for CSR reports when public companies don't issue them via shareholder resolutions, such as the one put in front of Apple to try get the company to issue a report.

This interesting shift in sustainability/corporate social responsibility reporting is reflected in data collected in 2008 by KPMG.[7] It looked at the inclusion of sustainability/CSR topics in the reporting mechanisms of the top 100 companies in the U.S. and found that twice as many top U.S. companies publicly released sustainability data in 2008 compared with only three years earlier. Delving a little deeper, KPMG found that ethics outweighed the economics for the first time as the primary reason for the disclosures:

> *Seventy percent of all companies studied wrote in their 2008 reports to stakeholders that ethical considerations were a primary driver for making [CSR] disclosures, while 50 percent cited economic concerns as the leading reason. By comparison, in 2005 the drivers were reversed, with economic considerations cited by 74 percent of the companies as the reason for reporting [CSR] data, compared with 53 percent of the companies citing ethical reasons for the disclosures.[8]*

And we are seeing more and more companies report on sustainability issues; 80% of the Global Fortune 250 companies now release CSR data, up from 64% in 2005. More than 2,700 public companies worldwide publish CSR reports. According to KPMG:

> *Three-quarters of the largest global companies' reports focused on a corporate responsibility strategy, including defined objectives, while 61 percent of the U.S. companies disclosing [CSR] data had a formal sustainability strategy.[9]*

These statistics reflect the fact that environmental and social issues are infiltrating businesses and playing a larger role in the evaluation of the organization's general risks and opportunities. Public and financial scrutiny is moving tomorrow's businesses to lessen their environmental impact while maximizing their social value. It's difficult to say how effective these programs will ultimately be, but they represent steps in the right direction—steps that will be supported in some part by the network and its capability to create a technology environment that enables more sustainable business practices.

CHAPTER 20

Is Broadband Really That Important?

Apple Store line for iPhone 3G

*Do not go where the path may lead, go instead where there is
no path and leave a trail.*
—Ralph Waldo Emerson

Can it be? Could the amount of broadband available to your country or state be as important as your roads? Or your schools? Or your environmental policies? Can the implications of the network be so far-reaching that the amount of broadband directly available to you directly affects the quality of your life and the opportunities for your happiness, success, and longevity?

This book exists to say that broadband *is* that important. This book predicts that the next 20 years hinge on broadband penetration and capacity—how to deliver more of it to more people. It's the Sustainable Network Law: the more broadband made available to network users, the faster sustainable network innovation occurs. To put it another way, broadband is the enabler of the sustainable network.

And if you haven't noticed, the world seems to agree. Broadband penetration is now one of the leading economic indicators analyzed when evaluating current economic performance and predicting future performance. In 2007 and 2008, countries such as Denmark, the Netherlands, and Iceland had the highest broadband penetration rates, while the U.S. ranked 15th, according to results produced by the Organisation for Economic Co-Operation and Development (OECD)[1] (see Figure 20-1). However, not everyone agrees with OECD's numbers; analysis by the Information Technology and Innovation Foundation (ITIF), put the U.S. in the 12th spot for global broadband penetration.[2] Regardless, most agree that broadband penetration is a relevant indicator of a country's overall vibrancy.

The results of analyses like the one shown in Figure 20-1 are one reason broadband has been high on President Obama's agenda. In a radio address back in November 2008, then-president-elect Obama said, "It's unacceptable that the U.S. ranks 15th in the world in broadband adoption, according to OECD. Here, in the country that invented the Internet, every child should have the chance to get online. That's how we'll strengthen America's competitiveness in the world."[3] Twenty years ago, no one would have believed that increasing the speed and connection of a populace's access to a network could lift the boat of an entire country. Today, it's helping to drive an agenda of growth, change, and improved living conditions for one of the world's superpowers.

Perhaps even more telling than the actual penetration numbers are the year-over-year broadband growth numbers, which represent the investment in broadband technologies made by each country (as shown in Figure 20-2). Perhaps surprisingly, countries such as the Slovak Republic, Greece, New Zealand, Norway, and Germany topped the list in growth from 2007 to 2008, while the U.S. was 15th, up from the 21st position the year before. Do you notice who's missing? Try some of the large oil-producing nations (Russia, Saudi Arabia, Venezuela) and the manufacturing-focused China. All of Africa is missing from the chart, as is most of the third world. There's plenty of work to do.

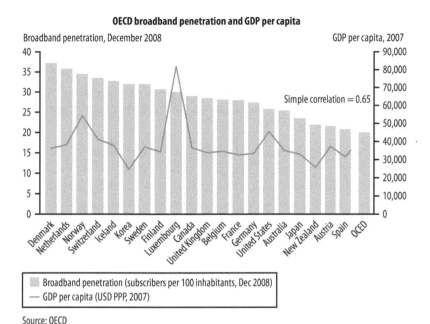

Figure 20-1. *Look carefully at how the Gross Domestic Product (the line) generally compares with the broadband penetration (the bar chart). Source: OECD, December 2008.*[4]

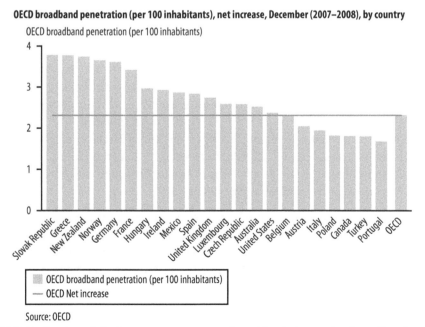

Figure 20-2. *Indicative of the investment a country is making in increasing broadband access. Source: OECD.*[5]

Countries around the world are looking at ways to change their growth trajectories, understanding that greater broadband penetration equates to greater economic opportunity and stability. It's why Australia is planning to build a national broadband network and why President Obama's economic stimulus package is focused on rolling out broadband. Initially, these broadband deployments will create short-term construction jobs, but more important are the long-term opportunities that will improve the overall competitiveness of the workforce.

There are estimates that the projected $10 billion investment by the U.S. government in the rollout of broadband (primarily in rural locations that have historically not had the access) could potentially create up to 500,000 new jobs in 2009.[6] But the more lasting economic stimulus would most likely come from the new businesses and entrepreneurial endeavors that are enabled by access to global marketplaces, as well as the improved efficiencies in business operations that online tools and services can provide.

Free Press, a media reform advocacy group, has been vocal in its support for broadband expansion, tying it directly to the economic potential of future performance. Josh Silver, executive director of Free Press, said the following:

> In our 21st-century society, having a connection to a fast and affordable Internet is no longer a luxury—it's a public necessity. Right now, more than 40 percent of American homes are not connected to broadband. This digital divide isn't just costing us our ranking as global Internet leader—it's costing us jobs and money at a time when both are urgently needed.[7]

If the intent of countries around the world is to ensure that broad sections of their populations can build skills and a knowledge base that allows them to better compete in the global economy, what does it say about those countries that can, but do not, promote broadband adoption? Clearly the goal of the developed world is to push broadband technologies into those countries that don't have access. And the response is encouraging. Take the mission statement of O3b Networks (*http://www.o3bnetworks.com/*), a company aiming to deploy a string of satellites over Africa by the end of the decade: "to make the Internet accessible and affordable to everyone on the planet. We will enrich lives and ensure equal and fair access to information through ubiquitous, high-speed connectivity to the world's content and applications."[8]

Broadband is truly an enabling technology. It opens access to the network, which leads to more applications, services, and innovations, which creates a self-fulfilling growth circle—this is the theory behind the Sustainable Network Law. On the other hand, if broadband access is unavailable, it can limit the usability of the network and in turn reduce its potency as a platform for change.

What happens when broadband access is severed? Recently, those of us living in the Bay Area found out, when someone cut some of the San Jose and San Carlos fiber-optic cables that deliver AT&T and Verizon telephone and Internet service to the region. With just a few snips, people and organizations everywhere felt the effects. The 911 emergency service was impaired (news agencies were used to distribute alternative phone numbers for the public); police and fire departments were unable to coordinate responses to incidents; hospitals and doctors' offices couldn't communicate with patients outside of their facilities; many companies shut down because work could not be conducted without phone and Internet access (IBM sent its employees home); and schools couldn't report attendance and had to revert to manual processes. The news went on and on about the reverberating effects those few snips had on businesses and social services. The county called a state of emergency and the local police notified the FBI, since tampering with telecommunications infrastructure is considered an act of terrorism. Again, all of this turmoil resulted because broadband access went down.

This is why TV commercials talk about broadband as manna from heaven. It's a gift, a boon, an advertising benefit for consumers of AT&T, BT, Sprint, Verizon, T-Mobile, or anyone else. The roster will get larger as broadband availability and capacity escalates, too. As cars, digital photoframes, bicycles, running shoes, and more connect to the network, soon they'll be advertised with the all-powerful descriptor: broadband. It's already a household word. It promises a world of transformation, and providers have caught on, plying it to a broadband-hungry world that cannot get enough.

It's not that there aren't other technologies, devices, protocols, and sciences involved in the sustainable network, it's just that broadband represents the first step to making it all possible. Ultimately, broadband provides the promise of the sustainable network. Its increased availability and capacity is critical to drive the transformational possibilities of the networked world forward. It really is *that* important.

CHAPTER 21

Sustainable Providers

People take different roads seeking fulfillment and happiness. Just because they're not on your road doesn't mean they've gotten lost.

—Dalai Lama

Given that this is a book about the network, I think it's fitting to take a look at the economic sustainability of the network providers—those who are investing and building out the network and driving direct revenues from that network. This industry is going through enormous changes and will most likely look much different in three to five years than it does right now.

In general, transitions are occurring within the network itself, as providers evolve their current infrastructure into next-generation IP networks (NGN) that can support the ever-expansive users, devices, and applications traversing it. And then there are the movements within the providers; there will be restructuring and consolidation, and whole new business models will emerge. Every few months, you'll see deals forged, mergers announced, and new providers taking a foothold.

But before showing you the forces shaping this industry, let's take a stab at categorizing these different providers. It will help with the discussion. There are many ways these organizations can be sliced and diced, and the reality is that these definitions are blurring so much and so quickly that they are almost becoming meaningless. Having made such a disclaimer, there are the traditional telephone companies, such as the AT&Ts, BTs, and NTTs of the world. Then there are wireless/mobile service providers, such as T-Mobile, Sprint, or Verizon Wireless. There are also cable/broadcast television provisioners, like Comcast here in the U.S. Finally, there are the "new" providers that focus on delivering services around content and search, or "in the cloud" offerings. Typical examples of these new providers, which is kind of an oxymoron because there is nothing typical about them, include Google, Yahoo!, eBay, and Amazon.

The pace of innovation is accelerating and changing the service providers' world indefinitely. Those that are able to quickly adapt their business models to meet customers' evolving demands will be able to monetize their networks and grow revenues. And what do those revenues look like? Telecommunications revenue is expected to grow from $2.1 trillion in 2008 to more than $3 trillion by 2013, a signal of the strength and fundamental ongoing growth of the network that supports these businesses.[1] Service providers that are unable to support the rapid roll-out of new services and applications to the market will be left fighting a cost-cutting battle that will be very hard to win. This isn't news to the service providers, by the way—it's well understood.

I mentioned earlier that it wasn't that long ago when we all received individual services from different, individual providers—for example, home phone service from the local telephone company, mobile phone service from a mobile phone provider, etc. At that time, all of the providers built out their networks to deliver a specific service to their customers and prided themselves on their ability to deliver that service well, with no interruption (what they call *high availability* of the network).

Several years ago, that all started to change—not the availability, but the compartmentalization of services. We, as customers, are increasingly relying on the network for both our personal and business lives, and don't want to deal with multiple providers. We started to demand the convenience of picking and choosing the services we wanted from a single source, so the providers raced to offer customers multiple services with the benefits of consolidated payment and simplified customer service.

The subtlety in this consumer shift, however, was much greater than superficial billing integration. We started to question why we couldn't have a single phone number that always went with us and why we couldn't access our TV programs from whichever device we wanted. What we were asking for was truly *converged services*, with the caveat, of course, that we wanted to receive the same quality and performance levels we were used to getting from each individual provider. We would not be satisfied with video that was pixilated, dropped phone calls, an inability to access email, or having to build a new address book for each and every service.

And so, to answer this demand, providers are now racing to offer seamless, personalized access to services from anywhere using any device or mode of connectivity. That is exactly what you demand from your new BlackBerry or iPhone, and why you are paying for that service plan with steep monthly minutes, plus data, plus texting, plus specials.

So, traditional phone companies, wireless providers, Internet service providers, and cable operators are scrambling to build and/or evolve their networks from a single service to one that can support this convergence of services. IP traffic is already increasing 30–60% on providers' networks without adding another single subscriber or service, so the traditional providers are struggling with how to simultaneously invest in the added capacity they need to support current customers, while rolling out new applications they need to attract new customers. (Oh, and as customers, we do not like to pay more for the same services we already have, so the providers have to do all of this for a price we feel is reasonable and sometimes cheaper than the single service we had before.)

Sounds like a dog-eat-dog world, eh? It is: at the end of the day, those who deliver all the services we want now and in the future will win. And that's a good thing, from this book's perspective, because it's driving the buildout of the network and increasing broadband, which gets us back to the Sustainable Network Law: the more broadband that's made available, the more new innovative applications and services are created, in a cycle that is ultimately making the network sustainable.

Sustainable providers? Very much so, as long as they are able to monetize the network, which in turn gives them ongoing incentive to continue to make the investments. But during the short term we are going to see a lot of change. As the service offerings increasingly overlap between different providers, it's going to be hard to tell who's who. You may have already noticed that the services many providers are marketing seem to be almost exactly the same. But there *are* subtle differences. You just have to know where to look.

Let's examine voice services. Take your basic old phone service, which we use to call a "phone" but now call a "landline." Traditional phone providers have spent decades building out dedicated networks to deliver a level of reliability that has been unmatched to date—you can always pick up your landline phone and get a dial tone. Yet, phone service providers are now finding their margins eroding because of competition for voice services as the industry shifts to an all-IP communications fabric, and, of course, because of competition from mobile phone and other providers.

The same voice services on your cell phone are definitely getting better, but it's not unusual to have disruptions. Cell phones are still in their infancy in comparison to traditional phones, and cell providers are in the process of building out their networks to expand their coverage while strengthening it. The mobile industry openly acknowledges some of these issues, with advertising slogans such as "Can you hear me now?", and by making fun of the fact that there are dead zones where coverage is simply nonexistent.

The voice services delivered by Internet providers (Earthlink, for example) are simply another application running over the network. While delivering many cost advantages, as well as integrating voice communications with other online applications, such as email, calendaring, unified messaging, conferencing, etc., it is important to note that you don't have all of the assurances with voice over IP (VoIP) that you are used to having with your traditional phone service. Because it is going over the public Internet, as opposed to the dedicated traditional public switched telephone network (PSTN), it is more susceptible to lag and to security breaches (any of the "baby Bells"). It is also going to provide only "best effort" voice quality, which could degrade if something affects the network connection. Again, these issues are being addressed, but it will take a little time. So, until the service quality of all voice services is equal among all types of providers (which it ultimately will be in the future), customers are picking and choosing their providers today based on the services and applications that are most important to them and the price for such all-in-one inclusion.

As a result of chasing customer demands, providers are moving from triple-play services, which consist of voice, video, and Internet, to *multiplay* offerings, which consist of an ever-broadening range of applications. And here is where the future is being built, ranging from standard video on demand to GPS to buying your groceries with your smartphone account. I need to point out here that a lot of this convergence is possible because of the convergence occurring in the devices themselves. For example, smartphones look more and more like computers, and video game consoles are being used to access the Internet and to play movies, so they are capable of supporting all of the different services and applications that providers are bringing to market.

Heard the Hype on Skype?

VoIP (pronounced as a single word: voip) lets people use the Internet to make phone calls without needing the service offered by traditional telephone lines. VoIP applications send voice data within IP packets that travel over your Internet connection, making it significantly cheaper than traditional phone service. Theoretically, you could make all the calls you want to anyone, anywhere in the world, without paying any more than the flat fee you pay for your Internet access. The main difference is that your Internet service is typically a single line item in your bill, while traditional phone calls are itemized, and you may even pay for each call you make via your landline (typically based on the time and distance of that call).

Skype is an example of a VoIP service. You can download the Skype software to your computer or mobile device (if it is supported by the mobile provider) to make voice calls and even video calls over the Internet. It's available in 28 languages in almost every country around the world. If Skype were a carrier, it would be the second-largest voice provider in the world (behind China Mobile), with 370 million users, 16 billion Skype-to-Skype minutes, and 2.2 billion Skype Out minutes, which allow users to call phones and cell phones for a small, fixed-minute fee.[2]

The dog-eat-dog world has further intensified if you're in the provider business because you're in the middle of network time (see Chapter 26), which relates to the accelerated speed at which you need to be able to identify and then capitalize on the changes all around you, rapidly adjusting your business models again and again, trying to increase the revenue you receive from customers, while attracting new customers and defending the ones you have. How do you do it?

Well, one way is through outsourcing. Some providers are trying to speed the delivery of the applications and services that customers want most by outsourcing all aspects of their businesses, even those that are considered core, such as network planning and design, the actual building of the network, ongoing maintenance, and even the service delivery itself. Outsourcing jumped in 2008, with particular strength in India and EMEA, with all indications that it will continue worldwide. Equipment vendors Ericsson and Nokia Siemens Networks are now the world's largest wireless operators due to the fact they are operating the networks of more than 355 million customers worldwide. Providers such as Orange, Sprint Nextel, and Vodaphone have turned over the management of their infrastructure resources in certain countries so they can cut their operating costs to be competitive in the market.[3]

Providers are also starting to share infrastructure and cooperatively manage network coverage in efforts to reduce and contain costs. It happens a lot in the U.S. between traditional phone companies and mobile providers, who merge their infrastructures to expand their geographical coverage and increase the types of services they are able to offer their customers. We have also seen this among mobile providers: it's not uncommon for providers to share cell sites or towers to increase coverage and overall reliability.

> In essence, one network provider will rent out a portion of its network to another provider, allowing it to expand its reach without needing to invest in the infrastructure to build it out.

Some providers will offer their infrastructures to other providers. In essence, one network provider will rent out a portion of its network to another provider, allowing it to expand its reach without needing to invest in the infrastructure to build it out. The new market term for this is network as a service (NaaS, if you're keeping track of new acronyms!). The owner of the network is able to better monetize its infrastructure, thus increasing its utilization. It becomes the infrastructure specialist, so to speak, typically using virtualization technology to partition capacity and securely allow separate, distinct organizations to leverage a common infrastructure.

And there are providers offering their infrastructures as a service (IaaS) to larger customers or enterprise-sized businesses (while the term "cloud" can encompass so many different types of offerings, it has also been used to describe the IaaS landscape). In these cases, the providers give customers the ability to use their infrastructure, so they don't need to build it out themselves. In addition, they will often offer customers a broad range of services that give them as much or as little direct responsibility and management over that infrastructure as they want. For example, Amazon.com lets software developers purchase processing power on its infrastructure (it also extends the model to its physical logistics and distribution services, allowing other retailers to use them).

Other providers include the service delivery that's on top of the infrastructure as a more complete "cloud" offering. For instance, the U.S. federal government is transitioning the USA.gov and GobiernoUSA.gov portals to a cloud provider that will host the sites for them; they estimate it will cost 80% less[4] than if they had to build and maintain the infrastructure to host the sites themselves. As a result of the opportunities, a diverse set of traditional and new providers is bringing a wide range of cloud offerings to market.

These cloud offerings give customers (typically businesses) the ability to scale operations or leverage technology without needing to invest in the underlying infrastructure. However, it also means relinquishing control, because they are relying on infrastructures that they are "renting" from the providers and don't physically own. As a result, another hybrid exists for those who want to maintain direct control of the network, yet still take advantage of some of the savings potentially associated with the cloud. In these cases, customers build their own private cloud networks and leverage the provider's public cloud offerings for different types of services and applications, depending on the scale or security needed.

Another business model was pioneered by the content providers Yahoo!, MSN, and Google. As they aggregated more and more content on their domains, they attracted the interest of advertisers looking for ways to reach consumers and capitalize on new online channels. They established a direct advertising–based business model as a viable route to the consumer that wasn't dependent on a monthly service plan. We, as customers, can log on from anywhere, and our content will be there waiting.

The network is the crux of all these businesses and business models (see Chapter 21, "Net Neutrality"). They all require a fast, reliable, and secure network infrastructure, with varying levels of policy and control to deliver the flexibility that providers need to quickly roll out new applications and services. There is a direct correlation between the network's ability to scale and adapt, and a provider's ability to seize new service, partner, or market opportunities.

The growth and opportunities created by all these new applications and services require an underlying network that can deliver simplicity and efficiencies at scale. Policy and control are key elements of the network, but have historically been lower on the list of priorities for network architects. This makes sense, given the single-service networks that providers provisioned in the past—it is much easier to predict bandwidth, quality of service (QoS), and overall requirements when delivering a single application or service over the network. Now, as these services (voice, video, data, etc.) converge, providers are finding that they need the visibility into the network traffic and a high degree of control over how that traffic is handled.

This issue has been compounded by the fact that everyone is now a potential publisher (uploader) of content. It used to be that the providers pushed the content to their customers, but with the advent of easy-to-use publishing tools, anyone can be a creator of content. Social networking sites count on this fact to create value for their communities. Grandma may be sharing her video diary with her extended family, or the local high school rock band may be posting its latest performance in hopes of being discovered. The dynamic nature of information flow has a tremendous impact on the communications infrastructure requirements needed to support it. This will be discussed more in Chapter 41, "Our Relationship with the Network."

Providers must now support unpredictable traffic demands with predictable experiences. And remember, this has all taken place over the past 10–15 years. The practice of putting the intelligence at the edge of the network, nearest the consumers, and overprovisioning the core just doesn't work. Who supports the onslaught of media-rich, latency-sensitive services and applications that are being published and consumed from every endpoint? To truly deliver the predictable and satisfying experience customers pay for and demand, providers must have control over the experience they deliver to customers from start to finish (in other terms, from edge to core and vice versa). It is not acceptable to release control and hope for the best as the traffic traverses any part of the network—it needs to be predictable, and the quality (not to mention security) must be maintained end to end.

The sustainable network relies on profitable providers and a vibrant networking industry.

It requires a network that can tie the packet-handling Physical layer of the network to the Applications and Services layers via policy and control (see Figure 31-2 to learn about the seven layers of the OSI model). For example, a residential customer with a triple-play package that includes an HDTV connection, a high-speed Internet connection, and local and long-distance calling, should be able to rely on said service no matter what time of day it is, how many services he is using, or how many other people are on the network. The provider that can deliver this should be able to charge a premium over one that offers variable service quality and drops off somewhere in the middle of the cloud for others to handle.

It's important for providers to integrate the policy and control layer with their operational management and billing systems so they can further monetize the network. The sustainable network relies on profitable providers and a vibrant networking industry. For example, if a gamer plays at home on his high-speed Internet connection and then goes to visit his friend, who doesn't have a high-speed connection, they should be able to quickly (through a portal or some user-friendly interface) ask and pay for higher-performance bandwidth for a specific period of time.

Which providers will be able to effectively optimize their networks to deliver the services that customers most want is still an open question. We are in a huge period of transition. What's clear is that a huge investment is needed to allow the network infrastructure to keep up with and support all the users, devices, and applications that are proliferating around the world. The companies that deliver the services and applications that let us leverage the network to its full advantage may come and go, morph and merge, be acquired or sold off in pieces, but network demand is not going anywhere but up. In the end, we need sustainable providers that can compete for our trust, loyalty, and dollars.

CHAPTER 22

Net Neutrality

It's difficult to make predictions, especially about the future.
—Yogi Berra

One wildcard in the network's sustainability revolves around *net neutrality*. The net neutrality debate has been raging for some time now. On the surface, it is about ensuring that everyone has access to the public Internet. It is the founding principle that all individuals should be able to use the network and be free to access the information and resources they want, without discrimination. There should be no preferential treatment in the handling of the traffic by the network of any person or type of service. So, your access is treated the same as your next-door neighbor's access to Internet services.

Sounds good, sounds right—after all, the network is the great equalizer. It's one of the reasons it is so well suited for sustainable change. However, when you dig deeper, net neutrality is actually about the economics of the network. In simpler terms, the debate revolves around the distribution of revenues generated via online activities. On one side of the debate are those who are paying to build out the network, and on the other side are those who are creating the services and applications that run on that network.

As we have discussed, broadband access is critical to the ongoing adoption of the network. It's required to deliver the high-performance connection that results in a satisfactory user experience and supports all the multimedia-rich services and applications we have come to know and love. But it takes investment to make sure broadband is available to all. In many cases, it necessitates adding capacity and upgrading the underlying network. In other scenarios, it is about extending the reach of the existing network to a greater percentage of the population.

Apart from some targeted government investments, that network infrastructure buildout to date has primarily been taken on by the private sector. Unlike the buildout of the transportation highways, which were funded by governments (or more specifically, taxes raised by governments), the bill to pay for the digital highway buildout is being paid by service providers. These organizations have spent billions of dollars creating many of the networks we use today, including the world's public Internet, with the tacit understanding that they will be reimbursed for that investment by charging for the services delivered via that network, hence your monthly data plan for that iPhone.

Today, however, these providers are struggling with how to monetize their network infrastructures to justify the ongoing investment required to support the increased usage patterns and demands that all the different applications are placing on the network. The reason providers are struggling is that the value chain of much of this content consumption completely bypasses the more traditional network providers. For instance, despite what the music labels would like you to believe, the providers that deliver your Internet access aren't getting anything from the songs you download or the video you stream, yet these providers are expected to support all of the traffic and treat it exactly the same.

The problem is that all of these transmissions are not the same. For example, video and email transmissions have very different impacts on the network. As you may remember, approximately one hour of HD video represents as much traffic as 25,000 email messages.[1] So, as more and more of your neighbors start to watch video online, the demands on the network are going to exponentially increase. For you to continue to use these online services in a satisfactory manner, the underlying infrastructure will need to be there to support it. And this is where net neutrality issues come into play. They can be boiled down to a debate on how money is made on the network and distributed among all the different providers.

Net neutrality is the proposed principle that network access should be free of restrictions—all content, all devices, etc. should be given equal access and all users should be able to expect a reasonable quality level in all their online experiences. The worry is that network providers have potential undue influence over the network and can affect the access of different types of users, content, or services.

Internet service providers, which are regulated by the government, typically collect flat monthly fees from customers for access to the network. The pricing structure may vary based on the type of connection that's available, but there is no real difference in price for the customer who uses the Internet to send a few email messages than for the customer who spends all his time playing *Halo* or *World of Warcraft* (media-rich video games). The difference to the provider, however, is distinct—the more customers who adopt these bandwidth-intensive applications, the more capacity and bandwidth the providers will need to add. The problem is that unless the service providers can identify additional revenue to justify the buildout, there will be no incentive for them to do so.

The service providers that are building the network would like to be compensated for the risks they are taking in investing in the infrastructure. They would like to be able to monetize the network and share in the revenue generated by all the applications and services they are ultimately supporting. They would like to be able to charge customers relative to their use, or at minimum, curb bandwidth hogs to ensure better access for all. The providers would also like to offer premium packages that would allow prioritization and a guaranteed level of service for applications that are more demanding than other best effort Internet uses—say, video versus email. This is one way they could share revenues generated by the content being consumed.

Providers have conducted several experiments on bandwidth management systems, some more successful than others. Comcast Corporation in the U.S. got in trouble for limiting peer-to-peer traffic that was consuming considerable bandwidth. Vodafone Hungary, however, seems to have been able to strike a balance in its efforts to limit excessive bandwidth consumption without cutting users off or seeming to punish them.

The pro–net neutrality advocates argue that any type of prioritization endangers equal, open access. They don't want any alterations or controls inserted into traffic transmission, fearing that any attempt to do so would negate the level playing field that a completely neutral Internet landscape provides. Content providers, such as the Googles of the world, have traditionally fallen into this "pro" camp. This makes sense, because these providers are collecting money directly from consumers for the services and applications they offer or from advertisers for the "eyeballs" they can deliver. They see themselves as the ones generating value for the network in the first place. Without them, there would be no network traffic and the service providers would be out of business. As such, they feel they are generating the revenue the service providers are currently collecting by creating demand for Internet access in the first place.

Net neutrality would ensure that content delivery doesn't degrade due to preferential treatment by network providers for specific applications (particularly, competitive applications). The problem is that if the traditional providers are not part of the content value chain in some way, they will not have the incentive to build out the network, which is critical to its ongoing sustainability (remember Chapter 6). We, as customers, are pretty fickle and if we have a bad experience (slow downloads or disrupted service) with any site, we are likely to go elsewhere. If this happens, it ultimately can affect the advertising premiums these content providers can command, giving the traditional providers an argument for why they are so critical to the success of the content providers. The reality is that some sort of prioritization is needed to protect everyone's connections. There needs to be a way to stop one customer from hogging all the bandwidth and degrading the performance of the network for everyone. There also needs to be a way to deliver consistent, high-performance service to customers—say, for video—that ensures that users have the experience they expect and don't give up on the online delivery. The irony is that once the network is upgraded to broadband connections, capacity will be much greater and the potential for favoritism will diminish, but if this favoritism isn't allowed, the networks most likely won't be upgraded or built. If this happens, the very thing that net neutrality is intended to prevent—zero-sum discrimination—is the very thing that will result.

To resolve the net neutrality debate, which seems to have come to a bit of a standstill, both sides must recognize that they need each other in a symbiotic way. They will need to find a way to work together to share the risks and rewards. Content providers need to make sure their users' experiences are satisfactory in order to get repeat business and continue to generate revenues. Network service providers should get something more for the applications and services that place greater demands on the network. The industry seems to be converging on a much more collaborative or shared model. It's starting to play itself out, even as you read this.

We have already started to see many content providers back down to a certain extent from their previously stoic stance on net neutrality, such as Microsoft, Amazon, and Yahoo!. And we are starting to see relationships blossom between service and content providers to more closely tie the services to the network's delivery capacity to gain greater control over the customer experience. For example, Sprint offers a dedicated, faster download service for Amazon's digital-reading device, the Kindle; Yahoo! has a digital subscriber line partnership with AT&T; YouTube has partnered with Verizon Wireless; and MySpace has signed a content deal with Cingular.

In addition, and perhaps a little ironically, we are also starting to see network service providers offer content, and we are seeing content providers hedge their bets and invest in their own private overlay networks. AT&T recently launched its own online video service, and Comcast has been fairly successful in forging deals that allow it to deliver distinctive content. NBC used the private LimeLight Networks to broadcast the 2008 Olympics, and there is much speculation around Google's network buildout, fueled in large part by its purchase of undersea fiber and the development of its own networking gear. Interestingly, these dedicated networks could end up doing exactly what the network providers are advocating—ensuring a consistent, good experience for users by installing controls that allow for better management of the overall traffic flow.

But as many have pointed out, these relationships and advancements could be wiped out, depending on where regulators come down on net neutrality. Its rules, price controls, and litigation could end up reducing the incentive to invest in building the infrastructure needed to support good user experiences and ultimately reduce the overall sustainability of the network. There must be guidelines to ensure that the innovative, entrepreneurial environment of the Internet is preserved, but deals must be allowed among all the providers to foster the continuation of the network buildout and promote greater value creation for all.

Of course, the basic tenets of net neutrality should be preserved to ensure that everyone is entitled to access to the network and no one is being "priced" out of the competitive landscape or given an unfair advantage. The network needs to be protected to sustain an environment that doesn't become exclusionary or unduly favor one type of service over another.

But an article in the *Wall Street Journal* points out, "Without many tens of billions of dollars worth of new fiber optic networks, thousands of new business plans in communications, medicine, education, security, remote sensing, computing, the military and every mundane task that could soon move to the Internet will be frustrated. All the innovations on the edge will die. Only an explosion of risky network investment and new network technology can accommodate these millions of ideas."[2]

Providers will only build it if they think there is the possibility to make a profit from it, and the world will only benefit from its possibilities if it is built.

CHAPTER 23

Tearing Down Economic Boundaries

Maureen receives a message saying there is money again, together with a pin code.

I am prepared to go anywhere, provided it be forward.
—David Livingstone

n late 1989, one of the last great boundaries between people was torn down—the Berlin Wall. It was a physical barrier that divided East Germany from West Germany, and its fall epitomized the end of an era (the Cold War). The news was carried on TV and radio and in the newspapers of the day. The Internet existed, but was not in the great public spotlight and hardly played a role. Fast forward to today. The Internet has been tearing down one boundary after another, without fanfare and without much conscious acknowledgment. It's been a quiet, systematic march as the network fans out and delivers information and opportunity freely into the hands of more and more people.

One dramatic barricade that has been lowered is the barrier of entry into the marketplace, as the network daily brings people who might have previously been shut out into the economic fold. We have seen everything rush onto the network in the past decade. Business-to-business transactions, global financial markets, the banking industry, the housing industry, and just about every other way to make or spend money can now be conducted online. The network is a tool that almost every individual, business, and government can use to change their economic models and sustain economic growth potential.

Skeptical? On my last vacation, I met a mule rancher, who, in my mind, confirmed without a doubt that this global transformation is real. Her family used to rely on cultivating personal relationships with customers in their home state of Idaho and neighboring states. Basically, their customer base was limited to anyone they could go and talk to about their first-class mules. Five years ago, when the kids joined the family business, they started a "new-fangled" website—nothing fancy, just a few photos and their contact information—to raise their profile and try to expand the reach of their ranch. Not too long after launching the site, they started to get calls from interested buyers in places as far away as Argentina and Spain. It turns out, good mules (which are the offspring of a donkey and a horse and are sterile, so they can't reproduce), are hard to come by throughout the world. Since starting the website, the business has tripled in size and it sells the majority of its mules to customers outside of the U.S. While admitting the logistics of delivering these mules worldwide has been "interesting" to navigate, the success has been both a surprise and a relief. The family is no longer tied to the whims or needs of a single customer or location, giving them much more peace of mind—and an opportunity to go on vacation and meet the likes of me, who never knew a thing about mules! And if stubborn mules can go international, I really don't see too many boundaries that can't be overcome.

The fact is, most large and many small (even family-run) businesses are multinational. They may be based in one country and have offices, employees, and partners around the globe. They likely source materials from multiple countries, manufacture in other countries, and sell to multinational customers located all over the world, starting the cycle all over again. These relationships, which billions of people are creating every day, are ultimately tying the economies of nations together, expanding the web of dependencies, regardless of any treaties or nationalistic policies that might or might not exist.

The Dark Side

The flipside to the possibilities opened up by the network is the detrimental impact that "no" network can have on economic prosperity. If network performance goes down or degrades, the effectiveness of the technology to sustain growth, development, and change significantly diminishes or vanishes entirely. This is why, when Bear Stearns collapsed in 2008, U.S. national intelligence agencies rushed in to study the effect it could have on freezing the entire market.[1] These agencies left the purely economic repercussions to the economists and focused on how the failure of one financial system and the potential "contamination" of accounting systems and overall confidence affected others. They looked at it as a potential page out of a cyberwarfare playbook to determine how best to protect against future "artificial" takedowns of critical financial institutions. While the markets froze on their own accord, it made real the worries that an attack on the networked financial systems or other significant business sectors could have on the greater economic sustainability.

For example, the network is reaching into the developing world through microfinance sites, such as MicroPlace and Kiva, to allow entrepreneurs to raise modest amounts of money to fund their business aspirations. The wall that divides poor third-world entrepreneurs from their western cousins would make the Berlin Wall look like a country fence. Tearing down this boundary did not take bulldozers and heavy cranes, but access to the worldwide network. For these people, boundaries no longer exist, and help in the form of money or manpower can come from anywhere. It's a symbol of what the network is doing elsewhere, or rather everywhere, as it levels the playing field completely flat.

Founded in 2005, Kiva lets people provide loans to those who need them (approximately 1 loan every 24 seconds,[2] generally in $25 increments) around the world. Just four years after funding its first loan in 2005, approximately 97,000 loans had been funded, totaling approximately $66 million, reaching borrowers in close to 50 different countries.[3] The Kiva website "lets you lend to a specific entrepreneur in the developing world—empowering them to lift themselves out of poverty,"[4] helping potential lenders determine who they want to help via borrower profiles. In mid-2009, Kiva extended its potential borrowers to include entrepreneurs in the U.S., picking up where traditional financing has fallen short, particularly during economic hard times. While not a new concept (microloans of this type were pioneered by Muhammad Yunus in 1976 with Grameen Bank), the network has made it easier than ever to connect people who have ideas to the money they need to make those ideas a reality.

As you can tell, I like Kiva as a networking success story, mainly because it has all the elements of a truly sustainable product of the network. The loans have helped entrepreneurs around the world go after their dreams. It is not a charity—Kiva is serious about creating business opportunities that have longstanding value, and it has proven itself to be a self-sustaining and -perpetuating model (just like the network) by the rate of repayment. Kiva's chief executive, Premal Shah, said, "Ninety-seven percent of our active loans are [paid] on time, and our default rate is less than 1%."[5] Once repaid, this money can be loaned again to another entrepreneur looking to finance an idea, making it a completely sustainable cycle. Kiva is a perfect example of how the network is tearing down traditional barriers of time, location, access, and money.

Sustainable Network Law: the more broadband that is made available to network users, the faster innovation occurs.

The network is leveling the playing field in other ways, too. Whether you dabble in the financial markets at home, sponsor political meetings using web conferencing, or merely email your opinion to an online newspaper an ocean or two away, you are equal to the greatest stock traders, politicians, or op-ed writers in terms of your access. And that access spawns opportunity, which leads to innovation. Remember the Sustainable Network Law: the more broadband that is made available to network users, the faster innovation occurs—all of which ultimately fuels the next generation of networking tools and applications that can take advantage of that broadband reach. So, let's drill into the innovation aspect for just a paragraph or two.

Instead of closely controlling the innovation process, the network allows innovations to come from anywhere and feed into the process, in essence distributing innovation among different individuals, entities, and geographies. A team in corporate headquarters in Munich can tap into the combined talents of a freelancer in New Jersey, a consulting firm in Bangalore, and a business partner in Singapore. These connections are changing the scope and relationships of constituents both inside and outside of the business, involving specialists, customers, partners, suppliers, and sometimes even competitors in the creative process as they innovate to create new products or incorporate refinements into next-generation offerings.

It's about extracting value versus having to create the value and control its development. This distributive model can help organizations overcome innovation barriers and bottlenecks and accelerate time to market. It can also help control costs by streamlining development, manufacturing, and distribution processes, giving companies that are able to leverage technology a potential advantage in the marketplace. It's one reason we are seeing more and more companies extending the collaborative process to their target customer bases to co-create solutions. This process allows customers to jointly develop products or services and weigh in on everything from functionality to packaging and marketing. Proctor and Gamble has a Connect + Develop program, which uses an online portal to collect customer ideas for "a game-changing product, technology, business model, method, trademark, package or design."[6]

Open, standards-based technologies further accelerate and enable greater innovation. They allow anyone with an idea to build extensions on the base technology, whether it is an application for a cell phone or the network itself. You have probably heard of the open application stores for cell phones. For example, in nine months, application developers outside of Apple had built 35,000 applications for the Apple iPhone, ranging from camera zoom functionality to a game called *StickWars* (it was the top downloaded application when I checked in April 2009—hey, I never said that everything is designed to be profound or enable the best in humanity!). Under normal circumstances, there is no way an organization would have the manpower to think up, develop, and bring to market 35,000 applications in a nine-month period. But with an open platform, innovations can come from anywhere, allowing individuals and businesses to create the applications and services they need to best serve their unique requirements.

Open source collaboration is often much more cost-effective than going out to find and hire the talent and intellect to work on an idea or problem. Open platforms that allow for collective problem solving can often accelerate advances and innovation that would be very hard to replicate if the burden were placed entirely on a single individual or organization's resources. For instance, it's not uncommon for someone to pose a question or idea in a chat room or specific developer or technical forum and receive a lot of valuable information that helps him find an answer or progress his understanding and thinking. Entire groups of people can also collaborate to develop a solution. Typically, some sort of prize or compensation is included as an incentive for those who significantly contribute or come up with the best solution. For example, the organization Innocentive provides companies with a community of more than 100,000 scientists ready to tackle problems, for which they are rewarded monetarily. Offering compensation helps organizations manage the timelines of these projects that do not offer contractual or clear obligations on behalf of those doing the work. We may find that these types of collaborations have implications on compensation models in the future (moving from paying for time spent on a project to paying for ideas, execution, and results).

How important is it to leverage new collaboration and innovation models? The analyst firm Gartner Group predicts that by 2015, companies will not be able "to build or sustain a competitive advantage unless it capitalizes on the combined power of individualized behaviors, social dynamics and collaboration."[7] McKinsey estimates that "in the US economy alone roughly 12 percent of all labor activity could be transformed by more distributed and networked forms of innovation."[8]

The network is also making it easier for people to take their ideas and translate them into viable successes. It is important to point out that ideas can encompass an expanded range of business ventures. As the digital information age has taken hold, it has borne a whole range of new Internet-based business models (including dot-coms); some are designed to serve the online world by improving a user's experience or enabling someone to garner greater value from connected information and resources; others are designed to create additional revenue streams or cost reductions for traditional offline businesses.

But the fact remains that the network is lowering barriers to entry and is allowing anyone to test and launch an idea with relatively little upfront capital investment. Traditional wisdom was that an entrepreneur who wanted to build a company would need a good idea and around $5 million to finance it. These investments would usually be made by institutional bankers or venture capital funds to get the business up and running. At minimum, it could take $1 million to get a product out the door.[9] Now, we are not talking about opening up a local store, restaurant, or service business—these are young companies with Fortune 500 aspirations; they want to be the next General Electric, Boeing, or Microsoft. With investments in the millions of dollars, the early returns need to be significant. This puts a lot of added pressure on the young business and its entrepreneurs (who are probably already not sleeping much!).

Internet-based companies require a lot of sweat equity to get off the ground and less hard cash. Therefore, returns can be more moderate to deliver success. There are hundreds of examples of companies creating online services or products that take only hundreds or thousands of dollars in financing to get off the ground. In general, the upfront capital goes toward business permits, website domains, computer or technical assets, and subsidizing the operating costs of the entrepreneurs, who are often working out of their homes or a shared workspace. In addition, if a product or service is digital, such as an online application, there are, for all intents and purposes, no manufacturing or distribution costs, making it significantly cheaper to bring the product to market. The network is the distribution channel, already in place and ready to support the next big thing.

For those who are developing physical products, the network can help reduce research and development costs, achieve operational efficiencies, and economize sales and marketing dollars. For example, through the Internet, business owners can find the talent and resources needed to get their ventures up and going. They can beta-test their ideas to validate them and reduce risk. They can conduct market research cost-effectively and find the best entry points for their products and services. They can reduce promotional costs, allowing customers to promote their products for them, leveraging viral marketing tactics that take advantage of word-of-mouth promotion.

To start a business 20 years ago, you needed a phone, a lawyer, a banker, an office, and lots of people. Today, you need a connection to the network and a computer. With that, you can incorporate yourself, search and apply for trademarks, get a domain name, start a new bank account, apply for payroll service, and do it all by the third or fourth coffee at a Wi-Fi-enabled café.

Faster to Fail

Time is a barrier to most new companies, but the Internet has also made it easier and less time-consuming for Internet-based companies to fail. This sounded strange to me when I first heard it mentioned as a benefit, but makes a lot of sense in the context of the upfront investments that need to be made for any new venture. In the past, when an entrepreneur started a traditional business, the time and financial wherewithal that she needed to commit and secure was often significant, in large part because of the production, manufacturing, and distribution that needed to be set up. Once a product was introduced and in the hands of the consumers, there was another period of time before feedback and true customer acceptance and/or relevance could be determined. Through this process, it could be years before the entrepreneur knew whether or not the product and company had a real chance of being successful.

With an online business, the cycles are significantly shortened and the investment significantly smaller. This makes it easier for online entrepreneurs to try something, quickly determine its potential for success, and then either go forward or cut their losses. This represents a significant benefit to the entrepreneur. The beauty of the Internet is that it has reduced the cost of entry and provides many different routes to market, many different business models, and many opportunities to take a risk—the perfect environment for innovative entrepreneurs to thrive.

Ventures that leverage the Internet require significantly fewer upfront investments, leaving more funds for what entrepreneurs do best—create. Y Combinator, a venture fund that specializes in supporting early-stage startups, provides many examples of how the network is changing the market entry landscape. Y Combinator mass produces startups, funding them in groups of up to 20 founders, twice a year. After an intensive screening process, the chosen founders are encouraged to move to Y Combinator's locations for three months, where they are given seed funding, often starting at around $5,000 (rarely more than $20,000), to try to get their ideas off the ground. Ten weeks into the program, they host a presentation day for potential investors and interested companies to hear and vet the ideas, products, or services. Since inception, Y Combinator has worked with more than 100 companies, many of which have gone on to be profitable or acquired by other companies. In its last batch of 20 companies, 4 were profitable on the demo day—that's quite amazing within a 10-week period, and yet quite familiar in the Internet landscape (just remember Kiva and its microloans).

Y Combinator, Kiva, and many other incubators for businesses and startups are actually modeled after the network itself. They remove barriers and allow funds, ideas, and access to flow into the newly leveled ground. The network is nothing other than a big Kiva for all of us. It connects buyers and sellers, writers and readers, borrowers and lenders, and allows us all to prosper by participating. The beauty of the network is that it has reduced the cost of entry to allow anyone and everyone to participate.

In one manner, the network is creating a global marketplace in ways we don't fully understand, mostly because we can't get far enough back to see the forest beyond the most visible, immediate trees. We know it is enabling a new economy by increasing the number of people who are able to join and participate in it. We know it is not only creating new market entry points, but also completely new markets. We know new online business models are emerging as traditional business models are evolving or simply being left behind. We know the network is helping drive efficiencies and is creating new products and service extensions. We know the talent pool is losing geographic restrictions, with individuals contributing, developing their skill sets, and finding their personal nodes in a new global economy. We know all this because we are in the middle of it, living it, watching the formation of all these new connections and relationships, but we don't fully understand it yet.

From market entry and expansion to workforce recruitment and development to competitive and productivity gains, the network simply reaches out and creates opportunity on a scale previously unknown and, in turn, influences the lives and livelihoods of all of us on this earth. The goal is to recognize and foster the opportunities so we can set our sights on the new horizons in a sustainable way. Oh, and if you want to buy a piece of the Berlin Wall, they're still available on eBay.

CHAPTER 24

Information Is King

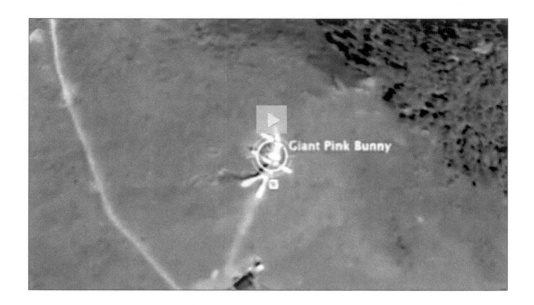

I am building a fire, and every day I train I add more fuel. At just the right moment, I light the match.

—Mia Hamm, women's soccer champion

In this digitized information age, every project, every product, and every service is an information-based business opportunity. Those with better information will be better prepared to compete. Those able to effectively leverage information will be able to create differentiated value. Those able to correlate and analyze the ever-increasing amount of digitized data will be able to improve their strategic decision making. Those able to manage the extremely rich dataset now available will reduce business volatility by improving their forecasting abilities and identifying predictive trends, and then acting quickly upon them.

Today, information can be both incredibly useful and overwhelming. Too much information (or as someone might text: TMI) can overload and fragment an unprepared operation. How do you weed out the noise? Where do you find the most pertinent information? How do you make sure information is serving to add, not be a detriment to, overall productivity? The term *data mining* comes to mind as the refined process of seeking patterns in mounds of information, but I like it more because of the image it brings to mind of men blackened by coal dust with helpful lamps attached to their safety helmets. Individuals and organizations that can mine the information and harness it to develop useful insights into opportunities and challenges will be better positioned to take advantage of all the Digital Information Age has to offer.

The network has brought a new level of transparency to almost every conceivable transaction because of the enormity of available digital data. For example, the ease with which customers can comparison shop means that organizations need to either compete on price or articulate and defend the value of their products and services. All within a few clicks of each other.

The same transparency exists in nonbusiness information—say, in government services, where any neighbor can now see and read your building permit without a trip to city hall. You can find out whether your neighbors contributed to a political party and how much they gave. Schools post tests, committees post their meeting minutes, and if you're a fan of Facebook or other social networking sites, you know that everyone posts everything. If information is king, transparency is the queen.

In the new networked world, where literally billions have access to the information you make transparent, extensive data collection and data analysis can be used to create customer profiles, correlating like inclinations and pain points that can open up new avenues for targeted communications and greater segmentation. A familiar example can be found at Amazon.com. It uses the data it collects to create profiles that are used to upsell more items to the customer. For example, when you buy a book, Amazon's automated profiles suggest additional books or movies purchased by other people who bought the same item you just chose. Buy a computer online, and you'll have to click your way through every possible accessory made before submitting your final approval.

It's the same as the paper fliers in your credit card statements, promoting products or services that are similar to those you bought during the billing cycle, except that the online ones use data stored on servers and programs that can compute and display within milliseconds.

But this book's question is, in this Digital Information Age, how is information exposed appropriately and used for greater benefit? It shouldn't be all about using the data to upsell more stuff, as we are seeing many do. There's an opportunity to use the information to do things differently—for example, mining all of the information that can be collected from all the networked interactions that take place during the course of a day to try to streamline processes and improve productivity. It's one reason that Project and Portfolio Management (PPM) tools are increasing in use. They attempt to bring order to decision making and provide collaboration, reporting, and governance tools that help organizations combine workgroups and workflows in a systematic way.[1]

If information is king, transparency is the queen.

One PPM tactic is to correlate the activities of a company's top-performing employees and map their activities to the rest of the employee base in an effort to identify and replicate best behaviors and practices. For instance, the information an organization gathers may indicate that workers tend to favor one communication mechanism over another (say, IM over email) or interacting on a regular basis (once a week) with 20 people versus 10, or subscribing to certain news feeds, or working more consistently on projects as an individual contributor or as a member of a collective group. By mining this information of online usage and communication habits, organizations can potentially identify patterns that foster a more productive work environment or create more meaningful work habits and organizational work streams or training opportunities. For example, data could reveal that all the employees avoid a particular logon system or fumble with the travel expense website or don't know how to reach the helpdesk. Once the pattern comes up, it can be addressed, and the organization can develop a solution, such as an online training session, a different navigation path, or embedded frequently asked questions and answer sections. Of course, on the flipside, there's the potential to identify employees who are spending all their time surfing the Web. While most of us in the ranks know who they are, they seem to be infuriatingly elusive to management!

Which brings us, probably not surprisingly, to the issue of privacy. Consumer advocates question the use of profiling on the Internet. They argue that it is an unnecessary invasion into the personal details of consumers. Recognizing that an abundance of information on an individual consumer could be very valuable, they are concerned it could be abused, or worse, compromised, and place the consumer's identity at risk. They make very good points that definitely need to be addressed, and we are seeing these questions start to bubble up worldwide. For instance, the European Union started legal action in 2009 to enforce data privacy rules that restrict the monitoring of Internet users for potential advertising purposes.[2]

> There used to be free time and work time, and now it's all jumbled together into free-to-work time.

But allow me to take the discussion in another direction. While IT departments would most likely argue that anything that takes place on a business-issued device belongs to the business, the reality is much different—much more, well, blurred. We make business calls on our mobile phones when we're at home and we routinely check email on our vacations; likewise, we take family calls during work and read personal email messages. As a full-time, working mother of two (who is writing a book in her spare time), I often see just the blur. I continue to answer email messages while at weekend barbecues and place party-supply orders from my office desk. And I don't think I am alone. There used to be free time and work time, and now it's all jumbled together (by the network, by the way) into free-to-work time.

And this is one of the beauties and simultaneous challenges of the Digital Information Age; it creates communication fluidity that allows people to take advantage of thoughts when they have them, wherever they have them, and to connect people to the resources they need whenever they need them. It is one of the reasons the network is such a great vehicle for innovation and holds the promise of producing breakthroughs and efficiencies wherever it goes. But it's also creating a whole new subset of problems that never existed before when you could walk out the door and leave work or home behind.

Many people are opting for the ties and actually prefer them because they allow work, play, family, and life to mingle in a much more realistic way. But when you mix privacy with free-to-work anytime, blend it with the adept mining of digitized information, and add to it our cultural need for the overall sustainability of the network (in our business and personal lives), it equals a need to set new boundaries around what's acceptable and what's not. Whether those boundaries are set by explicit agreements in business or by common courtesy in personal settings (use of cell phones in restaurants, for example), we are going to need to tackle what is and is not included in the realm of what's acceptable and what's completely off limits.

For instance, should someone's business career be affected by something posted on personal communications channels? What impact or relevance should photos on Facebook of your colleague dancing on the table at a club, or an account of the weekend's debauchery on a personal blog, have on career paths and options? The reality is that the same network is being used to stabilize a career as well as find a soul mate, so where do we draw the lines? If someone tracks your online usage and makes it public, has your privacy been invaded or just made public? What is all the information on the network then—public, private, secretive, or "ours, but don't tell"?

I have a colleague in sales who felt he couldn't ignore folks who wanted to connect to him from work on his social networking Facebook page (since sales is all about making connections), but he didn't really want to share photos of his family with people outside his intimate circle of friends. Now he's stuck with a mix of work and nonwork friends privy to his personal pages, so he doesn't post anything, which in turn gets both groups prodding him for updates. I think this is a perfect representation, albeit a small one, of the new types of issues that arise when information is king and transparency is queen.

New generations find value in sharing every bit of information about their lives, including their exact location every moment of the day, and sometimes that doesn't sit well with their elders, who don't understand why anyone would do that. Your financial history and credit ratings and medical history and family tree and high school antics and driving record and what you purchased last week are all available to the adept data miner. How can we make sure we use all of this information appropriately?

There are a lot of interesting questions around work ethics and our identities that will need to be answered. If the bosses expect me not to order party supplies while I'm at work, they should also not expect me to answer work email messages while I'm at home. Is it possible to maintain multiple levels of public and private, work and nonwork identities? Is splintering our identities reasonable, sustainable? Or is it creating a schizophrenic society?

It will take some time to work through this as more information becomes available, all of it transparent. I know it will require innovation and likely the next generation of our current social networking applications before we arrive at answers that are acceptable to all. When you think about it, we've never been able to truly harness information before in the way we can now; we could only generate it. So, to sustain it and really benefit from its powerful possibilities, we will need to balance its availability and protection.

CHAPTER 25

Evolution

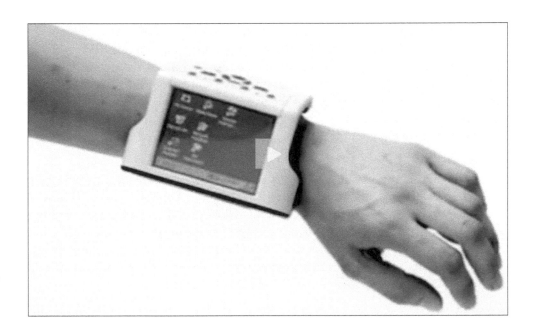

Failure is not fatal, but failure to change might be.
—John Wooden, basketball coaching legend,
University of California, Los Angeles

The network and all the applications and services it delivers are evolving business models, sometimes so rapidly that it's hard to predict where things will be in, say, 2015, let alone 2030. That's not the way investors like to fund startups. You're supposed to find your niche, acquire a few major customers (or a percentage of the public's awareness), and hammer away at the competition. But the underlying foundation that connects us all is changing, improving, molting, and moving (literally, given our newfound mobility). How can your business model keep up? How do you, as a consumer, keep up with a business whose model is constantly moving?

Remember the dot-com 1990s? Back then, anyone with a domain and the wherewithal to build innovative websites made millions in the temporary bubble. While the bubble inevitably broke, websites and Internet businesses continued to appear. For example, take any noun and put a ".com" after it, and there will be a business there (I just opened my browser and went to the sites of tennisshoe.com, faucet.com, and blouse.com). We now have aggregator sites and services that let you look do comparison shopping for all these nouns, providing all their prices, selections, services, and ratings. Then there are the aggregators of aggregator sites (Google or Bing).

So, if you started business in 1999 as tissue.com, you now provide a tissue application for iPhone, a blog on how to avoid the Swine Flu, and YouTube videos on how to correctly blow your nose. You also offer home delivery, and you sell every type of tissue conceivable, including electrostatically charged tissues to wipe the dust off a hundred device monitors. Why do this, you say? Why stay in business as tissue.com? Why put up with the shifting sands? The simple answer is that there's a 10-year history of opportunity and a new market potential the size of nothing you've ever seen.

Over the past decade or so, the network has lowered the barriers to entry in new markets and let businesses increase not only their reach, but also the depth of their customer relationships. New applications and new services created on the backbone of the network let businesses foster new relationships that are essential to growth and overall productivity, all the while taking costs out of traditional business operations to free resources and support further innovation. It's been the perfect storm for online business, and it is still in its infancy.

As I have already pointed out, the number of Internet users in developing countries is climbing at a rate that has or will soon outpace the number of users in the developed world (I have also tried to point out that every business is now a global entity, whether it wants to be or not). Innovative organizations that can develop services and applications tailored to meet the unique needs of customers in different regions can effectively tap into those emerging markets. Your tissue line may have to evolve again, but to double, triple, quadruple your customer base, how can you not?

In fact, online sales represents one of the few areas of growth for retail, particularly in today's challenging economic environments. According to figures released by the British Retail Consortium last December, in the midst of the recession, in-store sales fell by 1.4%, while online sales in the UK were up by 30%. Online sales grew 130% in China in 2008, according to iResearch, and amounted to about $19 billion. In the U.S., retailers racked up $141 billion in sales, according to Forrester Research, but that still represents only a fraction of the retail market. Overall, the online penetration of U.S. retailers is only at around 6%. Some online categories have a higher penetration, such as computer products at 45%; music, video, and books at 24%; and gift cards/certificates at 21%, but you could hardly say those markets are saturated and have peaked. When you look at markets such as sporting goods and apparel, with an 8% penetration, and the food, beverage, and grocery markets, with a 1% penetration, it's fair to say the opportunities are vast.[1]

Interestingly, basic trend lines show that whenever broadband access expands, retailers see a rise in online shopping. It's why virtually every brick-and-mortar retailer has an online presence. How could they not? Email blasts costs pennies per thousands and the email addresses are from known visitors. Customers can see different colors, styles, models, and makes with a click of the mouse, and businesses don't have to stock it all in every single location. And businesses can track and analyze their Internet visitors to customize their offerings to better cater to their shoppers. There is also evidence that an integrated online and offline presence can really help solidify the brand in consumers' minds. In Britain, Thinkbox conducted a study for the Internet Advertising Bureau and found that combining online advertising with TV campaigns resulted in 47% more brand "positivity" than either of those mediums in isolation.[2]

The network helps businesses foster new relationships that are essential to growth and overall productivity, all the while taking costs out of traditional business operations to free resources and support further innovation.

This is why everyone, from Levi's to Ford, is increasingly driving traffic to their online presence. Through traditional promotions (such as in-store, catalog, or media advertising), they build a compelling case for consumers to buy directly through their websites, presumably by offering savings garnered from the operational efficiencies they've achieved through networked business processes. But the most interesting point comes full circle back to the effect that broadband has on overall opportunity—when it extends, online activities and overall possibilities rise. This is definitely the case for both big and small entrepreneurs, who are able to reach out, connect to customers, and participate on a global scale like never before.

And here I want to pause for a second and look a little more at the case of the small entrepreneur, and more specifically the small online business, because it epitomizes what's happening in the entire network and our use of it. The success of small online businesses has traditionally been tempered by consumer preference for dealing with "known" entities. We, as customers, are wary (rightly so) of handing over financial information to unfamiliar organizations. But this is where the network steps in and turns hurdles into opportunities. Every time some threshold or hole appears, as here, when people's fears stop them from dealing with a company, something happens. This "something" is that someone comes up with a solution that overcomes this hurdle—in network time—and fixes or innovates right past it. It happens in every aspect of the network and in every chapter of this book, which is why I want to point it out—because it's evolution you can see. The network evolves and we, the people, follow right after it. It's one of the signs that the network is indeed sustainable, almost self-sustaining, as it finds a way to innovate and evolve using the resources of an entire globe to move forward.

> Every time some threshold or hole appears, there always seems to be someone ready to fill it.

So, what happens to small businesses that we don't know about or might distrust because they are not the big-box brands? Companies such as PayPal and Boku have evolved out of the natural business startup cycle to provide online payment services that let individuals pay anyone (another user, merchant, or unknown Internet website, etc.) in the way they prefer (via credit card, from their bank accounts, etc.), without needing to share any financial information with the receiver of that payment. So, online payment services remove one of the biggest hurdles for customers who would like to use online merchants but are hesitant to make the switch because they don't want to share financial data with unknown vendors. These third-party payment companies remove the uncertainty and provide some consumer protection, such as preserving privacy, that emulate the offline world. The "where there's a need, there's a way" network evolution has spawned online payment services and online shopping cart security testers, like McAfee Secure or VeriSign, which verify legitimate sites and give their seals of approval for nervous online shoppers.

And while everyone can use the network to create a global business, issues surrounding language, currency, and regulation can pose challenges to small companies operating on a truly global scale. Large business may have all the requisite lawyers, accountants, and expertise to handle these kinds of transactions, but for the small entrepreneur trying to sell a particular widget, it can make the proposition difficult, if not close to impossible, to navigate. So, you guessed it, the same evolution that we saw with payment services is happening, and new services that provide global logistic support (offered by a range of companies from UPS to American Express to IBM) have stepped in to fill the gap and move the network forward.

Businesses can also consider being a part of an existing retail platform service, such as those provided by Amazon or eBay, which offer the framework to serve consumers and conduct transactions beyond the boundaries of an individual business's geographical location. Or you can go back to PayPal, which offers its services in 190 markets and 17 currencies, meaning businesses can be conducted with customers around the world, with PayPal as the middleman, securing payment and exchanging currencies for both buyer and seller. This simply was not available 20 years ago. And these services do their part to help flatten the playing field, giving individual entrepreneurs a ticket to enter the global market. In PayPal's own words, it "enable[s] global ecommerce by making payments possible across different locations, currencies and languages."[3] And the service is definitely catching on—as of November 2008, PayPal had more than 164 million accounts worldwide. Not bad for a decade's worth of work.[4] In the third quarter calendar earnings of 2008, PayPal achieved $15 billion in total payment volume, representing year-over-year growth of 28% (that includes payments for eBay and non-eBay transactions). This might be interesting if you're a stockholder, but the real reason I bring it up is that it represents the sustainable network in action—thousands upon thousands of individual entrepreneurs and Internet transactions around the globe are making PayPal a success.

And it's not just about the individuals or small businesses. Most businesses, regardless of their size, want to expand and grow. The extensive reach of the Internet provides levels of scale that would previously have been unattainable, if not unthinkable. Today, businesses can expand faster than Starbucks can set up another coffee shop. They are not bound by traditional brick-and-mortar growth in the form of physical store locations and all the associated expenses (real estate, utilities, personalized sales staff, and training), and they can reach a larger audience, because, oddly enough, millions of people are searching for all these businesses. They are looking for the thing that will help them solve their problems or fill a need. Without adding a few hundred pages to this book, this is the reason behind the phenomena that are Yahoo!, Google, Bing, Cuil, and many more search sites that keep track of businesses as they expand their sites, products, content, and offerings.

To understand in more tangible terms what I'm talking about, let's look at the transformation taking place in the financial industry. This industry is increasingly using the network to create new service models, expanding its reach as it goes and driving costs out of its traditional offerings. Most banks have scaled back branch operations, favoring kiosks or smaller teller operations in locations of convenience for the customer, such as in grocery stores or shopping malls. The goal is to try to conduct as much of the simple transactional activity as possible without costly human intervention, while reserving the in-person interactions for the most complicated of transactions or for those situations and individuals that require handholding. It's interesting to look at how the financial industry evolved its business models to truly take advantage of online efficiencies, because it again shows the self-sustaining model of the network and how it evolves as needs and usage change.

The Internet was first seen as a tool for generating business leads. It was used to attract consumers to physically come to a bank or a brand or a company to do business. Then the Internet evolved by delivering efficiencies for businesses, by taking costs out of ongoing operations, enabling automation and reducing physical footprints and associated expenses by substituting them with online materials, forms, and communication tools. Now, there are innovative companies, such as ING, Inc. (founded as an online bank), offering many of the same services as traditional banks, but taking advantage of their different cost structures to offer lower fees and attract a wider range of customers. And the business tactics are paying off. In a Nielsen study, 29 million people used the Internet to make major financial investments and 16 million of those reported that the network played a crucial role in their financial decisions.[5]

And the line continues to blur between online banking and the place you used to go to wait in line to cash a check. The banking business model is changing in front of our eyes:

- People are increasingly swapping their traditional cheques and paper statements for online banking services and records. Online bill payment is so standard it can seem odd to write the occasional cheque. (Someday soon, these papers will be relics, going the way of the typewriter, so allow me my quaint British spelling a little longer.)

- Anytime, anywhere access to accounts helps people track their money and investments. You can transfer funds from one account to another using your mobile smartphone, even when you are in Amsterdam and your bank branch is in Arlington. Or, you can pay for stuff with your mobile phone using Boku or similar pay-by-mobile transaction companies.

- Online services allow financial institutions to reach and serve more people. This is particularly important in many developing countries, where access to the bank has been a barrier to individuals participating in the economy. Online access can eliminate the time and place restraints—sometimes the bank is physically too far away for regular visits. Online access also allows for changes in the bank's fee structure, which historically had to be higher to cover the operating expenses.

- Online trading has broadened the number of investors participating in the global stock markets. Buying and selling stocks and investing in bonds and funds are no longer reserved for the elite. From E*Trade to Charles Schwab, you can dabble in or make a living out of day trading. You can research account options, companies, markets, past investment histories, etc. Everything is readily available online, empowering you to make informed decisions on your banking and investment choices, without having to sit across a desk and rely on a salesperson.

- The cost to enter and invest in the world's markets is now just a flat monthly fee, paid to the brokerage house where you open and maintain an account. This simple evolutionary feature has allowed millions of people to participate in global markets and take more active roles in their financial investments (one of the many reasons why market fluctuations in one part of the world are felt globally).

- Mortgages brokers are also getting in on the action, prequalifying and preapproving customers for loans online, and letting customers complete entire transactions virtually. When the electronic/digital signature is recognized by the mortgage regulatory boards and the process becomes paperless, it will be a truly sustainable way to get a mortgage, saving a lot of operational, travel, and paper costs.

So, through network evolution, are we replacing traditional business models with ones that are better equipped to grow and drive unnecessary costs out of the business? It would appear so, if only because businesses that are able to effectively use the network to create and capitalize on opportunities are delivering value that is rendering businesses that are too slow to adapt unable to compete.

While it may be obvious, it should be explicitly stated that the network helps take costs out of operating models because of the shift from the physical to the digital (virtual storefronts are a lot less costly than physical ones). For example, this is the intent behind RiseSmart, an online company that works with organizations to help employees who are being laid off find new positions. Its value proposition? It leverages technology, underpinned by the network, to reduce the fees traditionally associated with outplacement companies. RiseSmart uses the network to do the upfront grunt work, such as searching relevant job postings that match a potential employee's needs, and reserves the high-cost, human touch for further refinement behind the scenes or in interactive online question-and-answer sessions with their clients. I am sure the sector will take on a few more innovators before it's all said and done, and will probably include virtual job interviews with your avatar (the virtual embodiment of you), or at least a screening.

The digital, however, is also opening up entirely new opportunities and business models. For example, in law, huge amounts of information need to be examined in the "discovery" phase to determine what may be relevant and admissible during the court's proceedings. With the digital world increasingly used as the main communications medium, and with everything being so interconnected, the amount of information and the potential links that may be of interest to either the prosecution or defense, are, can we say, immense. As a result, there are firms sprouting up that specialize in "e-discovery," priding themselves on their ability to uncover things that are pertinent to the case within the mound of possibilities.

And if you are worried that you don't have the technical expertise to best use the network to your advantage, whole new industries are sprouting up to fill this need. It's the promise of all the new "cloud" service offerings, such as Salesforce.com, which helps companies manage their customer relationships online, and Amazon's Web Services, which provides customers the infrastructure to support their online applications and services (see Chapter 41, "What Are They Doing to the Network?"). This gets us back to my earlier premise that when a challenge to the network's growth or potential appears, there always seems to be someone ready to conquer it. When holes pop up, someone comes along and invents a solution that can fill it so the network can go on to reach, connect, involve, and impact everyone and everything.

Now, I've been concentrating on the business world, but you can extrapolate the same principles to the public sector, to government services, to education and universities, to charities, and to civic organizations. Change is taking place everywhere. Established entities need to embrace it to thrive in this networked world and maintain relevancy as online entities drive at the heart of many of the traditional models. For their part, the continual innovations sustaining the network make it a platform that continues to extend your reach and potential. Success depends on being able to recognize opportunities and evolve to keep up with the wants and needs of your network users.

The million-dollar question, then, is what are we, the sustainable network users, evolving to?

CHAPTER 26

Network Time

Space and duration are one.

—Edgar Allan Poe, from the
essay "Eureka," 1848

Whether you are an individual, a business, or a government, the network is coming at you fast and furious. To be successful, you will have to adjust to network time. It's a major shift, a little like Einstein's spacetime,[1] that opened people's eyes to the workings of the universe. In network time, you will have to seize upon opportunity as it quickly presents itself in the online world, you will have to find new and meaningful ways to sync the online and offline worlds together and profit from those connections, and you *must* be able to recognize shifts in the preferences and consumption habits being shaped by the world's online experiences. Oh, and if you're in business, you'll have to do it all before anyone else has a similar chance in order to maintain your competitive advantage.

Network time is about speed, and broadband is the key to the whole concept. Speed in accessing information, speed in understanding its value, and then, of course, speed to market is more critical than ever. We like Internet speed. It is nice to hear a song, find it, buy it, and download it while the melody is still fresh in your head. Speed has always been an advantage, but in this connected world, it is an imperative for ongoing relevancy, which is to say that if you are slow, you risk being irrelevant. If you are not able to react in real time to new information, changes in the market, news in the world, perceptions of the populace, or trends in technology, you will not be able to fully capitalize on your opportunities. Network time can be applied to almost every industry, government, and organization, from computer chip design to your local PTA.

Don't believe me? Take your local restaurant. Every restaurant review I've ever seen is half about the food and half about how much time it takes to get the food. So, how can the network help? To cut down on wait times, some restaurants have implemented wireless networking solutions designed to minimize the time between a customer's order and getting the food to the table. The servers input food and drink orders into a wireless device that then queues up the orders for the chefs, enabling the most efficient prep and cooking time while improving the overall customer experience. Then there's the application on your iPhone that you can use to find the restaurant, read the reviews, and receive the directions to get there. And there's the reservation website that lets you reserve that table ahead of time, and a multitude of integrated network applications and tools involved to get the food and beverages on time to the restaurant's kitchen. Each of these time segments has been compressed through links and automation that increase efficiencies.

Supply and distribution channels have been completely redesigned to take advantage of the network's capability to improve the timeliness of deliveries. FedEx and UPS made their names by linking information related to the goods they ship around the world and feeding it into internal systems to both improve tracking and add automation to delivery processes. In addition, they externalized that information, giving customers the ability to check the status of their packages online at any time by simply inputting their shipping reference numbers, or receive a text or email when something's delivered.

And we've come to expect this level of information immediacy in almost everything we do. It doesn't matter whether you are a stockbroker who exists on up-to-the-millisecond pricing and trading information,[2] a store clerk who needs to check and locate inventory to close the sale, or a chef who's tracking the fresh seafood delivery truck to ensure that it can meet the needs of that party of 12 coming in 30 minutes, the ever-present access to real-time information is vital to your success.

For example, we have seen our supply chain and inventory management systems improve time to market to such a degree that we simply expect them to always deliver what we want when we want it. When's the last time you walked into a

If you are slow to adapt, you risk being irrelevant.

modern grocery store in the dead of winter and didn't see any strawberries? Retailers such as Wal-Mart and Carrefour have embedded tags into products (or asked their suppliers to embed them) to track real-time inventory levels and more efficiently manage stocking shelves to better meet customer buying patterns and needs. The concept of just-in-time inventory, where a purchase of a product automatically triggers the reordering of that product, reduces guesswork and the potential to overstock, all of which help companies manage their supply chains more efficiently and cost effectively. It also means you can always get the thing you want, when you want it. It's a form of network time. Just-in-time means companies used the network and its connections for the *just-in* part.

And rest assured, if you're not making the most of your time and seizing the opportunities, someone else will, thanks to this global community in which we all live and compete. However, while being first to market gives you an advantage, it still all comes down to providing what the customers need. The key is to make sure that you can meet those needs exactly when customers have them and *in the way they want those needs to be met.*

This is the concept behind products such as Amazon's Kindle, which is a portable wireless reading device. Amazon's major selling proposition is that it lets you think of a book and get it in less than a minute. Marry the fact that you have what customers want with the fact that you can quickly adapt and deliver it now, and you have success.

The compression of time by our always-on network is affecting everything. Just consider the compression of the news cycle. I was watching ESPN before bed on a Wednesday night—August 7, 2008, to be exact—when the news broke that the Green Bay Packers had reached an agreement with the New York Jets on the fate of Brett Favre, a future Hall-of-Fame quarterback (this is American football, by the way). After weeks of endless droning by sports analysts on what should, would, and could happen to Favre, he had finally made the decision that he was going to be playing the 2008–2009 National Football League season in a Jets uniform (note that his uniform was the subject of much discussion and changed again for the 2009–2010 season).

This, in and of itself, may not be particularly interesting, unless you were a Jets fan or Aaron Rodgers (the new Green Bay quarterback, who arguably had the worst position in sports), but what I found most amazing is the rapidity with which this news spread and the ripples it had in the communities that cared. Within minutes, the Jets organization had Favre memorabilia for sale, Fantasy Leagues had updated their draft rosters to include Favre, and bloggers were furiously blogging, with posts being read by hundreds and even thousands of interested and engaged sports fans. Speculation and analysis abounded, ranging from what this meant for the Packers and the Jets to where the Favres would live and whether or not they would find the amenities of New Jersey suitable. No topic seemed off limits and facts were added rapid-fire to the discourse as they became public. It was amazing to me to see how the conversations developed and how many people were participating on a national and international level, all on network time. The same thing happens to politicians and their scandals, the glitterati and their new amours, and even with what Apple is doing with the next iPhone.

Staying in the sports vein, another interesting intersection of the network and live events as they unfold occurred while I was writing this chapter (in *real network live time*, if you will). Fans who attended a baseball game at the new Yankee Stadium were not only able to sit down and enjoy an overpriced hotdog and beer while they watched the game unfold in front of them, but also were able to take in replays from every imaginable angle on video screens placed throughout the park. There are plans to allow fans to access game footage from their seats through their mobile devices, and there are even plans to include personal video monitors at every seat, which could be used to enable video chats between players and fans in the stands, or between fans and fans, or bloggers in the stands, and…well, you get it.

I saw some of this futuristic network live time piloted way back in 1998, when I was working in sports marketing. I was responsible for escorting the NFL film crew around Qualcomm Stadium in San Diego during Super Bowl XXXII. One of the stops we had to make during this great game (John Elway led his Denver Broncos to victory over the defending Super Bowl champions Green Bay Packers, 31–24, in case you care) was to a suite that had been provisioned with personal, interactive video screens. At that time, the functionality was fairly limited—fans could pull up statistics on the game and watch the live video feed, and the fans in the suite saw it more as a novelty than a tool, but the concept was there—the integration of the offline and online worlds embedded together in real time in an effort to enhance the overall experience and extend its reach (and ultimately, potential revenues).

I once heard the General Manager of the English Premier League football team Manchester United describe the team's future as resting on all the fans they had yet to reach (this is English football, by the way). In not so many words, he pointed out that only a finite number of fans could actually come to a game, so the team's challenge was to connect with all those people who would never have a chance to actually attend a live game. Its future depended on being able to reach fans in places outside of Britain in an effort to tap new markets.

So, back to the Yankees. The technology has finally arrived to make this integration a reality—it is why $16 million is being invested in the 53,000-seat Yankee stadium. The Yankee organization is hoping to deliver a premium baseball experience, ensuring that fans don't miss a moment of the action, offering traffic tips to help them navigate their way home, and making them feel an even bigger part of the game by allowing them to interact with the brand (players, coaches, etc.) at a much more intimate level.

> Network time is not just about speed—it's about making the time more relevant, getting people what they want, when they want it.

What's in it for the Yankees? Sure, ultimately this integration will create additional revenue as it uses the network to drive impulse purchases; using touch-screen IP phones to order food and instant merchandise with the day's final score emblazoned on a hundred different items. But long term, they expect it to generate persistent brand loyalty by extending the moment—yes, making the game, the event, much longer than it actually is, and taking every advantage with all those extra replays, commentary, and live blogging.

So, network time is not only pure speed, but also the ability to quickly provide your audience or customers what they need to engage with you and then stay connected to the moment (or brand). In essence, it means using bandwidth to maintain your relevancy. Time is compressing, and it relies on people getting what they want exactly when they want it. It represents a shift in expectations and a compression in timeframes whose time has come.

CHAPTER 27

Political Sustainability

Gilo work entrance to Jerusalem

A dream you dream alone is only a dream. A dream you dream together is reality.

— John Lennon

A nyone who lived through the 2008 U.S. presidential campaign knows that the network can help mobilize citizens and bring them together in meaningful ways to effect political change. The impact can be as simple as facilitating information sharing and as complex as impacting election outcomes. From Obama's massive Internet campaign contribution machine to the organizing tactics used by both the Republican and Democratic political parties, the 2008 U.S. elections were a vision into the future of how the network will affect the politics of tomorrow. It's a way for politicians to touch all their constituents, it helps create an informed population and is an enabling platform for their voices to be heard, and it also helps make politicians more accountable. To put it simply, the network is becoming the conduit for political sustainability.

We cannot underestimate the value and transformative change that can come from simply creating a repository of information that can be accessed on a global scale. Millions of people are turning to the Internet to become informed and to exercise their rights, using their connections to rally support, call attention to pressing needs, or uncover corruption and injustices, all of which can potentially create political systems that work better for the citizens they serve. The unfettered access to information can be used to exert pressures that can shift policy, influence spending decisions, or create a greater level of accountability within government bodies.

The network is causing this transformational twist in everything it touches, simply by allowing people and governments to access information that was previously unattainable. An article in the *Economist* made the supposition that Internet maps, "will do more than any political initiative in 2009 to determine exactly where money should best be spent in Africa."[1] The broad set of official and unofficial information posted by nongovernmental organizations (NGOs), watch groups, companies, and individuals can provide insights into the country's inner workings, which have been hard to come by in the past. "The kind of maps which in the past had been held to ransom by secretive African governments will pop up in African Internet cafés in less than a minute in 2009…they will serve to disseminate the findings of scientists to African policymakers and the public, changing the way money is spent."[2]

The network can help those who previously didn't have a voice have an entire platform. Political advocacy organizations are increasingly using the network to lay out the cold, hard facts of situations around the globe in efforts to educate and ultimately incite action, to help those in need. Just look at Amnesty International, which posts its annual report online so that anyone and everyone can see how each country ranks in terms of the world's human rights. Disseminating information on the ethical treatment of citizens, the accessibility of vital, basic services and the scope of police and military abuses by watchdog groups and NGOs can give a far-reaching voice to those who have traditionally been voiceless.

One such voice was amplified several years ago out of Mexico:

Claudia Rodriguez spent over a year in prison for the homicide of her would-be rapist—awaiting trial and the possibility of 15 years in prison for her act of self-defense. Women's organizations and activists in Mexico mobilized support for her case, declaring her innocence and recognizing the horrible legal precedent a guilty verdict would represent for all women and their possibility to defend themselves from assailants: "As long as Claudia is a prisoner, we are all prisoners."

The women's email activist network, ModemMujer, sent out Claudia's words and situation over the Internet to hundreds of women and women's organizations in Mexico, Latin America, and North America, with calls for letters to the president, the secretary of state, and the Department of Justice. Mobilization by women's organizations in Mexico City resulted in women flooding the hearing process and performing public protests. Letters were sent from all over Mexico, Cuba, Argentina, Colombia, Bolivia, Canada, and the U.S. Claudia was freed, although the verdict review stated that she had used "excessive force" in her self-defense, and the judge could have sentenced her to an additional five years in jail.

"The Internet did not free Claudia; her lawyers, community support, and the actions of the women's movement in Mexico and internationally did. The Internet is not a panacea for women's networking, information, and communication needs, but at least in Mexico, the Internet now plays a key role in women's strategizing."[3]

It's a role that has been adopted by groups around the globe, to create a voice or call to action for those who previously might not have had one.

And perhaps the role it plays is most evident when it's not there. A local Chinese official in Urumqi stated that protests in July 2009 were most likely unavoidable because the Internet had been down and remained unavailable to the population. Without the network, people had no way to voice their opinions and release their anger, so logic followed that they turned to raise their voices in the streets.[4]

And sometimes the network helps from the inside out. For example, when Iranians took to the streets in protest of the results of the presidential elections in 2009, the only way information reached the "outside" world was through those living it on the "inside." No media was allowed, yet stories flooded the airways. How were events being reported? Through the online "tweets" and mobile phone video posts from individuals recounting their experiences and documenting the activities of the day. It was reported that the government was actively trying to thwart the online communities, blocking sites and text messages, launching denial-of-service attacks on particular online services, and spreading misinformation, but as one anonymous poster to one of these sites pointed out, "You (government hackers) are completely outnumbered. There are thousands of Iranians who want to be free and people who support them for every one of you there is."[5]

The voice of the people remained a big part of the dialogue as events unfolded; they were not silenced, and that in and of itself represents astounding progress.

The same could be said as the events in the Gaza Strip conflict played out. The network was, in many instances, the only real-time view into what was going on in the region from the people that were living inside it. While the area was closed to most of the traditional media outlets, individuals within Gaza reached out to the world, telling their stories via phone interviews, videos posted on YouTube, posts on social media sites such as Twitter and Facebook, and blogs aimed at getting the word out on what was happening. Both sides used the network to try to tell their side of the story to influence greater public perception and reactions. Both sides were savvy in the influence and power of the network.

On the flipside, we saw Pope Benedict XVI, the head of the sovereign state of the Vatican, feel the pain of what happens when the influence of the network is underestimated during this Digital Information Age. He found himself in the middle of an online maelstrom in 2009 after announcing plans to lift the excommunication of four bishops. One of those bishops, Richard Williamson, had made statements denying the Holocaust and the mass extermination of the Jewish people by the Nazis in World War II. It appears that Williamson, instead of admitting the inaccuracy of his comments and providing an unequivocal apology, which was part of the conditions the Vatican set out for him, simply said he wouldn't have made the statements had he known "the full harm and hurt to which they would give rise."[6] He then went on to make other nonadmission, unapologetic statements via a posting on the website of a Catholic news agency (*www. dici.org*), which drew understandable ire from a multitude of communities.

These communities quickly began spreading the information online by linking to Williamson's statement, creating an upswell of public opinion that forced Pope Benedict XVI and the Vatican to make comments of their own. In response to the public's demand for an explanation, the Vatican released information that most likely, under other circumstances, would have remained private about the terms of the lifting of the excommunication, explaining that Williamson would not be able to function legally as a bishop of the Catholic Church without a mandate from the pope. The Vatican noted that in the future it would pay more attention to the Internet and public sentiment, and make sure to communicate its position to avoid any further misunderstandings.[7]

The network, however, does not represent just a platform to disseminate information and give a voice to the people; it can actually be an enabler for political activities, inciting and mobilizing action. We saw this in Iran, where online communities organized rally points and passed along protest details. We also saw this in India, after terrorist attacks shook Mumbai in November 2008, killing close to 200 people. Citizens of the city wanted to be heard. Tired of a political system controlled by politicians focused on supporting the status quo and maintaining the historic divisions created by the caste system, religion, and poverty, the citizens felt disenfranchised. They wanted change.

They wanted investment in infrastructure and, most of all, the opportunity to be heard and represented. The attack, which was the third such attack in five years, seemed to be the event that shook Mumbai's 16 million citizens into action. And it was the network that helped organize and bring meaning to the desire for action.

On December 2, 2008, text messages were sent and received all over the city, encouraging people to participate in a march on the state government headquarters the following day that would be peaceful but hard for the politicians to ignore. Thousands received the messages and turned out make their voices heard, many wearing "Enough is Enough" T-shirts and carrying signs that stated their feelings and their desire for change—"Some criminals come by boat, the others come by vote," and "Beware, politicians ahead."[8] The network helped mobilize the masses, spreading the word through viral text messages that friends sent to friends, family members, and people they worked with, energizing the population to make a stand. Many watching the area say the public protests may have marked a turning point in Mumbai's political history that, when it is all written, could be the key to substantive change in the region.

And the Internet is still being used to communicate and mobilize the population in India, as people post instructional lists on how to rebel against the status quo, including everything from tax revolts to starting a "Better India Fund" to privatizing the security of the infrastructure to creating a chief executive of the city.

These are just a few of the thousands upon thousands of ways the network is giving people new voices in their governments, communities, and schools. From your local PTA outreach to national political action sites, such as the liberal-leaning MoveOn.org or the conservative GOP.com, the network is allowing unprecedented numbers of citizens to band together for common causes. The network can provide both a voice and immediacy to that outcry, no matter the cause or

The network is allowing unprecedented numbers of citizens to band together for common causes.

the ideology. And vice versa, too, as governments increasingly use online tools to inform citizens and explain the impacts and roles government can have in their lives. Just look at the Recovery.gov website, which describes the U.S. economic stimulus spending programs.

Certainly a reason the network makes such a good platform for voicing opinions is that it offers a level of anonymity that makes it possible for people, who might otherwise be silenced, to have a voice. They can share their opinions, relay injustices, and get involved in the politics of their communities. It allows people to make statements or to express opinions under screen names or nicknames that are less conspicuous, and in some cases, shelter them from certain political recourse. It's important to note, however, that there's a limit to this sheltering. There are many instances in which bloggers have been tracked down or text messages traced to the source—those authors have been labeled as dissidents and persecuted or prosecuted (depending on how you look at it) by their governments. So, let's be clear: people who use the anonymity of the Internet are not, in fact, anonymous—there's just a separation that can protect them to a degree and give them the courage to participate.

Sometimes the network can even provide its own form of civil disobedience. For example, in Tibet, acts of defiance have been enabled by a subtle mechanism of the network—the cell phone ringtone. Tibetan government officials are cracking down on "reactionary" digitized ringtones, which citizens are downloading to their phones and using to express themselves and show signs of support for exiled leaders. Here, the network is literally allowing citizens to be heard, which draws smiles and sometimes cheers from fellow supporters when they go off (luckily, it turns out it's hard to prove the true intent of a ringtone in courts of law).

While never intended to be a catalyst for change, the network is helping people reach out to others and bring them into the political process. The network is the accidental catalyst, the platform for politics and governing. Time will tell how much the network continues to influence, but with network adoption rates soaring and new devices tearing down the barriers for admission, it depends more on how those in power listen and react to what they are hearing and learning from the general population.

If substantial transformations result from the recent activities in Mumbai and the outpouring of commentary on the Gaza strip, the network could be seen as a viable platform to enable peaceful change. It can be used as a measuring stick on the needs and mood of the population, which can help set direction and policy emphasis. If politics, however, stagnate in the regions and the population grows more frustrated and discontent, the network relevancy could be minimized and digital activism transferred to more dramatic "offline" actions.

The network is the accidental catalyst.

It's interesting to think back in time and ponder how the world's political struggles may have been different if the network had been around during history's key inflection points. It's a "what if" game. It goes something like this: what if the world had been "flat" during the days of the U.S. Revolution? If the citizens and politicians were able to regularly communicate across the pond, perhaps things wouldn't have come to a boiling point. The direct dialogues and relationships enabled by the network might have been capable of addressing the seemingly disjointed governance of the British Empire over all its colonies. If so, it's interesting to think of how the world would be different today.

And what if Marie Antoinette and the French aristocracy and politicians of her time had been able to really understand the frustrations and life struggles of the French population, say, by watching videos posted on YouTube or reading their blogs? Perhaps they wouldn't have been so disconnected and could have been able to stem the seemingly inevitable tide of revolution.

Would these events have been different if they had taken place in the Digital Information Age? Maybe, maybe not. Human nature will always be human nature, and war and atrocities continue throughout our world today. However, it's plausible that the access to information and the platform for change that is now available via the network can and does influence events and political agendas. It won't be too long before the symbiotic relationship between the government and the network is so commonplace it's indiscernible. It's only natural, as one is in power and one is all-powerful.

Rocking the Vote

Rock the Vote uses music, popular culture and new technologies to engage and incite young people to register and vote in every election… and take action on the issues that affect their lives, and leverage their power in the political process.

—Part of the Charter of RocktheVote.com

The rules are changing in politics, and what's driving that change is the demographic. Let's recap just a little of the Internet history we examined back in Chapter 2:

- It was just 40 years ago, in 1969, when Leonard Kleinrock developed the concept of Arpanet, which was the idea to connect computers over phone lines.

- By 1981, Arpanet had 213 hosts, with a new host added every 20 days. The following year, the term *Internet* was first used to describe these interconnections among hosts.

- By 1995, the Internet was in entirely commercial hands with 6.5 million hosts and 100,000 "www" sites.

- By 2008, there were 1.5 billion users of the Internet.

So, if you were born in 1969 or later, your entire life has evolved with the network. And that line in the sand is moving each and every year. If you are a politician, this means that your constituency "gets it" and is using it more and more with each passing year.

Creating a Facebook page or a Twitter account is becoming part and parcel of the political process. Progressive politicians get it and are using the network to create connections to constituents, making themselves accessible and their positions understood in an ongoing online dialogue. And they've discovered that it can have a huge impact on their ability to engage and inspire constituents (even if they do text or Twitter during rollcall or their opponent's speeches!). On the flipside, there are some who are disenfranchised by the technology adoption and are struggling with how to create meaningful connections that can be turned into support and, better yet, votes. The network is becoming an influential tool that can make or break politicians, helping them get elected or, by its absence, making it harder and harder to get into and stay in office.

How is a wire- and router-filled network doing this? Essentially, the network is rocking the vote by expanding the dialogue. The world is so interconnected that what happens in one state or region or country can affect (or be a model for) other locations. Instantaneously. The network lets people from around the world witness and even participate in elections, inasmuch as they can share opinions or question and endorse ideas and candidates. The entire network phenomenon has the potential to lead to a place we haven't seen in many years—electoral participation. And that should make politicians sit up and take note. Some may tend to sweat a little more.

It's not coincidental that both the most recent and the largest examples of how the network is changing the road to political office took place in the 2008 U.S. presidential election. A 44-year-old politician took the U.S. by storm using social networking, Internet canvassing, and a host of modern networking technologies and application uses. And you know what? It was easier than ever for the world to take an interest. Not just because Barack Obama was a dynamic, young, African American, skillful orator, but because coverage and conversations took place globally in an unprecedented way, often in real time, streaming from the Internet into literally millions of laptops and mobile devices. It was easily the first big election of the Digital Information Age. As such, it is fair to drill down into the set of statistics that has surfaced around the election, to give you a sense of how the network can play a pivotal role in politics going forward. And not just in the U.S., either.

Political success depends on a candidate's ability to get his message out and rise above the clatter of the election. This simple fact cannot be underestimated, and Barack Obama had the edge over and over again. For starters, his technical savvy was pointed out as one of the reasons why he, a senator from Illinois who had only served half a term, received the Democratic presidential nomination over the more favored and seasoned Hillary Clinton. Mr. Obama could mobilize his millions of supporters almost at will, using his websites, social networking, text banks, email blasts, and video streams. He created communities of influence and campaign relevance, while Clinton only dabbled in online engagements that were neither substantive nor inspiring, for example, using the network to solicit input to help her pick a campaign theme song.

The 2008 U.S. presidential election was the first time we had political pundits blogging, texting, and appearing online as fast as the offline polling numbers could be posted.

A Pew Internet study of voters in the primary elections was very telling in this regard:

> Led by young voters, Democrats and Obama supporters took the lead in their use of online tools for political engagement. 74% of wired Obama supporters have gotten political news and information online, compared with 57% of online Clinton supporters. In a head-to-head matchup with Internet users who support Republican McCain, Obama's backers are more likely to get political news and information online (65% vs. 56%). Obama supporters outpaced both Clinton and McCain supporters in their usage of online video, social networking sites and other online campaign activities.[1]

The 2008 election was the first U.S. presidential (or other) election in which the online world and influence was measurably felt. It was the first time we had political pundits blogging, texting, and appearing online as fast as the offline polling numbers could be posted. It was also the first time we heard experts talking about the online world's impact. People and the press got it. Those over 40 years old either relished the new powers and parameters of this first full-network election, or seemed to struggle with the concept of how texting 10 people you know in a stadium of 100,000 supporters could have any impact. Many predicted that the absence of a vibrant online presence would have a negative impact on the candidates' resulting success, which makes sense when you consider that 28% of wired Americans said that the Internet made them feel more personally connected to the campaign, and 22% said that they would not have been as involved in the campaign if not for the Internet.[2]

A record-breaking 46% of Americans (total population 305,097,669) said they used the Internet, email, or text messaging to get news about the campaign, share their views, and mobilize others.[3] Garret Graff, editor at the *Washingtonian* magazine, noted that "text-message reminders helped increase turnout among new voters by four percentage points, at a cost of only $1.56 per vote—much cheaper than the $20 or $30 per vote that the offline work of door-to-door canvassing or phone banking costs."[4]

A lot of discussion—OK, more like trainloads of talk—occurred within the media and political pundits on the sheer volume of contributions Obama received from small donations, which, in political terms, is anything less than $200. Mr. Obama received considerably more small contributions than Mr. McCain or any other candidates in the past. In fact, 49% of his campaign contributions were less than $200. But when you look at the overall numbers of large donors, Obama's numbers ended up being not that different from McCain's. Why the disconnect? Data from the nonpartisan Campaign Finance Institute (CFI) revealed that large donors still made up almost half of Obama's campaign fundraising (he only had 12% fewer large donors than McCain),[5] which highlights a more interesting point—Obama was able to get many of his supporters to give more than once. I think that speaks volumes in terms of Obama's ability to leverage online pledge efforts to get his supporters to contribute several times to his campaign.

Obama's ability to cultivate his online communities and repeatedly generate both monetary and political support from them was unprecedented, aided in large part by websites, the mobile phone, and social networking tools (by the way, it continues as this book is being written, as President Obama repeatedly returns to his donor lists to try to generate core support for his presidential initiatives). Obama raised $742 million for his campaign, in comparison to McCain's $367 million.[6] By the end of the campaign, Obama had 10 million people on his mail and email lists, of which 4 million had donated. In marketing terms, that is a phenomenal conversion rate. Just for the record, marketing campaigns typically expect 2–4% conversion from an email blast or mailer, and anything verging on or above 10% is considered highly successful, if not promotion-bound, for us marketers. So, a 40% conversion is something many don't even dare to dream about.

And while Obama did have many large donors, little has been made of the fact that much of his success was attributable to "bundlers" using the tools of the network. Bundlers are people who reach out and collect contributions from the wide network of individuals they know within an organization or community, generally leveraging social networks they have cultivated. You know them; they are the friends or colleagues who send you email messages asking you to go to a website and donate to support them in their efforts to raise money for a cause (leukemia research, breast cancer awareness, etc.) via an organized activity (triathlon, walkathon, bake-off, etc.). Social causes have relied heavily on bundlers for years because they turn out to be some of the most successful fundraisers.

Obama's was the first presidential campaign that successfully mobilized these bundlers for political fundraising. The campaign even offered training programs (via campaign finance director Julianna Smoot) to help bundlers craft their "asks" from their friends and acquaintances, using the network tools available to everyone. It worked. According to information collected from the campaigns by the Center for Responsive Politics (CRP), 561 bundlers had raised a minimum of $63 million for Obama by mid-August (that's more than $110,000 per bundler).

Obama wasn't the only one who was able to successfully mobilize online communities to raise money. Sean Tevis, the first-time candidate for a Kansas state house seat, started his fundraising going door to door. However, after tough canvassing, he had only raised a whopping $25 using the tried-and-true traditional methods. Experts say that running a good race of this size—for a house seat with 11,000 registered voters in the district— would take approximately $25,000. So, Mr. Tevis was 1/1,000th of the way to his goal.

Instead of getting discouraged, Tevis turned to the Internet. He got a lot of coverage in the 2008 election, including coverage by outlets such as the *Wall Street Journal*, *Los Angeles Times*, and National Public Record (NPR).[7] Mr. Tevis started posting stick-figure cartoons of what it was like to raise money to run for office (as shown in Figure 28-1). Before long, he started getting more and more traffic, to the point that he had to upgrade his server to handle the load. He was soon getting individual donors, many of whom weren't even from Kansas, pledging money for his campaign.

Figure 28-1. Stick figures on the Internet raised more money than the plumper kind standing behind Kansan screen doors (courtesy of Sean Tevis; http://seantevis.com/kansas/3000/running-for-office-xkcd-style/).

Close to election time, Mr. Tevis had raised more than $100,000 from supporters, significantly more than Arlen Siegfreid, the incumbent candidate, who raised close to $46,000 from corporations and lobbyists. While Tevis lost his bid by four percentage points (408 votes), he more than proved the point that the network is a powerful tool to get the message out and garner support.

While the use of the network is generally positive in its influence, it should be noted that it also has potentially negative impacts. The network can highlight and accelerate the negative campaigning that gives political races a bad name. Hundreds of online sites and communities were responsible for spreading negative messages about candidates—some erroneous, and many outright lies that inflicted heavy damage—if only because of the Internet's speed and reach. Many blame online content for perpetuating the rumors that Obama was a Muslim or not of American birth. You can pick any political party and find hundreds of examples of political mischief published by the other side, all of it streamed or posted within seconds of dispatch. And once something is on the Internet, it can go anywhere and last indefinitely. When talking about civic solutions, research, or insightful analysis, I like to call the network sustainable, but for things like rumors, innuendos, and sex tapes, "sustainable" turns very quickly into "wag the dog."

An entire book could be written on what the network has done to news cycles and how traditional and new media are coping with it. Newspapers and the network are colliding like two galaxies running into each other. It's still in motion as I write, and where it's going will be of interest to us all.

Perhaps by examining the 2008 election and how the news was digested from these new sources and who knew what at which times will give a clue to where it's all going. For example, Obama made it a point to send text messages to millions of his supporters with newsworthy announcements first, bypassing the press or media entirely (reporters had to sign up to be supporters to get the texts firsthand, a brilliant tour de force in my mind).

The ripples from the 2008 U.S. general election gave rise to the first new voices and new network distribution paradigms of this Digital Information Age, going beyond the traditional media of the previous century. In September 2008, HuffingtonPost.com (HuffPo) had 4.5 million unique visitors, a whopping 474% over September 2007, and Politico.com had 2.3 million unique visitors, representing 344% growth from a year before (attracting a slightly older population—23% aged 55 or older). These fledgling, relatively new media sites rivaled and even outperformed longstanding political blog champ DrudgeReport.com, which did grow 70%, but stagnated at 2.3 million unique visitors (however, 40% of the visitors earned over $100,000 per year). Others, like DailyKos (+381%), TownHall (+117%), and TalkingPointsMemo (+1,321%), all grew far ahead of the overall Internet expansion in the previous year of only 4%.[8]

Thousands of websites catered to the politics of the 2008 U.S. election from all angles and all political ideologies. And this specialization made these websites ideal destinations for the political junkies we all seemed to become in this monumental election. Even Google wasn't fast enough. If you were on Huffington Post and just saw a new speech by a politician, then Googled the query, it wouldn't show up. It had just taken place, and the Google spiders hadn't reported it yet. Some of these sites, admittedly, were more interested in being first than being right, a trend that will hopefully and ultimately needs to correct itself, given our increasing reliance on the Internet for our news.

And therein lies the next big thing, the next ripple to a connected world that will soon be a 24/7 campaign: how will the next generation get instant links to real-time events and accurate reporting? The answer may be a combination of

Even Google wasn't fast enough.

traditional and Digital Information Age approaches. While political blogs may seem like competition for the traditional magazines and their own political blogs, sites like HuffPo and Drudge cross-linked and referenced commentary and posts throughout the media ecosystem, representing potential opportunities for innovative media companies in future elections.[9] It should also be noted that after the election, many of these sites saw their readership fall, giving rise to the potential need for the more dynamic content business models.

Something to note is that while the sustainable network is good at helping people find others with their same interests or inclinations, it can also make it harder to receive differing viewpoints. Because people can seek out the information they want (which often is in line with their political leanings), it may be more difficult to ensure that everyone gets a balanced viewpoint or hears counterpoints to any particular issue. This is potentially detrimental to the whole process because it's only within an environment of freely exchanged thoughts and information that meaningful political discourse and change can occur.

From the blogosphere to YouTube to volunteer phone banks using Skype from the individual homes of volunteers, the election of 2008 will be viewed as the one that truly began the 21st century and this Digital Information Age. Regardless of whether the Internet was used to promote positive messages or misinformation, it's clear that it had an impact on how voters got involved in and informed about the race. Look at how the three online activities grew during the presidential primary campaigns:

- 35% of Americans say they watched online political videos, a figure that nearly tripled the numbers collected by the Pew Internet Project in the 2004 presidential race.

- 6% of Americans made political contributions online, compared with 2% during the entire 2004 campaign.[10]

- 10% say they used social networking sites, such as Facebook or MySpace, to gather information or become involved.

Granted, the growth of all these activities stems from a small base, but it's a glimpse into the future. Just examine the use of social networking sites. They are popular with younger voters, who are increasingly participating and influencing the political dialogue, and who will naturally inherit the political system in the next few decades. A phenomenal two-thirds of Internet users under the age of 30 have a social networking profile, and half of them use social networking sites to get or share information about politics or the campaigns. Twelve percent of online 18–29-year-olds have posted their own political commentaries to an online newsgroup, website, or blog.[11]

In general, the use of social media has grown substantially since the first time Pew Internet probed this issue during the U.S. 2006 midterm elections.[12] Eleven percent of Americans have contributed to the political conversation by forwarding or posting someone else's commentaries about the race, and 5% have posted their own original commentaries or analyses.[13] These are all significant demographics that all candidates in the near future should read and reread several times over, then create permanent IT positions on their campaign committees, if they don't already have them.

The fun question is, where is this wired-to-the-teeth generation going to take us? What new applications and network innovations can increase the participation of a nation's people in its own elections? Despite all the Internet mud-slinging, these participation demographics are the bright blue sky of a newer, improved democracy. It's a new kind of question we have never had to answer before: what happens when individuals participate in an election unlike ever before?

The 2008 U.S. general election demonstrated how the network can make any democracy more powerful, more personal, and even more inspirational by allowing its citizens to participate on a grand scale. The digital tools were the force behind the phone calls, door-to-door canvasses, email messages, and text messages used to persuade the undecided and implore everyone to go to the voting polls. The digital world was instrumental in informing, driving, reminding, and incentivizing people to directly contact other people to get them to participate in the process. While a common perception is that the low popularity of George W. Bush allowed the radical changes that got Barack Obama elected, I think it was the network, and the intelligent use of those network resources, that elevated a relative newcomer to the national and international political scene to a winning position. In the end, the old world could not push the paper fast enough to engage so many. It needed everyone to be a node on the network.

And yes, quality journalism still counted.

Of course, in an era of constant media bombardment, part of the challenge of making any democracy more democratic via the sustainable network is to provide customizable data that can be made more personal and engaging for users. Things didn't have to go Hollywood, but anything interactive helped, such as maps that showed real-time tallies of who was winning in each state and within each county within each state, or simply allowing users to create lists of which races they wanted to track. CNN, for instance, let visitors track any combination of 35 different races among the presidential, congressional, and gubernatorial votes. The MyVote.com site allowed visitors to do something similar with statewide races. If you were fast to the Web with breaking info, you had a lot of followers. If you lagged behind the news curve, you had to provide interactivity, customization, or some flash, to somehow draw and keep the increasingly jittery user. And quality journalism was still a draw, as people regularly flocked to the outlets that delivered well-researched, thoughtful analysis on the political issues and candidates. (There was also a role for those who simply provided witty commentary and poked fun of the political controversies of the day, as attested to by the popularity of shows such as *The Daily Show with Jon Stewart* and *Saturday Night Live*.)

Hundreds of thousands of people posted videos of their voting experiences and thoughts about the 2008 U.S. general election online, and many of those were foreign citizens in foreign lands. Everyone was granted a voice on the network. Video Your Vote Project, a joint production of PBS's NewsHour and YouTube, encouraged people to film their voting experiences and submit them online to be part of an election experiences repository. They provided video cameras to 1,000 first-time voters to try to get a flavor of what was energizing people to go out and vote, with the theory of using those videos to encourage others to get out and exercise their right to vote. The project was simply overwhelmed with blogs, videos, dispatches, texts, tweets, websites, and comment boards, not from 1,000 first-time voters, but by literally millions of them. The entire network was a Post Your Vote experience.

While not every country will have an election of such worldwide focus, the good news for any democracy in the world is that the network showed itself as the ultimate tool for political sustainability. In short, it is much harder to hide in a digital world and the network makes it much easier for individuals to make a difference. Not only did the network bring the voters to the voting booth, it also watched the booth.

Initiatives such as the Twitter Vote Report Project and sites like 866OURVOTE.org were aimed at empowering all voters to become election monitors. Basically, users could tweet in real time about any voting issues they encountered, and the Election Protection Coalition would work to immediately deploy legal volunteers to polling locations to resolve problems when necessary. Also, the political machines (election boards, etc.)

were under scrutiny, making it more important than ever for them to respond to any claims of fraud, voter intimidation, and election site inadequacy to maintain public confidence in the process and the legitimacy of the outcome—we didn't want any more hanging chad incidents!

It doesn't take much creative nudging to see that the network could be both the election tabulator and the monitoring system for any election, anywhere. Votes in Somalia could be counted in Brazil and announced in Montreal. Cell phones with video cameras could record and monitor the voting process. Secure connections could eliminate local gerrymandering. New voter registration could be by fingerprint and video capture for countries without adequate identification methods (like the U.S.), and the databases held securely out of the country to avoid voter fraud.

You only make that kind of change with a little help from your friends.

Remember the Sustainable Network Law: the more broadband that's made available, the more network innovation that takes place. Well, apply this to the democratic principles of "one person = one vote," and that's where we'll hopefully be in a few more decades.

The crux of any good political system lies in people's trust of it and what they perceive as their ability to hold those in power accountable. Trouble results when people are fed up and feel powerless and uninspired by those who are leading them—it's the stuff of riots and revolutions. This is a lesson we saw in the recent elections in Iran and even more recently in Afghanistan—perhaps the country could have benefited from a more networked election process, or at least leaving the network turned on.

I believe the world's global network can create a new level of participation in the political process. The network truly gives people a platform to be heard. And that, in turn, encourages greater participation in the political arena. Ask Barack Obama. In August 2005, he visited the British Prime Minister at 10 Downing Street as a Senator from Illinois, without a crowd and without fanfare. He was part of a visiting caucus. After the visit, he supposedly walked the streets of London back to his hotel, stopping for a beer.[14] In April 2009, not even four years later, he revisited 10 Downing Street as President of the United States, amid hundreds of journalists and admirers, to represent the U.S. at a G20 summit. You only make that kind of change with a little help from your friends, all connected by one large sustainable network.

CHAPTER 29

The Right to Network Usage

There is a real danger of a Virtual Curtain dividing the Internet, much as the Iron Curtain did during the Cold War, because some governments fear the potential of the Internet and want to control it.

—Human Rights Watch

This entire book is about how the sustainable network is changing the world and laying the foundations of our future. And it's all because of access and the power that this access creates. But what if you don't want that access? What if your task is to block it? There may be some legitimate reasons to block Internet traffic. For example, you may wish to protect your children and block pornographic and other nefarious sites on your home computer. Businesses may want to prevent nonbusiness bandwidth consumption and protect themselves from potential lawsuits relating to "unfriendly" work environments. These considerations aside, the real value of the network comes in unfettered access to information.

But is this openness of the network concept a singular view? And, as long as we're asking so many questions, how open do you really want it to be?

It is clear that there are parts of the world and many governments that don't view unfettered access as a value, and they are going to great lengths to stifle and restrict the connections to the world's resources. In principle, this is nothing new, but it is counter to how the network has been built. It is counter to the phenomenon that is the sustainable network, and any one country, no matter how large, is tiny compared to the billions of people, devices, and websites that are connected by the worldwide infrastructure of this global network. As such, it's easy to suppose that governments will not be able to maintain a "closed" network environment forever. After all, the network is designed to find ways to permeate, persist, and connect. If citizens want to reach out and connect to the rest of the world, they will find a way, a network, or a new device to do so. People will find a way to be inclusive.

In the meantime, a quick look at Reporters Without Borders, which monitors press freedom around the world, is a good indicator of the world's latest offenders trying to stifle communications. China is well known for its many attempts to block unwanted digital content. In 2009, the Chinese government issued a directive that required the installation of filtering software, nicknamed "Green Dam," on every PC sold in the Chinese market, under the auspices of protecting children from harmful Internet content.[1] It was sharply criticized by governments around the world, which protested the requirement on a variety of grounds, from free speech impingement to potential security compromises to free-trade violations, because the reality is, if actually loaded onto every PC, it would give the Chinese government unprecedented control over every individual's personal computing use.[2] While China backed off of its deadline (July 1, 2009) for implementation, it's not certain for how long or how successful international pressure will be in getting the Chinese government to rethink its approach.

It would be quite a capper to a long list of methods the Chinese government has employed to clamp down on access. It has used technological tricks and some good old-fashioned coercion measures, from fines to complete shutdowns to pressuring content owners, to keep content in line with what the government deems acceptable. It employs thousands of government workers in these efforts, and to date, they have been fairly successful in achieving the results they desire.

Google executives were criticized for censoring some of its search results in China, and Yahoo! was questioned by Congress in 2007 for turning over email messages that led to the imprisonment of Chinese dissidents. That same year, during a meeting of the Communist Party Congress, which coincided with the awarding of a Congressional Gold Medal to the Dalai Lama, YouTube was shut down by the Chinese government, presumably to avoid any glimpses of the medal presentation.

> A handful of bloggers whose commentaries were unfavorable to China were detained.

In 2008, Cisco Systems was also questioned by Congress after it was suggested, based on a Cisco sales presentation, that Cisco was potentially helping the Chinese government modify its networking equipment to block and censor Internet traffic (this was an accusation Cisco vehemently denied).[3] Also in 2008, the year the summer Olympics took place in China, it was discovered that China had been monitoring Skype communications. A handful of bloggers whose commentary was unfavorable to China were detained, and probably not so coincidentally, their postings were blocked or removed.

In June 2009, the Chinese government shut down Google, citing that the search engine was contaminating the country with pornography. This followed an incident in March, when YouTube traffic came to a halt in China. Though no specific reason was released by the government, most commentary pointed to video clips that were posted (presumably by the Tibetan government in exile) of the previous year's riots against Chinese rule in Tibet.[4] Not surprisingly, the shutdown lasted through the anniversary of the Tiananmen Square massacre (along with the blocking of Twitter). By the way, this is not the first time the Chinese government has "attacked" Tibet citizens virtually; it has used botnets to monitor the communications of individuals and organizations to identify dissidents or others deemed of interest.

But China is not alone in its efforts; the governments of at least a dozen other countries have blocked various sites from their citizens. Iran has bought Internet monitoring and blocking software,[5] and spent much of 2009 trying to thwart online activists who questioned the presidential election results and the legitimacy of the ruling party. Thailand blocked YouTube in 2007 when a video appearing to mock King Bhumibol Adulyadej, an offense expressly against Thai law, was posted. In February 2008, believing YouTube was distributing offensive content not in line with the values deemed appropriate for its citizens, the Pakistan Telecommunication Authority directed the country's Internet service providers to block the site. We know this is true because when Pakistan's ISPs blocked the site, they altered YouTube's Internet routing information, rendering it briefly inaccessible for many other countries as well. Oops.

In 2009, Bangladesh blocked YouTube for approximately 36 hours after recordings of a meeting between the prime minister and army officials discussing a mutiny by border guards were posted.[6] In most of these instances, the content providers agreed to filter the offending content, which it was argued broke the laws that govern that particular country, before service was restored. It doesn't mean the content was removed—it is generally viewable by people around the world—it is simply not available for users originating from the countries in question.

There are also instances in which citizens have voiced their approval for this kind of censorship. Take Saudi Arabia, where 25 members of the Communications and Information Technology Commission (CITC) monitor and then block websites that are not in line with what the country believes its citizens *should* view, ranging from porn and gambling sites to sites that call for political change. One local blogger, Fouad al Farhan, was jailed in 2008 for advocating political reforms. While Farhan wrote under his own name, most of the country's estimated 2,000 bloggers post anonymously to avoid potential persecution (one would rightfully assume).[7] The CITC claims, however, that only 40% of citizens of Saudi Arabia say they are concerned and some actually favor filtering/blocking by the government.[8] This explains how Saudi Arabia can solicit the help of its citizens, who send around 1,200 requests a day to have sites blocked.[9]

> Australia's federal government proposed a national Internet filter, dubbed a "Net Nanny."

And it's something we should all take note of, as many citizens potentially view filtering and blocking content as a legitimate responsibility of government. Even countries that are proud of the freedoms they protect for their citizens are being forced to take a look at their stands. The European Union started legal action early in 2009 against Britain for not applying EU data privacy rules that focus on restricting the monitoring of Internet users for potential advertising purposes, and simultaneously issued warnings that it was going to force social networking sites, such as Facebook and MySpace, to hide minor profiles from search engines.[10] While many would vehemently agree with the concept of protecting minors and ensuring that an individual's activities online remain private, these issues highlight how tricky it is to decide where the lines need to be drawn.

There is no international standard, nor universal agreement, on what is acceptable or not; we are all treading in uncharted waters. And as individuals, information, and services become increasingly and inextricably linked, we will need to be sure that we understand exactly where and how we want to bound them. Questionable restrictions on the network can lead to potential fettering of its possibilities. For example, Australia's Federal Government proposed a national Internet filter, dubbed a "Net Nanny" that would cover all web users.[11] The initial intent, which has been in effect since 2006, was to protect against child pornography, but it is being extended to any website that authorities view as controversial—a very hazy space. Who will be deciding what is acceptable? Who programs these filters? Exactly where are the lines drawn?

Are social networking sites that provide a platform for people with common interests responsible for policing and controlling all the content that is posted on their sites? What's considered freedom of expression, and what's considered detrimental to the good of our societies? At what point does something turn from a healthy debate of controversial topics to a conversation that inspires hate or is malicious in its intent? How do we protect freedom of speech and separate it out from truly dangerous interactions? It can be a slippery slope, but it's one that we need to climb.

What do you do in your own home? Do you block websites from your children, often called *parental control* settings in your web browser? If you don't, why not? If you do, how do you keep track of all the new things that are out there? Do you use a service? How does that service decide what to block and what not to block? I, for one, would block any site (as well as want to put its owner in jail) that has anything to do with child pornography. So, I assume everyone has a line somewhere separating total freedom from regulation.

The information and communications technology (ICT) industry is looking at the whole blocking issue and how technology can potentially be used to stifle expression and personal freedoms. Unfortunately, the bevy of declarations, codes, and initiatives that ICT companies can point to as a framework to guide their behavior in the near future still needs a lot of work. There's the United Nations Universal Declaration of Human Rights, drafted in 1948,[12] which provides a basic framework but little practical guidance in this Digital Information Age.

Which leads us to attempts by the technology industry itself, such as the Global Network Initiative (GNI). Technology companies including Google, Yahoo!, and Microsoft worked with human rights groups, such as Human Rights First, and organizations focused on corporate responsibility advocacy, such as Business Social Responsibility, to form a common set of principles on how they will do business in countries that have a propensity toward censorship and free speech restrictions. The GNI requires the evaluation of each country's track record to look for evidence and repeat offenses of stifling personal freedoms and expression. It then requires the technology companies to promise to protect the personal information of users, to "narrowly interpret and implement government demands that compromise privacy,"[13] and to assess any potential human rights impacts of their actions in countries in which they do business. The companies also agree to be monitored by independent experts on their progress and compliance.

The GNI represents a step in the right direction, but it doesn't go far enough. There's no definition of which areas of the world it should be implemented within and whether all the countries are treated similarly. There's also no mention of milestones nor a clear understanding of what would constitute progress, and it does not outline repercussions associated with violating the principles.

Then there's the wildcard of country-specific legislation, which can either augment or confuse any industry-wide or international efforts. For example, there's the U.S. Global Online Freedom Act (Gofa),[14] which was first proposed in 2006 but has yet to make it on the statute books. Gofa's aim is "to promote freedom of expression on the Internet, to protect United States businesses from coercion to participate in repression by authoritarian foreign governments, and for other purposes."[15] Unfortunately, while it sounds good, the devil is in the details, which to date have been very nonspecific, though they do potentially include fines of up to $2 million USD on U.S. companies that provide technology to help restrict Internet services.[16] There's also another bill planned for introduction in the U.S. Senate in 2009 that would bar foreign companies who sell technology to monitor or block Internet traffic to governments such as Iran from receiving U.S. government contracts.[17]

> The right to network usage and the right to connect freely without government interference should be central to the discussion.

These kinds of regulations could force companies to draw lines specifying with whom they will and will not do business (realistically, they'll most likely make these decisions based on deal size and monetary opportunities). And while it might put pressure on governments that have a propensity to censor by making it harder for them to build out a reliable Internet infrastructure, it is just as likely to have the opposite effect. These kinds of retributions (fines or withholding government contracts) could create a situation in which citizens in censor-prone countries have even less freedom. It could force companies to pick sides, and it follows that the companies that decided to provide the Internet infrastructures to censor-prone governments become entirely beholden to those governments (for their monetary success), making them unwilling to push back or join international efforts to protect free speech and individual human rights.

These issues should attract the attention of activists and pragmatic folks alike. There is a lot to debate, with the goal to create more definitive processes to not only safeguard, but also promote, human rights worldwide. The right to network usage and the right to connect freely without government interference should be central to the discussion. However, it should be an inclusive rather than divisive dialogue; one that combines the technology capabilities with both sound policy and economics.

As a platform that can deliver opportunity to users around the world and enable (and actually protect) freedom of expression, the network can't be beat. If we can work on the connective spirit of the network and see that it is honored and cultivated, and if we can agree on frameworks that allow the free exchange of information, we'll all be able to participate in a changing-the-world-for-the-better era.

We really are on the cusp of such a revolution, powered by the billions of users on the network. It's quite simple. Using the network, the connective power of the many can overcome the stifling governing by the few.

CHAPTER 30

Challenges of the Networked World

One of Google's first servers...

Just because you know where you want to end up doesn't mean you will not be faced with obstacles, or challenges along the way. Instant success rarely happens.

—Catherine Pulsifer

You've seen or heard the headlines: "Transit delays due to network outage ground passengers for hours," "Upgrade prematurely cancels service," "Socialite's address book posted on Web," "Outage bumps market exchange off the Internet," "Crash embarrasses company, causes stock to plunge."[1]

However, seldom do you see the headline, "Network unlocks power of computing devices, creates goodwill, economic prosperity, and social change." Maybe the sustainable network isn't a headline. Maybe, instead, the news is the gaps, holes, and openings for activities with a detrimental impact.

The network's capability to support so many different users, devices, and applications and to extend the reach of all who use it also makes it a harder environment to control and protect. Mixed in with all that good is bad or malicious traffic, and this traffic can degrade or bring down the network, and allow people to steal, alter information, or perpetrate a variety of other crimes. Any disruption can be costly. It's estimated that large businesses lose an average of 3.6% in annual revenue due to malicious network downtime each year,[2] with an impaired network estimated to cost companies $3 million per day or more.[3]

The people who perpetrate online attacks and crimes come in all shapes and sizes, with all types of motivations. Here, the virtual world really does mimic the physical world. It may be someone outside trying to gain information or someone on the inside looking to disrupt operations or vindicate a wrong. It can be a teenager in her bedroom going through her rebellious phase or a member of an organized crime cartel, halfway across the world, looking to pull off an extortion scam or sell financial or personal identity records. Just as in the physical world, you need to know about the dangers that exist online so you can better protect yourself against them (or at least look both ways before crossing).

There's a tendency to paint the picture of the risks associated with the Internet as a doom and gloom landscape. There are stories of online crime rings holding owners of websites hostage for ransom, not all that dissimilar to the Somali pirates hijacking cargo boats in the Indian Ocean. Convicted hacker Robert Moore, who was part of a sophisticated Voice over Internet Protocol (VoIP) fraud scheme, stole and then sold more than 10 million minutes of telephone service, netting more than $1 million from the scheme.[4] This does not look that different from other recent white-collar crime schemes, such as Bernard Madoff's investment ponzi scheme exposed in late 2008.

There are attackers stealing credit card information from online databases that look a lot like the identity theft rings that specialize in making physical copies of your credit card information in the alleyways and back rooms of restaurants and retail shops. Actually, contrary to public perception or the news reports you hear about, the Computer Security Institute's (CSI) annual Computer Crime and Security Survey Report found that the majority of information criminals use to perpetrate identity fraud still comes from stolen personal belongings (waste, copies of bills, etc.) and information gathered from telephone calls, rather than online information.

This is not to say that your risk is diminished online. To the contrary, one of the benefits of the sustainable network—the far-reaching nature of the network—also means the potential attacker base is far wider than what you would be subjected to in your hometown. So, now you can be attacked by someone surfing in Peoria or Manila or Minsk! Plus, attacks are becoming more automated, giving attackers greater range in the number of targets they can go after. On the flipside, because an attacker's list of potential targets has grown so vast (the world), if you protect yourself, it might work in your favor, diminishing the probability of a specific online attack against a specific individual. Remember, you're small potatoes compared to CitiBank or General Electric, but if you are linked to any of those bigger targets, you may get caught in the attacker's net.

This might be one of the most disconcerting aspects of the risks associated with using the network. Much more of your personal information is becoming digitized and linked in ways you may not even know about, creating the potential for far-ranging damage and implications. Just think about all the different types of organizations with which you share personal information—everyone from mortgage brokers to retail stores, from your tax assessor to the local DMV. They all have databases with your name, along with potentially millions of other names. Then there are your online activities. Do you do online banking? Is your health provider online yet? Buy your car online yet? None of these is inherently dangerous; in fact, many represent the potential of the network. The point is to be aware of your key personal data and understand how and to whom you are making that information available. Awareness is the first step in protecting yourself.

> **Be aware of your key personal data and understand how and to whom you are making that information available. Awareness is the first step in protecting yourself.**

Online crime is on the rise. Just about every security firm reports that. For example, in the four months from August to November 2008, IBM's security experts detected a significant increase in the attack activity among its managed security service clients. It saw the number of web and network security incidents surge by 30% during that period, from 1.8 billion to 2.5 billion[5] (representing thousands of attempts a second).

The other thing that security experts point out is that the nature of the attacks is evolving. It seems that the stories of the dumb bank robber, such as the one who patiently stood in line with ski mask on and note to teller in hand, don't apply online. Attacks are getting more automated and sophisticated, and they are poised to have a larger financial impact than historically reported. There are predictions that there is more *malware* out there than ever, and it is being designed and programmed for data theft.[6] *Spyware*, which is software that covertly gathers information on user activity and then transmits that information without the user's knowledge to someone or someplace else, is on the rise. Particularly, spyware with a criminal intent, which represents the most severe threat as opposed to that used for targeting marketing purposes, was found to be doubling every month.[7] Google researchers found that 1 in 10 web pages they looked at contained malicious code, such as spyware, that could infect an individual's computer.[8] The study also found that gangs were able to hijack web servers, effectively taking over and infecting all of the web pages hosted on the computer.[9]

You Might Think Twice...

Ever bought things directly through the Internet from sites you've just discovered? Have you ever opened an email message from a friend that contained an email recipient list a mile long? Do you use an email alias given to you by your home service provider as your identifier on other websites? You want to make sure you don't make it easy for people you don't know to get your personal information. Do everything you can to protect it.

It might mean you take a few extra steps—using a certified online payment system (such as PayPal) to make purchases from sites you don't know that much about, checking with your friends before opening anything within messages that contain long recipient lists (to ensure that they are not the result of a virus or worm that infected your friend's account and is trying to do the same to yours), signing up and using an email address that can't be directly tied to your home location, etc. It will be worth it. You wouldn't provide personal information to strangers you meet on the street—don't provide it to those you come across on the digital information highway.

According to CSI's survey results, 27% of respondents experienced a targeted attack on their businesses. As of November 25, 2008, the Identity Theft Resource Center (ITRC) reported 585 data breaches, which exposed over 33 million records, a fairly significant rise from the 446 data breaches reported by ITRC for all of 2007. (It's not clear, however, how much of this 31% rise can be attributed to a general increase in the reporting of incidents or an actual uptick in the crimes perpetrated.) These numbers are just the tip of the iceberg, as demonstrated by the 2009 bust of Albert Gonzalez, who hacked into the databases of some of the U.S.'s largest companies and stole the financial information of more than 130 million individuals. We need to be prepared for the potential scale of these online crimes because, like the opportunities enabled by the network, they are unlike anything we have ever seen before.[10]

What to do? The first step is to *understand* your risk level. In other words, what do you have to protect that is accessible online, and how would a successful attack that compromised those assets affect you, both in hard and soft costs? As an individual, this can be a fairly easy assessment—you probably have a variety of financial accounts and all the information associated with your personal identity. You can also probably easily inventory the ways in which those assets could be compromised (beyond the information that is stored in the databases of all the companies/entities you deal with that is out of your direct control). There's your home computer, maybe a laptop or two spread across your family, your cell phones, and potentially your home router, which hopefully has the firewall up and running. But then again, are you sure you know exactly what is running on all of these devices? Do you know what your teenager is running on his laptop? Or what he downloads from servers? Do you know what all the applications do that you and your family members have loaded onto your phones? When was the last time you looked or asked? Did you let your houseguests use your computer to go online? Did that guest download anything? I don't want to imply that any friends or family are doing anything that they shouldn't be doing, just that any unknown variables can be potential risks, simply because they are unknown.

You can imagine the problems are compounded for businesses, governments, and the public sector. Understanding exactly what is in use in their IT environments is probably one of the biggest troubles they face today. A survey estimated that approximately 25% of all devices in a company's IT infrastructure are undocumented and unprotected by maintenance contracts. In addition, 75% of network devices are out of compliance with corporate policy, while 30% of network devices are no longer sold, and 20% are no longer supported by the manufacturer.[11] These statistics are both astonishing and unsettling.

> It is increasingly difficult for any organization to keep a current, accurate inventory of all the users, devices, applications, and services running on their network.

How can this be?

Just visualize all the people who come in and out of a business's facilities, from employees to contractors, from partners to customers, all of whom may introduce their personal devices into the IT environment. Or think of a large university, and imagine 30,000 students, each with a laptop, iPhone, or another Wi-Fi device, in addition to the devices of the faculty and visiting lecturers, as well as the computing system and research facilities of the campus itself. Do you think all of these people alert the IT department when they connect to the network with these devices? Do you think they tell them exactly what they are going to do with their access?

Then visualize all the new applications and services required to keep a business competitive or a university running. A study by Aberdeen Research Group found that companies expect to increase the number of business-critical applications running on their networks by 67%.

Combine these trends with a relatively flat IT budget, and the result is an IT department that is often struggling just to keep pace with the immediate needs of the business or government agency. In fact, 70% of IT's time is spent on "keeping the lights on," with only 30% of the IT budget going toward growth and transformative projects.[12] This is what is referred to as the "Chief Information Officer's Dilemma"—the CIO is tasked with keeping everything going, while simultaneously freeing up resources to allow the business to grow and innovate safely.

The average business enterprise spends just as much of its IT budget on the network communications services as it does on network management and administration of that network (approximately 11% each).[13] Companies that are able to get their network monitoring under control and take a more proactive stance to network management end up spending a smaller percentage of their budgets just keeping things running (60–65%), compared to those with a reactive or more chaotic approach (75–80%).[14] Keeping up with the growth of the network, as we've seen in the worldwide adoption rates of the past decade, is a full-time job that doesn't come with the luxury of knowing who's exactly on and why.

There are many IT management tools available to support the discovery, ongoing management, and control of all these endpoints and assets, but it's definitely a fluid process and one that does not promise to get easier anytime soon. As a result, network management is rising on the priority list of almost every large organization and business.

> ## Do you ever want to face your service provider's tech support phone tree again?

Understanding what is on the network, including users, devices, and applications, and knowing where there are potential bottlenecks or weaknesses, is crucial to ensuring optimal network performance—whether the organization is Ohio State University or Hertz Rental Car Corporation. It's an imperative for the sustainable network. Maintaining its availability, reliability, and security is more important than ever, even in the face of the fact that it is also more difficult.

Think about the last time your home DSL or cable network connection went down. How much did it disrupt your life? Remember the hours you spent with tech support? Maybe it was your home router and you suddenly had to go to a local café to log on; or maybe your spouse needed the connection because of a deadline she was facing and you somehow became the cause of her stress. The kids were mad, the TiVo didn't connect, and, well, on and on. How long did you last like that? Or better yet, how long do you think you could last?

So, you can understand that for businesses there is an increasing lack of tolerance for network downtime. A study by the Strategy Group found that almost one-third (32%) of enterprise respondents said that they had zero tolerance, and the average response of the group was that they could tolerate just 1.8 hours of downtime. In addition, roughly

10% of respondents estimated the costs of a network outage at more than $10 million in damages and lost revenue per day.[15] Plus, the negative consequences of a network outage can go beyond financial, with 69% of respondents citing "decline in corporate image" as their biggest concern, followed by loss of customers at 47%.[16] If you work out of your home, running your own business, you never again want to face your service provider's technical support phone tree.

You should also care about what all these enterprises that have databases containing your information are doing in the area of security, because you place your trust in them every time you do business with them and share your personal information. You want to know that your personal data is well protected and not at risk. You don't want to recognize that company's name in a nightly TV news report about a security breach that compromised its data.

Take It to the Top

A Carnegie Mellon study on directors serving on U.S. public company boards found that only 36% indicated that they have any direct involvement with oversight of information security. The study also found that boards were only involved approximately 31% of the time in assessment of risks related to IT or personal data (which could trigger security breach notification laws that are designed to ensure that any individuals that could be affected by the breach are informed of the potential risk).

The survey also found that only 8% of respondents' companies had a risk committee that was separate from the audit committee, which calls into question whether appropriate attention is being paid at the highest levels to network security issues. The survey suggested that these issues need to be treated as enterprise risk management rather than lumped into IT.[17]

All of this brings us back, somewhat breathlessly, to the point that in order to protect all the networked assets, you (either as an individual or a business owner) must do a risk assessment. You need to chronicle your most critical assets, your potential vulnerabilities (exposure), and ultimately itemize the costs if those assets were compromised.

Every asset connected to the network has an associated risk level. That risk level can be low, medium, or high, and is determined by the ways that the asset can be compromised and the likelihood that it will be attacked. So, loosely speaking:

Risk = Asset Value × Threat × Vulnerabilities (Figure 30-1)

Just as there is no silver bullet for many of the problems the sustainable network faces today, there is no one-size-fits-all solution for the security of the current 1.5 billion connected network users. It is important to realize that there will always be some level of risk associated with the network and all the digital assets connected to it. The key is to find an *acceptable level of risk* and develop security measures that help you achieve that level.

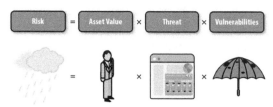

Figure 30-1. The risk of getting wet equals the value of you keeping dry times the threat of today's weather forecast times that old umbrella with the patched holes.

For example, let's say you have $10 in one hand and $10,000 in the other. The asset value of the $10 is probably low, because it wouldn't have a huge impact on your life if it was lost or stolen. However, if something happened to the $10,000, that would be a different story. Criminals would likely target the $10,000, so the threats would be higher for that sum of money compared with the $10. The vulnerabilities for both are equal, since they are the same asset type—money—and can both be taken by pickpockets, frauds, or heists. The end result of this assessment is that the overall risk level for the $10 is low versus the $10,000, which is high. To achieve an "acceptable level of risk," you will probably go to greater lengths to protect the $10,000 (and heck, just go spend the $10 and stop worrying). You may decide, because you understand the vulnerabilities, to deposit the money in a bank whose deposits are insured. The same principles apply to the network and all of the assets it connects.

However, if you are going to use the sustainable network, and every indication is that you are probably doing so if you're reading this book, you must realize that security is not an achievable end state. It is a continual cycle and constantly needs to be reevaluated to ensure that it matches your tolerance for risk. It is vital for individuals, companies, and governments to actively manage and protect their information and digital assets in the same vigorous fashion as they do for many of their physical assets.

By going into the virtual world with eyes wide open, users can create a safe, productive environment and benefit from being connected to the world's resources. If you understand where the risks are, you can try to avoid them. Many of the upcoming chapters in this book show you how and where to look. This is important, because the asset value of the sustainable network far outweighs the risk of using it. Indeed, the result of not using the network represents the greatest risk of all.

CHAPTER 31

Network Defenses Depend on How Traffic Is Sent

... an Enigma machine

*The wind and waves are always on the
side of the ablest navigators.*
—Edward Gibbon

For the network to appropriately handle all the traffic it transmits, it must have some visibility into what that traffic is and understand it to a certain extent. If you paid any attention to the first part of this book, you might think this is a tall order, what with all the different types of applications running over it, all the different types of devices connecting to it, and the ever-spiraling adoption rates. The concept that the network can just be a "dumb pipe" is a relic of the past, although to be fair, "the past" might be as long as you've had your most recent job. The network needs to understand the *intent* of the transmission so it can deliver service guarantees, provide an experience commensurate with your expectations, and perhaps most importantly, restrict or ideally remove anything malicious or nefarious.

All of which is easier said than done.

Transmitting traffic is complex. As we have discussed earlier, and you have no doubt committed to memory, there are standard, well-established protocols to ensure that each network component can do its part in aiding a predictable transmission across the network. The Transmission Control Protocol (TCP) and Internet Protocol (IP) are a couple of the key underlying protocols used to connect all computing devices on the Internet and allow them to transmit data and communicate with one another. There are a host of other protocols that govern how specific applications or devices interact with one another (for example, HTTP is the underlying protocol for the Web, defining how messages are formatted, transmitted, and ultimately handled by the web servers and browsers that store and present the information). All of these other protocols are supported by TCP/IP to ensure that information is transmitted appropriately across the Internet.

With that tidbit as a foundation, let's revisit the mail analogy we used in Chapter 2 when describing how the network works to better understand traffic transmission.

When you write a letter, put it in an envelope, and post it, imagine that the post office takes it, cuts it up into several pieces, numbers those pieces, and then sends them through the system to the letter's intended recipient. Magically, the letter reassembles itself just before delivery to the recipient. In a sense, this is what happens on the network. When information is transmitted over the network, it is split into numbered TCP segments that are sent as packets across the network. In an ideal world, the packets would be transmitted in sequence and without loss (see Figure 31-1A). But unfortunately, that's not the case. When a message is transmitted, the network will make its best effort to deliver the packets (which can come out of sequence, as shown in the bottom of Figure 31-1B) or even smaller pieces of data (called *fragments*), which are broken down by networking devices, such as routers, to further facilitate the ease of transmission. The receiving system, such as a mail server, is responsible for reconstructing the packets into a stream of information. The server will acknowledge which packets it has received, and the sending system will retransmit those that were not acknowledged (the missing packets), so that the entire message can be presented to your application, such as email, as a whole entity.

Figure 31-1 only represents a single flow from the client (your computer application) to the server (the device connected to the network). In reality, most client-to-server communications consist of two flows, one from the client to the server, and another one from the server back to the client, as the communications go back and forth. Imagine the complexity as hundreds of thousands to millions of these transmissions flow over the network at any given point in time. Plus, there are multiple types of connection architectures adding to the complexity. Connection architectures, you say?

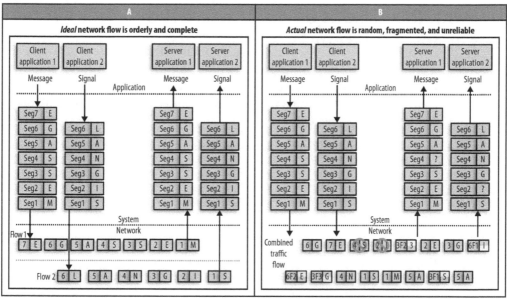

Figure 31-1. The ideal network flow of traffic is fast, direct, and unbroken; the actual flow of network traffic can cause you to say, "You mean you never got my email? How strange."

Yes, connection architectures. Initially, the *client-server* architecture dominated early network traffic flow, where the client is the application (such as email), running on a computing device (say, a computer or PDA), and interacting with a server, which is a dedicated device that manages the resources necessary to perform the application's operations. In this case of email, the server acts like a virtual post office that sends, receives, presents, and stores the messages for your email application.

Increasingly, however, applications such as instant messaging (IM) leverage *peer-to-peer* (P2P) connection architectures. These connection architectures allow computing devices on either end of the connection to have the same capabilities and responsibilities. In the case of IM, users can chat back and forth in real time via text messages. There are also P2P file-sharing applications, such as BitTorrent and eMule, which enable users to easily share files and information. These types of applications have gotten a lot of press because people use them to share music and videos, which can result in potential copyright infringement violations. However, because of the direct connections enabled by P2P, its popularity continues, and it has broadened to include movies, software, video, and music. In fact, the Yankee Group estimates that P2P accounts for roughly 60% of all traffic on the Web today.

How does the network cope? How does it deal with the millions of packets at any one instant?

Also, you'll soon hear about the promise of Service-Oriented Architecture (SOA), which allows a client from any device to interface with any kind of service to perform business functions. These can be highly automated processes, such as just-in-time merchandizing, where the scanning of a barcode in a store will trigger the automatic ordering of that item from the stocking warehouse and a subsequent shipment of a replacement to the store. In the next few years, some analysts expect SOA to be used in more than 80% of new, mission-critical applications and business processes.

So, back to our real-world network traffic flow, with all of these connections flowing through the network, originating from myriad different devices, and leveraging a variety of architectures. There is a lot, and I do mean a lot, of potential for error. How does the network cope? How does it deal with the millions of packets at any one instant?

First, you must remember that the network and its usage have somewhat grown together over the years, with many engineers around the world developing the tools to ensure accurate traffic processing that will continue to support ongoing adoption. For starters, quite a bit of information can be garnered from just the *headers* of each of the packets, providing the source, destination, any quality of service (QoS) requirements, and an indication of the type of traffic contained within the packet, for example, whether it is web (HTTP), mail (SMTP), or voice (VoIP). The network also uses a variety of techniques to eliminate the misinterpretation of data that can occur during transmission.

Such network processes for ensuring traffic delivery include:

- *IP defragmentation*, the capability to properly combine fragments of packets into packets;

- *TCP reassembly*, the capability to properly reassemble the TCP segments in the right order, while removing duplicate and overlapping data;

- *Flow tracking*, the capability to track flows (client-to-server flow and server-to-client flow) and associate them with a single communication session;

- And *normalization*, the capability to interpret and, if necessary, remove encoded representations and special characters from the reassembled message.

You may never need to know these terms, but they could come in handy when that coworker claims she sent you an email that never arrived. ("But I'm sure your email would have been defragmented, reassembled, and delivered to me had you indeed sent it.") OK, maybe not, but the point is that the network is doing a lot of work to make sure it reliably gets the traffic where it needs to go, and this is important because it is the underlying work that goes into protecting against attacks and misuse.

Because once these packets are processed and reconstructed, the traffic can be analyzed so appropriate action can be taken. Recall that to understand the "purpose" of the traffic, you have to look much further. Deep inspection of traffic requires an understanding of the actual application and an ability to interpret the intent of each piece of that communication. This is sometimes called Layer 7 intelligence, referring to the top layer in the Open System Interconnection (OSI) model, which is a framework used to describe the structure of the interactions and dependencies of all network components (Figure 31-2).

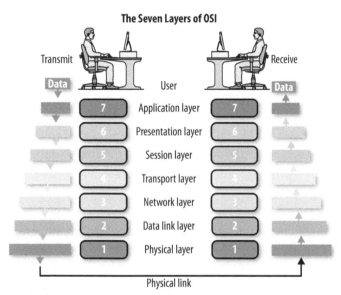

Figure 31-2. You and I live and work and play in the Application layer of the OSI model, and when you're crawling around under your desk to reinsert the DSL jack your dog pulled out while scratching, you're a Layer-1 kind of user. Now for the pun: dog-ear this page because I refer to it quite often in this book.

The bottom layer (Layer 1) is the *Physical transport* layer—the wires (or lack thereof if we're talking about a wireless network), the connectors (the devices used to join the electrical circuits together), and the signaling characteristics that make up the physical structure of the network. The second layer is the *Data link* layer, controlling the initial access to the network and furnishing the host (computer) information to enable transmission. Layer 3 is the *Network* layer, which creates the logical paths between routers, switches, and more, and so on up the OSI stack until you reach Layer 7, which is the *Application* layer, supporting the functions of the application itself and the end-user processes. It is at this seventh layer that most of the advanced network security mechanisms operate.

These security measures can include technologies that sit on the devices themselves or within the network, but they all try to inspect the traffic deeply. The types of security categories can include—among other technologies—firewalls, antivirus, antispam, and intrusion prevention solutions (IPS) that are all designed to *control traffic to a certain extent* and try to mitigate a broad range of security breaches from theft, manipulation, or accidental leakage of data to network shutdowns, system takeovers, and financial loss.

Many attacks try to evade detection by fooling the detection mechanism into seeing different data than the target host will see, often referred to (appropriately) as the victim. This allows an attacker to attack the host without being detected, a time-tested scenario that also includes the wolf dressed as Grandma with a picnic basket.

As we have already discussed, transmission in the network can be complex, so the devices in the network need to understand exactly how the target host/application is going to reconstruct and react to the data it receives. Look at the upcoming Figure 31-3. Application 1 generates information as a stream of data (MESSAGE). The operating system breaks that stream into segments (TCP segments) and sends them to the network. The receiving operating system collects the TCP segments and converts them back to a stream of data (MESSAGE), which is then presented to the receiving application. Since the underlying network does not guarantee delivery of the TCP segments, the receiver tells the sender which segments it has received, and the sender will retransmit any that have not been received.

TCP reassembly is the process of collecting TCP segments in the order that the sending application sent them and extracting the application data stream from them (the data stream is the relevant information required to deeply inspect and determine the intent of the transmission). Attackers may use various techniques to create ambiguous segments to try to evade detection. One of the most common is to take advantage of wiggle room built into the protocols that outline the conventions for the interactions among computing devices. For example, when you say "hello" to someone, you typically expect the person to say "hello" back. And if you ask a question such as, "Where are you from?", you might expect a response that includes some sort of city, town, or general locale. These are predictable behaviors (protocols) that facilitate a progressive dialogue between people. The same can be said for the network. When information is sent across the network, the receiving devices expect it to be in a predictable format and to follow a predictable sequence of events. When something falls out of the norm, deep inspection can often identify the wiggle and call it out.

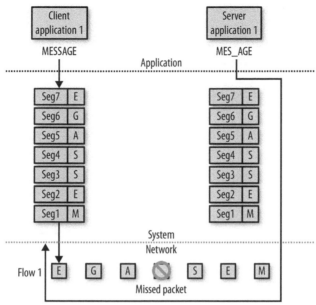

Figure 31-3. If Little Red Riding Hood examined the picnic basket and quickly compared it to her Grandma's picnic list, she would have noted the missing sandwich and that it was, indeed, not her grandmother.

The rules for network etiquette are defined by open protocols and published standards (such as RFCs, or Requests for Comments), as well as vendor-defined specifications for communication between networked devices, making it possible for a lot of different devices provided by a lot of different vendors to interact in a predictable way. However, because the published standards need to cover a lot of different scenarios, they are quite complex and must leave room for interpretation by the implementer (a wiggle). In addition, some TCP implementations have deliberately or accidentally deviated from the specifications. The result is that the same TCP segment can be accepted or rejected by different TCP stack implementations, providing attackers with many opportunities to construct ambiguous TCP segments.

An attacker can send varying contents in overlapping TCP segments, for example, two of the same segments that contain different data, as depicted in Figure 31-4. Different TCP stack implementations interpret the order differently—some use the first received, while others use the last received. For example, Windows takes data from the older segment, while Solaris takes it from the newer one. BSD and Linux (other operating systems) are not consistent—sometimes they prefer the older TCP segment and sometimes they prefer the newer one. Without knowing the exact behavior and circumstance of the victim's TCP implementation, the network device can have trouble determining what the right behavior is and whether or not to send an alarm. There. You just read and understood your first network attack scenario, and it is no more complicated than being able to identify the guy who goes to the restaurant and pretends he made reservations, arguing that the maitre d' is the one at fault.

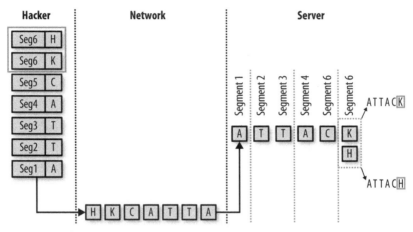

Figure 31-4. This example illustrates how a hacker, by sending overlapping data, causes problems. The hacker application sends the first five segments normally, then purposely creates two different Segment 6 packets and sends them both to the server. Different implementations of the TCP stack would interpret the data differently. Most operating systems will resolve the data to "ATTACH," but Windows NT and Solaris will see "ATTACK."

The good news is that it is relatively easy to detect ambiguous packets (and lying restaurant patrons) and stop them, because rather than trying to figure out what the attacker is trying to do, you simply stop the packet from ever reaching its destination (rather than listening to the solicitor at the door, just close the door). As a result, the attacker will never have the chance to access the target or victim and perpetrate his attack.

To date, there are a variety of technologies on the market that can help prevent or contain an attack to minimize its damage and maximize the availability and integrity of the network and all its resources. Some are better than others, and it's not unusual for a wide range of technologies to operate in concert to try to achieve broad coverage. We'll bring them up from time to time, with the key takeaway being the understanding that the network is a series of devices that read and forward traffic to the next point in its path to its final destination. Inspection of that traffic at different levels is necessary for secure delivery.

The key for the sustainable network will be trying to stay a step ahead of, or at least in step with, the ever-evolving risk and attack landscape to ensure that the promises of the network are not stymied by nefarious activities.

CHAPTER 32

I Am on the Net,
Therefore I Am Vulnerable

Where there's a will, there's a way!
—Proverb

E very network has vulnerabilities—even the smallest network, such as your home wireless network. These vulnerabilities can be exploited to compromise network resources and all the information available on them. Given our increasing reliance on all of these online resources, it's vital to protect the sustainable network. It's important to understand and then guard against any vulnerability to maintain the integrity and availability of the network and all the digital assets it connects.

These vulnerabilities represent *holes* in the devices connecting to the network or the actual network itself, and attackers can use them to slip in and screw things up. When a vulnerability is exploited, the resulting attack can vary in impact from annoying to significantly damaging, and ultimately, to crippling. These exploits can allow someone to steal or change information, shut the whole thing down, or even take complete control.

In 2008, a survey[1] asked Internet providers to rank the threats that pose the largest problems to their networks over a 12-month period. *Bots* and *botnets*, which are networks of compromised systems that can be used to launch other attacks, took the top spot, followed closely by DNS *cache poisoning threats*, which can redirect web traffic to the incorrect destinations, and *Border Gateway Protocol* (BGP) *route hijacking*, which is an Internet routing protocol that, when tampered with, can render sites inaccessible. Figure 32-1 shows all of the concerns, which, if you are a worrier, should give you something to mull over the next time you go online.

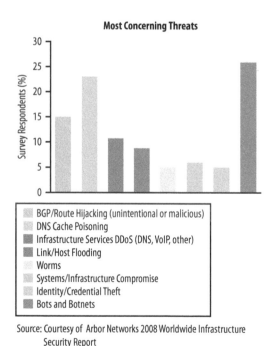

Source: Courtesy of Arbor Networks 2008 Worldwide Infrastructure Security Report

Figure 32-1. See what's on the minds of some of the best network security engineers in the world, from worms to floods.[2]

All of these attacks stem from the exploitation of vulnerabilities in the network and the network's connected computing devices. It's important to note there are really two types of vulnerabilities. The first are inherent within the devices and inner workings of the network itself, and the second are the result of the humans behind the machines. It turns out that while system errors are responsible for about 25% of network outages, human error is to blame for 50–80% of network outages,[3] bringing new meaning to the phrase "to err is human."

The Machines

In almost every piece of software, including the operating system of a device (phone, computer, router, server, printer, etc.) and the applications (email, video, voice, word processing, etc.), there are defects or unchecked boundary conditions that can be exploited. When a vulnerability is identified, the developers of the software typically create a patch to protect against the exploit of that vulnerability and issue it to the users of the software. Seems simple enough—if you have a hole in your screen door, you fix the hole so mosquitoes don't fly in, right?

But there is a long-fought battle between security experts about when such vulnerabilities should be made public. On one hand, the argument says it's vital not to call attention to a vulnerability and invite hackers to create attacks that could pose a risk to all systems that leverage the underlying software. On the other hand, there is the belief that openness is the only way to achieve true security, forcing software developers to quickly fix vulnerabilities.

While public policy and sentiment have come down in favor of each position at different times, the tide has turned recently toward the "openness" side, as evidenced by the evolving field of network and computing law. In 2008, in two separate cases on two separate continents, courts sided with security researchers who were trying to talk about security flaws they found. In one case, the Massachusetts Bay Transportation Agency (MBTA) attempted to prevent three MIT students from talking about the vulnerabilities they found in Boston's transit fare card system, known for its "Charlie Card." The other case had NXP Semiconductors hoping to prevent researchers at Radboud University in the Netherlands from publishing details about security flaws in one of its transit system cards, specifically one used by the London transit system (the MIFARE Classic card).[4] In both cases, the courts sided with those who wanted to make the vulnerabilities known, rather than the companies trying to stifle the openness of the information.

> A single attack can be used again and again—it's more "productive."

Obviously, the risks associated with a software vulnerability can vary dramatically, depending on what the software is and how many people or devices are using it. Typically, the software in greatest use is a bigger target because an attacker would have greater potential for gain. A single attack can be used again and again—it's more "productive" (and economically attractive) for attackers to figure out a way to infiltrate the 90% of the population using that software versus the 10% using something else.

And the potential exploit enabled by any particular vulnerability is often reflected in the urgency of the vendor's patch release timing. You may have seen alert windows pop up on your laptop screen asking to update your software with a security patch, in which case, it is most likely in your best interests to patch it immediately. Other patches are issued on a more regular schedule. For instance, Microsoft does batch patches for vulnerabilities that pose minimal risk to the ongoing operations of its software. Apple issues security updates fairly regularly, but you need to turn on the System Preferences setting for Auto updating for timely notice.

What it ultimately comes down to, however, is what we all do with that information. Ultimately, protecting the network comes down to the people who are on it.

The People

Users tend to be the root cause of most network vulnerabilities, because they either don't know or are unaware of how they are impacting the network's security. We buy a device that has more power and communication capability than the first space shuttle, and we're allowed to go online without a lesson or rulebook on how to behave ourselves. It's easy to see why we're responsible for 50–80% of all the network vulnerabilities. All too often, it's the way systems are configured or implemented by humans that creates the overall risks to systems and networks. Users may turn on features during configuration or leave settings on by default that are simply more vulnerable to attack. As a result, it's important to understand how a user's configuration of a device can affect the overall security of that device or system and, ultimately, the network.

Sometimes it just means that users and businesses need to take a more conservative approach when setting up their systems, turning everything off and only enabling features when there is an explicit need in an effort to reduce the attack vector's surface. For example, you may have already done this when you set your web browser to block pop-up windows.

Other times it's about making sure we keep current. When you learn of patches, how quickly do you install them? When a vulnerability is discovered that can have serious implications, a patch will be issued posthaste. Sometimes, it must be noted, hackers are sitting around playing *Grand Theft Auto*, waiting for a good idea when they see an issued patch. It can be a window of opportunity, because if a patch is issued, it tends to indicate a big hole and easy pickings for the hacker. You should be aware of any vendor-issued patches that resolve software bugs and apply these patches, no matter how seemingly innocuous, as soon as possible to minimize exposure to that particular vulnerability and any attack that might exploit it.

How do I do that, you ask?

- Both Microsoft and Apple have software update preference settings in their devices' system preferences or system settings. Make sure your computer or laptop has some kind of "auto" setting that downloads security patches automatically or at least alerts you of new ones.

- If you can't remember the last time you updated your computer's software system, you're probably vulnerable. You should put this book down for a while and do yourself a favor.

- Smartphones from Palm, Apple, BlackBerry, and phone carriers such as Sprint and Verizon have supporting websites where you can sign up for new software update alerts. When they are issued, take the time to update your device.

- Most modern applications have a preference setting to automatically check for updates—make sure this is enabled, too. Some applications from Microsoft, Adobe, and many of the smaller vendors usually have a menu item to enable automatic update checks.

- If you work for a mid-size or large company, check with your IT group. Most have Network Access Control policies and some have remote device scanning capabilities that can help you identify issues and keep your devices free from malware.

- Finally, there are some malware-checking programs (to check for viruses, worms, Trojans, botnets, etc.) from companies such as Symantec, TrendMicro, and FireEye that scan new applications and the information you download from the network for known attacks.

And Sometimes It's Just Good Hacking

In 2008, it was discovered that there were deficiencies in the Internet's DNS protocol and common implementations that would actually facilitate DNS cache poisoning attacks.[5]

DNS is responsible for resolving all the domain names of websites in the world into actual IP addresses that the routers use to forward the traffic. For example, when you type "www.company.com" in your web browser's address field, a DNS server does the lookup and translation of that alphabetical address to the actual numerical IP address, which might look something like "123.123.123.2." These DNS servers can get a little busy, so to speed address resolution, DNS servers keep the name-to-IP address resolution mapping in cache memory, thus keeping frequently used results obtained from other DNS servers readily available to reduce latency.

In a cache poisoning attack, the DNS server is tricked into accepting incorrect information into memory (thus poisoning the cache of the DNS server). The DNS server then responds to domain name queries with that incorrect information. First, the attacker gets the DNS server to ask it a question about where a particular IP address is located. Then, in response to that question, the attacker answers a completely different question that contains a different address to which the attacker wants the server to resolve. The DNS server caches that answer and then uses it the next time it is asked about that IP address, resolving to the incorrect one, as illustrated in Figure 32-2.

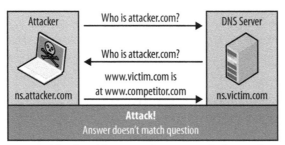

Figure 32-2. *Sometimes a good hack is like a good magic trick that makes a machine believe in something that's merely an illusion.*

A DNS cache poisoning attack exploits the DNS server's willingness to accept responses for questions it didn't ask. In Figure 32-2, the attacker asks the DNS server, "Who is www.attacker.com?" The DNS server tries to resolve by getting the information from the authority on the domain, which is the attacker. In response to the DNS query, "Who is www.attacker.com?", the attacker answers, "www.victim.com = www.competitor.com."

DNS cache poisoning itself is not new, but this specific vulnerability, which, in essence, provides the entry point to poison the cache, is a unique implementation that exploits the fact that the DNS server reuses the same source port instead of a randomly assigned one for all outgoing queries. A CSI survey released in 2008 found that 8% of respondents had experienced some sort of DNS incident. By the end of the year, one in four DNS servers were still vulnerable.[6] There are proposed DNS Security Extensions (DNS-SEC) designed to bolster DNS against these types of vulnerabilities and prevent attackers from hijacking and redirecting web traffic. Basically, they use digital signatures and public-key encryption technologies to allow websites to verify their domain names and corresponding IP addresses.[7]

In addition to inherent software vulnerabilities and those created from specific implementations, it's important to recognize that some applications are themselves inherently dangerous. Some applications create opportunities for attackers simply because of what they are designed to do. For example, P2P file-sharing applications are designed to make it easy for people to exchange files, but by their very nature, they also make it easy for anyone on the Internet to grab files from users' computers. This is why it's so important to be cognizant of all the implications associated with everything you load onto your devices when connected.

You can also create vulnerabilities when you create your own programs. When developing programs, consider all of the repercussions and recognize that there may be security tradeoffs when building unique extensions to a system in the business world or when using the latest gizmo or cool application in your personal life. These things seem to draw the hackers because they represent new terrain that has not been updated; patched systems tend to be more protected because they've been around longer and had more opportunity to find and resolve potential vulnerabilities.

For instance, the proliferation of the new open application stores, which allow users around the world to create applications for specific devices and platforms (such as Apple's iPhone or Google's Android Browser), promises to accelerate innovation and deliver new and interesting uses for the devices and the network. Do you need to guess who else they attract?

Fortunately, there are many checks and balances in place to minimize the chance that these open applications will create opportunities for security breaches, but it also isn't unrealistic to presume that a particular application's developer may not have been a security expert; she may not have created and tested her application with security in mind. As a result, it is possible she unwittingly created holes in the system that attackers could exploit. While the benefits of open platforms and open application development far outweigh the potential detriments, it's important to be mindful of the potential impact that anything loaded onto a device or system could have.

If you are on the network, are you vulnerable? Yes. If you are not on the network, are you vulnerable? Yes. That's because information about you and your family is somewhere on the network, in the government's database, a credit card or mortgage company's database, or your local Little League website. So, I suggest you take matters into your own hands and do all you can to protect yourself. Keep reading, and start to use the openness of the network to research and then leverage all the resources that are available to help you protect yourself. After all, the sustainability of the network is dependent on our ongoing ability to confidently use it in all of our daily activities.

CHAPTER 33

Antisocial Network Engineering

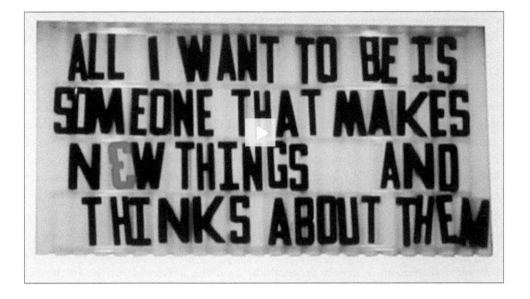

Trickery and treachery are the practices of fools that have not the wits enough to be honest.

—Benjamin Franklin

As we are so often reminded, we are all human and capable of making mistakes. In this regard, the virtual world is no different from the physical one, and it's what attackers are counting on. If you zoomed through Chapter 32, you might have missed the tidbit that 50–80% of network device outages, which disrupt the availability of the network, are attributable to benign human factors.[1]

Sometimes these network compromises are the product of poor management practices or inadequate checks and balances. They could be the result of data retrieved from a lost or stolen device, which can easily happen. Consider that 22% of employees[2] carry corporate data on portable storage devices outside of the office, or take the case of the Bank of New York Mellon employee who lost a backup tape containing the financial records of approximately 10 million customers while en route to have it destroyed.[3] Oops. The attackers could be playing the numbers game, throwing their nets wide in hopes of catching unwitting victims. Like when your teenager goes to a site recommended by one of her friends and downloads strange stuff that ends up dragging down the home network every time she boots up. And then there are the exploits conducted by people with specific criminal intentions. One example is the bank trader who was familiar with the access controls associated with the inner workings of Société Générale and is now charged with fraud, forgery, and attacks on an automated system that resulted in losses of approximately 4.9 billion ($7.2 billion USD at then-current exchange rates) in January 2008.

So, let's dwell for just a little bit on the scammers and con artists of the virtual world who take advantage of the trust and goodness of people to get them to unknowingly provide information or create vulnerabilities on the network. Just as in the physical world, some virtual scams are more obvious than others and some illusions are more elaborate in their scope. You may have received the email message from a prince from Africa who is worth millions but needs your help to get him and his money out of the country. Just send him your bank account information, and he will deposit his millions and allow you to keep a portion for your troubles. While there's a high probability that you are *not* going to hand over your bank account information, this scam must work with someone, because this email message "gets around." The trickier scams, as in the physical world, are the more involved schemes—the ones that look like truly legitimate operations that work to build a trusting façade so that you lower your guard and unveil information they can use. They don't need your bank information, they just need to gain access to your laptop. All your banking information and more can be had in seconds once access is granted.

This is the crux of *phishing* scams. Phishing lures users into visiting an official-looking site by getting you to click on a link or open an attachment, such as an innocuous-looking holiday card, a store coupon, or any of a thousand enticing hooks that click-happy users seem incapable of ignoring. Your click takes you to a fake website that may look exactly like the legitimate one, where the attacker tries to collect information on you, such as your username and password. Or perhaps you end up downloading a worm, a virus, or a Trojan horse on your laptop, giving the attacker further opportunity to collect information or disrupt general operation.

With the rise of *Web 2.0* (referring to the second generation of web development and usage) and all the user-generated content that is flying around the digital world (think YouTube and Facebook pages), you can get a sense of the vast potpourri of attacking options available to attackers. Criminals and scammers have a whole set of channels, or vectors, they can use to perpetrate their attacks. For example, they are no longer relegated to getting you to click on an email attachment—they may be able to entice you via postings in blogs and forums that contain links to images or other content that could unwittingly infect a user. Several good examples of such scams were in the news while I was writing this book.

A botnet is a network of multiple individual devices that have computer programs that can run automatically or when triggered by a remote command from an attacker.

Twitter was recently targeted by a phishing scam (Twitter.com is a social networking site that lets people broadcast text messages, everything from the mind-numbing to the profound). Fake and often inappropriate messages were posted on the Twitter accounts of Britney Spears, CNN anchor Rick Sanchez, several Fox News anchors, and other high-profile personalities.[4] How did this occur? The attackers reset the victim's passwords by exploiting the tools the Twitter support team uses to help Twitter users who can't remember their passwords.[5] The attackers then tricked users into logging on to a page that masqueraded as the Twitter front page, thereby capturing their personal login and password information. They used that information to make false posts that appeared to be coming from the users themselves, all in an effort to put their foot in the door and get more users to eventually download infected material and collect more personal information.

As I have mentioned previously, the new U.S. administration has garnered worldwide interest, so it's no surprise that hackers took advantage and tried to capitalize on U.S. President Barack Obama's inauguration. They tried to impersonate Obama's website and entice people into clicking on the story "Barack Obama has refused to be a President." When users clicked, the site would download all the files on the victim's computer so it could be used to host the fake site and perpetuate the scam. Ultimately, this attack was intended to infect as many machines as possible in an effort to grow a botnet ("bot" is short for "robot"—yes, "robot"; we are definitely in the 21st century). Is it as scary as it may sound? Perhaps.

A botnet is a network of multiple individual devices that have computer programs that can run automatically or when triggered by a remote command from an attacker. The botnet can execute without user involvement and can tell its host device exactly what to do and when to do it. Basically, the attacker creates a backdoor on your networked device that he can access and then use to control your machine whenever he wants. If you're infected, you'll probably never know it (sometimes you may notice a slowdown of your system), but the attacker can use your computer, and hundreds of others, to launch serendipitous attacks from his network of self-running robots. Some scams use thousands of compromised computers and laptops, so only a tiny fraction of each device's bandwidth is needed, thereby avoiding detection.

Network criminals may be using as many as a quarter of the computers on the Internet.

Worms and Trojans are other familiar infection mechanisms. They are similar to and sometimes used interchangeably with bots, as they, too, install onto a target computing device and can then be used to launch other attacks without the computer's user ever knowing. The distinction comes in the level of interaction involved—worms tend to be self-perpetuating, while Trojans tend to involve more interaction with the attacker. Just as the name hints, the attacker uses a Trojan to get into your system and then gather useful information.

So, what do these botnets do, once ensconced? Well, many are used to launch Denial of Service (DoS) attacks against specific resources or servers, flooding them with so much traffic that they can't keep up and process the requests, ultimately rendering the devices unable to provide access to their resources (see Chapter 37 on 21st-century warfare for some specific examples). There are many variations of what a DoS attack can do once the attacker gains control of the computing resource (computer, server, mobile phone, etc.), from sending a file to reformatting the hard drive to launching yet another attack. Basically, a successful DoS attack can give an attacker complete control over that resource and ultimately the network to which it is attached. There are predictions that as many as a quarter of the computers on the Internet may be used by cybercriminals in botnets,[6] and, unfortunately, it seems as though the growth of the largest botnets continues to outpace containment efforts and infrastructure investment.[7]

The largest distributed DoS (DDoS) attacks, which typically leverage multiple botnets to converge on a particular resource, server, or router to overwhelm and render it unattainable, have now grown a hundredfold to break the 40 Gb barrier in 2008.[8] Additionally, 57% of service provider respondents to a survey conducted by Arbor Networks in 2008 reported attacks larger than 1 Gb in a 12-month period.[9] These can place great strains on the network and eat up valuable bandwidth that could otherwise be put to much better use.

On October 20, 2008, John Markoff of the *New York Times* reported on an experiment held at the Microsoft campus in Redmond, Washington, in which an unprotected computer running Windows XP was allowed to connect to the Internet without a firewall or other protection. A cybercrime researcher and investigator carried out the experiment, and in exactly 30 seconds, the computer had been found by a botnet and was infected.[10]

Now, that experiment is a little different than you plugging into the network. Most work, home, and even Wi-Fi networks have built-in firewalls and protection, and the Redmond experiment probably also had some unique characteristics built into the computer system to make it attractive. But there are basic things you can do to protect your systems from becoming infected by malware and part of a botnet:

- Resist the urge to click on unknown or potentially dubious links.

- When you receive an email or text message that prompts you to visit a site, even if it looks like it comes from a legitimate source, don't click on the provided link. Instead, you should physically type the address of the site in your web browser. This way, you can make sure you go to the official, legitimate site and not a fake location.

- Remember, it is the embedded link in the email or text message that leads users astray, because they don't notice or don't know that the link doesn't lead to the official website you're intending to visit. Phishers have gotten increasingly sophisticated in their mimicry of legitimate sites, so often the only way you will know is to look very carefully at the web address. So, don't hide this field in your web browser and, again, make sure you manually type in all web addresses.

- Always connect to the network from behind a firewall.

- Run a complete suite of security software, including firewall, antivirus, URL filtering, and antispam technologies on your devices.

Remember, scammers and attackers are looking for a way in. Once they have a foothold, they can use it almost any way they want. They can capture valuable account information, so, when you surf online, make sure you are safe. Go only to places you can trust and be careful what you communicate to whom. In general, use the same precautions you would when you're out of town driving around looking for a restaurant. If it's sketchy or makes claims ("best steak ever") that look too good to be true, just say, "no, thank you." If you know someone who recommends it, sure, go ahead and try it, but always walk in with your eyes open and be ready to spot a rat.

CHAPTER 34

Protect the Net

Now we know! And knowing is half the battle!
—Animated G.I. Joe Public Service Announcements
on U.S. television for children, 1985–1986

W e know that the sustainable network is connecting people all over the world, and we would like to concentrate on the infinite realm of opportunities it provides, but as you know, not everyone uses the network's tools and information for good. Just as in the physical world, there are individuals motivated by personal gain, greed, power, ideologies, or other nefarious ends.

This is a circumstance of human nature and not the sustainable network, and it runs so deep that the connections and information sharing we conduct over the network *must* be protected. There are plenty of precautions and measures that we can take to maintain the integrity and privacy of the data flowing through the network and its global communications infrastructure, but the question is, how much do you want to know about it? How stuff works can be boring at times. It takes your undivided attention and, as with all things in network engineering, it suffers from an overuse of acronyms. But if you are aware of how someone could infiltrate your laptop, find your online banking passwords, and play havoc with your hard-earned money, you can at least make it difficult for attackers to do.

There are dozens of different technologies that individuals, businesses, and governments deploy to protect the integrity of the data flowing across the public network (Internet) and within their internal networks. There are security technologies built into the applications themselves to try to ensure proper use and security solutions for deployment on individual hosts to protect the specific devices, and still others that are designed to sit in the network to protect all the traffic flowing through it. There are so many acronyms (i.e., SSL VPNs, IPSec, and NAC) that you may wonder whether it's a whole separate effort to keep the criminal mind from seeing the defenses!

Any good security strategy will layer in a variety of technologies that do the following:

- Ensure that all the devices and applications on the network have been developed with security in mind, don't introduce unnecessary risk, and have been patched appropriately to address known vulnerabilities.

- For the most critical resources, such as servers that house intellectual property or sensitive information, there are mechanisms in place to monitor activity and ensure proper usage.

- Ensure that the sophistication of the security measures mirror the sensitivity and criticality of the information flowing over the network. Businesses and governments will be taking precautions and going to levels that most of us would never conceive of attempting.

As individuals, we typically rely on scaled-down versions of many of the government- and business-grade technologies, such as personal firewalls, antispam software, URL filtering, and antivirus software, to try to keep the information we store on our computing devices safe. A software firewall is usually built into your home DSL or cable modem, requiring you to provide a username and password when you install it. The same is available in most Wi-Fi devices that provide home or small-office wireless connectivity. The username/password combination is like the lock and key to the front door of your home. It attempts to control who enters, especially when you're not there. There are additional techniques to further validate that you are who you say you are, from rudimentary security questions to more sophisticated key *fobs* (devices you keep on your person that display a randomly generated alphanumerical code that can be used in combination with a personal identification number [PIN] to authenticate a user). Others are just designed to make sure you are human and not a bot—like *CAPTCHAs*, which are those crazy words that some sites ask you to type in before you are granted access.

The firewall, or access control device, is often the first layer of defense, determining which traffic to allow or deny. It does this by applying a *policy*, a set of actions composed of "accept" and "deny" rules. These rules are based on various criteria, such as the traffic source, the destination, and the networking protocol the traffic is using. Most firewall polices allow protocols that let you conduct your business with your friends and coworkers on the Internet, while keeping out traffic that is known to pose a threat to your systems. Some of the protocols commonly allowed include mail (SMTP), file transfers (FTP), VoIP (SIP), web access (HTTP), and DNS.

Think of a firewall as a bouncer for a nightclub: a big guy with tattoos and a shaved head. When you approach, the bouncer will take a cursory look at you and determine if you can enter based on whether you meet the club's criteria, such as whether or not you are wearing shoes. The bouncer might do a quick patdown to ensure that you are not concealing something that is not allowed, such as a weapon or drugs. However, as we all know, there is a lot that the bouncer can miss because he's really there to control traffic, not necessarily spy on it.

This is where technologies such as antispam, URL filtering, antivirus, and government- and business-grade Intrusion Detection Systems (IDSs) and Intrusion Prevention Systems (IPSs) come into play. These technologies are like the metal detector just beyond the bouncer that identifies people trying to sneak in the stuff they shouldn't. They may simply sound alarms (giving you warnings that something may not be right) or they may take it one step further and kick the traffic off the network, akin to the bouncers physically removing troublemakers from the premises—their job is to make sure very little gets through.

Let's start with the most sophisticated first; IDS/IPS solutions process the traffic flowing through the network in an effort to understand the intent of that traffic and determine what it is doing at the Application level (Level 7, remember? Refer back to Figure 31-2), so it can identify and stop attacks on the network. The goal is to minimize the time and costs associated with attacks and intrusions. These intrusion prevention technologies look at the traffic that the firewall allows in the network (see Figure 34-1), looking for the bad stuff.

While there is intelligence in all these systems, it tends to be more of the brute force kind. It's not uncommon for the IDS and IPS alarms to go off when there is nothing actually malicious, just like when metal detectors sound an alarm for your belt buckle, watch, or the keys and coins in your pocket. As a result, all of these IPSs offer response mechanisms that allow administrators to control the exact response for specified types of attacks in different parts of the network, with the ability to make adjustments in what the system should look for and how it should respond. But it takes quite a bit of monitoring and security know-how to fine-tune and make best use of these technologies, which is why they are most commonly found in business and government settings. It's also a reminder that security is a process and not a destination. There is no single solution or silver bullet, and the more technologies and techniques that are layered in, the better the chance for success.

Role of firewall

| Denied traffic | **Drop rules:** Anything not explicity allowed below |
| Allowed traffic | **Allow rules:** SMTP, FTP, HTTP, DNS, B-B VPN |

Role of Intrusion Detection Prevention

| Bad traffic | Detect Notify Take action |
| Good traffic | |

Figure 34-1. A firewall is like a bouncer, but an IDS/IPS device examines all the swill the firewall lets through in the normal course of business and network use, frisking and prodding into engineering constructs you don't even want to learn about.

So, since your household probably doesn't have or really need an IPS device (unless you're one of the many network engineers reading this book who happens to have a broom closet full of routers, switches, firewalls, and the like just for fun and upping the electric bill), you might familiarize yourself with technologies such as antispam, URL filtering, and antivirus that can help protect your computing devices and information. The function of these software solutions on your laptop or computer is to filter out things that are known to be bad or unwanted. Antispam and URL filtering focus on keywords that the user or program defines as "bad," otherwise known as *blacklists*. Antispam can be applied to combat the proliferation of unsolicited messages and is typically used to reduce unwanted (junk) and dangerous email messages in a user's inbox (it should be noted that more and more service providers have spam filters on their ends that do an amazing job, so it may not be necessary to invest in your own solution). URL filtering, also known as web filtering, content-control software, or even the overly hokey *censorware*, is designed to restrict content delivered via the Internet. Some URL filtering is built right into the computer and sometimes into the browser, such as Internet Explorer,

Apple's Safari, or Firefox. Parents might use it to ensure that their kids are not going to inappropriate or potentially dangerous websites where they could infect the whole household network. Another benefit of URL filtering is that you can actually reduce the chances of something bad being downloaded on your computing device, since dubious websites are more likely to be infected with malware (which could be viruses, worms, Trojans, and other nasty stuff).

With any of these security technologies, when "bad" words are detected (in a website address or an email message's address, subject, or body), the system will get rid of or quarantine the traffic. Remember our bouncer analogy? Well, if you have been blacklisted from a club, the bouncer can check his list and see your name, and you will be denied access. You won't be dancing there tonight—or for as long as your name is on the blacklist. Some systems use *whitelists* instead, defining everything that they want to accept (and, by default, denying everything else), which is the equivalent of an approved guest list the bouncer checks when deciding whether or not you get into the club.

Antivirus is a critical component of your individual security plan because viruses pose a major threat to the integrity and functionality of computing devices. In essence, they're deadly, but it's surprising how many people don't employ antivirus software on their devices. The culprits take their name from the physical world's viruses, partly because of the sustainable network's capability to spread the infection quickly and indiscriminately. Computer viruses are typically carried in files and are generally aimed at damaging end user systems, using various email and web servers for propagation. Consequently, it is important to detect viruses while they are being uploaded or downloaded to mitigate and hopefully prevent any damage.

> Dubious websites are more likely to be infected with malware.

Just as physical viruses are catalogued and characterized so that doctors can recognize and appropriately treat them, so it is with our virtual vigilantes. Security experts can actually recreate the attack patterns used by computer viruses and then create attack-matching *signatures*. They use these signatures to identify network viruses and the types of attacks that are happening in real time. Once identified, devices can implement the safeguards to thwart the viruses. So, our tattooed bouncer now has a list of specific "do not let in under any circumstances" paparazzi, and when a match is found, he blocks entry to the club and probably literally bounces them down the sidewalk.

Antivirus software typically scans files in your email application and in your miscellaneous web traffic looking to find a match for any of its attack signatures. Because it relies on signatures, a virus must be identified before it can be protected against. For this reason, you should always allow your antivirus software to perform automatic updates, whereby it connects to its home support center and downloads the latest signatures.

You should also be aware that some antivirus programs have the capability to fix the files that have been infected by viruses, while other programs can prevent the damage of a virus by not only alerting the user to its presence but also stopping the virus from loading and running itself on the computer or system. Antivirus is part of a larger group of file-level protection measures, so if you're shopping around for security solutions, you should look for the capability to extract files within traffic and inspect them to detect a variety of malware (Trojans, bots, worms, and viruses).

If you think this is all a headache to implement in your home or small office (and sometimes it is), be thankful you're not a big business. Or a university. Or any level of government using the network to aid its constituents. When you become a big network, or even just a bigger network, the security aspects begin to snowball and our bald-headed bouncer becomes a single guy at one of the entrances to New York's Grand Central Station. The sheer number of users, devices, and applications flowing through a business or government entity's environment, coupled with the growing sophistication of attacks, demands the need for a multilayered security strategy that can protect the organization at every level. While the amount of resources that can be applied to create a secure environment is much greater, so too are the number of avenues needing protection.

It used to be that there was a fairly defined network "perimeter" that the business worked to protect—its outside wall to the world and its connection to the Internet. But with the advent of the increasingly mobile network and the distributed enterprise model with people working and interacting from any- and everywhere, that is no longer the case. Businesses, governments, and other organizations need a multitiered approach that includes security measures on both the devices connected to the network (laptops, servers, phones, printers, and so on) and the network itself. The perimeter approach to network security has seemingly been turned inside out, creating a gelatinous security nightmare with not only external threats, but also internal *and* remote access threats. The pervasiveness of the sustainable network means you can be attacked from anywhere.

This is all why in the past 10 years, or even the past 5, if you are a white-collar employee working in a large office, you've become familiar with such things as keycards, encryption mechanisms, secure ID tokens, VPNs, specialized application firewalls, security incident management systems, and the list goes on and on. It's part of your day, part of your work life, so much so that you may not even recognize them as security measures. One of the more talked-about security mechanisms in recent years is network access control (NAC) solutions.

NAC, also referred to as Network Access Protection (NAP), is the consistent application of network access policies (a set of rules governing who can log in to the network) to meet the challenge of insider threats to organizations and their networked resources. In fact, NAC-like solutions can be found in the top three of many businesses' IT initiatives.

This is presumably due to the rise in threats that result from the increasingly distributed number of people who need to access business networks. Just think of how telecommuting, off-shoring, and outsourcing practices (to name a few) are changing both the boundaries of businesses and its participants (remember Chapters 23–25). These trends will be even more prevalent in the future as broadband continues its global outreach and workers can be anywhere and everywhere, thereby increasing the demand for technologies such as NAC, which help organizations make access decisions based on the answers to the following:

- What is the relationship of the user to the organization? Is the user a customer, a full-time employee, a partner, etc.?

- What are the potential risks associated with the devices that are currently accessing the network? What about those that are attempting access? Are they under the company's control? Are they up to date on all relevant software patches, etc.? Can they be scanned?

- What is the location of the connection? Is the user in an airport using an unsecured connection, or is he in his office cubicle?

- What is the time of access? For instance, is it during work hours or after hours? What is the user's time zone?

A total NAC solution must use all this information to create a global policy that grants access to only the appropriate users at the appropriate time, using only the devices that adhere to the organization's security parameters. Used in combination with other security devices on the network, such as firewalls, rate-limiting switches (which help prevent traffic overloads and contain attack impacts), and IPSs, access can be adjusted based on the real-time activities taking place on the network. For example, if an IPS identifies an attack on the network coming from a new user, the IPS can send an alert and the NAC solution can shut down or quarantine that user to prevent further spread or damage. NAC solutions are bouncers on steroids, flexing their muscles and working in coordination with the other enforcers to ensure that people in the club are doing only what they should be doing.

Did you understand that last paragraph? If you did, welcome to the 21st century! The fact that you are reading network acronyms and understand what they mean and what they do is a great milestone. Get ready for more network security jargon to enter the common vocabulary. Perhaps you'll lead the charge!

All of these measures, policies, and detection can control, at a fairly granular level, the type of traffic that is flowing on the network to mitigate threats to the network's resources. Because these devices are digital, they create lots of logs and pages upon pages of information on what they have seen or processed. The logs are important because they can be correlated to figure out what is really going on in the network. As the threats and attacks become more sophisticated, they are often not easily recognized from a single data point or attack vector. As a result, organizations are trying to figure out how best to compile and make sense of all this information to help identify weaknesses in the network and create up-to-date attack signatures that can be used to fortify the network against future exploits. They contain great information about what happened and can help predict what's to come.

But figuring out what happened and protecting any one network may be too insular. All the information contained in the logs can also serve as documentation of the events for criminal prosecution. However, referring to CSI's annual security survey, only 60% of respondents attempted to identify the perpetrator of an attack, using the logs and other status information. Most respondents focused on the remediation activities—patching security holes, installing additional security software, changing security policies, etc. And while there has been a big push within law enforcement to follow up and try to arrest the culprits and put them in jail (hopefully without Internet access), only 27% of CSI respondents actually reported incidents to a law enforcement agency of any kind. The respondents cited that incidents were either too small to bother reporting, they didn't believe law enforcement could help, or they wanted to avoid any negative publicity.

There's no switch you can simply turn on to protect yourself.

But the sustainable network will most likely depend on thousands of "formal" public investigations in order to thrive and survive. To be sustainable, the network needs to be above reproach. People need to be able to trust it and believe that it is governed by rules of law that set boundaries similar to those in the physical world. The only way that can happen is if those who threaten and actually damage it are held accountable for breaking those laws. Unfortunately, it may take some gargantuan financial loss or cataclysmic event to occur, as many security analysts predict, for organizations to start putting resources into attacker identification and prosecution. Most of the data is logged—it just has to be mined a little and then used to take external action.

Let me reiterate: today, as you're reading this book, there are billions of dollars' worth of equipment protecting the integrity of the network on an hourly, if not minute-by-minute, basis. While different attacks use different methods to exploit vulnerabilities throughout the network, each time an attack occurs, it actually strengthens the network with the information its attack vectors give us. But given the adoption rate and ultimate power of the sustainable network in just the near future, the network's security will require an even greater multitiered approach that is coordinated and all-encompassing.

We will have to work together to both protect the Net and police it, with cyberpolicing and network law becoming steadfast at a federal and worldwide level.

There is no silver bullet, however. There's no switch you can simply turn on to protect yourself if you're connected to the network. Security is a process, not an end state, and it is absolutely critical that it continues to evolve and keep pace with both the inventiveness of the hackers *and* the innovation of the users. You must be aware of the risks and the preventive options available, the same as if you were crossing a busy street. Don't be afraid to take that step, just make sure you look both ways. Protect yourself. Protect your data. Make sure those you interact with (businesses and friends) do the same. Be vigilant. The alternative threatens the overall growth and benefits of the sustainable network.

The Last Best Place to Attack: Your Mobile

It turns into a car if I have to make a quick getaway.

—President Barack Obama, about the
special-issue BlackBerry he carries

n a world where being connected at all times is almost imperative, it would seem logical that the president of the United States would want always-available access to the network. But advisors and security experts saw it as too risky—they couldn't guarantee that his messages wouldn't be intercepted. Not unfounded worries for such a public figure. Remember when socialite Paris Hilton's cell phone was hacked and her celebrity friends' phone numbers were exposed? I know, the horror! But it's easy to see how a president's phone may pose some worries.[1] President Obama was able to enter the Oval Office with a government-fortified BlackBerry on his hip, after promising to keep the messages on it strictly of a personal nature.

While mobility is extending the access of the network to far-flung reaches of the globe and opening doors for great swaths of the world's population, including a president or two, it is also creating possibilities for attackers and openings for exploitation by criminals and many others with less than admirable intentions. Attacks are no longer relegated to the wired network or the domain of traditional computers. Just as the wired networks are transitioning to an "all IP" environment, the traditionally siloed wireless networks are also converging onto IP (as discussed in Chapter 21), making the differences between them increasingly negligible. In fact, you could say the network is again leveling playing fields, as vulnerabilities are becoming quite equitable, whether you access the network from your landline or mobile phone. The main difference is that now, with the mobility of network, criminals can attack your devices from afar with little risk of being caught or even detected. A criminal no longer has to break into a secure facility, but only has to find a radio wavelength to attack otherwise secured dignitaries.

It was not that long ago that I remember driving to a meeting in Silicon Valley with a security expert who was able to jump onto the "secure" wireless networks of the companies we passed, simply because they left their wireless network wide open. This type of hacking is called *wardriving*, and it is a form of wireless reconnaissance that involves driving around to locate target networks and gather information about their authentication, encryption keys, and so forth. I want to assure you that the expert was just proving a point and logged off as soon as the network was penetrated. But the point remains relevant—wardriving continues. Load up the laptop and some other hardware in your car with applications like Netstumbler, Kismet, and Wireshark (free and open source sniffers and network analyzers), and you can find wireless networks to penetrate. A new generation of tools such as Aircrack and Karma in the hands of talented hackers can analyze your wireless traffic, inject data into the stream, and pretend to be legitimate access points, compromising all the information that passes through it.

And the information that's now flowing over mobile networks, created by the ever-growing number of mobile subscribers using their mobile devices to do everything from talking to banking to running their businesses, looks very lucrative to would-be attackers. Forecasts place the number of smartphones expected to ship in 2013 at over 430 million, with 1.7 billion new mobile phone sales between 2008 and 2013.[2] That's a lot of opportunity, as these devices carry more and more personal information and play increasingly critical roles in our business and personal lives.

Traditionally, security on the mobile phone has always taken a backseat to usability. That wasn't necessarily the wrong approach. To date, malicious activity on mobile phones has been relatively negligible, consisting of attacks with only limited impact.[3] This can be explained by the fact that initial mobile networks (1G and 2G networks) only supported voice. This meant the

We can expect that mobile attacks will become increasingly sophisticated and more frequent.

value of any personal information was very limited (relating to the user's contact list and phone calls) or derived from the minutes themselves that could be stolen to get access to the network. With a single application going over a single network, the attack vectors and risks to the service were fairly low and contained. Now, however, with the addition of data, video, and other multimedia applications and the proliferation of device types that can traverse the mobile network, the risks have multiplied. In addition, the amount of information stored on mobile devices has increased exponentially. While phones used to house simple contact lists and an application or two, newer smartphones can expose a user's entire email inbox, GPS location information, account numbers, financial statements, and other information.

We can expect that, just as in the "wired" world, mobile attacks are going to become increasingly sophisticated and more frequent. And these attacks can come from anywhere and from anyone, including the users themselves. Remember, we're talking about the mobile network—all the characteristics that make it so useful also make it vulnerable. The worst part about mobile-based attacks is that your device could be transmitting personal information to an attacker or used in an active DoS attack, all unbeknownst to you while the device is sitting in your pocket.

As a result, users of mobile networks have found themselves increasingly the targets of activities traditionally confined only to computers and the wired networks. For example, a survey in the UK found that 66% of UK mobile phone users have been victims of spam, with the number of 18–24-year-olds targeted as high as 75%. Nearly 1 in 10 of those who received spam have been targeted by phishing attacks, which try to trick the victims into providing personal data; 38% received a text message containing a link to another site; and 45% received a text message that tried to trick them into calling a premium rate phone number.[4] We have also seen *vishing* (a hybrid term for voice phishing), in which an attacker calls a victim and tries to lure him into revealing personal data.

In addition to all the information now flowing across the mobile network, the entry of many nontraditional phone providers, such as Microsoft and Google, is further evolving the mobile threat landscape. Some might argue that their entry is potentially driving OS consolidation, sometimes referred to as "creating a monoculture." In agricultural terms, a monoculture relates to using crops that are genetically similar and have the same growth patterns to garner greater yields. In an OS, it relates to using the same source code and architectural and design principles to create underlying software that can be used by multiple systems. In turn, this could create bigger, more productive targets for attackers. The potential is greater for an attacker to create a single exploit that has far-ranging implications across multiple network environments.

To explain, the OS is the underlying software that runs on your computing device—in this case, the smartphone—and supports the smooth operation of all the applications and services that are delivered by that device. With the entry of companies that already have large OS market share in other arenas—such as Apple and Microsoft, who are known for dominating traditional computing environments—it is not a huge leap that all the knowledge attackers have developed for any vulnerability associated with Apple and Microsoft can be potentially associated and exploited in their mobile versions. And as more and more traditional applications are adapted for mobile devices, any underlying vulnerabilities in the OS could get translated as well. It has already happened. An image-processing vulnerability in an older version of Mac OS X made it into version 1.1.1 of Apple's iPhone firmware, allowing users to load and execute open source software directly onto the iPhone. Because the vulnerability was already well known, crafting an exploit was much easier and quicker to accomplish.[5]

It should be noted, however, that OSs developed specifically for the mobile world, such as Symbian or Google's Android mobile platform, are just as likely to be targeted as the mobile versions of OSs from traditional software vendors, as they gain users. We have seen evidence of this—there was a 400% growth in the number of Trojans seen in the wild for Symbian and Windows Mobile alone.[6] In February 2009, the "Sexy View" worm targeted Symbian mobile phone users in China. The worm spread via text messages that sent a link offering pictures of "naked girls" to everyone on the recipient's contact list—the first step toward a mobile botnet scenario touched upon in Chapter 33.

This is a very scary development—to think that attackers can amass the increasingly prolific and powerful mobile devices to launch attacks. The real kicker is that a subculture of wireless and mobile hackers exists, and its members use the sustainable network to compare techniques, stories, and swap utilities to further their own hacking efforts. The dramatic increase in mobile threat activity, albeit starting from a small base, is probably indicative of what's to come. And the timeframe seems to be getting shorter and shorter between vulnerability discovery and time to exploit. It took approximately two weeks for hackers to get into the first-generation iPhone, and one month before the tools were available that allowed general users to unlock their phones. The next-generation 3G iPhones were unlocked in a matter of hours.[8]

All of these factors are creating what some have called a perfect storm for attackers to start to really try to exploit. Because the phones are now running a mainstream OS, hackers are much more familiar with the smartphones than they used to be with the proprietary OSs of older "dumb phones." At the same time, the number of users turning to these cheap and powerful devices is growing, and the amount of personal data kept on the devices or going across the mobile networks is growing exponentially.

It's the multibillion-dollar bull's-eye. More personal information is migrating over to the mobile network, so much so that while ID fraud in general may be falling,[9] the lure of all this personal information will make the mobile phone and the mobile network prime targets. Why fool around targeting one individual at a time in the physical world when there is so much low-hanging fruit in the mobile world? Those tasked with dealing with security threats—CIOs, Chief Information Security Officers (CISOs), and Chief Security Officers (CSOs)—cited viruses, worms, and spyware as the IT security threats keeping their teams up at night, with more than half attributing those risks to mobile devices and remote workers, a worry that is up significantly compared with a year prior.[10]

All of the potential attacks that traverse a traditional IP-based wired network are also viable for the mobile network, which is evolving to use this same IP-based infrastructure to support the newer 3G and soon, 4G applications. The good news is that the general security measures developed to mitigate virus infections, spyware, and other types of attacks on other IP networks can be modified and applied to securing the users and handheld mobile devices in operation today.

Some experts say that we shouldn't be using IP, but that ship has already sailed. AOL tried to build a more secure network without using IP, and it succeeded, but it also lost a huge chunk of market share. Consumer demand forced AOL to adopt IP and say hello to the public Internet.[11] The reason everyone is leveraging IP is because it provides a universal, cost-effective, vendor-agnostic platform that has demonstrated an unprecedented ability to reach out across all boundaries and connect people and resources like never before (IP is one of the foundations of the sustainable network and its unbelievable adoption rates in the past decade). To stop using IP would be to stop forward progress. Therefore, assuming the inevitable (ongoing adoption of the network), the trick is to realize the potential vulnerabilities so they can be identified and resolved.

It is a problem that mobile device providers are well aware of and have been going great lengths to address. While they are concerned about reliability and protecting consumer trust in their brands, it's important to point out these vendors are also commercially motivated to add layers of security to their mobile devices to thwart attempts to unlock their subsidized devices and protect their contracts with media distributors (e.g., the carriers and application stores).

Physical security is still probably the most important thing that anyone can do to protect the private data on a mobile device.

The mobile carriers, who are responsible for managing the network and ensuring a satisfactory user experience, need to maintain the integrity of the data flowing through the network to protect the relationships they have with customers. With increasing competition from all different types of network providers, they can't afford breaches that could provide incentives for users to switch to other providers. Mobile providers understand that to ensure the continued growth and revenue potential of the mobile network, they need to provide assurances that users and their personal information will be protected. For example, a survey of British mobile consumers found that 28% blame their operators for unwanted communications, and 44% would consider changing networks because of mobile spam. This figure rises to 65% as soon as the frequency of unwanted messages hits one or more a month.[12] Imagine what the percentage would be if consumers were told about lost or compromised data sent over the network.

So, it's no wonder that mobile providers are investing in measures that protect their mobile networks. Analysts predict that spending by service providers for network security appliances and software will hit $889 million worldwide in 2011.[13] The mobile security client software market is predicted to hit $1.6 billion in 2013.[14] Mobile providers are implementing a multilayered security approach to protect the mobile network, with technologies such as access control, authentication, authorization, firewalls, and real-time dynamic threat management. However, all these measures can't protect the consumer's mobile device if your phone falls into the hands of someone else.

While the device manufacturers and network operators do their part, we each also need to do ours. If you haven't already noticed, mobile devices are very easy to lose, easy to steal, and easy to leave on the café table or on the seat of the train. More and more thieves target iPhone and BlackBerry users in urban settings and find them easy prey because they are distracted and are not watching their surroundings. Physical security is still probably the most important thing that anyone can do to protect the private data on a mobile device. BlackBerry phones have a number of enterprise features designed to "nuke" the phone if it's lost, stolen, or even falls off the network for a long period of time. Apple is beginning to follow with its 3GS phone, with features designed to instantly and remotely wipe the phone at the touch of a button.[15] But the best defense is to make sure the bad guys never get the chance; keeping the device safe is your optimal protection.

However, there are a few other things you should keep in mind to protect yourself. For starters, consider that everything you do on your phone is as vulnerable as the activities you conduct online and should be protected the same way. Would you post naked pictures of yourself on your Facebook page? No? Then don't send them using your phone, because they can be forwarded and persist just as they can when posted online.

Would you send someone your bank account information? No? Then don't send it from your phone—make sure you are conducting any financial activities via a secure mobile connection (typically, the entity you're interacting with will provide a secure connection for any legitimate transaction). There are also a few other things you can do to protect your phone from an inexperienced attacker or at least slow down and annoy a more experienced one (who will ultimately be able to do whatever he wants with your phone once it is in his possession). Ask yourself the following questions:

- Do you have a *killpill* scenario? If you lose your smartphone, do you have a way to remotely erase or lock it?

- Do you password-protect your phone or smartphone? How often does it require keying in?

- Does your mobile have easy passwords (most do, since it's difficult to key in long sequences)?

- Do you keep passwords in your smartphone?

- Does your mobile's network browser automatically log you in at startup?

- Do you follow your company's access policies when you use your mobile for company business?

- Do you keep your home address and phone numbers under titles such as "Home" or "Family?" If you do, change them or else thieves, stalkers, or others can easily find your home address.

There are dozens of smartphone applications that can perform remote erasing, locking, and secure data encryption. Next time, skip the downloadable game and secure your phone and its content. At the very least, create a password to open and turn on the device (if lost or stolen, this can force the new owners to erase and delete all data in order to make it work).

A secure mobile network requires us all to do our part to protect its integrity. It begins with everyone using their phones appropriately and keeping them physically secure. It includes device manufacturers creating strong security features for these increasingly sophisticated and powerful devices, to protect them from compromises. And it includes mobile operators deploying a multilayered security architecture to stop and mitigate attacks on the voice, video, and data that passes through the mobile network. As mobile devices become the means through which the world enters and interacts online, it's important that it's secure enough to allow the network to continue operating as a sustainable platform for change.

CHAPTER 36

Government's Role in Protecting the Network's Integrity

*There can be no friendship without confidence, and no
confidence without integrity.*

—Samuel Johnson

FEMA *phones hacked; calls made to Mideast, Asia: Racked up about $12,000 in calls to the Middle East and Asia.* This was an Associated Press headline on August 20, 2008. While I wouldn't personally choose to hack into the phone system of the Department of Homeland Security (DHS), someone did, and the takeaway is that it can be done. If banking, transportation, electric power distribution grids, and government networks themselves are disrupted or infiltrated, the new, networked world and all the relationships it enables are in jeopardy. It means problems aren't just localized—they can now have ripple effects across the country and even the world, reminding us that an insecure network is not sustainable. For the network to be the effective underlying communications infrastructure of this Digital Information Age, it needs to be reliable and secure, which means threats to it must be thwarted and risks mitigated to protect its integrity.

This is why security is on the top of the list for most governments. Outages, compromises, or attacks to the network can be deadly. Network interruptions can adversely affect economic growth (currency goes down, for example) and the overall security of the nation's sensitive information and resources. Much of the world's critical infrastructure relies to some degree on the network and its digital assets; there's no such thing as a safe haven or island of calm. Remember, everything is connected.

If any particular network is impacted or even attacked, think of what could be affected—agriculture, water, public health, emergency services, government, defense, industry, information and telecommunications, energy, transportation, banking and finance, chemicals and hazardous materials, postal and shipping industries—the list goes on and on. For example, by simply changing a few network passwords, Terry Childs, a San Francisco network administrator, took the San Francisco network hostage, impeding service availability for days.[1] And all because he was afraid he might be laid off. While his actions didn't actually help his job security, imagine if he really wanted to be destructive.

Because of the value of the information flowing through networks (and government networks in particular), they are likely targets for attackers. U.S. government agencies reported 12,986 cybersecurity incidents to the U.S. Homeland Security Department in fiscal year 2007, and noted that incursions on the military's network were up from the year before by 55%.[2] So, it probably goes without saying that there needs to be a plan in place to protect sensitive information flowing throughout the network and contained in the world's databases.

But one of the biggest problems associated with cybersecurity is the vastness of its scope and the procedural lines it crosses. Identifying and protecting against any single incident often can involve many different governmental agencies, private-sector industry participants, and potentially even international bodies. The irony here is that the pervasiveness of the network, which makes it such a great tool that can be leveraged by all, is also what makes it relatively difficult to protect. It has a way of morphing that is both endearing and incredibly frustrating.

The simple solution would seem to be to make a single entity responsible for the security of cyberspace. However, the reality is that the problem is too large for any one organization to handle. There have been international efforts to try to tackle the issues, such as the Council of Europe's Convention on Cybercrime that, since its origination in July 2004, has signed 39 member states of the Council of Europe and 4 nonmember states. Twenty-one countries have ratified the Convention, which means they agree to establish laws against cybercrime in their own countries to ensure that law enforcement officials have the appropriate procedural authority in place to investigate and prosecute computer-related offenses and to extend international cooperation to others to combat cyberthreats.

At the country level, most governments are evaluating how best to handle threats to the network's infrastructure and streamline chains of command and control to maximize network availability and minimize recovery time. This was the reasoning behind the U.S. National Infrastructure Protection Plan (NIPP), which was released in 2006. It was a multiyear, multisector planning process consisting of 17 critical infrastructure sectors, including the IT sector, focused on creating strategies to make the nation safer and more secure. (Note that refinement and planning continues today, because as the threats evolve, so do the measures needed to identify threats, vulnerabilities, and potential consequences across sectors and geographies, as well as the corresponding protection mechanisms.)

The number of acronyms, regulations, and governmental agencies that own different pieces of the cybersecurity puzzle in each country is enough to make your head spin. General sentiment, however, is that no country is doing enough or has the visibility and security it needs to truly understand and protect against the dangers to the network. If you remember the nature of network routing, you'll quickly understand that attacks can come from thousands of routers outside your borders, all at once, one every millisecond, or in such a coordinated mishmash fashion that it defies comprehension.

For example, a report produced in 2008 by the Center for Strategic and International Studies Commission on Cybersecurity (ISCC) made the following observation: "...cybersecurity is now one of the major national security problems facing the U.S...only a comprehensive national security strategy that embraces both the domestic and international aspects of cybersecurity will improve the situation." The report calls for "minimum standards for securing cyberspace, to ensure that the delivery of critical services in cyberspace continues when we are attacked," and updating old cyberspace laws "written for the technologies of a less-connected era." It makes recommendations that span the technical, such as "requiring better authentication," and the overall processes, such as "appoint[ing] an assistant for cyberspace and establish[ing] a Cybersecurity Directorate that absorbs existing Homeland Security Council functions."

> **Cyberattacks were identified as one of the most serious economic and national security challenges we face in the 21st century.**

These process and governance recommendations were echoed in large part in a report released in March 2009 by the Government of Accountability Office (GAO). In evaluating the status of the U.S. cybersecurity programs, the GAO used input from a panel of public and private cybersecurity experts. The panel recommended the articulation of a clear national strategy, executive branch responsibility, an operational model that can drive day-to-day activities and longer-term strategy and alliances, greater cooperation between public and private sectors, elevated awareness and investment in cybersecurity education and research, improved enforcement, and greater attention to global cyberspace matters.[3] In a report issued in May 2009 by the National Security Council (NSC), cyberattacks were identified as one of the most serious economic and national security challenges we face in the 21st century.

I don't want to paint too dire a picture because, while it's a serious concern, there is hope for cybersecurity. For example, in the U.S., President Obama announced the creation of a cybersecurity coordinator, whose responsibility is to orchestrate a wide array of federal cybersecurity policies and agendas to ensure that resources are working in concert. And it's estimated that the U.S. federal government will spend a little over $100 out of every $1,000 requested for IT spending in fiscal year 2009 on IT security, representing approximately $7 billion. This is an increase of almost 10% over 2008. It is indicative of the attention that the world's governments are starting to pay to cybersecurity concerns. There is also a $17 billion, five-year program currently in place focused on defensive cybersecurity efforts, and these will most likely see expansion in some form or another under the current administration. It has been estimated that in a six-month period, the U.S. government has spent close to $100 million to respond to and investigate online probes and attacks on military systems.[4]

In addition, there are certification programs for manufacturers to ensure that products deployed in government networks meet specified security levels. For example, Common Criteria is a set of internationally recognized and accepted standards that let vendors test and validate their products by an approved third party via a well-established process. Another example is the Federal Information Processing Standards (FIPS), which was developed by the National Institute of Standards and Technology (NIST), and has been recognized and adopted by other governments around the world to oversee the security of algorithms and cryptographic functions.

But these standards bodies take time to develop. It takes meeting after meeting, paper after paper, acceptance, and review. During the time you were learning how to set up your home wireless DSL modem and keep it working, the network has morphed into the sustainable worldwide network and cybersecurity efforts have tried to evolve along with it. The question is, have those efforts been able to stay ahead of, or even just keep up with, the attacks on the network?

Looking forward, there is an increasing recognition that the protection of the network is just too big for any one organization, sector, or even country. Remember, the network is only as strong as its weakest link, so it requires continued efforts from both public and private industries. And this is where the government or the market (or the public) must demand a greater level of cooperation that has heretofore been hard to come by. The reality is that the increasing complexity of the network infrastructure is making it necessary for government agencies to rely on equipment vendors and professionals to provide the expertise and materials, giving credence to the fact that network evolution seems to be happening at a rate that is faster than any government can react.

For real progress, it is apparent that public and private sectors must build and fortify a relationship of trust. An inability to trust and communicate can hamper protective measures and create potentially unnecessary levels of risk within cyberspace. For example, in a recent cybersecurity hearing, a former government official acknowledged that:

> An effective national cybersecurity effort must leverage intelligence community's superior acumen but is in grave peril if controlled by intelligence community…In recent examples, adversary Internet addresses used in attacks and their various attack methods have been classified to the point they were not broadly available for defensive purposes or provided through channels. In numerous cases, this roadblock prevented information from being used effectively in cyber defense and provided further advantage to our adversaries. If you cannot or will not share useful information with cyber defenders (from private industry) their job is made far more difficult.[5]

So, today, efforts are moving in the direction of solving these communication problems and establishing collaboration for the greater good between the public and private sectors. There are a variety of organizations and initiatives designed to solidify best practices and processes for identifying, stopping, and recovering from a potentially devastating incident or attack that could affect the nation's critical infrastructure.

For example, Cyber Storm events (Cyber Storm II was held in March 2008) is run by the Department of Homeland Security in conjunction with government representatives from "friendly" nations such as Britain, Canada, Australia, and New Zealand, and private industry experts. These events simulate coordinated attacks on critical infrastructure, both physical and virtual. Another coordinated set of events is the TOPOFF exercises, which include top officials at every level of the U.S. government, as well as representatives of the international community and private industry. TOPOFF participants conduct terrorism preparedness exercises to test how organizations work together to respond to incidents such as a climatic natural disaster, a chemical spill, or an act of terrorism. The exercises simulate the potential effects of an attack on the physical infrastructure, which includes the network and all its digital communications and resources, so that participants can go through a coordinated assessment of the damages, identify containment measures, and then work (speedily) to recover. The most recent event, TOPOFF 4, was held in October 2007 and included more than 23,000 federal, state, local, and private sector participants, as well as representatives from Australia, Canada, and the UK, coordinated by the Federal Emergency Management Agency (FEMA).

How the Network Can Help Efforts

Interestingly, the network itself is one of the best tools at the disposal of governments and businesses when disaster strikes. In governmental jargon, the ability to stave off or quickly recover from a disaster is referred to as *Continuity of Operations* (COOP). The goal is to prevent interruptions in mission-critical services and, in the event that they occur, to reestablish those services as quickly as possible. There are local and national frameworks in place to help deal with disastrous events, be they natural (such as a hurricane) or manmade (such as a terrorist attack) and cover everything from policy and procedures to manpower and technology mobilization. The network plays a central role in these plans and efforts to keep operations running as normally as possible in the event of an emergency or catastrophic event.

A survey by Juniper Networks[6] found that 62% of government employees across all sectors believe that *telework*, or secure remote access to data and information sharing capabilities, is a critical part of an agency's COOP capability, particularly when preparing for scenarios that require "social distancing," as in the case of a pandemic flu, where limiting exposure is necessary to stem the spread of the disease. In these instances, connectivity is central to the agency's ability to stay connected to what's going on and achieve some degree of normalcy (facilitating ongoing activities) in the event of a global pandemic event, such as the "swine flu" that hit the world in 2009. Regions under quarantine can interact with the outside world via the network; businesses and government agencies can continue to operate, leveraging telecommuting employees; and governments can keep constituents informed and the situation under control with a myriad of online tools at their disposal to communicate and track activities.

Knowing exactly what's needed in a disaster is almost as important as getting it. So when natural disasters hit, such as earthquakes, tsunamis, and blizzards, the network can help get the word out and speed recovery, providing updates and letting vital services get to where they are needed most. Most disasters don't take place with all the necessary first respondents sitting waiting for something to happen. The ability to connect from home and get orders and directions online in a coordinated fashion means quick recovery. Many organizations and businesses can use the network to access backup facilities (data centers) located outside the region to retrieve the digital information and resources they need to resume operations. After Hurricane Katrina hit, temporary cell towers were erected to help agencies coordinate activities and to provide general mobile phone service so people could let others know if they needed help and locate loved ones.

When an attack or disaster hits and a region is struggling to get things under control, maintaining communication channels and access to digital information and resources speeds the return to normalcy. Of course, as with anything, the best way to prepare systems to work under stress situations is to use and test them regularly. While 79% of government workers surveyed reported that their agencies support telework in some form, only 28% actually utilized telework on a routine basis. This has been identified as a potential weakness in the strategy. Only 8% of respondents reported that their agencies were "very ready" to respond to a variety of scenarios. And while 63% reported that their agencies were modifying their IT infrastructures to support COOP, only 32% reported that they have committed financial resources.[7]

> **Most disasters don't take place with all the necessary first respondents sitting waiting for something to happen.**

This is probably why, in the U.S., two bills have been introduced (the Telework Improvements Act and the Telework Enhancement Act) to formalize telecommuting policies and programs. The Office of Personnel Management (OPM) took pages from these bills and announced a telework plan in the first half of 2009 for government employees as part of its effort to adopt a more flexible work environment that is better prepared to maintain continuity of operations in the event of a disruptive event.

Of all the things that can happen—be it a cyberattack, a tornado, a kidnapping, or a Katrina-level hurricane—having the network operational is paramount. The goal is to leverage the network to maximize the availability of its resources while minimizing the risks to those resources. That's a very difficult thing to do. It requires continual investment; unbiased, close cooperation; and recognition of how important this network really has become. If the network is going to sustain our governments and the underlying infrastructure that supports our economic and social activities, its availability and integrity need to be protected.

CHAPTER 37

21st-Century Warfare:
Cyberattacks

*This [cybersecurity] has got to be in the top five national
security priorities.*

—Jerry Dixon, former Director of the National Cyber
Security Division at the Department of Homeland Security[1]

On August 8, 2008, an attacker activated an unspecified number of computers across the globe that had been infected with malware. All these unsuspecting systems were used to perpetrate an attack, sending so much traffic over the network to Georgia's government data center that it overwhelmed the country's network infrastructure, and all the networks went down in Georgia. Virtually no one could get through. The few users who could get access saw images on their screens that drew similarities between Hitler and Georgia's president, Mikheil Saakashvili. Under the cover of this network communications blackout, Russian tanks rolled into Georgia.

The network attack, which was traced back to Russia, served the same purpose as strategic air strikes on enemy radars and communications antennae before a massive air attack. The assault on Georgia's computer networks cut the country off from external communications and support. It was designed to cover the invasion, and it was the initial thrust of a coordinated military attack.

The motivation of North Korea's attack on 22 South Korean and U.S. government sites in July 2009 is less clear. It might have been a demonstration of political muscle, an act of defiance, or perhaps the actions of rogue activists. We may never know why hackers took control over 12,000 computers in South Korea and 8,000 international computers to launch a cyberattack that successfully took down or created access problems for key sites in South Korea (Blue House, Defense Ministry) and the U.S. (Secret Service, Treasury Department, Federal Trade Commission).[2]

What we do know is that these kinds of incidents are becoming more and more frequent, prompting many nations to reconsider cyberwarfare and asking questions. What level of aggression does an attack of this nature represent? When is it deemed an act of war? What are appropriate responses? Do the laws of war apply in cyberspace? How do the rules of engagement change? Are innocent bystanders and civilians off limits, or do they become the targets because that is where the greatest devastation can be inflicted (attacking the financial, energy, or transportation systems of a nation)? Most of these questions are still being explored because they have no simple answers. But it is plainly evident that all nations need to be prepared to protect their network and IT systems.

> **They are training personnel in the finer points of cyberwarfare.**

Cyberwarfare brings interesting new dimensions to the battlefield. In fact, it is an entirely new battle space, because it's dynamic and not restricted to any single location. However, that doesn't mean it can't blur into the real (physical) world. For example, the *New York Times* reported that under former U.S. President Bush, American forces were authorized to covertly hack into Al Qaeda computers and change information to lure operatives into a trap in the physical world.[3]

Cyberwarfare also shifts boundaries, and the concept of striking range becomes a non-issue. Attacks can be launched from anywhere to anywhere, and the attackers are often decentralized and anonymous. And perhaps most frustrating, power can rest with individual users, who can cause maximum disruption and potential devastation with minimal upfront investment.

The attack on Georgia, while the best-documented cyberattack, may not have been the first. Many blame Russia for a similar attack on the Estonian networks in 2007; perhaps Russia was the obvious culprit, since the timing coincided with Estonia's deliberation over the movement of a Soviet-era monument. One thing is for certain—it will not be the last. It's estimated that a cyberattack such as the one perpetrated against Georgia costs approximately $.04 per machine,[4] putting it within the reach of even cash-strapped nations. You don't need to have a lot of money in the coffers or be part of a well-endowed crime syndicate to fund these kinds of attacks. As such, network attacks on nations are definitely a part of the arsenal of the 21st-century army, and virtually no one is immune.

According to a "for official use only" intelligence report issued by the Homeland Security Department and obtained by the Associated Press[5] in August 2008, there are no effective means to prevent a similar attack on U.S. websites (a situation that evidently still applies, as we saw this summer during the aforementioned takedown of key U.S. government sites by North Korea). In fact, all countries are vulnerable, and all governments agree that any widespread disruption has the potential to be devastating, so they are desperately learning how to identify, block, and then counter such attacks on their network infrastructures. They are training personnel in the finer points of cyberwarfare, including efforts to create a defensible position and to potentially launch offensive counterattacks. Look for Sun Tzu's classic text *The Art of War* to be modified soon for IT thrusts and parries.

There are reports that the U.S. government has been working on a highly classified replica of the Internet (the National Cyber Range) to try to understand and ultimately prevent attacks that could take down the system. The goal is to create better defensives against inevitable online weapons. Due to potential sensitivities and the international cooperation that would need to be negotiated to create a truly representative model of the world's largest network (including domestic and international sites), it is unclear where the program will go under the new administration.[6]

Every military and intelligence agency around the world already uses the network to keep authorized personnel in constant contact. Allied nations share military and counter-terrorist intelligence and databases over secure networks to improve high crime and military intelligence operations. And all military personnel in hostile or combat situations, where a few seconds' delay in information or orders could be the difference between life and death, rely on portions of the "public" network at times. While all of the details of these military networks are highly confidential, they do cross and mingle with our sustainable network, probably more frequently than we realize.

To reduce the number of intersections between military and public networks (for reasons of both security and bandwidth reservation), the U.S. Department of Defense created a Global Information Grid (GIG), which is a worldwide network-centric information system that allows appropriate military and government personnel located around the globe to access to critical information resources. In turn, the Air Force, Army, Navy, etc. all have their own network strategies, with links to GIG, to increase overall proficiency. For example, the U.S. Air Force has Command and Control Constellation initiatives and the U.S. Army has coined its network strategy LandWarNet.

> While world peace may be a potentially unattainable state, digital losses are a more palatable alternative to human losses.

The U.S. Army has stated that it plans to become a knowledge-based, net-centric force that can ensure that personnel have all the information they need to complete their missions. One component of the Army's plan is an on-the-move (OTM), high-speed, high-capacity backbone communications network that links soldiers in tactical ground units with commanders and the GIG system. The range of applications, such as identification and location tracking, mobile net-centric tracking of units, and "friend or foe" identification, are designed to protect those on the ground and maximize their overall effectiveness. And the U.S. Air Force, which runs the Predator drone program in Afghanistan and parts of Pakistan, does so from satellite links to the drone's pilots, who are sitting in war rooms in the western U.S. The pilots have joysticks for controls and a computer monitor for eyes. Each drone costs about $4 million, while a typical fighter jet costs $150 million.[7]

For better or worse, the network is changing the way military operations are carried out and managed by governments around the world. As a proponent of leveraging the network for sustainable means, I find this particular topic uncomfortable to contemplate (especially as I can only imagine all the things I don't know about that the network is being used to do against other people—it completely tests my naive concepts of netiquette).

However, it is important to acknowledge all sides of the equation. Cyberwarfare is a part of the overall network story. We, along with future generations, will need to grapple with and shape what it means. The network can be used to hurt, maim, and destroy other people, countries, and freedoms, but it can also be used to thwart such actions and promote sustainable growth, development, and good.

My ultimate opinion, which may put me at risk for sounding like a beauty pageant contestant responding to a world-in-peril question, is that while world peace may be a potentially unattainable state, digital losses are a more palatable alternative to human losses. So, anything the network can do to preserve life is well worth it.

CHAPTER 38

Social Sustainability

Can humanity be mobilized by an inanimate object?
—Sarah Sorensen

T his is one of the hardest chapters to write, because how do you even start to summarize all the direct and follow-on influences the network is having on the way we think and the way we interact with the world? Everything in this book has a social aspect, a social impact that could be explored in depth for dozens of pages. In the time it took for me to write this sentence, or perhaps for you to read it, millions logged on and uploaded, downloaded, or accessed something that wasn't there 20, 10, or even 1 year ago. Every second, these effects are felt around the world. How do you write about that in a book?

The network can help create many small changes that can ultimately make a big impact in the lives of an individual, a family, a neighborhood, and even a country. Take the citizens of Estonia, who wanted to do something about the trash that had been accumulating in their forests and natural habitats. They created Teeme Ära and launched the "Let's Do It" campaign, which challenged Estonians to join in the effort to clean up the 10,000 tons of waste that littered their country. Oh, and by the way, they wanted to do it in a single day. It started with just 20 volunteers and grew to more than 600 volunteers, and then more than 500 official partners, and so on, all of whom were energized by the effort and started rallying and organizing support. Using Google and other free software, more than 700 volunteers took and sent photos with their mobile phones of the actual trash, creating a visual, virtual garbage map of more than 10,000 trash sites. On May 3, 2008, more than 50,000 people, representing 4% of the 1.3 million citizens of Estonia, came out and cleaned up the country in five hours. In total, it cost 500,000 Euros. It's estimated that if the government had to do the same thing, it would have taken three years and 22.5 billion Euros.[1]

While this example is specific to Estonia, there's nothing that says its principles can't be replicated on smaller or larger scales around the world. They already are (just go to Google and type in the search words "Save Our," and you will find hundreds of thousands of individuals and organizations trying to create change). What could you do in your neighborhood to help connect people to an issue and then coordinate a response? How could you better mobilize your own network of friends, families, and colleagues to participate in solving problems and making a difference?

With projects such as United Devices[2] Grid platform or IBM's World Community Grid (WCG), you start to get a sense of the scale and potential the network can deliver to support social advancements and improvements worldwide. United Devices hosts a virtual screening program for cancer research and is the largest computational chemistry project in history, leveraging the processing power of more than 2 million computers around the world. The WCG connects more than 1 million computers from 400,000 members worldwide and makes this computing power available to help public and not-for-profit organizations advance their knowledge and share information to progress their research.[3]

Grid Computing

Grid computing, sometimes called distributed computing, combines the idle or unused CPU processing power and/or free disk space of computers that are voluntarily connected via a network. People join the grid, which means they volunteer their computers' processing power when they are not using it, putting it to work for the greater good when it would otherwise be idle. This kind of collaborative computing is most popular in science and research institutions that require intense computer processing.

One of the projects leveraging the WCG computing resources is "Nutritious Rice for the World," which aims to understand the structure of rice to help farmers breed better rice strains that deliver "higher crop yields, promote greater disease and pest resistance and utilize a full range of "bioavailable" nutrients that can benefit people around the world."[4] The research relies on a 3D modeling program that requires a lot of computational power to improve the accuracy of the information. It's predicted that the WCG will be able to shorten discovery time from the 200 years it would have taken using traditional experimental approaches to less than 2 years. And it doesn't stop there—the WCG is tackling all sorts of monumental projects that are simply too big for any one of us to solve. But once connected, the power of the many—well, you know the rest.

The assistance of the many is how we now help communities when disasters strike. This is vital as people try to understand the needs of an area that's been devastated and to give appropriately, whether it's money, donations, volunteer time, or expertise. For instance, the American Red Cross was able to amass $63.4 million in online donations in the wake of the terrorist attacks on the U.S. east coast on September 11, 2001[5] to support the victims and their families. After the tsunami in Asia and Hurricane Katrina in New Orleans, many people turned to the Web to see how they could help. Groups spanning all parts of the globe banded together to raise money and support relief efforts. Philanthropic and relief sites, such as those run by the Red Cross, as well as online communities ranging from groups of students to concerned mothers to industry consortiums, were able to collect donations (close to $1 billion in the U.S. and more than £500,000 GBP in the UK alone was raised for tsunami victims; over $4 billion was collected from donors around the world by philanthropic organizations for Hurricane Katrina victims), mobilize teams of rescue and relief workers, and subsequently support rebuilding efforts by matching needs with resources.

And the role the network plays continues to grow. Just take the earthquake in Italy in 2009—within minutes, and I mean literally minutes, photos and news of the devastation were posted online; maps of the area and scientific explanations of the fault lines involved were linked to real-time views from witnesses and first-hand accounts of the quake. Simultaneously, calls for aid went out and philanthropic organizations began mobilizing a response by sending out information to first responders and using their websites to post information about how to contribute. And this is what is so powerful about the network that personifies the many—it allows people to get involved in small ways that can ultimately make a big difference.

Sites such as *www.globalgiving.com*, where you can locate humanitarian needs based on project (or event), country, or even cause, encourage people to make small donations, with the idea that enough small donations add up to big changes, as captured by its tagline, "a million little earth-changing ideas." Its Italy Earthquake Relief and Recovery Fund was launched the same day as the disaster and, through $10, $25, $50, $100, or "other" increments, reached half its goal of raising $50,000 within two months. These efforts were replicated throughout the Internet, as organizations raised large and small sums to support recovery efforts in the region. Unfortunately, there is no shortage of tragic events around the world that need humanitarian aid, but the good news is that the network is helping connect people to these causes and to make it easier for people to provide support.

The network breaks down isolation and it can lessen loneliness.

Besides the access to all types of information and resources, another social benefit of the network is that there is always someone online somewhere that you can talk to or connect with, and that simple fact can be very powerful. There are groups that you can join, both passively and actively, that share your interests and passions (fears and worries, and so on) without geographic limitations. And finding someone who has the same illness as you, who's going through the same things you are dealing with, can provide comfort, reassurance, and confidence. It's the reason that many self-help and support groups leverage online tools—to help people maintain a constant connection to others who can understand.

The network breaks down isolation and it can lessen loneliness. It is, from one valuable perspective, a giant (and vital) support system for those in need. During the current economic downturn, in which many people are finding themselves out of a job, the network provides a meeting place to share stories and commiserate, not to mention to look for new work (the search term "jobs" has even surpassed cars, games, and porn in popularity!).[6]

Everywhere in this book, I've talked about connecting people to information that helps them get what they need. You and I may take this information for granted, but its impact can be profound. Do you know that many people on the African continent have never had access to basic geographical information pertaining to their communities? Maps on Google and other sites, while general in nature to most readers of this book, can help disseminate valuable community information to people who have never previously had access to it. From street names to school enrollment and rankings, from livestock density to incidents of illnesses and deaths among different populations, and from rainfall to community services and even civil unrest, all of this information is a powerful thing. An online map that is available to all and is constantly refreshing based on the data it is mapping can make a significant difference in the lives of individuals within those communities.

While using all of these digital tools to locate resources and interact with people is amazing, it's important to recognize that these connections are not the same as those made in the physical world. And, as with almost everything, there may be unintended consequences associated with substituting this virtual world for real-world activities. A motto that comes to mind is "everything in moderation." We are just starting to see studies on the physiological and psychological effects that all of this connectedness has on the way we behave and think about the world, so it will be interesting to see where this goes.

For example, to explain the greater hostility that is exhibited online, psychologists point out that our mirror neurons aren't triggered in these less-personal online interactions. This means that because we don't see the faces of the people we are dealing with, we don't feel the empathy that we potentially would if we were right in front of them. As a result, people feel emboldened to be more aggressive or even hurtful in their communications. In addition, subtle nuances that people pick up when they are talking to someone through hand gestures or voice inflections are lost online; words are monotone, leaving interpretation up to the reader. This is why it's good practice to always ask yourself, "Is this something I would say if I were looking that person in the eye? Would it be OK if it were attributed to me in perpetuity?"

We have also started to see studies that explore the differences the network is creating between generations. What's different in problem-solving abilities of those who grow up connected to the network compared with those who grew up with the Dewey decimal system, for instance? The ease with which we can access information may ultimately end up affecting how we store and think about that information. The *New York Times* recently wrote a story on a study being conducted by neuroscientists that focuses on the effects all this easily accessible information can have on the brain. It seems that folks who have had to "maintain complex mental maps of the world, like London taxi drivers, have an enlarged hippocampus," which is thought to be where people store their internal maps.[7] The question is, as we rely more and more on our online maps and GPSs, will these mental muscles diminish? Will the network end up affecting the way we generally navigate the world?

What about our social abilities? How will our relationships be different as we conduct more and more of them through our smartphones and social networks? Research has started to identify the role that the network, primarily cell phones and the Internet, is having on the family unit. Participants cited the network as promoting more connectedness among family members, allowing them to stay in touch and be informed of the minutiae of one another's days. And a quarter of the respondents said the Internet has decreased the time they spent watching TV. However, instead of translating to greater quality time, this same research found that "tech-using" families are less likely to share meals and less likely to be satisfied with their leisure time. One of the main explanations for this seeming disconnect is the blurring of the lines between work and home. The findings revealed that, "when they spend more time working, people tend to give their remaining free time to their families…at the expense of time spent relaxing or engaging in hobbies or other activities."[8]

It's clear that there is still a lot to understand and explore about the social impacts of the network, some of which are obvious and others obscured. After all, the network is ultimately about people—not machines, cables, and devices—and people are complicated. It's opening up new lands and exposing people to new ideas and cultures. It is making it easier for people to sustain connections and develop relationships that can expand their horizons and opportunities. For the first time, we have something that ties us all together instantly, creatively, equally.

CHAPTER 39

The Health Net

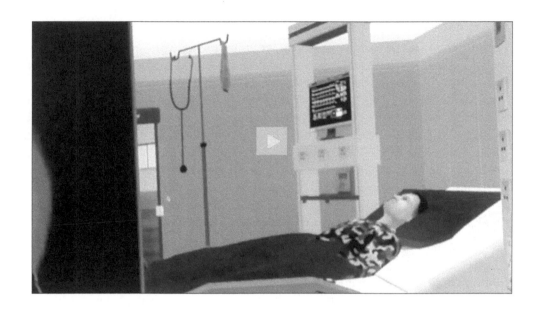

The greatest wealth is health.
—Virgil

have already suggested how the network is playing an enormous role in 21st-century research, connecting the world's intellect and bringing collaborative resources to bear on some very tough problems. Beyond facilitating our understanding of the inner workings of the complex human body, the medical and healthcare fields can use the network to advance the everyday health and wellness of individuals around the world. There are clear social benefits to be derived from the existing network. In fact, the past two decades have seen the network support general healthcare system efficiencies that eventually lead to better treatments and overall improvements in a patient's health. So, let me skip a stone across it to highlight where the network makes a difference.

For starters, many healthcare providers are using the network to help patients manage their own health. Users can keep track of their daily food intake, access tips for healthy living, query suggestions on daily life, and gather information on reducing their symptoms and managing their illnesses. Doctors now have online office hours. Many actually perform virtual visits and chat with their patients to answer their nonemergency health questions or concerns, such as, "I have poison ivy, what do I do?" There's a wealth of medical research now available to anyone. Medical libraries are searchable, and it's amazing how much user-friendly information can be at your fingertips to help you become better informed or to administer basic-quality homecare. When I get the dreaded, "Mom, I don't feel good," I immediately go to WebMD.com to research the new ailment or ache that has come along. If Mom can't fix it, I can then make an appointment online.

I'm not alone. More and more people are understanding their own bodies and getting comfortable with their options and choices. In fact, in a survey of people who used the Internet to deal with a major personal illness, more than half of the respondents said it was crucial in their own applied healthcare.[1] One reason it is playing such a critical role is that you can use the network to confirm symptoms and diagnoses, learn what to expect, figure out what to ask your doctor, and prepare yourself to ask the questions that will help you find out what you want to know if you don't get the answers you were expecting. And if the illness is severe enough, you can find support and connect to others who are going through the same things as you. This access to information and support just wasn't possible 20 years ago. If I stopped right here, it would be a grand step forward in our ability to take better control of our health.

But as you know, the network never stops—it keeps progressing and drives innovation, enabling a new model in healthcare, dubbed Health 2.0 (after the popular Web 2.0 principles of social media and online access). Health 2.0 brings patients together and makes them real partners in the process, allowing them to control their own care at a level never seen before. For example, critically ill patients are coming together to participate in treatment trials, leveraging online resources to input their information and share findings with their common community. They can chart their own medical histories, keep daily journals, or compare notes with others in the trial, all of which expands the scope of the information and the speed with which researchers can receive and analyze it.

20/20 into the Future?

Considering that there are 4 billion cell phones in use around the world, it's not hard to envision a time when everyone will also carry electronic medical records with them. It's easy to see how portable medical records stored on a cell phone (securely) could prove invaluable if a user is involved in an emergency health situation. With your medical records on your phone, regardless of whether you are physically able to communicate, you can be assured that healthcare providers will have immediate access to key information on your medical history. To start, try using the ICE sticker, described at the end of this chapter, to let providers know how to access medical information on your phone.

Then there are the benefits associated with simply extending the reach of healthcare. Take a simple video monitor used to provide face-to-face interactions with doctors. These video capabilities can allow remote clinics to link to larger facilities or hospitals and gain access to the extensive resources and expertise at those locations. Remote patients can consult with experts on tough cases or receive guidance on treatment plans. Some facilities have linked all the real-time information generated by the patients' networked machines to give doctors a real-time view of what's going on at all times. For instance, doctors can take the information generated by a heart monitor or fetal scan, couple it with live video feeds from those patient rooms (typically only those most critical), and present them at central monitoring locations. Doctors can then keep track of the progress of multiple patients at once, receiving real-time information, both statistical and visual, thereby making their on-call time that much more efficient. In fact, all of this data can be collected at one point and networked to another point (presumably stored in some kind of a database) and analyzed or monitored by a doctor from almost anywhere. We have seen this successfully implemented with X-rays, as technicians halfway around the world read and report on what they see in order to cut down on response time. With a little innovation, the possibilities are endless.

However, the healthcare industry as a whole has been slow to embrace new technologies. This is why, in 2009, President Obama called for an investment to modernize the U.S. healthcare system. "It won't just save jobs, it will save lives," he said. "We will make sure that every doctor's office and hospital in this country is using cutting-edge technology and electronic medical records so that we can cut red tape, prevent medical mistakes, and help save billions of dollars each year."[2] The nonpartisan U.S. Congressional Budget Office (CBO) estimates that, as a result of this push, approximately 90% of doctors and 70% of hospitals in the U.S. will be using electronic medical records within the next 10 years, with standards that include enhanced security and patient privacy, developed by Health and Information Technology (HIT), by 2010.

A nationwide electronic medical records system, with hospitals connected to one another, has the potential to deliver huge cost savings that can be significant when applied to the trillions of dollars countries around the world spend on their healthcare systems every year (the U.S. system is estimated to cost $2.3 trillion). For starters, processing paper claims costs twice as much as processing electronic claims,[3] and there are predictions by the CBO that a national electronic healthcare system could generate tens of billions of dollars in savings and an overall reduction in private health insurance premiums for families.

> Electronic records could potentially help reduce the estimated 98,000 preventable deaths that occur in U.S. hospitals each year.

A networked medical system also has the potential to create efficiencies that can lead to improved care. Time to delivery can be of critical importance in medical care, and the network's ability to connect healthcare professionals with the information they need exactly when they need it, or connecting patients to the specialists they need in emergency situations, can save lives. Mobile, portable healthcare solutions can enhance care by bringing clinical expertise to patients when they most need it, such as during a stroke, heart attack, or seizure.[4]

Medical records stored on paper, containing a variety of doctor chicken-scratches made throughout the years, are more difficult to search quickly and extract pertinent patient history and information. They are also harder to share for the purpose of coordinating treatments and are more prone to cause medical errors. For example, there are estimates that 17% of U.S. physicians use some basic electronic health records (EHRs), with only 4% using fully integrated, functioning EHRs. There are estimates that 98,000 preventable deaths occur in U.S. hospitals each year.[5] Electronic records could potentially help reduce this number, particularly if they are linked to medical treatment information.

For instance, hospitals that have instituted electronic labeling systems on medications—in essence, putting a barcode on each and every bottle or syringe—and linked that information to patient records have been able to reduce the number of medication mistakes (such as those related to incorrect prescriptions or dosages or drug interaction errors) to 0%.[6] That's worth noting! The way it typically works is a nurse or doctor uses a wireless device to scan the medication and then scan the intended patient's medical record number, which correlates the information to verify it is in fact what is prescribed and the correct dosage, and flags any potential adverse drug interactions based on the patient's history. Assuming the medication and patient records are input correctly, it is easy to see how this could potentially prevent incorrect dosages or medications.

The UK's National Health Service (NHS) is "embracing ICT to improve efficiency, responsiveness, and access to services."[7] It has pointed to inefficiencies such as incomplete and inaccurate patient information as causes of potentially fatal errors. It found that more than a quarter (27%) of the health service's errors were derived from poor information, which has led to close to 1,200 deaths a year in England and Wales.[8]

The NHS aims to provide a single, up-to-date, accessible electronic healthcare record for each patient in England by 2010, dubbed the NHS Care Records Service (CRS). The goal is to develop a fully integrated system that will allow health professionals to access patient data and maintain a single record of care that is housed electronically to reduce duplication or holes in information, resulting in "better quality, more responsive and coordinated patient care, as well as reducing costs and improving safety, confidential safety, confidentiality and efficiency."[9] It has also enlisted British Telecom to support a range of NHS services, including NHS Direct and NHS 24, that give patients access to advice 24 hours a day, seven days a week, both online and via telephone.

Another huge benefit to electronically linked healthcare systems is the creation of a massive database of healthcare information, from symptoms to prescriptions to medical strategies, to procedures and treatments of health problems, illnesses, and diseases. This kind of database has the potential to shed light on the science of medicine the same way the Human Genome Project shed light on the human genome. At any given moment, you could get live data on any set of factors: Latino women, cigarette smokers, with two or fewer children, in their 40s, born with a fraternal twin.

Let's be clear: there are significant privacy and information ownership issues to be worked out. I always assume that the information on my health is my own, but that may not be evident to everyone. You may be surprised by the answer your doctor or health-care provider gives. There are also issues around patient confidentiality that need to be closely guarded. And effective regulations must be put in place to ensure that doctors are free to make medical decisions and treat each patient individually. But the potential that can come from such sharing of generic information, en masse, about healthcare successes and failures throughout the world, could extend and improve the lives of all.

Finally, in addition to transforming the operations of medical systems and organizations, the network is impacting how information feeds into those systems. When the swine flu outbreak occurred in late spring 2009, online tracking systems were used to help people see where confirmed cases were located and to potentially identify trends. Although there are kinks to work out, sites such as HealthMap (*www.healthmap.org*) maintained updated information on the swine flu, combining feeds on confirmed cases, symptoms, and geographical distribution (from Google Maps) among other things, in an innovative structure of networked information. In the future, tying this information to timelines or other potentially meaningful data, such as suspected sources of infection, could provide even more insight into the patterns and spread of infectious diseases. We've hardly started to climb the mountain of healthcare data that could be tied together. After all, each of us has something to share.

Healthcare is one area where the Internet truly can deliver unequaled value, providing empirical data to the masses delivered in real time, free from potential biases created by cultural or motivational differences. This information can be leveraged to create sensible action plans and policies. There are ethical and moral questions to be answered, and legislative and regulatory processes that must be agreed upon, but as healthcare systems evolve worldwide, it is critical that they effectively integrate technology into their delivery and maintenance.

The goal is really simple: create a more effective and sustainable system that can help keep you healthy, with a greater quality of life.

What You Can Do

- Ask healthcare providers about their plan to move to digital medical records. For a sense of the direction that more progressive healthcare providers are taking, you can check out Kaiser Permanente's website at *www.kp.org/future*.

- Put an ICE sticker (In Case of Emergency) on your cell phone and create an ICE contact for rescue workers to use in case of an emergency (*www.icesticker.com*).

- Take part in your health provider's website and web tools; email your doctor, take online health courses, get online test results quicker, etc. Let your provider know what is useful and where there's room to improve.

- If your parents are getting elderly, get them online to a healthcare provider's site so they can actively seek help and get support. Some local elder care businesses can help, too. Try a Google search ("elder care <zip code>").

- Before your next doctor visit, go online and research what ails or aches you, so you can be prepared with any questions or concerns.

- Research drugs and prescriptions online to make sure you understand potential side effects of said drugs, and know what to look for in case of an unintended reaction.

- Try an application on your laptop, iPhone, or BlackBerry that tracks eating, calories, and fitness. It doesn't matter which one, as long as you get into the habit of using a device to help you do the counting.

- Consider signing the Declaration of Health Data Rights, designed to make sure that personal data records are the property of the individual patient (*www.healthdatarights. org/home*).

CHAPTER 40

Not by Accident:
Social Networking

A wealth of information creates a poverty of attention.
—Herb Simon

S ocial media is a catchall term for all the different types of online applications and sites that let people engage in more dynamic, personal interactions with one another. And there are a lot of people doing it (social networking, that is). Even animals are getting in on the action. Don't believe me? Just check out Romeo, a cat with hundreds of followers who's been raising money for charitable works ($3,500 in case you're wondering).[1]

IBM estimates that by 2012, the number of unique monthly visitors to online social networking sites will surpass 800 million.[2] Nielsen Online reported that social networks and blogs have already surpassed email in global popularity and are growing at a rate that's more than three times as fast as the Internet's overall growth (1 million new blogs[3] are posted every day!).

So what is it? Besides a heavy use of abbreviations for typed communications, such as LOL (laughing out loud) and a new hip vocabulary that includes "tweets" and "diggs," the impact and possibilities of the connectedness enabled by social media networks and applications are simply inspiring. Once you emerge from the terminology fog, in very basic terms, social networking creates ways for individuals with something in common to come together online and interact. A social network service offers people an online community built around a shared interest, activity, or experience. Some examples of the most popular are Facebook, Twitter, MySpace, and LinkedIn in North America; Friendster, Cyworld, and Wretch in the Asia Pacific region; and Skyrock, Bebo, and Hi5 in Europe (there are many, many more for you to discover online). These services allow people to meet up with others who like the same music, share the same political views, or went to the same elementary school—there is no limit to the type of communities that can exist.

Through these social networking services, people knowingly create links with others, share information, rally and organize, and develop new connections (often known as the very revered online "friend"). They use social media tools to interact online and develop relationships and ties to the community. These social media tools can facilitate one-to-one communications, such as email or instant messaging, or one-to-many communications, in the form of posts, blogs, or feeds. These one-to-many tools facilitate the automatic distribution of an individual's thoughts, comments, and stories to the many people (known as friends or followers) who have requested those updates as soon as they are available. There are even social media aggregator sites (like Streamy and Bebo) that help individuals collect and see all the updates from all their news feeds, friends, and community groups in a single location (sometimes referred to as *lifestreaming*).

Items that are posted in online communities are easily linked to other posts and can be passed along to even more people and places. If you remember, that is the value of the network—to help people connect to the resources and information they need. Well, the beauty of the social network is that it makes it even easier to find relevant online content. So, once something is on a social site, it can go anywhere and last indefinitely. This can be great when you're talking about works of art or insightful research, but for things like sex tapes, not so much. It doesn't take long for people to find themselves in the middle of a much larger network that spans the globe and in front of many, many people they probably wouldn't care to meet.

A good rule to follow is to never write, post, or send anything you don't want to see on the home page of another website. And this goes for anything that traverses the network, whether it's a blog or a photo from your mobile phone. And with the visibility recently given to a number of crimes in which the criminals used social net-

A typical user will spend approximately 4.5 hours a month on Facebook.

working sites to find information and establish relationships with intended victims (such as the "Craigslist killer"),[4] everyone should be careful of what they put on these sites. Everyone should understand the dangers of putting too much information out in the public domain, including addresses, phone numbers, and personal identification information. Gone are the days when you could use your alma mater or dog's name as your password, because anyone can do a quick search and figure those things out! So, while social networking is about making it easy to share everything, you need to make sure you consciously decide what *everything* actually is.

But what a phenomenon! Facebook.com has seen its user base skyrocket over the past year. The more than 200 million active users[5] spent over a billion hours on the site in June 2009, with typical users spending more than 4.5 hours a month.[6] The site has been reportedly growing at approximately 5 million new users a week![7] Just a little more than six months earlier, it had 132 million, up from 52 million in 2007.[8] The site traditionally appeals to a more affluent teen (12–17 years old) and young adult (18–34 years old) following, but is increasingly attracting users over 35 (in the first half of 2009, U.S. Facebook users over 35 nearly doubled),[9] as well as a greater international audience. Facebook more than quadrupled its number of users in Europe and Asia after introducing versions of its site in Spanish, German, and French in 2009, helping to compensate for slowing growth in the U.S. Visitors to social networking sites grew 9% in North America from 2008–2009, compared with 25% globally.[10]

Likewise, Twitter saw a flurry of news articles in 2009 on its popularity and, in turn, saw its popularity rise even more to become a household name. Twitter allows people to post questions, comments, or updates on their lives in communications called "tweets" that are no longer than 140 characters. Over time, people can follow the tweets of their "friends" either online or via their cell phones anytime those friends post a new communication.

When you visit Twitter.com (and you should), you may find it a bit disconcerting that you can be "friends" with everyone from MC Hammer to Lance Armstrong to 10 Downing Street, and sometimes it's hard to understand why anyone cares that Joe is "heading to the coffee shop now," or that Jane "couldn't muster the courage to talk to the cute guy at the train station." However, there is something about the service that is catching on. More than 9.3 million visitors went to Twitter.com in March 2009, an increase from the 5 million visitors in February, representing a 131% increase.[11] By April, it had 17 million unique users, representing 83% growth in a single month, and a quadrupling of its audience over that two-month period.[12]

It could be that media attention on the service just happened to hit Twitter's target market, fueling interest and use. Interestingly, Twitter users tend to visit the top online news sites two to three times more often than nonusers. It seems you can't turn on the TV, listen to the radio, or read the news (either online or off) without someone mentioning Twitter. News anchors use it (along with other social networking sites) as a major source of information in the coverage of everything from the very serious riots in Iran over the 2009 presidential elections to how people are beating the heat during the summer. But as with everything, there are doubters who say the numbers are inflated and don't necessarily represent the breadth of the population that may be assumed when you hear 17 million. The average user is young, white or Asian, with no children and lower income, though there is a sizeable number of Twitter users with an annual household income of $100,000 or more. There are also statistics that point to only a 40% retention rate, referring to users who continue to return to the service after a month. The people who do actively use Twitter are hooked; some estimate these users tweet, on average, 105 times a week![13]

Even if the actual business models of social networking are fuzzy, there is no doubt that it could be classed as big business. In the middle of an economic downturn that is unlike any most of us have experienced in our lifetimes, where lending is tight and venture funding virtually nonexistent, Twitter received an additional $35 million in venture capital (in February 2009). This is after a reported offer of $500 million in stock that Facebook made for the company in the latter half of 2008. This, by the way, could be seen as pocketchange for Facebook, which once had a valuation of approximately $15 billion, a number that was extrapolated after Microsoft bought a 1.6% stake in the company in 2007 for $240 million.

It's important to realize that what's making Twitter attractive to users—namely, its reach and real-time, viral nature—also makes it an attractive target for attackers. In April 2009, a worm spread on Twitter, generating close to 10,000 spam tweets and compromising almost 200 accounts.[14] The attack indicates that hackers see social networking sites as good places to try to steal passwords and account information from vulnerable communities of people.[15]

Then there is what many predict will be the next evolutionary step for social networking in 3D virtual worlds. It's epitomized in *Second Life*, which is a virtual world, complete with restaurants, shops, parks, corporate office buildings, and anything else you can imagine. Akin to a game-like environment, you create your own *avatar*, which is the virtual embodiment of yourself (though it doesn't need to look anything like you, and in fact can look like whatever you would like it to). Your avatar interacts with other avatars in a virtual world. You can hang out at a club or café, attend a tradeshow, host a press conference, conduct a business meeting, take a virtual job to earn virtual money that you can use to purchase virtual merchandize and even property. The "inworld" unit of trade is called the Linden dollar, after Linden Labs, which originated and developed the *Second Life* concept, and can be converted to U.S. dollars for the offline world at one of the online Linden dollar exchanges.

As someone who has a hard enough time keeping track of my first life, the concept of living a second one is a little mind-boggling to me. However, many people are immersed in these virtual worlds. Numbers are hard to come by, but at the end of 2008, Linden Labs reported that visitors had spent over 600 million hours in *Second Life* since its inception in 2003 and the world had crossed the threshold of 70,000 concurrent users. That is considerable, considering that in January 2007, more than 1.5 million people had logged in to *Second Life* at least once, but the number of users who returned within 30 days was only a little over 252,000. It seems that the idea of "living" or participating in different aspects of a virtual world is certainly becoming more mainstream. As of October 2008, there were 15 million registered "residents" of *Second Life*, which had more than 230 TB of data and 2 billion virtual items to view. The average user spent 33 minutes per month in the world, with approximately $1 million in user-to-user transactions conducted daily, representing a 67% increase in a 12-month period. And there are many virtual gaming worlds, too, from *World of Warcraft* to *Eve Online* (whose banking entity, it should be noted, was caught red-handed in June 2009 with its hands in the virtual till—hey, I guess it really is like the physical world!).[16]

These social networking services and virtual world environments are becoming more popular and starting to seep, just as the network is prone to doing, into all aspects of our personal and professional lives. Corporations such as Cisco and IBM have virtual campuses that are manned by employees who can provide visitors information on the products and services they offer, using these sites to help identify potential customers and cut down on sales travel. Universities have virtual lectures, and tradeshows offer virtual exhibits. 3D architectural models in the virtual world have been used to help raise the money needed to build new hospitals and community centers in the real world, giving visitors an opportunity to walk virtually through the facilities and get a sense of what it will look like when it's done.

You can argue about the social benefits of social networking sites, such as helping users build confidence, making connections, or escaping from trying real-world lives or problems. You can also argue some potential detriments, such as the tendency of users to exhibit greater aggression or for the sites to amplify isolation and delinquency. The reality is that growth rates and adoption of the virtual world are soaring. Social networking is not just a trend, but is increasingly part of our material world going forward.

We are at a turning point in the Digital Information Age, one that creates a more inclusive and interactive online world that will be vital to our collective conscious and problem-solving efforts. These social networking services and applications represent the new ways we are groping with the vast libraries of information that are being created or transferred to the network. They are evolutionary innovations of how we can use the network to do virtual things that allow us to be better informed and make better sustainable decisions. Social networking is just the beginning of a vast parade of new innovations using the virtual constructs that the network creates. The possibilities are only limited by the imagination.

CHAPTER 41

Our Relationship with the Network

Do unto others as you would have others do unto you.

—The Golden Rule

The network is here to stay. And it will continue to be inextricably linked to the way you live your life. You can argue about the growth rates, the number of users, devices, digitized content, services, applications, and capacity, but one thing is for certain—it is growing exponentially in reach and importance.

And the more important these networked services and applications become, the more we require from them—anytime, anywhere access, using whichever device we want—precisely because they are part of our lives. These services have infiltrated our businesses, families, and civic lives—they are part of the inner sanctums of who and what we are. We want the persistent connection to all that is ours, whether it is shared, purchased, or created. And, as the network is increasingly able to deliver these things and we find new and innovative ways to integrate it into our daily lives, our reliance is only going to increase.

The world as we know it is changing, and it is the network doing it.

I've tried to show you that you use the network every day, whether you realize it or not. Most obvious is when you go on the Internet, but the network also facilitates a majority of all the other day-to-day transactions we conduct, in ways that you may not have even realized (from connecting with friends to facilitating money transfers to doing inventory management in the stores in which you shop). If you've reached this far in this book, you have gone through the multitude of examples and some rather dry network statistics that hopefully demonstrate its role in our lives. Now you know why it's so important. It's not just the use of the network that has increased over the past years, but our reliance upon it and its ability to help us effect real change.

I believe we have just reached the tipping point of this Digital Information Age. I can't pinpoint the exact date, of course, but in terms of the criticality of the network in our work, civic, and personal lives, we're there. We have now reached a confluence of all the trends I have been discussing. The technology has matured, its adoption has grown, the ways in which the network can be integrated into what we do have risen exponentially, and we, in turn, have created complex interdependencies with the network that we probably will never completely comprehend.

The variety of services and applications available to users has evolved significantly over the past decade. Services have gone from static, one-way transmissions, where you look at content on a web page, to dynamic, interactive communications, where you meet and chat in real time with others on a social networking site. These types of interactions place different requirements on the network and create new expectations from the people who use them.

Innovative applications and services continue to change the landscape of the network (many of which have been touched upon in this book, including web services, SaaS, Web 2.0, and cloud computing). Keeping up with the trends and all the new terminology can be difficult, even for those of us in the industry, but in a nutshell, they are all about using the scale and efficiencies of the network to increase the number and effectiveness of our connections. They are designed to make it easier for individuals, governments, and businesses to take advantage of the opportunities made possible by the network.

All these new applications and services are helping expand the breadth and depth of the network, which in turn increases the demand for access to it in the self-perpetuating cycle that has been described (probably ad nauseum) in this book. One thing to note, however, is that while all these innovative new services and applications make it easier to use the network to its best advantage, they also put a strain on it. As these services and applications evolve from basic data to increasingly advanced real-time exchanges, they require much more rigorous performance and capacity levels.

Juniper Network's Chairman and former CEO, Scott Kriens, used an analogy once to describe to me the changes in scale and composition taking place in today's digital world. He compared the network to the predictability of an automobile freeway system. All the traffic on one side of the freeway travels the same direction. It all consists of commercial and passenger vehicles. You can identify traffic patterns and try to prepare for high traffic volumes. For example, during commuting hours, drivers know to expect a longer commute due to congestion. You can also predict how traffic is going to ebb and flow on and off the freeways, and you can use metering lights to help with traffic integration and try to minimize disruptions.

This is how the network used to be, approximately a decade ago. It was a much more predictable system. Most of the data was flowing downstream. In other words, users were typically downloading content from a web page or from a service. Users were the consumers of the data that was primarily owned by the content/service provider, so the vehicle was pretty well understood. There was also predictability in the general traffic patterns. Network provisioners

High-speed, universally accessible networks deliver the experiences of the sustainable network in a perpetual cycle.

knew what to expect from users of different applications. For example, they could predict the amount of traffic load email would place on the network. Also, a little congestion (or couple seconds' delay) was tolerable and potentially expected by the user.

Now (and moving forward), the landscape has changed and we need to reinvent the rules. With all the different users, devices, and applications traversing the network that are being introduced to the digital world by more interactive two-way Web 2.0 sites, the predictability is gone from the system. There are different types of "vehicles" on the network—not just cars and trucks, but airplanes (mobile devices that are connecting from anywhere) and hovercrafts (cloud computing and all the hybrid models they enable) are all in the mix. All of these vehicles are going north and south on the freeway, as users are increasingly uploading and downloading content. This means traffic is traveling in all directions. It can come from everywhere—it is as if there are an infinite number of freeway on-ramps, placing unprecedented demands on the system. Plus, there is the expectation that everyone needs to get where they are going immediately, so there is no tolerance for lag or congestion.

High-speed, universally accessible networks are ultimately going to deliver the experiences that generate ongoing and increasing demand for the network in a perpetual cycle. At the beginning of this book, I simply called it broadband. Now you know what broadband means, and you know how important it is to the sustainability of the network. If we want to use the network to create progress, change, and action, we are going to need to foster its development and do our part to support its buildout and protect the connections we establish through it.

The network is our best chance to set in motion changes that can be shaped to deliver a 21st-century definition of the greater good. It has all the elements: it is pervasive, reaching across the globe and connecting people to information and opportunity; it can reduce our material consumption and conserve precious natural resources; it can make governments accountable to the people they serve; it can level the playing field and lower barriers of entry to the entire global marketplace; it can mobilize people so they have a voice; and it can foster collaboration, accelerate innovation, and spur the development of solutions to some of the world's toughest problems.

It's also presenting us with challenges: we need to maintain its integrity and impact; we need to ensure the security of all information; we need to look deep within ourselves to define privacy, free speech, and personal freedoms; we need to break down barriers of intolerance to ensure that opportunity remains open to everyone; we need to find value in a global digital marketplace and be willing to adapt to the fast-paced, competitive landscape. And we need to get several billion people to join us online.

The accidental answer for this troubled planet isn't a static thing. Just like you, it's on a continuous journey, with twists and turns and ups and downs. It's a continuous, self-perpetuating system, always on, always there, and always presenting us with possibilities. It's not about cables, routers, or the latest buzzwords—it's about humankind being connected for the very first time and making the most of those relationships. If we can embrace the potential of the network and use it to tackle the challenges we face head-on, I am certain we can create a more sustainable planet.

Glossary: A Quick Cheat Sheet of Common Terms

3G

Third-generation mobile network. The types of applications, capacity, and speed supported by the mobile network are based on the "generation" (G) of the network. 1G is an analog network and 2G is a digital personal communications service (PCS) network. Both are voice-centric, with the main difference in the voice quality, although 2.5G networks support some data services, such as mobile instant messages (IM) and push-to-talk (PTT) services. To date, most mobile broadband is offered via 3G networks, which offer improved voice quality, spectrum utilization, and additional data capacity. 3G networks typically support data stream rates of 3–14 Mbps. The next evolution is 4G mobile networks, which promise to deliver speeds up to 100 Mbps and are positioned to better support the applications and services of the near future than their hardwired brethren.

Antispam

Software that combats the proliferation of unsolicited messages to reduce unwanted (junk) and dangerous email messages that contain malware.

Antivirus

Software that scans files in your email application and miscellaneous web traffic to find a match for specific attack patterns, referred to as *signatures*, that pose a risk to computing systems. File-level protection measures can detect a variety of malware, including but not limited to viruses, worms, and Trojans.

Avatar

A virtual persona that you can create for yourself to enter and participate in the virtual world.

Backbone

The core of the service provider's network. Virtually all traffic passes through the backbone.

Bandwidth

The capacity and speed of a connection.

Barroso's Principle of Proportionality

States that energy consumption of a device should be proportional to the traffic load that device is handling. This principle was proposed by Luiz André Barroso, a distinguished engineer at Google, who advocates energy proportionality as a means to dramatically improve server efficiency in real-life use.

Broadband

A high-speed network connection.

Cell site/base station

The fixed transmitter that receives traffic sent from a mobile device over the radio access network (mobile network).

Cloud

The basic concept of the "cloud" is that people and organizations can leverage the Internet to access applications and services that are run in giant data centers hosted by "cloud" service providers. At the highest level, clouds enable users to share the costs associated with building out and running such a large data center–like environment. It also enables users to scale their applications and services and handle ebbs and flows in demand more efficiently without needing to overprovision or potentially waste resources to reduce energy consumption.

Cloud computing provides users or businesses access to resources, e.g., storage or databases, without having to build out, pay for, or own the infrastructure that supports the resulting functionality. It is sometimes likened to grid computing, which allows users to share computing resources and spread intensive data processing activities across these shared/pooled resources, thus minimizing the burden on any one. As the Internet is often referred to as "the cloud," the concept follows that the links between these computing resources are made via the Internet.

Cyber

Cyber is a prefix that's fallen out of favor lately, banished to B-movies and their cyborgs and cyberorganisms. The prefix is formally used to suggest control, or control of processes on a large scale.

Dennard's Scaling Law

Every new generation of silicon packs more performance in a smaller energy budget, derived from the observation that all key figures of merit in integrated circuit design—such as layout density, operating speed, and energy efficiency—will improve, provided that geometric dimensions, voltages, and doping concentrations are consistently scaled to maintain the same electric field. This law was formulated by Robert Dennard in 1974.[1]

Digg

Allows people to aggregate content of their choosing (by submitting links from their favorite news sites or authors) from anywhere on the Internet. These articles are voted on by the user population.

Energy conversions

Energy conversions [2]

1 kilowatt hour (kWh)	3412 Btu (btu)	3'600 kilojoules (KJ)	
1 megawatt (106 W)	1'000 kilowatts (103 W)		
1 megajoule (MJ)	0.001 gigajoules (GJ)		
1 gigajoule (GJ)	0.9478 million Btu (million btu)	277.8 kilowatt hours (kWh)	
1 Btu (btu)	1'055 joules (J)		
1 million Btu (million btu)	1.055 gigajoules (GJ)	293 kilowatt hours (kWh)	
1 therm (therm)	100'000 Btu (btu)	0.1055 gigajoules (GJ)	29.3 kilowatt hours (kWh)
1 horsepower-hour (hp-hr)	2545 Btu (btu)	0.7457 kilowatt-hour (kWh)	

Mass conversions

1 pound (lb)	453.6 grams (g)	0.4536 kilograms (kg)	0.0004536 metric tons (tonne)
1 kilogram (kg)	2.205 pounds (lb)		
1 short ton (ton)	2,000 pounds (lb)	907.2 kilograms (kg)	
1 metric ton (tonne)	2,205 pounds (lb)	1,000 kilograms (kg)	1.102 short tons (tons)

Firewall

A security technology designed to control access to resources based on the source, destination, and type of traffic.

Googlization

One of the many terms inspired by the search engine Google, it refers to making sure something is "searchable" on the Internet, meaning it can be linked to and resourced from other online locations.

Internet

Also known as the World Wide Web, the Internet is the world's largest public network.

IDS/IPS

A security technology designed to try to identify attacks in the traffic flowing through the network and alert or take action to try to mitigate the effects of an attack.

Lifestreaming

Social media aggregator sites that allow individuals to collect all the updates they receive on all the different social media services they use, from their friends, community groups, news feeds, etc. in a single location.

Moore's Law

Loosely, it states that computing hardware capabilities are doubling every two years because the number of transistors that can be put on an integrated circuit is doubling approximately every couple of years. It has continued for half a century and is not expected to stop for another decade at least and perhaps much longer. It was first observed by Intel's cofounder, Gordon E. Moore.

Net neutrality

The proposed principle that network access should be free of restrictions. All content, all devices, etc. should be given equal access and all users should be able to expect a reasonable quality level in all their online experiences.

Network Access Control (NAC)

A tool that can help organizations manage the endpoints that come into their networks. While servers and other IT assets are handled by other solutions, NAC tackles the very difficult problem of trying to control exactly what individuals can access on any particular network based on who they are, where they are located, the devices they are using, and a variety of other factors.

Network attacks (most common)

Attack type	Description	Potential loss	What you can do about it
Spam	Unwanted, unsolicited communications and messages.	Loss in time. In addition to being a nuisance, these messages often contain malware or phishing attacks.	Filter your email and text messages and never open something from an untrusted/unknown source.
Malware	General descriptor of malicious software loaded onto a computing device without the owner's explicit consent. It can represent spyware, viruses, worms, Trojans, bots, etc.	Can ultimately take over the computing device and steal or change information.	Never open or click on links from unknown sources; install a security suite that includes a firewall, spam filtering, antivirus, and web URL filtering; install updates.
Spyware	Program designed to collect and send personal information about users.	Personal information and details about your browsing habits (where you go and what you do).	Never open or click on a link from an unknown source; install a security suite that includes a firewall, spam filtering, antivirus, and web URL filtering; install updates.
Virus	Computer program that can infect a computing resource and then replicate and spread to other devices.	Can eat up bandwidth and corrupt or destroy files.	Never open or click on a link from an unknown source; install a security suite that includes a firewall, spam filtering, antivirus, and web URL filtering; install updates.
Worm	A self-replicating computer program. A worm is similar to a virus, but it doesn't need to attach itself to a program to spread.	Can eat up bandwidth and corrupt or destroy files.	Never open or click on a link from an unknown source; install a security suite that includes a firewall, spam filtering, antivirus, and web URL filtering; install updates.
Trojan	A program loaded onto a computing resource (typically without the owner's knowledge) that allows the attacker to access and interact with the device.	Attackers can use Trojans to steal or change information or take complete control over the computing device.	Never open or click on a link from an unknown source; install a security suite that includes a firewall, spam filtering, antivirus, and web URL filtering; install updates.
Phishing	Attempts to trick people into giving out sensitive information.	Usernames, passwords, and credit card information.	Never click on links embedded in messages, and don't give personal information to any untrusted source.
Denial of Service (DoS)	An attack designed to flood a resource with so much traffic that it is overwhelmed and can't respond.	Eats up bandwidth and can ultimately make the network or the networked resources unavailable. A successful DoS attack may also be able to take control of the resource.	There are DoS protection technologies, but the reality is that if the attacker has more computing resources than you, there's not much you can do.
Botnets	A network of many individual devices that have computing programs (bots) loaded onto them (generally unwittingly) that will run when triggered to perpetrate an attack.	Can take over a fraction or the whole computing resource, typically to launch a DoS attack. They can grant the attacker access to the infected device and all its information.	Install a security suite that includes a firewall, spam filtering, antivirus, and web URL filtering; install updates.

Node

Any connection point on the network.

OSI model

A framework used to describe the structure of the interactions and dependencies of all network components. It includes seven layers, starting at the Physical Transport layer and moving up to the Application layer.

QoS

The quality of service that is typically guaranteed by the network service provider to ensure the delivery of a specific experience type—for example, no jitter or latency in your video feed.

Power types and modes[3]

Online power: Provides energy over a wired network to a power sink from an energy source (such as a power grid) available for general use.

Offline power: Provides stored energy to a device until the storage is depleted (such as that provided by a battery). It's assumed that the device is disconnected from any power grid.

Disconnected: The device is disconnected from all of its power sources and is not using any electrical power.

On/full power mode: The device is connected to a power source and is working at expected (normal) capacity.

Off: The device is completely turned off, but if it's connected to one or more power sources (plugged in), it may still draw some power.

Idle: The device is connected to a power source and is turned on and potentially operational, but is not serving its primary purpose due to lack of utilization.

Standby or *sleep mode*: A mode of operation for partial or complete temporary shutdown of systems and power sinks, albeit with some consumption of power. This mode may be manually invoked by operator intervention or automatically invoked based on a power management policy. This mode can be used to save hardware wear, battery or other offline power capacity, or online power consumption. Generally, the operating environment state is preserved in standby mode, but this state is maintained in regular volatile memory, thus typically using some power.

The EPA estimates that if all office computers and monitors in the U.S. were set to sleep when not in use, it would save $4 billion in electricity costs and the emissions equivalent of 5 million cars.

Low power mode: Partial standby mode for equipment with power management capabilities, offering reduced processing power and/or other resources. This mode is considered to be an "on" state.

Hibernation mode: Similar to off, but with the operating environment maintained. In this mode, the system is not shut down, so the activity at the time of hibernation is stored and can be reestablished on exit of hibernation mode.

RSS

A data/news feed format that subscribers use to receive updated content directly to their cell phones or another online location of preference. It's mainly used to distribute links to ordinary web pages.

SaaS

A service that allows companies to receive the functionality of different applications remotely via the Internet. SaaS eliminates the need for the user or business to purchase and maintain the software, resulting in potentially significant cost reductions, yet with all the benefits of the full breadth of functionality that application would offer were it located locally.

Second Life

A virtual world, created by Linden Labs, complete with restaurants, shops, parks, corporate office buildings, and anything else you can imagine (akin to a game-like environment).

Smart grid

A grid designed to modernize energy generation and distribution to make it more efficient and more reliable by connecting different types of power sources to different power draws. The goal is to create a real-time view of supply and demand that allows individuals/entities to understand how they are using power and make informed decisions or recalibrate their use.

Smartphones

Phones with advanced features that increasingly mirror PC applications over mobile broadband connections.

Social media

Online applications and sites that allow people to engage in dynamic, personal interactions with one another. A social network service offers people an online community built around a shared interest or activity or experience. Some examples of social media services are Facebook, Twitter, MySpace, and LinkedIn in North America; Friendster, Cyworld, and Wretch in the Asia Pacific region; and Skyrock, Bebo, and Hi5 in Europe.

Throughput

A bandwidth measurement that quantifies the rate at which data can be transmitted from one device to another, typically measured in derivatives of bits and bytes.

Twitter

An online application that allows people to post questions, comments, and updates on their lives in communications that are no longer than 140 characters. These posts are called "tweets." People can be notified online or via cell phone whenever a friend posts a new communication.

Tweets

Communications (posts) on the social networking site Twitter (no more than 140 characters in length).

URL filtering (also known as web filtering)

Designed to restrict content delivered via the Internet. It can also help reduce risks, since dubious websites are more likely to be infected with malware.

Voice over IP (VoIP)

Technology that uses the Internet for phone service, without needing the service offered by traditional telephone lines (PSTN). VoIP applications send voice data within IP packets that travel over your network connection.

VPN

Virtual networks that essentially overlay a private network on top of the public Internet network infrastructure. Some common flavors include IPSec, which is focused on security and creates an end-to-end encryption overlay network; MPLS, which is focused on QoS and builds on the routing infrastructure to control how traffic is forwarded; and SSL, which is focused on the security of specific applications and leverages web browser to establish a secure connection.

Web services

Sometimes called application services, web services let businesses interact with one another via the Web without needing a detailed understanding of one another's IT infrastructures. Web services can increase overall business efficiencies by enabling the sharing of business logic, data, and processes across the network without needing user involvement; rather, the application is directly interfacing with another application.

Web 2.0

A term that refers to the next generation of the web development. It represents a number of dynamic, collaborative applications (cloud computing, SaaS, web services, etc.). It is the transition from simply going to the Internet to retrieve static data (from a web page) to using the Internet to collaborate and interact. It encompasses social media sites and applications that are designed to facilitate personal interactions and community development through a variety of interactive tools (posts, blogs, wikis, chat rooms, etc.), as well as web services.

Notes

Chapter 3

1. "Smart 2020," commissioned by the Global eSustainability Initiative (GeSI), with analysis by McKinsey & Company (*www.SMART2020.org*).

Chapter 4

1. *http://www.kiva.org/app.php?page=businesses&action=about&id=9250*

2. *www.kiva.org/about*

3. Computer History Museum's "Internet History." More milestones can be found at *www.computerhistory.org/internet_history/*.

4. "Mouse Inventor Strives for More," BBC News, November 5, 2001 (*http://news.bbc.co.uk/2/hi/science/nature/1633972.stm*). During an interview, Engelbart said, "SRI patented the mouse, but they really had no idea of its value. Some years later it was learned that they had licensed it to Apple for something like $40,000."

5. *The World Fact Book*, U.S. Central Intelligence Agency, 2008 (Skyhorse Publishing).

6. Top 10 emerging markets: China, India, Russia, Brazil, Mexico, Turkey, Indonesia, Iran, Poland, and Saudi Arabia. Top 10 developed markets: U.S., Japan, Germany, UK, France, Italy, Spain, Canada, South Korea, and Australia; source: IMF, ITU, Morgan Stanley Research.

7. Informa Telecoms & Media

8. Gartner Group as reported in "Broadband to reach 77% of U.S. households by 2012 Gartner says: Broadband penetration currently reaches just over half of U.S. homes," Brad Reed, Gartner Group, *Network World*, July 24, 2008 (*www.networkworld.com/news/2008/072408-broadband-penetration-gartner-study.html?hpg1=bn*).

9. "Broadband to reach 77% of U.S. households by 2012, Garner says," *Network World*, Brad Reed, July 24, 2008 (*http://www.networkworld.com/news/2008/072408-broadband-penetration-gartner-study.html?hpg1=bn*).

10. Dave Clark

11. 3G Americas press release, December 22, 2008 (*www.3gamericas.org/index.cfm?fuseaction=pressreleasedisplay&pressreleaseid=2077*).

12. "Two billion new Bourgeois using cell phones," Stephane Teral, Infonetics Research, March 24, 2009.

13. "Is Silicon Valley Losing Its Magic?", Steve Hamm, *BusinessWeek*, January 12, 2009.

14. "Boom in the Bust," *Economist*, March 7, 2009.

15. "Apple's Ambitious iPhone 3G Plans," Peter Burrows, *BusinessWeek*, August 22, 2008

16. Rajesh Jain, NetCore Solutions Ltd., Web 2.0 Conference presentation, 2008.

17. "Two billion new Bourgeois using cell phones," Stephane Teral, Infonetics Research, March 24, 2009.

18. Rajesh Jain, NetCore Solutions Ltd., Web 2.0 Conference presentation 2008.

19. "More than 633 million mobile subscribers in China," ilinca, unwired view, January 6, 2009 (*www.unwiredview.com/2009/01/06/more-than-633-million-mobile-subscribers-in-china/*).

20. "Two billion new Bourgeois using cell phones," Stephane Teral, Infonetics Research, March 24, 2009.

21. "China Mobile Subscribers Surpass Total US Population," eMediaWire, April 6, 2007 (*www.nextbillion.net/news/china-mobile-subscribers-surpass-total-us-population*).

22. For the month of November 2008, as reported by *www.unwiredview.com/2009/01/06/more-than-633-million-mobile-subscribers-in-china/*.

23. The ICT industry refers to the full range of devices and applications that play a role in digital communication; ranging from monitors and cell phones to PCs and storage devices; all the different applications that enable the sharing or use of information, from email and online services to spreadsheets and video games; and the hardware and software needed to operate the networks that transmit the information, from the smallest home office to the largest global networks.

24. "China Mobile Subscribers Surpass Total US Population," eMediaWire, April 6, 2007 (*www.nextbillion.net/news/china-mobile-subscribers-surpass-total-us-population*).

25. "Poorer Nations Go Online on Cellphones," Tom Wright, *Wall Street Journal*, December 5, 2008 (*http://online.wsj.com/article/SB122844530354182063.html?mod=todays_us_marketplace*).

26. "Brazil Telecom and Service Provider Router Market," Synergy Research Group, 2008.

27. "Brazil Telecom and Service Provider Router Market," Synergy Research Group, 2008.

28. "Service Provider and Enterprise Telecom and Datacom Equipment Market Share and Forecasts," Infonetics Research, July 2008.

29. According to CIA World Factbook, as reported by Nationmaster, which pools statistics taken from sources such as the CIA World Factbook, UN, and OECD (*www.nationmaster.com/graph/med_tel-media-televisions*).

Chapter 5

1. "Video Surge Divides Web Watchers," *Wall Street Journal*, August 14, 2007.

2. A helpful website you can use to translate between bits and bytes is *www.matisse.net/bitcalc/?input_amount=1&input_units=gigabits&notation=legacy*.

3. "Broadband to reach 77% of U.S. households by 2012 Gartner says: Broadband penetration currently reaches just over half of U.S. homes," Brad Reed, *Network World*, July 24, 2008 (*www.networkworld.com/news/2008/072408-broadband-penetration-gartner-study.html?hpg1=bn*).

4. "Global Broadband Subscribers hit 400 million," CBS MarketWatch, November 2008 (*www.marketwatch.com/news/story/Global-Broadband-Subscribers-Hit-400/story.aspx?guid=%7bFB19043A-A38C-480F-BECD-CF90E0CDF447%7d*).

5. HeavyReading

6. "The Coming Exaflood," Bret Swanson, *Wall Street Journal*, January 20, 2007 (*http://online.wsj.com/article/SB116925820512582318.html*).

7. "FCC redefines "broadband" to mean 768 Kbps, "fast" to mean 'kinda slow,'" Nilay Patel, March 19, 2008 (*www.engadget.com/2008/03/19/fcc-redefines-broadband-to-mean-768kbps-fast-to-mean-kinda/*).

8. "Fiber in the Last Mile," Pyramid Research (*www.pyr.com/downloads.htm?id=1&sc=LR020909_FBR*).

9. Fiber to the Home Council and Infonetics Research

10. "Fiber in the Last Mile," Pyramid Research

11. Wireless Intelligence Report, September 2008

12. HeavyReading

Chapter 6

1. "The Coming Exaflood," Bret Swanson, *Wall Street Journal*, January 20, 2007 (*http://online.wsj.com/article/SB116925820512582318.html*).

2. 2008 Cisco Systems, Inc., Cisco Visual Networking Index, "Approaching the Zettabyte Era," June 16, 2008.

3. 2008 Cisco Systems, Inc., Cisco Visual Networking Index, "Approaching the Zettabyte Era," June 16, 2008.

4. "Juniper Networks Helps Laboratory of Neuro Imaging Double Network Performance, Cut IT Management Time in Half: Juniper's High-Performance Network Infrastructure Accelerates the Deployment of Applications and Services for Conducting Cutting-Edge Research," press release, December 3, 2008 (*www.juniper.net/company/presscenter/pr/2008/pr_2008_12_03-16_53.html*).

5. "Network management: Tips for managing costs," Karen D. Schwartz, *Computerworld*, August 27, 2008 (*www.computerworld.com/s/article/9113604/Network_management_Tips_for_managing_costs?taxonomyId=14&pageNumber=1&taxonomyName=Management*).

6. "Video Surge Divides Web Watchers," *Wall Street Journal*, August 14, 2007.

7. University of Minnesota and Cisco Systems

8. comScore global in September 2008 and Morgan Stanley Research

9. New Tee Vee conference stats for the month of September 2008

10. "Video Surge Divides Web Watchers," *Wall Street Journal*, August 14, 2007.

11. "Approaching the Zettabyte Era," 2008 Cisco Systems, Inc., Cisco Visual Networking Index, June 16, 2008.

12. "The Coming Exaflood," Bret Swanson, *Wall Street Journal*, January 20, 2007 (*http://online.wsj.com/article/SB116925820512582318.html*).

13. Bernstein Report, 2007

14. "It's Personal: Similarities and Differences in Online Social Network Use Between Teens and Adults," by Amanda Lenhart, The Pew Internet and American Life Project, May 23, 2009 (*www.pewinternet.org/pdfs/PIP_Teens_Social_Media_Final.pdf*).

15. Bernstein Report, 2007

16. *www.tvturnoff.org*

17. *www.tvturnoff.org*

18. Minnesota Internet Traffic Studies (MINTS), March 2009 (*www.dtc.umn.edu/mints/home.php*).

19. TelecomView, "Telecom 2020: TransformationStrategies," October 2008.

20. *www.tvturnoff.org*

21. "It's Personal: Similarities and Differences in Online Social Network Use Between Teens and Adults," Amanda Lenhart, The Pew Internet and American Life Project, May 23, 2009 (*www.pewinternet.org/pdfs/PIP_Teens_Social_Media_Final.pdf*).

22. "It's Personal: Similarities and Differences in Online Social Network Use Between Teens and Adults," by Amanda Lenhart, The Pew Internet and American Life Project, May 23, 2009 (*www.pewinternet.org/pdfs/PIP_Teens_Social_Media_Final.pdf*).

23. "Internet Interrupted: Why Architectural Limitations Will Fracture the 'Net," Nemertes Research, November 2008.

24. "How did Michael Jackson's death affect the internet's performance?", Emma Barnett, Telegraph.co.uk, June 26, 2009 (*www.telegraph.co.uk/scienceandtechnology/technology/5649500/How-did-Michael-Jacksons-death-affect-the-internets-performance.html*; "News sites swamped following Michael Jackson's death," cnet, Greg Sandoval, June 25, 2009 (*http://news.cnet.com/8301-1023_3-10273325-93.html*).

25. *Globe and Mail* (Toronto), September 17, 2008

26. "Customers Angered as iPhones Overload AT&T," *New York Times*, Jenna Wortham, September 2, 2009 (*http://www.nytimes.com/2009/09/03/technology/companies/03att.html?_r=1&scp=15&sq=network%20security&st=cse*).

27. "Inauguration Crowd Will Test Cellphone Networks," Matt Richtel, *New York Times*, January 19, 2009 (*http://www.nytimes.com/2009/01/19/technology/19iht-19cell*).

28. "Inauguration Crowd Will Test Cellphone Networks," Matt Richtel, *New York Times*, January 19, 2009 (*http://www.nytimes.com/2009/01/19/technology/19iht-19cell*).

29. "Online inauguration videos set records," John D. Sutter, CNN, January 23, 2009 (*www.cnn.com/2009/TECH/01/21/inauguration.online.video/*).

30. "Worldwide Telecommunications Equipment 1H08 Market Share Update," IDC, #214275, Volume: 1, September 2008.

31. Tom Nolle, CIMI Corp., Netwatcher, 18.1% of service provider CAPEX is on infrastructure and 3–5% of that is on IP.

32. Moore's Law states that the number of transistors on a chip will double about every two years (*www.intel.com/technology/mooreslaw/*).

33. Over a three-year time period. "Stress Fractures in the Internet by 2012," Nemertes Press Release, November 19, 2008 (*www.nemertes.com/press_releases/nemertes_press_release_stress_fractures_internet_2012*).

34. "Broadband subs hit 400 million, 'Net bending under the weight," FierceTelecom, November 19, 2008 (*www.fiercetelecom.com/story/broadband-subs-hit-400-million-net-bending-under-weight/2008-11-19*).

35. "A Broadband Stimulus Plan," Michael Mandel, *BusinessWeek*, January 6, 2009 (*www.businessweek.com/bwdaily/dnflash/content/jan2009/db2009015_446050.htm?link_position=link1*).

36. Nemertes Research

Chapter 7

1. ITU, 2009 press release

2. T-Mobile, April 2009

3. "Mobile Planet Connecting the World," Guy Daniels and Ian Channing, 2007.

4. "Mobile Connections Reach 4 Billion Worldwide," 3G Americas Press Release, December 22, 2008.

5. Informa Telecoms & Media's Global Mobile Forecasts (*www.intomobile.com/2008/12/14/informa-5-billion-mobile-subscribers-to-generate-1-trillion-in-revenues-by-2013.html*).

6. "Mobile/WiFi Phones and Subscribers report," Infonetics Research, March 24, 2009.

7. "Netbooks Surge Forward in Adoption," CiOZone, jmottl (*http://bx.businessweek.com/tech-trend/view?url=http%3A%2F%2Fwww.ciozone.com%2Findex.php%3Foption%3Dcom_myblog%26show%3DNetbooks-Surge-Forward-In-Adoption.html%26Itemid%3D713*).

8. Informa Telecoms & Media

9. "Mobile Broadband Cards, Routers, Services and Subscribers, 4Q08," Infonetics Research, March 10, 2009. Infonetics Research defines mobile broadband to include W-CDMA/HSPA and CDMA2000/EV-DO.

10. Informa Telecoms & Media

11. "Mobile Broadband Cards, Routers, Services and Subscribers, 4Q08," Infonetics Research, March 10, 2009. Infonetics Research defines mobile broadband to include W-CDMA/HSPA and CDMA2000/EV-DO.

12. "Mobile Connections Reach 4 Billion Worldwide," 3G Americas press release, December 22, 2008.

13. "Mobile Connections Reach 4 Billion Worldwide," 3G Americas press release, December 22, 2008.

14. Morgan Stanley, 2008

15. "Unwired: The Decline of the Landline," *Economist*, August 13, 2009.

Chapter 8

1. "Presence Based Services Market 2008–2013," Insight Research Corporation, December 2008.

2. "Location Based Services Market, 2008–2013," Insight Research Corporation, October 2008.

3. "Spies in Your Mobile Phone," Heather Green, *BusinessWeek*, January 13, 2009 (*www.businessweek.com/print/technology/content/jan2009/tc20090112_390493.htm*).

4. "Spies in Your Mobile Phone," Heather Green, *BusinessWeek*, January 13, 2009 (*www.businessweek.com/print/technology/content/jan2009/tc20090112_390493.htm*).

5. Pew Internet Research, 2008. Six percent of cell phone owners read a news story on a cell phone and 7% of BlackBerry, iPhone, or other smartphone users used the device to read a news story.

6. "The Mobile Phone and Financial Applications Worldwide, 2009–2014," Insight Research Corporation, April 2009.

7. "Broadband Wireless Sector Analysis Report," New Paradigm Resources (NPR) Group, December 2008. Twenty and a half percent of smartphone users perform mobile banking; among users with basic cell phones, it's only 2.7%. Currently, 24% of all cell phones in the U.S. market today are smartphones.

8. According to a survey conducted by research, data, and strategic analysis firm The Kelsey Group in conjunction with research partner ConStat.

9. "Smartphone Adoption Accelerates Mobile Local Search," The Kelsey Group and ConStat (*www.marketingcharts.com/interactive/smartphone-adoption-accelerates-mobile-local-search-6672/*).

Chapter 9

1. Gartner Symposium/ITxpo: Emerging Trends (*www.gartner.com/it/page.jsp?id=503867*).

2. *www.SMART2020.org*

3. "Green ICT: Banking on a software solution to climate change," Rikki Stancich, Climate Change Corp, October 22, 2008, (*www.climatechangecorp.com/content.asp?ContentID=5727*).

4. "Current Technology Could Reduce Emissions 55 Percent Below 1990 Levels by 2030," Business Wire *(www.businesswire.com/portal/site/home/email/headlines/?ndmViewId=news_view&newsLang=en&div=-564504432&newsId=20090126006105)*.

5. "A Climate Risk Report: Towards a High-Bandwidth, Low-Carbon Future. Telecommunications-based opportunities to reduce greenhouse gas emissions," Climate Risk (*www.climaterisk.net*).

6. Edward L. Glaeser is a professor of economics at Harvard University, a City Journal contributing editor, and a Manhattan Institute senior fellow. His article describes research jointly performed with Matthew Kahn of UCLA.

Chapter 10

1. "Defra 2007: Act On C02 Calculator Public Trial Version - Data, Methodology and Assumptions," United Kingdom's Department for Environment, Food and Rural Affairs.

2. "Study: Trees absorb one-fifth of CO2 gas," UPI.com, February 19, 2009. (*www.upi.com/Science_News/2009/02/19/Study_Trees_absorb_one-fifth_of_CO2_gas/UPI-11191235069651/*).

3. "Everyday tips to reduce your carbon footprint," Kristi King, WTOP Radio, February 23, 2009 (*www.wtopnews.com/?nid=220&sid=1608351*).

4. "The Illusion of Clean Coal," *Economist*, March 7, 2009.

5. Broadcast on National Public Radio (NPR), February 26, 2009.

6. Edward L. Glaeser is a professor of economics at Harvard University, a *City Journal* contributing editor, and a Manhattan Institute senior fellow. His article describes research jointly performed with Matthew Kahn of UCLA.

7. "Everyday tips to reduce your carbon footprint," Kristi King, WTOP Radio, February 23, 2009 (*www.wtopnews.com/?nid=220&sid=1608351*).

8. Greenhouse Gas Emissions, EPA (*www.epa.gov/climatechange/emissions/ghgrulemaking.html*).

9. "Benefits of Trees in Urban Areas" (*www.coloradotrees.org/benefits.htm*).

10. "Study: Trees absorb one-fifth of CO2 gas," UPI.com, February 19, 2009 (*www.upi.com/Science_News/2009/02/19/Study_Trees_absorb_one-fifth_of_CO2_gas/UPI-11191235069651/*; *http://www.sightline.org/maps/charts/pollu_co2transp_ooh*).

11. "'Eco-generosity' To Make Waves in 2009," Environmental Leader, January 21, 2009 (*www.environmentalleader.com/2009/01/21/eco-generosity-to-make-waves-in-2009/*).

Chapter 11

1. IBM Television Advertisement, CBS, March 21, 2009.

2. Center for Urban Transportation Research, Federal Highway Administration, Texas Transportation Institute. U.S. drivers spent 4.2 billion hours sitting in traffic in 2005 alone.

3. EU Intelligent Car Initiative Brochure

4. IBM Television Advertisement, CBS, March 21, 2009.

5. IBM Television Advertisement, CBS, March 21, 2009.

6. "A Climate Risk Report: Towards a High-Bandwidth, Low-Carbon Future. Telecommunications-based opportunities to reduce greenhouse gas emissions," Climate Risk (*www.climaterisk.net*).

7. *www.eyeonearth.eu/EN/Map/Pages/default.aspx?EEARating=1&UserRating=1*

8. "Powerful Systems Bring Efficiencies to Roads, Rail, Water and Food Distribution," Steve Lohr, *New York Times*, May 30, 2009.

9. *www.ead.ae/en/?T=4&ID=3999*

10. "Promoting energy efficiency in the developing world," Diana Farrell and Jaana Remes, *McKinsey Quarterly*, February 2009 (*www.mckinseyquarterly.com/Economic_Studies/Country_Reports/Promoting_energy_efficiency_in_the_developing_world_2295*).

11. "Promoting energy efficiency in the developing world," Diana Farrell and Jaana Remes, *McKinsey Quarterly*, February 2009 (*www.mckinseyquarterly.com/Economic_Studies/Country_Reports/Promoting_energy_efficiency_in_the_developing_world_2295*).

12. "Promoting energy efficiency in the developing world," Diana Farrell and Jaana Remes, *McKinsey Quarterly*, February 2009 (*www.mckinseyquarterly.com/Economic_Studies/Country_Reports/Promoting_energy_efficiency_in_the_developing_world_2295*).

13. *www.siliconvalley.com/greenenergy/ci_6086258?nclick_check=1*

14. "High-Tech, Low Carbon: The Role of the European Digital Technology Industry in Tackling Climate Change," EICTA and INTELLECT, April 2008.

15. *The McKinsey Quarterly*, 2008

16. *http://logisticsviewpoints.com/2009/02/04/walmart-developing-a-more-sustainable-trucking-fleet/*

17. David Lewis presentation from Nokia Siemens

Chapter 12

1. "Encourage the Rebels," Vinod Khosla, *Newsweek*, December 15, 2008 (*www.newsweek.com/id/171909*).

2. Advanced Metering Infrastructure from Itron (*www.itron.com/pages/solutions_detail.asp?id=itr_016422.xml*).

3. *www.itron.com/pages/solutions_detail.asp?id=itr_016422.xml*

4. "Data Center Overload," Tom Vanderbilt, *New York Times Magazine*, June 8, 2009.

5. The Green Power for Mobile program is spearheaded by the GSM Association.

6. The North American Network Operations Group

7. Greenhouse Gas Protocol

8. IBM Advertisement, Monday, November 24, 2008, *San Jose Mercury News*, page 10A

9. IBM Advertisement, Monday, November 24, 2008, *San Jose Mercury News*, page 10A

10. *http://earth2tech.com/2008/11/10/a-reliable-green-grid-could-need-2-trillion/*

11. *http://www.siliconvalley.com/news/ci_11682442?nclick_check=1*

12. Source: Nielsen Survey—3Q08

13. *www.energy.gov/recovery/index.htm*

14. "Google looking to go green is the right kind of power grab," Eric Schmidt, *San Jose Mercury News*, September 2008 (*www.siliconvalley.com/latestheadlines/ci_10838269*).

15. "The Climate for Change," Al Gore, *New York Times*, November 9, 2008 (*www.nytimes.com/2008/11/09/opinion/09gore.html?_r=3&partner=permalink&exprod=permalink&oref=slogin*).

16. BCC Research

17. "Google unveils software to cut household energy waste," Matt Nauman, *San Jose Mercury News*, February 10, 2009.

18. "Google unveils software to cut household energy waste," Matt Nauman, *San Jose Mercury News*, February 10, 2009.

19. "Enterprise And SMB Hardware Survey, North America And Europe, Q3 2008," Forrester Research. Hardware technology decision makers from North American and European enterprises (percentages may not total 100 because of rounding).

20. Lux's definition of the "power web" market includes smart-metering hardware and software, networking technologies, energy storage (including batteries for both the grid and electric vehicles), flywheels, and supercapacitors, as well as alternative grid-connected power sources, including fuel cells. The definition excludes renewable generation systems like solar, wind, and tidal power, and the electric vehicles themselves (*www.luxresearchinc.com/info/smr?power_smr*).

21. Morgan Stanley says the sector is composed of advanced metering infrastructure, demand response, and transmission and distribution automation.

22. "Powerful Systems Bring Efficiencies to Roads, Rail, Water and Food Distribution," Steve Lohr, *New York Times*, April 30, 2009.

23. "Google unveils software to cut household energy waste," Matt Nauman, *San Jose Mercury News*, February 10, 2009.

24. "CIA Admits Cyberattacks Blacked Out Cities," Thomas Claburn, *InformationWeek*, January 18, 2008, citing Tom Donahue.

25. "Top 10 Security Stories of 2008," Thomas Claburn, *Information Week*, January 2, 2009, (*www.informationweek.com/news/security/attacks/showArticle.jhtml;jsessionid=ZPM0NRJ TPC2OCQSNDLOSKHSCJUNN2JVN?articleID=212700286&pgno=4&queryText=&isPr ev=*).

26. "U.S. Cyber Infrastructure Vulnerable to Attacks," Yochi J. Dreazen and Siobhan Gorman, *Wall Street Journal*, May 6, 2009 (*http://online.wsj.com/article/SB124153427633287573. html*).

27. These reliability standards were developed by the North American Electric Reliability Corporation (NERC), which the FERC has designated as the electric reliability organization (ERO).

Chapter 13

1. "Energy Efficiency in Telecom Networks," August 27, 2008; and Green Telecom and IT Summit at CTIA, "Greening the Network," Nokia-Siemens presentation, David Lewis, Director of Customer Marketing in North America, Light Reading Webinar, September 10, 2008.

2. "Environmental Implications of Wireless Technologies: News Delivery and Business Meetings," Michael W. Toffel and Arpad Horvath, Environmental Science and Technology (*http:// pubs.acs.org/doi/abs/10.1021/es035035o*).

3. "The Carbon Footprint of Email Spam Report," McAfee report, released April 15, 2009 (*www.icfi.com/*).

4. *www.gxs.com/gxs/newsroom/pr/2008/09182008.htm*

5. Environmental impact estimates were made by GXS using the Environmental Defense Fund Paper Calculator. For more information, visit *www.papercalculator.org*. Additional gallons of gasoline calculations were made by GXS using EPA data.

6. "E-Invoicing Solution Selection Report," Lesley Keene and Jeff Pikulik, Aberdeen Group, December 2005.

7. "Sector-Specific Issues and Reporting Methodologies Supporting the General Guidelines for the Voluntary Reporting of Greenhouse Gases," Energy Policy Act of 1992. The Department of Energy puts average tree cover at 700 per acre.

8. *www.turbotax.com*

9. David Lewis, Nokia Siemens

10. Dr. Shyue-Ching Lu, Chunghwa Telecom's chairman and CEO, 2008.

Chapter 14

1. GeSI (*www.theclimategroup.org/assets/resources/publications/Smart2020ReportSummary.pdf*)

2. Center for Urban Transportation Research, Federal Highway Administration, Texas Transportation Institute

3. CDP6 Report, 2008 (*www.cdproject.net*).

4. Center For Urban Transportation Research, Federal Highway Administration, Texas Transportation Institute

5. Dr. Alex Wissner-Gross, Harvard University physicist (*www.telegraph.co.uk/scienceandtechnology/technology/google/4217055/Two-Google-searches-produce-same-CO2-as-boiling-a-kettle.html*).

6. John Buckley (*www.telegraph.co.uk/scienceandtechnology/technology/google/4217055/Two-Google-searches-produce-same-CO2-as-boiling-a-kettle.html*).

7. Chris Goodall (*www.telegraph.co.uk/scienceandtechnology/technology/google/4217055/Two-Google-searches-produce-same-CO2-as-boiling-a-kettle.html*).

8. Google spokesperson (*www.telegraph.co.uk/scienceandtechnology/technology/google/4217055/Two-Google-searches-produce-same-CO2-as-boiling-a-kettle.html*).

9. Dr. Alex Wissner-Gross (*www.telegraph.co.uk/scienceandtechnology/technology/google/4217055/Two-Google-searches-produce-same-CO2-as-boiling-a-kettle.html*)

10. The average car in the U.S. produces 98 pounds of carbon for every 100 miles (*www.terrapass.com/carbon-footprint-calculator/*).

11. Energy Saving Trust (*www.energysavingtrust.org.uk/*)

12. Carbon abatement of approximately 1,144 pounds for the year.

13. Referenced by Chunghwa Telecom, study conducted in 2007.

14. Szomolanyi, K. (ed.), Greenhouse gas effect of information and communication technologies, 2005.

15. Center for Urban Transportation Research, Federal Highway Administration, Texas Transportation Institute.

16. Center for Urban Transportation Research, Federal Highway Administration, Texas Transportation Institute.

17. "A stress test for good intentions," *Economist*, May 16, 2009.

18. *www.informationweek.com/news/management/trends/showArticle.jhtml?articleID=212201924*

19. *www.sustainIT.org*

20. Cisco Systems, WebEx advertisement, April 9, 2009.

21. Aberdeen Group

22. Gartner Group, May 2008

23. "Hosted UC: Latest Market Numbers and Trends," Frost & Sullivan, Melanie Turek, May 4, 2009 (*www.nojitter.com/blog/archives/2009/05/hosted_uc_lates.html;jsessionid=QEVRGZMAMWPJUQSNDLOSKH0CJUNN2JVN*).

24. "Growth of Unified Communications Services to Dwarf Products Growth," *MarketWire*, January 9, 2009.

Chapter 16

1. 2008 Global e-Sustainability Initiative (GeSI) report

2. "Green Telecom East: Verizon's Thermal Ware," Dan Jones, Unstrung, June 17, 2009.

3. "Green IT Initiative in Japan," METI, October 2008 (*www.meti.go.jp/english/policy/index_information_policy.html*).

4. "METI (Ministry of Economy, Trade and Industry) Takes Aggressive Lead to Reduce Power Consumption of IT Device Starting Next Year," Asahi Shimbun, 2007. The goal of Japan's METI "Green IT Project" is to reduce router power consumption by 30%.

5. "High Tech: Low Carbon: The Role of the European Digital Technology Industry in Tackling Climate Change," EICTA, April 2008.

6. CIMI, Netwatcher, 2009

7. Unstrung Insider, Light Reading, vol. 7, no. 8, December 2008.

8. Cisco Systems

9. *www.computerworld.com/action/article.do?command=viewArticleBasic&articleId=331868&source=NLT_MGT*

10. "Being Ecologically Sound Makes Economic Sense," Sun's Eco Innovation Initiative, 2008.

11. IDC Multiclient Study, Server Virtualization On the Move 2007.

12. *www.nspllc.com/*

13. *www.sustainablelifemedia.com/*

14. *www.globaltestmarket.com/survey/sframe.phtml?PHPSESSID=vipqejdcnq7shoca2oa7juj4j6&change=1&COLS=*,70%&frame_loc=http://www.sustainablelifemedia.com&inverted=0*

15. "RPA Calculator Analyzes Cost Savings of Reusable Packaging," *Environmental Leader*, March 19, 2009.

Chapter 17

1. "Data Center Overload," Michael Manos (then GM of Data Center Services for Microsoft), *New York Times Magazine*, June 8, 2009 (*www.nytimes.com/2009/06/14/magazine/14search-t.html?pagewanted=2&_r=2&partner=rss&emc=rss*).

2. "Building, Planning and Operating the Next-Generation Datacenter," IDC, 2008.

3. Nemertes Research

4. Advanced Micro Devices

5. "It: Slashing the Digital Carbon Footprint," Institute for Sustainable Communication, *Fortune*.

6. British Telecom

7. According to a report by management consulting firm McKinsey & Company and the Uptime Institute.

8. Anson Wu, Market Transformation Programme figures based on projected 2007 server consumption as a proportion of 2006 total UK electricity consumption (excluding transport), updated from 2005 DUKES energy consumption, as reported in "High Tech: Low Carbon: The Role of the European Digital Technology Industry in Tackling Climate Change," EICTA, April 2008.

9. Dutch Ministry of Economic Affairs, as reported in "High Tech: Low Carbon: The Role of the European Digital Technology Industry in Tackling Climate Change," EICTA, April 2008.

10. Zukunftsmarkt energieeffiziente Rechenzentren, PD Dr. Klaus Fichter, 2007 (*www.border-step.de*), as reported in "High Tech: Low Carbon: The Role of the European Digital Technology Industry in Tackling Climate Change," EICTA, April 2008.

11. According to a report by management consulting firm McKinsey & Company and the Uptime Institute.

12. The North American Network Operations Group

13. "Enterprise And SMB Hardware Survey, North America And Europe, Q3 2008," Forrester Research. Hardware technology decision-makers from North American and European enterprises (percentages may not total 100 because of rounding).

14. "How Much Time, Once the Cooling Fails," Rich Miller, Data Center Knowledge, Hosting365, February 8, 2008, (*www.datacenterknowledge.com/archives/2008/02/08/how-much-time-once-the-cooling-fails/*).

15. "High Tech: Low Carbon: The Role of the European Digital Technology Industry in Tackling Climate Change," April 2008.

16. "Cool More with Less in Your Data Center," Paul McGuckin, Gartner Group, October 2008.

17. "Sun's Green Efforts Teach a Lesson," Internetnews.com, January 28, 2009 (*www.internetnews.com/infra/article.php/10796_3799011_1*).

18. *www.vmware.com/company/news/releases/customer-survey-vmworld.html*

19. "Microsoft to Cut Carbon Footprint by 30 percent," Environmental Leader, March 16, 2009.

20. *www.businessweek.com/technology/content/mar2009/tc20090315_857456_page_2.htm*

21. *www.juniper.net/us/en/company/press-center/press-releases/2008/pr_2008_11_10-20_1.html*

22. "High Tech: Low Carbon: The Role of the European Digital Technology Industry in Tackling Climate Change," EICTA, April 2008.

Chapter 18

1. *www.theclimategroup.org/assets/resources/publications/Smart2020ReportSummary.pdf*

Chapter 19

1. "Stanford Business School Study Finds MBA Graduates Want to Work for Caring and Ethical Employers," Press Release, Stanford Graduate School, July 26, 2004 (*www.csrwire.com/press/press_release/20993-Stanford-Business-School-Study-Finds-MBA-Graduates-Want-to-Work-for-Caring-and-Ethical-Employers*).

2. "Corporate Ethics and Fair Trading – A Nielsen Global Consumer Report," Nielsen, October 2008.

3. CDP surveyed 87 individuals at 80 finance institutions (all of whom are CDP Signatory Investors) including Allianz, AXA Group, BlackRock, Goldman Sachs, Hermes Investment Management, and Swiss Re to assess how CDP and other climate change data is used (*www.cdproject.net*).

4. The U.S. added 4 companies from its *2008 tally* for a winning total of 20 companies, knocking the UK to second, with 19 (down from 24 in 2008). Japan added 2, to total 15 companies this year. Rounding out the top 5 were France (8) and Germany (7), while Canada, Finland, and Sweden each had 5 companies on the list. Two-thirds (65/100) of the 2008 companies remained on the list in 2009, and 46 of the 100 companies have been in existence for at least 100 years.

5. *www.corporateknights.ca/special-reports/70-the-global-100/354-the-2009-list.html*.

6. "Cisco Faces Down Questions on China Record" (*http://redir.internet.com/rss/click/www.internetnews.com/infra/article.php/3784951*).

7. *www.kpmg.com/Global/IssuesAndInsights/ArticlesAndPublications/Pages/Sustainability-corporate-responsibility-reporting-2008.aspx*

8. *www.kpmg.com/Global/IssuesAndInsights/ArticlesAndPublications/Pages/Sustainability-corporate-responsibility-reporting-2008.aspx*

9. *www.kpmg.com/Global/IssuesAndInsights/ArticlesAndPublications/Pages/Sustainability-corporate-responsibility-reporting-2008.aspx*

Chapter 20

1. Nielsen/NetRatings (*www.websiteoptimization.com/bw/0705/*).

2. ITIF added speed and price to the broadband penetration equation to demonstrate what it believed to be a more complete picture of a nation's broadband rankings.

3. "Obama: Broadband, Computers Part of Stimulus Package," Grant Gross, IDG News Service, December 8, 2008.

4. See the OECD broadband portal for more information on data sources and notes.

5. See the OECD broadband portal for information on data sources and notes.

6. *www.businessweek.com/bwdaily/dnflash/content/jan2009/db2009015_446050.htm?link_position=link1*

7. "Obama: Broadband, Computers Part of Stimulus Package," Grant Gross, IDG News Service, December 8, 2008.

8. *www.o3bnetworks.com/mission.html*

Chapter 21

1. "The Future of Telecommunications 2008–2013," The Insight Research Corporation (*www.insight-corp.com/reports/futuretel08.asp*). According to this report, estimates and predictions include narrowband and broadband landline, wireless, and cellular services, as well as Internet communications.

2. eBay Q308 earnings and Morgan Stanley Research

3. *www.telecomseurope.net/article.php?type=article&id_article=8374&utm_source=lyris&utm_medium=newsletter&utm_campaign=telecomseurope* and "Nokia Siemens to run Orange networks in Britain, Spain," Tarmo Virki, Reuters, March 18, 2009 (*www.reuters.com/article/rbssTechMediaTelecomNews/idUSLI58032920090318*).

4. "Federal CIO Vivek Kundra Sees Potential of Cloud Computing," *InformationWeek*, Mary Hayes Weier, April 24, 2009.

Chapter 22

1. "Video Surge Divides Web Watchers," *Wall Street Journal*, August 14, 2007.

2. "The Coming Exaflood," Bret Swanson, *Wall Street Journal*, January 20, 2007.

Chapter 23

1. "U.S. Steps Up Effort on Digital Defenses," David E. Sanger et al., *New York Times*, April 28, 2009.

2. According to Kiva.org website, April 30, 2009.

3. *http://kivadata.org/summary.html*, April 30, 2009.

4. *www.kiva.org/about*

5. "When Small Loans Make a Big Difference," *Forbes*, June 3, 2008 (*www.forbes.com/entrepreneursfinance/2008/06/03/kiva-microfinance-uganda-ent-fin-cx_0603whartonkiva.html*).

6. "Proctor and Gamble Connect + Develop web site," (*www.pgconnectdevelop.com/pg-connection-portal/ctx/noauth/PortalHome.do*).

7. "Gartner: Four Disruptions That Will Transform the Software Industry," Thomas Wailgum, *CIO Magazine*, October 15, 2008. (*www.cio.com/article/454930/Gartner_Four_Disruptions_That_Will_Transform_the_Software_Industry*).

8. "Eight business technology trends to watch," James M. Manyika et al., December 2007, McKinsey Quarterly (*www.mckinseyquarterly.com/Information_Technology/Applications/Eight_business_technology_trends_to_watch_2080*).

9. Incubator 2.0 Session at Web 2.0 Summit, November 5–7 with Dave McClure, 500 Hats; Jeff Clavier, Softtech VC; Ron Conway, Angel Investors; Josh Kopelman, First Round Capital; Paul Graham, YCombinator.

Chapter 24

1. "Infrastructure Slideshow: IT Trends for 2009," Baseline (*www.baselinemag.com/c/a/Infra-structure/IT-Trends-for-2009/*).

2. "EU to sue Britain for not applying Internet privacy rules on Phorm advertising tracker," Aoife White, AP, Brussels, April 14, 2009.

Chapter 25

1. "The State of Retailing Online," Forrester Research, 2008.

2. "Simultaneous Surfers," Burt Helm, *BusinessWeek*, May 25, 2009.

3. From PayPal's website (*www.paypal-media.com/aboutus.cfm*).

4. The company was founded in 1998 and then acquired by eBay, the world's largest online marketplace, in 2002 in a transaction valued at approximately $1.5 billion.

5. U.S.-based Pew Internet Project Study, 2007.

Chapter 26

1. Wikipedia's definition of spacetime is "any mathematical model that combines space and time into a single continuum. Spacetime is usually interpreted with space being three-dimensional and time playing the role of a fourth dimension that is of a different sort than the spatial dimensions" (*http://en.wikipedia.org/wiki/Spacetime*).

2. "Stock Traders Find Speed Pays, in Milliseconds," Charles Duhigg, *New York Times*, July 24, 2009 (*www.nytimes.com/2009/07/24/business/24trading.html?_r=2&hp*).

Chapter 27

1. "Putting Africa on the map," Jonathan Ledgard, Economist.com (*www.economist.com/dis-playstory.cfm?story_id=12494557*).

2. "Putting Africa on the map," Jonathan Ledgard, Economist.com (*www.economist.com/dis-playstory.cfm?story_id=12494557*).

3. "Mexican Women's Movement Makes the Internet Work for Many Women," Erika Smith, November/December 1998 (*www.isoc.org/oti/articles/1197/smith.html*).

4. "Reporter's notebook: Boiling emotions in China," Jaime FlorCruz, CNN, July 8, 2009 (*www.cnn.com/2009/WORLD/asiapcf/07/08/china.uyghurs.florcruz/index.html*).

5. "Iranians dodging government's Internet crackdown," Doug Gross, CNN, June 18, 2009 (*www.cnn.com/2009/TECH/06/18/iran.dodging.crackdown/index.html*).

6. "Pope Demands Bishop Recant Holocaust Position," NPR, February 4, 2009, and "Pope Acknowledges Vatican Mistakes in Bishop Case," NPR, March 12, 2009.

7. "Pope Acknowledges Vatican Mistakes in Bishop Case," NPR, March 12, 2009.

8. "Outrage – and a Plea for Business to Lead," Manjeet Kripalani, *Business Week*, December 15, 2008.

Chapter 28

1. "The Internet and the 2008 Election," Pew Internet, June 2008.

2. "The Internet and the 2008 Election," Pew Internet, June 2008.

3. "The Internet and the 2008 Election," Pew Internet, June 2008.

4. "Text the Vote," *New York Times*, Garrett M. Graff, August 12, 2008 (*http://www.nytimes.com/2008/08/13/opinion/13graff.html*).

5. The Campaign Finance Institute (*http://www.cfinst.org/Default.aspx?aspxerrorpath=/pr/prRelease.aspx*)

6. "Banking on Becoming President, Politicians & Elections," OpenSecrets.org, (*www.opensecrets.org/pres08/index.php*).

7. August 12, 2008

8. September comScore numbers

9. "Politics Makes New Bedfellows," Steve Smith, minonline, October 24, 2008 (*www.minonline.com/news/8950.html*).

10. "The Internet and the 2008 Election," Pew Internet, June 2008.

11. "The Internet and the 2008 Election," Pew Internet, June 2008.

12. "The Internet and the 2008 Election," Pew Internet, June 2008.

13. "The Internet and the 2008 Election," Pew Internet, June 2008.

14. "Eyes of the World Are on Obama," Jeff Zeleny, *New York Times*, April 2, 2009.

Chapter 29

1. "Beijing Delays Rule on Software Censor," Michael Wines, *New York Times*, June 30, 2009 (*www.nytimes.com/2009/07/01/technology/01china.html?_r=2&partner=rss&emc=rss*); "China's Information Dam: Should Yahoo!, Google and Microsoft help the censors?" *The Washington Post*, June 29, 2009 (*www.washingtonpost.com/wp-dyn/content/article/2009/06/28/AR2009062802398.html*).

2. "China's Green Dam: The Implications of Government Control Encroaching on the Home PC," OpenNet Initiative (*http://opennet.net/chinas-green-dam-the-implications-government-control-encroaching-home-pc*).

3. "Cisco File Raises Censorship Concerns: Document Implies Support for China," Glenn Kessler, *Washington Post*, May 20, 2008 (*www.washingtonpost.com/wp-dyn/content/article/2008/05/19/AR2008051902661.html*).

4. "Google caught up in China censorship debate," John Boudreau, *San Jose Mercury*, June 28, 2009 (*www.mercurynews.com/ci_12691151?IADID=Search-www.mercurynews.com-www.mercurynews.com*).

5. "Cost of Selling 'Net Monitoring' to Iran," Bob Brewin, nextgov, June 29, 2009 (*http://whatsbrewin.nextgov.com/2009/06/cost_of_selling_net_monitoring.php*).

6. *http://www.siliconvalley.com/news/ci_11985934?nclick_check=1*

7. "Internet Censorship, Saudi Style," Peter Burrows, *BusinessWeek*, November 13, 2008 (*www.businessweek.com/magazine/content/08_47/b4109068380136.htm*).

8. "Internet Censorship, Saudi Style," Peter Burrows, *BusinessWeek*, November 13, 2008 (*www.businessweek.com/magazine/content/08_47/b4109068380136.htm*).

9. "Internet Censorship, Saudi Style," Peter Burrows, *BusinessWeek*, November 13, 2008 (*www.businessweek.com/magazine/content/08_47/b4109068380136.htm*).

10. "EU to sue Britain for not applying Internet privacy rules on Phorm advertising tracker," Aoife White, AP, Brussels, April 14, 2009.

11. "Strewth! Will stickybeak Oz pollies come a gutzer over shonky web censorship plan?" Martyn Warwick, October 31, 2008.

12. "The Universal Declaration of Human Rights" (*www.un.org/en/documents/udhr/*).

13. "Google, Yahoo, Microsoft Set Common Voice Abroad," Jessica E. Vascellaro et al., *Wall Street Journal*, October 28, 2008 (*http://online.wsj.com/article/SB122516304001675051.html*).

14. A good summary of the Act can be found at *www.govtrack.us/congress/bill.xpd?bill=h111-2271*.

15. *http://thomas.loc.gov/home/gpoxmlc110/h275_ih.xml*

16. "Obama urged to punish US firms for aiding internet censorship," Bobbie Johnson and Daniel Nasaw, *Guardian*, June 30, 2009 (*www.guardian.co.uk/world/2009/jun/30/us-firms-aiding-censorship*).

17. Bill proposed by Sens. Charles Schumer, D-NY and Lindsey Graham, R-SC, as reported in "Cost of Selling 'Net Monitoring' to Iran," Bob Brewin, nextgov, June 29, 2009 (*http://whatsbrewin.nextgov.com/2009/06/cost_of_selling_net_monitoring.php*).

Chapter 30

1. Actual headlines: "Canadian grocery chain Sobeys' software crash lasts 5 days," "British Telecom BT SurfTime upgrade prematurely cancels service," "Network Solutions outage bumps Nasdaq off the Internet," "Skype outage hits 220 million users," "Program glitch disrupts 619 calls (So.Cal) for most of day," "eBay embarrassed by crash and 22-hour outage, plunge of stock; traced to absence of upgrade," "Amazon S3 Outage Casts Cloud on Cloud Computing," "Google's GrandCentral Service Suffers Outage, Downtime."

2. Study by Infonetics Research

3. Annual Ziff Davis Enterprise Editorial Research survey, 2008. The Strategy Group conducted a survey in July 2007 that included 173 respondents from Ziff Davis Enterprise database. These respondents were all manager-level or higher working in organizations with more than 100 employees.

4. "Interview With A Convicted Hacker: Robert Moore Tells How He Broke Into Routers And Stole VoIP Services," Sharon Gaudin, *InformationWeek*, September 26, 2007 (*www.informationweek.com/news/internet/showArticle.jhtml?articleID=202101781*).

5. Information garnered from IBM's 3,700 corporate clients, December 2008 (*www.informationweek.com/news/security/management/showArticle.jhtml?articleID=212201984&cid= nl_IWK_daily_H*).

6. "Top 10 Security Stories of 2008," Thomas Claburn, InformationWeek, January 2, 2009, (*www.informationweek.com/news/security/attacks/showArticle.jhtml;jsessionid=CZFRF QUNSZCPOQSNDLOSKHSCJUNN2JVN?articleID=212700286&pgno=5&_requestid=441505*).

7. According to the Aladdin eSafe CSRT study in 2008.

8. "Google Searches Web's Dark Side," BBC News, May 11, 2007 (*http://news.bbc.co.uk/2/hi/ technology/6645895.stm*).

9. "Google Searches Web's Dark Side," BBC News, May 11, 2007 (*http://news.bbc.co.uk/2/hi/ technology/6645895.stm*).

10. The indictment of Albert Gonzalez can be found at *http://media.nbclocalmedia.com/documents/Indictment.pdf*.

11. Annual Ziff Davis Enterprise Editorial Research survey, 2008. The Strategy Group conducted a survey in July 2007 that included 173 respondents from Ziff Davis Enterprise database. These were all manager-level or higher working in organizations with more than 100 employees.

12. Annual Ziff Davis Enterprise Editorial Research survey, 2008. The Strategy Group conducted a survey in July, 2007 that included 173 respondents from Ziff Davis Enterprise database. These were all manager-level or higher working in organizations with more than 100 employees.

13. Infotech Research Group

14. Annual Ziff Davis Enterprise Editorial Research survey, 2008. The Strategy Group conducted a survey in July, 2007 that included 173 respondents from Ziff Davis Enterprise database. These were all manager level or higher working in organizations with more than 100 employees.

15. Annual Ziff Davis Enterprise Editorial Research survey, 2008. The Strategy Group conducted a survey in July, 2007 that included 173 respondents from Ziff Davis Enterprise database. These were all manager-level or higher working in organizations with more than 100 employees.

16. Annual Ziff Davis Enterprise Editorial Research survey, 2008. The Strategy Group conducted a survey in July, 2007 that included 173 respondents from Ziff Davis Enterprise database. These were all manager-level or higher working in organizations with more than 100 employees.

17. A Carnegie Mellon University CyLab survey of 703 individuals (primarily independent directors) serving on U.S.-listed public company boards corporate board directors, 2008.

Chapter 32

1. Survey by Arbor Networks of 66 self-classified Tier 1, Tier 2, and other IP network operators from North America, South America, Europe, and Asia, 2008.

2. Courtesy of "Arbor Networks 2008 Worldwide Infrastructure Security Report"

3. InfoTech Research Group

4. "Top 10 Security Stories of 2008," Thomas Claburn, *InformationWeek*, January 2, 2009 (*www.informationweek.com/news/security/attacks/showArticle.jhtml;jsessionid=CZFRF QUNSZCPOQSNDLOSKHSCJUNN2JVN?articleID=212700286&pgno=5&_reques-tid=441505*).

5. US-Cert, Vulnerability Note VU#800113. There are several other existing vulnerabilities (CERT Advisory CA-1997-22 BIND, CERT Vulnerability Note VU#109475) that attackers can exploit to poison the cache.

6. *www.informationweek.com/news/security/vulnerabilities/showArticle. jhtml?articleID=212001825*

7. *www.networkworld.com/news/2009/022609-commerce-secretary-internet-emergencies. html?page=2*

Chapter 33

1. Study by Infonetics Research

2. "Study: Routine Misbehavior by End Users Can Lead to Major Data Leaks," Tim Wilson, Dark Reading, September 2008.

3. *www.informationweek.com/news/security/attacks/showArticle.jhtml;jsessionid=CZFRFQUN SZCPOQSNDLOSKHSCJUNN2JVN?articleID=212700286&pgno=5&_requestid=441505*

4. "Twitter accounts of Obama, Britney Spears attacked," CNN, January 6, 2009 (*www.cnn. com/2009/TECH/01/05/twitter.hacked/index.html?iref=newssearch*).

5. Twitter cofounder Biz Stone wrote on the site's blog at *www.twitter.com*.

6. Davos World Economic Forum, Vint Cerf, January 2008.

7. Survey by Arbor Networks of 66 self-classified Tier 1, Tier 2, and other IP network operators from North America, South America, Europe, and Asia, 2008.

8. *www.networkworld.com/community/node/35360*

9. Survey by Arbor Networks of 66 self-classified Tier 1, Tier 2 and other IP network operators from North America, South America, Europe, and Asia, 2008.

10. *New York Times*, October 20, 2008.

Chapter 35

1. "Top 10 Security Stories of 2008," Thomas Claburn, *InformationWeek*, January 2, 2009 (*www.informationweek.com/news/security/attacks/showArticle.jhtml;jsessionid=CZFRF QUNSZCPOQSNDLOSKHSCJUNN2JVN?articleID=212700286&pgno=5&_requestid=441505*).

2. "2009 Mobile/WiFi Phones and Subscribers biannual market size, share, and forecast service," Infonetics Research, March 24, 2009.

3. "Top 9 security predictions of 2009," Derek Manky, ZDNet Asia, January 5, 2009 (*www.zdnetasia.com/news/security/0,39044215,62049756,00.htm*).

4. "Two thirds of Britons victims of 'mobile spam' according to survey," Cloudmark, April 22, 2008, (*www.cloudmark.com/en/company/release.html?release=2008-04-22*).

5. Jonathan Zdziarski, author of *iPhone SDK Application Development* (O'Reilly, *http://oreilly.com/catalog/9780596154059/*).

6. "The Network Security Industry is Thankful for..." Infonetics Research, December 23, 2008.

7. "Google fixes Android root-access flaw," David Meyer, ZDNet UK, November 11, 2008 (*www.zdnetasia.com/news/security/0,39044215,62048148,00.htm*).

8. "Google fixes Android root-access flaw," David Meyer, ZDNet UK, November 11, 2008 (*www.zdnetasia.com/news/security/0,39044215,62048148,00.htm*).

9. Visiongain, 2008

10. Network World, 2008

11. Jonathan Zdziarski, *iPhone SDK Application Development* (O'Reilly, *http://oreilly.com/catalog/9780596154059/*).

12. "Two thirds of Britons victims of 'mobile spam' according to survey," Cloudmark, April 22, 2008, *www.cloudmark.com/en/company/release.html?release=2008-04-22*.

13. "Security Appliances and Software for Mobile Networks and Devices," Jeff Wilson, Infonetics Research, July 8, 2009.

14. "Security Appliances and Software for Mobile Networks and Devices," Jeff Wilson, Infonetics Research, July 8, 2009.

15. Jonathan Zdziarski, *iPhone SDK Application Development* (O'Reilly, *http://oreilly.com/catalog/9780596154059/*).

Chapter 36

1. "Top 10 Security Stories of 2008," Thomas Claburn, *InformationWeek*, January 2, 2009 (*www.informationweek.com/news/security/attacks/showArticle.jhtml;jsessionid=CZFRFQUNS ZCPOQSNDLOSKHSCJUNN2JVN?articleID=212700286&pgno=5&_requestid=441505*).

2. "E-Spionage: A BusinessWeek Investigation," Brian Grow et al., *BusinessWeek*, April 21, 2008.

3. *www.networkworld.com/community/node/39557?netht=rn_031109&nladname=031109dai lynewsamal*

4. "U.S. Steps Up Effort on Digital Defenses," David E. Sanger et al., *New York Times*, April 28, 2009.

5. Amit Yoran, chairman and CEO of NetWitness and former director of the National Cyber Security Division of the Department of Homeland Security, in a statement made in March 2009 before the House Subcommittee on Emerging Threats, Cybersecurity, Science and Technology, which is part of the House Committee on Homeland Security, as reported in "Cybersecurity Hearing Prompts Calls For Leadership, Laws," Thomas Claburn, *InformationWeek*, March 11, 2009.

6. Juniper Networks, COOP Government Action Survey, U.S. Government's third quarter in 2007.

7. Juniper Networks, COOP Government Action Survey, U.S. Government's third quarter in 2007.

Chapter 37

1. "Public, private sectors at odds over cyber security," Joseph Menn, *Los Angeles Times*, August 26, 2008.

2. "Officials: N. Korea believed behind cyber attacks," Hyung-Jin Kim, Associated Press, July 8, 2009 (*http://news.yahoo.com/s/ap/20090708/ap_on_re_as/as_skorea_cyber_attack*).

3. "U.S. Steps Up Effort on Digital Defenses," David E. Sanger et al., *New York Times*, April 28, 2009.

4. Bill Woodcock, research director for Packet Clearing House, The New York Times Company, 2008.

5. Pamela Hess, AP reporter, Washington Bureau

6. "U.S. Steps Up Effort on Digital Defenses," David E. Sanger et al., *New York Times*, April 28, 2009.

7. "Drones Are Weapons of Choice to Fight Al Queda," Christopher Drew, *New York Times*, March 16, 2009.

Chapter 38

1. *www.youtube.com/watch?v=A5GryIDl0qY*

2. Grid.org

3. IBM.com

4. *www.worldcommunitygrid.org/projects_showcase/rice/viewRiceMain.do*

5. "Online Donations Make Gains," Nicole Wallace, The Chronicle of Philanthropy, June 12, 2003 (*http://philanthropy.com/free/articles/v15/i17/17002001.htm*).

6. jobs2web (*www.jobs2web.com/resources/*)

7. "The Cellphone, Navigating Our Lives," John Markoff, *New York Times*, February 16, 2009 (*www.nytimes.com/2009/02/17/science/17map.html?pagewanted=2&_r=1&src=linkedin*).

8. "Networked Families," Pew Internet and American Life Project, October 19, 2008, 202-419-4500 (*www.pewinternet.org*).

Chapter 39

1. U.S.-based Pew Internet Project Study, 2007.

2. "Obama: Broadband, Computers Part of Stimulus Package," Grant Gross, IDG News Service, December 8, 2008.

3. *www.barackobama.com/issues/technology/#transparent-democracy*

4. *www.polycom.com/company/news_room/press_releases/2009/20090406_1.html*

5. "Senate Mulls Stimulus Funds for Health IT," Kenneth Corbin, InternetNews, January 15, 2009 (*www.internetnews.com/government/article.php/3796636/Senate+Mulls+Stimulus+Funds+for+Health+IT.htm*).

6. Oprah.com, June 9, 2009

7. NHS.org

8. NHS.org

9. NHS.org

Chapter 40

1. "Fundraising, Via Twitter (With Cats!)," David Pogue, March 4, 2009 (*http://pogue.blogs.nytimes.com/2009/03/04/fundraising-via-twitter-with-cats/?ref=personaltech*).

2. "Changing Face of Communications," IBM, January 2009.

3. Statistics collected by medialab for 2008 (*www.scribd.com/doc/11481779/Social-Media-2008-Statistics*).

4. For a list of some of the Craigslist crimes, read "'Craigslist Crimes'" Piling Up: Will Recent Horrifying Examples Spur Action?" Javier Lavagnino, June 8, 2009 (*http://blogs.findlaw.com/blotter/2009/06/craigslist-crimes-piling-up-will-recent-horrifying-examples-spur-action.html*).

5. "Facebook gets $200 million investment from European firm," Scott Duke Harris, *Mercury News*, May 26, 2009.

6. According to Nielsen, as reported in "Chart of the day: Users Spent A Billion Hours on Facebook," Nicholas Carlson and Kamelia Angelova, *The Business Insider*, Silicon Alley Insider, July 14, 2009 (*www.facebook.com/ext/share.php?sid=101403592053&h=eXyIw&u=hdIo-&ref=nf*).

7. "How Facebook is Taking Over Our Lives," Jessi Hempel, *BusinessWeek*, March 2, 2009.

8. Reston, Virginia–based researcher ComScore, November 2008.

9. "Number of US Facebook Users Over 35 Nearly Doubles in Last 60 Days," March 25, 2009 as reported on "Inside Facebook: Tracking Facebook and the Facebook Platform for Developers and Marketers" (*www.insidefacebook.com/2009/03/25/number-of-us-facebook-users-over-35-nearly-doubles-in-last-60-days/*).

10. Facebook addicts (11%) of the service make up approximately 62% of its traffic, with regulars (53%) accounting for approximately 34%. Quantcast, December 2008 (*www.quantcast.com/facebook.com#demographics*).

11. ComScore Media Metrix data for March 2009

12. ComScore Media Metrix data for April 2009

13. *www.quantcast.com/twitter.com*, April 30, 2009

14. *www.informationweek.com/news/internet/social_network/showArticle.jhtml?articleID=2165 00968&cid=nl_IWK_daily_H*

15. *www.cnn.com/2009/TECH/01/05/twitter.hacked/index.html?iref=newssearch*

16. "A Virtual Bank with Real Woes," Rob Cox, *New York Times*, June 14, 2009.

Glossary

1. More information can be found at *www.ieee.org/portal/site/sscs/menuitem.f07ee9e3b2a01d-06bb9305765bac26c8/index.jsp?&pName=sscs_level1_article&TheCat=6010&path=sscs/07 Winter&file=Bohr.xml* and *http://en.wikipedia.org/wiki/Robert_H._Dennard*.

2. Greenhouse Gas Protocol Conversion Factors

3. Information from International Telecommunication Union (ITU) Focus Group on ICT & Climate Change meeting held on November 24–28, 2008, which sets out to provide the standard definition of possible power types and modes of ICT/Telecom equipment, served as the base for these definitions.

Index

Latitude, 49, 53
Layer 7 intelligence, 233
leveraging mobile phones, 53
lifecycle carbon footprint
    label, 68
lifestreaming, 294, 306
LimeLight Networks, 167
Linden Lab's Second Life, 104
LinkedIn, 294
linking things together, 6–8
Local Area Network (LAN),
    10
London transit system, 239
loneliness, 284
Long Term Evolution (LTE),
    33
Loopt, 53
low power mode, 309

M

Madoff, Bernard, 222
Malta, national smart grid
    network, 87
malware, 223, 307
malware-checking programs,
    241
manufacturing efficiency, 78
Markoff, John, 249
Massachusetts Bay
    Transportation Agency
    (MBTA), 239
McAfee Secure, 186
McCain, John, 208
Measuring a Footprint, 63
Media Access Control (MAC)
    address, 10
medical records system,
    electronic, 290
megabit per second (Mbps),
    29
megabyte per second (MBps),
    29
Metropolis, 73
microfinance, 171

MicroPlace, 171
Microsoft, 167
MIFARE Classic card, 239
Mikogo, 103
Ministry of Economy, 141
mobile access, 46–50, 52–56
    Google, 52
    portability, 47
    roaming, 47
    What Is Mobility?, 47
mobile applications
    collecting personal
        information, 53
    leveraging mobile phones,
        53
mobile attacks, 262–268
    Google's Android, 264
    Symbian, 264
    vishing, 263
    wardriving, 262
mobile broadband, 32
mobile marketing companies,
    54
MobileMe, 52
mobile network operators,
    117
mobile networks
    base station, 33
    cell site, 33
    commercial mobile
        broadband networks,
        48
    Green Power for Mobile, 81
    secure, 267
ModemMujer, 199
Moore, Robert, 222
Moore's Law, 118, 306
MoveOn.org, 201
MPLS VPN, 110–111
MSN, 161
Multiprotocol Label
    Switching (MPLS), 43
Mumbai, India, 200
MySpace, 167, 212, 218, 294,
    310
MyVote.com, 213

N

National Cyber Range, 279
natural climate, 64
natural gas, 63
net efficiencies, 72–78
    Abu Dhabi, 74
    Glimpses into the Future...,
        72
    Metropolis, 73
    supply chain's carbon
        emissions, 77
Netherlands, carbon footprint
    reduction, 67
Net Nanny, 218
net neutrality, 164–168, 306
    content delivery, 166
    defined, 165
Network Access Control
    (NAC), 256, 306
Network Access Protection
    (NAP), 256
network adoption, 22–26
    Brazil, 25
    China, 24
    India, 24
network as a service (NaaS),
    160
network attacks, 307
network efficiencies, 119–125
    Barroso's Principle of
        Proportionality, 120
    breakthroughs, 121–125
    lifecycle, 123–125
    optimal peak performance,
        119
    virtualization, 122
network energy consumption,
    114–126
    A Country View—Japan,
        115
    Adaptive Link Rate (ALR),
        121
    Barroso's Principle of
        Proportionality, 120
    cell phones, 117

W

WalMart, 77
wardriving, 262
Waste Electrical and
    Electronic Equipment
    (WEEE) directive, 140
Web 2.0, 311
WebEx, 103
web filtering, 310
webinars, 102
web services, 311
What Is Mobility?, 47
What You Can Do
    dematerialization, 95
    detravelization, 105
    energy grids, 90
    healthcare, 292
    network energy
        consumption, 125
Where.com, 53
whitelists, 255
Wide Area Network (WAN),
    10
World Congress on IT, 141
World Economic Forum, 141
World Information
    Technology and Services
    Alliance (WITSA), 141
world's ecological footprint,
    70
worms, 248, 307
Wretch, 294

Y

Yahoo!, 69, 156, 161, 167
    censorship, 217
Y Combinator, 176
You Might Think Twice…,
    224
You Might Want to Know (or
    Not), 29
Your Unsmart Home Grid, 84
YouTube, 38, 167, 184
    Bangladesh blocking, 218
    Chinese government, 217
    King Bhumibol Adulyadej,
        217

About the Author

Sarah Sorensen is the principal of Sorensen Consulting and an associate of Two Tomorrows, a sustainability consultancy. Prior to that, she spent eight years at Juniper Networks in a variety of product and corporate marketing roles. Most recently, Sarah created and managed the company's Corporate Citizenship and Sustainability strategy and was a founding member of the company's Green Taskforce, which is responsible for driving energy efficiency initiatives within the engineering and product teams. During her tenure, she also managed Juniper's business announcements, crisis communications, and public sector outreach, and spent half a decade marketing the company's network security technologies.

A graduate of UCLA (1996), where she majored in English and was a member of UCLA's Division 1 women's soccer team, Sarah has focused her career on branding, marketing, communications, and public relations for both startups and Fortune 500 companies. She has developed and written dozens of whitepapers, byline articles, and presentations on and about the networking and security industries.

Colophon

The cover and heading font is Frutiger; the body text is Sabon.

Get even more for your money.

Join the O'Reilly Community, and register the O'Reilly books you own. It's free, and you'll get:

- $4.99 ebook upgrade offer
- 40% upgrade offer on O'Reilly print books
- Membership discounts on books and events
- Free lifetime updates to ebooks and videos
- Multiple ebook formats, DRM FREE
- Participation in the O'Reilly community
- Newsletters
- Account management
- 100% Satisfaction Guarantee

Signing up is easy:

1. **Go to: oreilly.com/go/register**
2. **Create an O'Reilly login.**
3. **Provide your address.**
4. **Register your books.**

Note: English-language books only

To order books online:
oreilly.com/store

For questions about products or an order:
orders@oreilly.com

To sign up to get topic-specific email announcements and/or news about upcoming books, conferences, special offers, and new technologies:
elists@oreilly.com

For technical questions about book content:
booktech@oreilly.com

To submit new book proposals to our editors:
proposals@oreilly.com

O'Reilly books are available in multiple DRM-free ebook formats. For more information:
oreilly.com/ebooks

O'REILLY®

Spreading the knowledge of innovators   oreilly.com